American Debates on Sexual Equality

American Debates on Sexual Equality

by
Sanford Kessler and Traciel V. Reid

B L O O M S B U R Y
LONDON • NEW DELHI • NEW YORK • SYDNEY

Bloomsbury Academic

An imprint of Bloomsbury Publishing Plc

50 Bedford Square	175 Fifth Avenue
London	New York
WC1B 3DP	NY 10010
UK	USA

www.bloomsbury.com

First published 2013

ISBN: HB: 978-1-4411-5403-3
PB: 978-1-4411-8864-9
ePDF: 978-1-4411-6670-8
ePub: 978-1-6235-6940-2

Library of Congress Cataloging-in-Publication Data
Kessler, Sanford, 1945-
American debates on sexual equality / by Sanford Kessler and Traciel V. Reid.
pages cm
Includes index.
ISBN 978-1-4411-5403-3 (hbk. : alk. paper)– ISBN 978-1-4411-8864-9 (pbk. : alk. paper)
1. Women's rights–United States. 2. Women–United States. I. Reid, Traciel V. II. Title.
HQ1236.5.U6K4747 2013
305.420973–dc23
2012044383

Typeset by Fakenham Prepress Solutions, Fakenham, Norfolk NR21 8NN
Printed and bound in the United States of America

To our students

CONTENTS

CONTENTS   ix

Education

Employment

Pay Equity

Pregnancy

INTRODUCTION

Although today's Americans generally support sexual equality in principle, they differ sharply over questions regarding sexual equality in practice. Should the US Constitution, for example, require full legal equality between the sexes, or does the current, less rigorous constitutional standard suffice? If women enjoy the same civil rights as men, must they fulfill the same civic duties, including the obligation to register for the draft? Should the crime of rape be redefined to include sexual assaults against men? Should men have an equal voice in abortion decisions, or must women always have the final say? Should the right to marry belong to heterosexual couples only, or to same-sex couples as well? Our answers to these and other such questions reveal much about how we view ourselves as individuals, as family members, and as citizens of a democratic republic.

American students are intensely interested in these questions regardless of their personal and professional goals, partly because they know that sex affects destiny. Most students, for example, are or will be involved in intimate relationships with gender-related role expectations; most recognize that public policies regarding sexual equality will shape their educational and employment opportunities; and most know that in wartime men and women have different civic responsibilities that could determine whether they live or die.

Despite these facts, most classroom discussions regarding sexual equality tend to generate more heat than light. Most students are largely unaware of the various factors that bring particular issues involving this principle into public consciousness and that shape American law, public opinion, and even their own thinking on these issues. Many also tend to respond emotionally to such issues and thus have difficulty fully understanding their opponents' views and concerns.

Similar problems exist when discussions about sexual equality occur outside of the classroom. Controversies regarding hot-button topics such as abortion rights and same-sex marriage fuel the sometimes vicious "culture wars" that continue to divide Americans on moral, religious and political grounds. It is therefore difficult for either public figures or ordinary citizens to discuss these controversies dispassionately—that is in ways that foster genuine listening and understanding rather than posturing and intellectual rigidity.

In this book, we use a debate format to help dismantle these formidable barriers to learning. Our debates contain the best available arguments— pro and con, feminist and anti-feminist—on the most important sexual equality issues of our time. These arguments appear in a broad selection of readings from various sources: polemical writings, judicial opinions, works of political theory, social science research, newspaper articles, public documents, and private correspondence. Our authors include historical figures such as Alexis de Tocqueville, Frederick Douglass, and Elizabeth Cady Stanton; scholars such as Catherine MacKinnon, Susan Moller Okin and Steven E. Rhoads; and leading jurists such as Justices Sandra Day O'Connor, Antonin Scalia and Ruth Bader Ginsburg.

In selecting the readings for this book, we were mindful of both its purpose and the diverse nature of its intended audience. Thus, we chose readings whose arguments, for the most part, are rationally defensible rather than scripturally based, that are accessible both to college students and to the general public, and that represent divergent points of view. We have sought to present all positions—including those with limited support in the "marketplace of ideas"—fairly and objectively in order to promote critical thinking. We believe that even unfashionable ideas can enhance our understanding and often contain more than a kernel of truth.

We have also sought to help you, our readers, understand these debates by placing them within a broad interpretive framework. We think that a number of intersecting factors—religious, political, sociological, sexual, and racial—tend to shape American controversies regarding sexual equality and that a comprehensive discussion of this principle must take these influences and more into account. One cannot understand the current storm over same-sex marriage, for example, without considering the various factors that shape American law and public opinion on this subject. These include the views of conservative and liberal Christians, our current social and political climate, the increased visibility of gays and lesbians in American life, and the actual or perceived links between the fight for same-sex marriage today and the civil rights struggles of the past.

Yet we believe that one important, oft-neglected question provides an indispensable key to understanding most current debates on sexual equality: do the biological differences between the sexes have moral, social, and political significance? Virtually all Americans know that men generally tend to be physically stronger than women and that only women can carry, give birth to, and breast feed children. Yet we differ sharply over how relevant these physical differences are to our current lives. Do these differences, for example, foster distinct masculine and feminine virtues, or are these character traits the products of socialization? Should we ever take biology into account when assigning men and women the rights and duties of citizenship or their roles within family life? And, finally, what bearing do these biological differences have on our understanding of equality, the great moral touchstone of our society?

These and similar questions appear and reappear in the readings that follow. When discussing such questions, we refer to those authors who hold that biology shapes our sexual identity as "traditionalists" because most Americans historically have held this view. We call those who stress the role of society or history in shaping our sexual identity "reformers" because they, like most feminists, seek to discredit natural difference arguments on the grounds that they use biology unfairly to restrict sexual equality.

Traditionalists tend to believe that the concepts of masculinity and femininity are grounded in nature, that men and women are naturally fitted to play somewhat different roles in life, and that some degree of sexual inequality is necessary for our personal wellbeing as well as for the public good. Reformers tend to believe that the concepts of masculinity and femininity are largely artificial constructs, that most non-physical distinctions between the sexes impose unfair burdens on women and, to some extent, on men, and that we should strive for greater sexual equality in all spheres of life.

This division between traditionalists and reformers is by no means hard and fast. While traditionalists use natural difference arguments today, for example, to argue against registering women for the draft, reformers use natural difference arguments to justify maternity leaves which increase employment opportunities for women in civilian life. Indeed, the courts have also used natural difference arguments to curb the rights of men. While a mother can legally end a pregnancy against a father's wishes, this same father is legally obliged to provide for the upkeep of his newborn whether he wants to or not.

We have used the biological difference question to help us determine what issues to feature, what readings to include, and how to organize and present these readings. The readings are divided into six chapters which are further subdivided into units. The first chapter explores the natural difference controversy as it appears in early American history while the next five chapters highlight current substantive, policy-oriented debates regarding sexual equality. We conclude the book in a seventh chapter with some final observations on the current state of sexual equality and on what the future might hold for this principle.

In order to orient our readers to the debates and arguments of this book we briefly introduce each reading selection and also begin each substantive chapter with a short essay which places its reading selections in context. We have also included a list of questions and a short bibliography at the end of each chapter. The list of questions highlights the most salient issues raised in the chapter while the bibliography guides interested readers to additional relevant source materials.

We, as editors, sometimes disagree regarding the substantive issues raised by the debates in this book. Yet we have tried to speak with one voice when discussing these issues in order to help readers reach their own, independent conclusions regarding them. We have also tried to achieve neutrality in our use of language, and especially with respect to the terms "sex" and "gender." Most scholars use "sex" to refer to the biological differences between men and women and "gender" to refer to the differences between the sexes which are socially or historically constructed. Not surprisingly, traditionalists tend to use "sex" more frequently in their writings while reformers tend to favor "gender." We use both words in our book although we use the term "sexual equality" rather than "gender equality" in our title because most of our readings focus on the relevance or irrelevance of biology in explaining how American men and women differ.

We conclude this introduction by briefly summarizing each chapter of the book so that you, our readers, can choose your own point of entry into the debates. We hope, of course, that you will eventually read them all.

1 Early American Views on Sexual Equality

Our first chapter focuses on how early Americans understood sexual equality in relation to the principles of the Declaration of Independence. The chief question at issue was whether the natural differences that exist between the sexes justify assigning men and women different, fixed roles in life. Supporters of this position, which historians call the "doctrine of separate spheres," argued that the family is the basic unit of society and that women can best secure their natural rights through marriage. Opponents argued that women are first and foremost individuals and, therefore, deserve to enjoy the same civil rights and opportunities as men.

2 Sexual Equality: A Constitutional Perspective

This chapter considers the natural difference question in relation to efforts by American courts to define sexual equality under the US Constitution. The key point at issue here is whether state and federal laws can be grounded on sex-based differences and, if so, under what circumstances. Today, the Constitution requires governments to treat groups which are alike similarly. Thus, when judges and justices examine policies that discriminate on the basis of sex, they must determine when men and women are presumptively alike and when they are presumptively different.

3 Rights and Duties of Citizenship

Chapter 3 continues to explore the understanding of sexual equality in the US Constitution by examining how the natural differences between men and women affect their respective rights and duties as citizens. To what extent, our authors ask, should American citizenship have an identifiable gender or sex-based component? As we shall see, the natural difference question fueled earlier controversies regarding suffrage and jury duty for women and continues to drive the current debate over the role of women in the military.

4 Equality of Opportunity in American Society

This chapter explores how natural difference arguments affect educational and employment prospects for men and women. Americans used these arguments in the past to limit the types of school, job and athletic opportunities that were available to women. As our readings show, sex-based differences continue to shape current disputes regarding college sports and employment issues such as parental leave after childbirth.

5 Violence

Chapter Five explores how American law deals with the twin evils of domestic violence and rape. Our prevailing legal narrative tends to characterize women as victims and men as aggressors. Yet, as our readings show, this narrative is now being challenged on two distinct, but interconnected fronts. Some authors argue that efforts to protect female victims of domestic violence are often counterproductive and disempowering. Others advocate a more neutral approach to sexual violence on the grounds that male victims of this evil deserve as much sympathy and support as female victims.

6 Marriage and Parenthood

This chapter examines three highly charged controversies regarding the institutions of marriage and parenthood as they exist in the United States today. The first concerns the value of assigned sex roles within marriage. Traditionalists tend to favor maintaining sex-based roles in some form while

their opponents argue that these roles foster injustice and should be eliminated. The second debate concerns the legal status of same-sex marriage.
Should the law treat gay and straight unions equally? Not surprisingly,
those who favor legalizing same-sex marriage tend to downplay the natural
differences between the sexes while those who oppose same-sex marriage
stress them. The third debate, which concerns the relationship between
parents and children, highlights the mostly unsuccessful efforts of fathers to
challenge laws and policies regarding custody and procreation which favor
women on natural difference grounds.

7 Sexual Equality in America—Now and in the Future

In the last chapter of the book, we briefly assess the state of sexual equality
in America today and offer some thoughts regarding the future. While
certain controversies regarding sexual equality have now ended, we believe
that many of today's critical debates regarding the scope and meaning of this
principle are still unresolved. We predict that these debates will continue to
shape our private and public conversations for many years to come.

Acknowledgments

We would like to thank those who have assisted us in bringing this project
to fruition: David Estrin for helping us to complete our original book
proposal; Karen O'Connor of American University for convincing us that
this book should be published; our editors at Bloomsbury Press, Marie-
Claire Antoine and Ally Jane Grossan, for all their constructive help; our
colleagues and friends Elias Baumgarten, Sinikka Elliott, Christian Pierce,
James Zink, and Sheva Zucker; the Political Science Department at North
Carolina State University for enabling us to co-teach a seminar on sexual
equality in America; and finally, the young men and women in this seminar
for allowing us to test different readings, arguments, and teaching strategies on them. These students, who became a true community of learners,
convinced us that Americans can discuss controversial issues regarding
sexual equality from a variety of different perspectives with insight, civility,
humor, and grace. We therefore dedicate this book to them.

1

Early American Views on Sexual Equality

Introduction

Perhaps the best starting point for understanding virtually all American debates on sexual equality is the Declaration of Independence, the document which sets forth the basic principles of our regime. Its key principles are that "all men are created equal," and are endowed by God with the natural rights to "life, liberty, and the pursuit of happiness." Scholars today disagree over whether the Founders understood the term "men" in the phrase "all men are created equal" to refer exclusively to white males, or to refer generically to all human beings, black as well as white, female as well as male.[1]

Abraham Lincoln endorsed this latter view in his famous speech on the Dred Scott decision (1858), arguing that the Founders' God did endow all individuals with equal natural rights although He did not create us equal in all respects—in intellect for example.[2] Sojourner Truth, an African–American abolitionist and feminist, used this distinction to argue for women's rights in "Ain't I a Woman?" (1851): "What's that [referring to intellect] got to do with women's rights or Negroes' rights? If my cup won't hold but a pint, and yours holds a quart, wouldn't you be mean not to let me have my little half measure full?"[3]

Yet the greatest controversy regarding sexual equality in early American history was not about language, but about how women could best secure their natural rights. The Founders clearly believed that men and women should strive to safeguard these rights differently. Men best accomplish this aim, they believed, by engaging in economic and political activity, while women do so by consenting to marry the men of their choice. This choice, if wisely made, enables them to rely on their husbands for protection, for their economic wellbeing, and for their ability to pursue their natural vocations as wives and mothers. The Founders' views on this matter were incorporated in what historians now call the "doctrine of separate spheres," a doctrine based on the then widely held view that the biological differences between men and women shape their respective social identities.

Alexis de Tocqueville summed up the doctrine of separate spheres near the end of *Democracy in America* in a chapter entitled "How the Americans Understand the Equality Between Men and Women." Americans, he wrote, believed that "nature had established such a great difference between the physical and moral constitution" of the two sexes that it clearly intended "to give a different use to their different faculties." Thus, they "carefully divided the functions of man and woman," to enable them to perform "the great work of society" in harmony with nature's intentions. Tocqueville did not explain what these natural physical and moral differences were, perhaps because he considered them obvious to most of his readers.[4]

The Founders, however, helped to illuminate these perceived differences by referring to them at various points in their writings. They considered men physically stronger and more independent than women, and thus better able to provide for the material wellbeing of their families and of society as a whole. This greater strength and independence, in their view, formed the natural basis for what they called the masculine virtues which include assertiveness, ambition, and "valor" or physical courage. These virtues enabled men to perform their assigned economic and political roles.

The Founders considered women naturally dependent on men because of their "delicacy," or vulnerability resulting from their physical weakness and their role in having and caring for children. This dependence, in their view, fostered the feminine virtues which helped them successfully perform their assigned tasks as wives and mothers. These virtues include "tenderness" or kindness and compassion, "modesty" or shyness, discretion and sexual reserve; and "sensibility" or moral awareness and emotional responsiveness.[5]

Men, according to the doctrine of separate spheres, were expected to work outside the home and to exercise civil rights connected with their economic and political responsibilities. Women, on the other hand, were confined to the "peaceful circle of domestic occupations," as Tocqueville put it, and denied civil rights on the grounds that their husbands effectively promoted their interests.[6] Founder James Wilson defended this inequality by arguing that the public sphere exists chiefly to serve the private one. "In the just order of things," he noted, "government is the scaffolding of society: and if society could be built and kept entire without government, the scaffolding might be thrown down, without the least inconvenience or cause of regret."[7]

Tocqueville also defended this inequality, claiming that women contribute more to healthy political life than men do by shaping the mores, or habits, sentiments, and ideas, which make free government possible. American clergymen generally agreed, maintaining that God made woman dependent and weak precisely in order to help her wield this "mighty power." It is the "consciousness of that weakness," the pastors of the General Association of Massachusetts maintained in 1837, "which keeps her in those departments of life that form the character of individuals and of the nation."[8]

Early American feminists strongly rejected such arguments. Sarah Grimké maintained in 1838, for example, that these pastors used flattering language in order to give men despotic power over women. While Grimké conceded that men are physically stronger than women, she strongly denied that this physical disparity requires women to be dependent on men, that it fosters two different sets of virtues, and that it has any bearing on the rights and duties which God assigned equally to both sexes. "Men and women were CREATED EQUAL;" she asserted, in that "they are both moral and accountable beings, and whatever is *right* for man to do, is *right* for woman."[9]

The American feminist movement formally began in 1848 at a women's rights convention organized by Elizabeth Cady Stanton and others in Seneca Falls, NY. The convention issued a "Declaration of Sentiments," which was a revised version of the Declaration of Independence written chiefly by Stanton herself. According to this document, the tyranny of American men over women extended from the political arena, to the marketplace, to the household, and, finally, to the bedroom. Under these circumstances, no woman could be truly free unless she enjoyed civil rights, and especially the right to vote, the "first right of a citizen."[10] Later in life, Stanton discussed the philosophical basis for her views on civil rights in "The Solitude of Self," an address she delivered before committees of the US House of Representatives and the US Senate.[11]

Frederick Douglass, the great African–American statesman, attended the Seneca Falls Convention and linked its activities to his own work as an abolitionist. "Standing as we do upon the watch-tower of human freedom," he wrote in *The North Star*, we endorse "any movement, however humble, to improve and elevate the character of any members of the human race." Douglass considered the "Declaration of Sentiments" as "the basis of a grand movement for attaining the civil, social, political and religious rights of women" despite the unpopularity of feminism among both men and women during his time.[12] In this respect, he was more than prescient. The authors of this document inaugurated perhaps the most successful social revolution in American history, one that dramatically changed law and public opinion regarding sexual equality and accomplished virtually all of its concrete aims.

Although Tocqueville lacked Douglass' foresight regarding the future of sexual equality, he indirectly offered one possible explanation for feminism's great success. Tocqueville saw the arc of history moving sharply toward equality for all Americans as the result of an unstoppable worldwide democratic revolution. The "passion for equality," he argued in *Democracy in America*, is the chief passion of modern times, "attracting to itself and sweeping along in its course all sentiments and all ideas."[13] Tocqueville knew that this powerful passion could weaken the doctrine of separate spheres and its institutional supports. Indeed, some Europeans whom he cited in the *Democracy* already argued that men and women should be "not only equal but alike," that they should "mix together in all things—work, pleasure, public affairs," and that they should have the same "functions ... duties ... and ... rights."[14]

Tocqueville believed that Americans were too inherently conservative to ever embrace what he considered such ill-conceived notions. Indeed, no early American feminists went quite as far as their European counterparts in rejecting the doctrine of separate spheres. Yet, as we shall soon see, the passion for equality utterly transformed America, leading us today to embrace key elements of the European version of sexual equality that our ancestors rejected. Indeed, this passion has helped destroy most of the legal and moral supports for the doctrine of separate spheres and has put today's traditionalists clearly on the defensive.

Notes

1   See, for example, Thomas G. West, *Vindicating the Founders: Race, Sex, Class, and Justice in the Origins of America*. Lanham, MD: Rowman & Littlefield, 1977, xii; and Conor Cruise O'Brien, *The Long Affair: Thomas Jefferson and the French Revolution, 1785–1800*. Chicago: University of Chicago Press, 1996, 319.

2   Abraham Lincoln, *Selected Speeches and Writings*, ed. Gore Vidal. New York: Vintage Books/The Library of America, 1992, 120.

3   Sojourner Truth, "Ain't I a Woman?" Delivered 1851 at the Women's Convention in Akron, Ohio. feminist.com, http://www.feminist.com/resources/artspeech/genwom/sojour.htm 1–2.

4   Alexis de Tocqueville, *Democracy in America*, trans. Stephen D. Grant, ed. Sanford Kessler. Indianapolis: Hackett Publishing Company, 2000, 265.

5   See, for example, West, *Vindicating the Founders*, 84–7.

6   Tocqueville, *Democracy in America*, 266.

7   James Wilson, "Chapter I: Introductory Lecture. Of the Study of the Law in the United States," *Collected Works of James Wilson*, vol. 1. Indianapolis: Liberty Fund, The Online Library of Liberty, 2007, http://oll.libertyfund.org/title/2072/156454 19, 1–32.

8   Pastoral Letter of the General Association of Massachusetts, June 28, 1837. http://www.wfu.edu/~zulick/340/pastoralletter.html 2, 1–4.

9   Sarah Grimké, "Letter III," *Letters on the Equality of the Sexes and Other Essays*, ed. Elizabeth Ann Bartlett. New Haven and London: Yale University Press, 1988, 38, 37–44.

10 Elizabeth Cady Stanton, "Declaration of Sentiments and Resolutions: Woman's Rights Convention Held at Seneca Falls, 19–20 July 1848," *The Elizabeth Cady Stanton and Susan B. Anthony Papers Project,* http://ecssba.rutgers.edu/docs/seneca.html 3, 1–6.

11 Elizabeth Cady Stanton, "The Solitude of Self: Address Delivered . . . before the Committee of the Judiciary of the United States Congress, Monday, January 18, 1892," http://www.wfu.edu/~zulick/340/solitude.html.

12 Frederick Douglass, "The Rights of Women: The North Star, July 22, 1848," *Uncle Tom's Cabin and American Culture,* http://utc.iath.virginia.edu/ 1–2.

13 Tocqueville, *Democracy in America,* 202.

14 Ibid., 265.

READINGS

James Wilson (1742–98)

James Wilson was an important American Founder. He served in the Continental Congress, signed the Declaration of Independence, helped draft the US Constitution, and served as one of the first Associate Justices of the U.S. Supreme Court. He wrote the *Lectures on Law*, from which the following selection is taken, after becoming the first professor of law at The College of Phildelphia in 1790.

James Wilson, "Chapter I.: Introductory Lecture. Of the Study of the Law in the United States," *Collected Works of James Wilson, vol. 1* (Indianapolis: Liberty Fund, The Online Library of Liberty, 2007) http://oll.libertyfund. org/title/2072/156454, 1–32, (Excerpts: pp. 18–20)

Methinks I hear one of the female part of my audience exclaim—What is all this to us? We have heard much of societies, of states, of governments, of laws, and of a law education. Is every thing made for your sex? Why should not we have a share? Is our sex less honest, or less virtuous, or less wise than yours?

* * *

Your sex is neither less honest, nor less virtuous, nor less wise than ours. With regard to the two first of these qualities, a superiority, on our part, will not be pretended: with regard to the last, a pretension of superiority cannot be supported.

I will name three women; and I will then challenge any of my brethren to name three men superior to them in vigour and extent of abilities. My female champions are, Semiramis of Nineveh; Zenobia, the queen of the East; and Elizabeth of England. I believe it will readily be owned, that three men of superior active talents cannot be named.

You will please, however, to take notice, that the issue, upon which I put the characters of these three ladies, is not that they were *accomplished*; it is, that they were *able* women.

This distinction immediately reminds you, that a *woman* may be an able, without being an accomplished female character.

In this latter view, I did not produce the three female characters I have mentioned. I produced them as women, merely of distinguished abilities-of abilities equal to those displayed by the most able of our sex.

But would you wish to be tried by the qualities of our sex? I will refer you to a more proper standard—that of your own.

All the three able characters, I have mentioned, had, I think too much of the masculine in them. Perhaps I can conjecture the reason. Might it not be owing, in a great measure—might it not be owing altogether to the masculine employments, to which they devoted themselves?

Two of them were able warriors: all of them were able queens; but in all of them, we feel and we regret the loss of the lovely and accomplished *woman*:....

For these reasons, I doubt much, whether it would be proper that you should undertake the management of publick affairs. You have, indeed, heard much of publick government and public law: but these things were not made for themselves: they were made for something better; and of that something better, you form the better part—I mean society—I mean particularly domestick society: there the lovely and accomplished *woman* shines with superiour lustre.

By some politicians, society has been considered as only the scaffolding of government; very improperly, in my judgment. In the just order of things, government is the scaffolding of society: and if society could be built and kept entire without government, the scaffolding might be thrown down, without the least inconvenience or cause of regret.

* * *

... Female beauty is the expression of female virtue. The purest complexion, the finest features, the most elegant shape are uninteresting and insipid, unless we can discover, by them, the emotions of the mind. How beautiful and engaging, on the other hand, are the features, the looks, and the gestures, while they disclose modesty, sensibility, and every sweet and tender affection! When these appear, there is a "Soul upon the countenance."

* * *

If nature evinces her designs by her works; you were destined to embellish, to refine, and to exalt the pleasures and virtues of social life.

To protect and to improve social life, is, as we, have seen, the end of government and law. If, therefore, you have no share in the formation, you have a most intimate connexion with the effects, of a good system of law and government.

Alexis de Tocqueville (1805–59)

Alexis de Tocqueville travelled to the United States in 1831–2 with his friend Gustave de Beaumont, ostensibly to study the American prison system, but with the deeper aim of scrutinizing all aspects of American life. The fruit of this labor was a two-volume masterpiece, *Democracy in America* (1835; 1840), which is perhaps the greatest work on the United States ever written. The selection below is from Volume II of this work.

Alexis de Tocqueville, "How the Americans Understand the Equality of Man and Woman," *Democracy in America,* trans. Stephen D. Grant, ed. Sanford Kessler (Indianapolis: Hackett Publishing Company, Inc. 2000), 265–8. (Excerpts: pp. 265–6, 267–8).

I have shown how democracy destroys or modifies the different inequalities that society brings into being. But is that all, and does it not finally succeed in acting upon this great inequality between man and woman, which has seemed up until our time to have eternal foundations in nature?

I think that the social movement that brings son and father, servant and master, and, in general, inferior and superior, nearer to the same level, will raise up woman and is bound to make her more and more the equal of man.

But it is here, more than ever, that I feel the need to be well understood; for there is no subject on which the crude and disordered imagination of our time has given itself a freer rein.

There are men in Europe who, confounding the different attributes of the sexes, claim to make of man and woman beings who are not only equal but alike. They give to both of them the same functions, impose on them the same duties, and grant them the same rights; they mix them together in all things---work, pleasure, public affairs. One can easily conceive that by endeavoring to make one sex equal to the other, both of them are lowered, and that this crude mixing of nature's works can never produce anything except weak men and indecent women.

It is not in this way that the Americans have understood the kind of democratic equality that can be established between woman and man.

They have thought that since nature had established such a great difference between the physical and moral constitution of the man and that of the woman, its clearly indicated aim was to give a different use to their different faculties; and they have judged that progress did not consist in making beings that are dissimilar do more or less the same things, but in arranging for each of them to perform their tasks as well as possible. The Americans have applied to the two sexes the great principle of political economy that rules industry in our day. They have carefully divided the functions of man and woman in order that the great work of society be better done.

America is the country in the world where the most constant care has been taken to mark out clearly separated lines of action for the two sexes and where they are obliged to march at the same pace, but always in different paths. You do not see American women govern the external affairs of the family, manage a business, or, finally, enter the political sphere; but neither does one encounter any of them who are obliged to engage in the rough work of ploughing or in any hard work that demands the development of physical strength. There are no families so poor that they make exception to this rule.

If the American woman cannot escape from the peaceful circle of domestic occupations, she is not, on the other hand, ever constrained to go out of it.

From this it results that American women, who often display a masculine reason and a very virile energy, conserve in general a very delicate appearance and always remain feminine in their manners, even though they sometimes show themselves to be masculine in mind and in heart.

Nor have the Americans ever imagined that the consequence of democratic principles was to overturn marital authority and introduce a confusion of authorities into the family. They have thought that every association, in order to be effective, had to have a head and that the natural head of the conjugal association was man. They therefore do not refuse to the latter the right to govern his wife, and they believe that, in the small society of husband and wife just as in the larger political society, the object of democracy is to regulate and to make legitimate necessary powers and not to destroy all power.

This opinion is not peculiar to one sex and opposed by the other.

* * *

Thus, the Americans do not believe that man and woman have the duty or the right to do the same things, but they show the same respect for each of their roles, and they consider them as beings of equal worth, although their destiny is different. They do not give to woman's courage the same form or use as man's, but they never doubt her courage; and if they think that the man and his wife must now always employ their intellect and their reason in the same manner, they consider, at least, that her reason is as sure as his and her intellect as clear.

The Americans, who have allowed woman's inferiority to survive in the society, have thus raised her with all their power, in the intellectual and moral world, to the level of man; and in this they appear to me to have admirably understood the true notion of democratic progress.

For myself, I will not hesitate to say it: even though in the United States the woman scarcely leaves the domestic sphere, and she is, in certain respects, very dependent within it, nowhere does her position seem to me higher; and if, now that I am approaching the end of this book in which I have pointed out so many remarkable things accomplished by the Americans, I were asked to what I think must be principally attributed the remarkable prosperity and growing strength of this people, I would answer that it is to the superiority of their women.

Sarah Grimké (1792–1873)

Sarah Grimké was born into a prominent slaveholding family in South Carolina. Disgusted by slavery, she and her sister Angelina moved North where they became America's first female abolitionists in the 1830s. In 1837, the Grimké sisters lectured extensively in the greater Boston area. While Massachussetts religious leaders generally opposed slavery, they also opposed women speaking in public. Thus, they issued a pastoral letter implicitly attacking the Grimké sisters for violating the doctrine of separate spheres. While the two sisters retired into domestic life in 1838, Sarah continued to work for women's rights privately until her death in 1873. The selections below include portions of the pastoral letter and of Sarah Grimké's response to it.

Pastoral Letter of the General Association of Massachusetts, June 28, 1837 http://www.wfu.edu/~zulick/340/pastoralletter.html, 1–4 (Excerpts: pp. 2–3)

Brethren and Friends,

Having assembled to consult upon the interests of religion within this commonwealth, we would now, as Pastors and Teachers, in accordance with the custom of this Association, address you on some of the subjects which at the present time appear to us to have an important bearing upon the cause of Christ.

* * *

III. We invite your attention to the dangers which at present seem to threaten the female character with widespread and permanent injury.

The appropriate duties and influence of women, are clearly stated in the New Testament. Those duties and that influence are unobtrusive and private, but the sources of mighty power. When the mild, dependent, softening influence of woman upon the sternness of man's opinions is fully exercised, society feels the effects of it in a thousand forms. The power of woman is in her dependence, flowing from the consciousness of that weakness which God has given her for her protection and which keeps her in those departments of life that form the character of individuals and of the nation. There are social influences which females use in promoting piety and the great objects of Christian benevolence, which we cannot too highly commend. We appreciate the unostentatious prayers and efforts of woman, in advancing the cause of religion at home and abroad:--in Sabbath schools, in leading religious inquirers to their pastor for instruction, and in all such associated effort as becomes the modesty of her sex; and earnestly hope that she may abound more and more in these labours of piety and love. But when she assumes the place and tone of a man as a public reformer, our care and protection of her seem unnecessary, we put ourselves in self defence against her, she yields the power which God has give her for protection, and her character becomes unnatural. If the vine, whose strength and beauty is to lean upon the trellis work and half conceal its clusters, thinks to assume the independence and the overshadowing nature of the elm, it will not only cease to bear fruit, but fall in shame and dishonor into the dust.

We cannot, therefore, but regret the mistaken conduct of those who encourage females to bear an obtrusive and ostentatious part in measures of reform, and countenance any of the sex who so far forget themselves as to itinerate in the character of public lecturers and teachers.

* * *

Sarah Grimké, Letter III, *Letters on the Equality of the Sexes and Other Essays*, ed. Elizabeth Ann Bartlett (New Haven and London: Yale University Press, 1988), 37–41. (Excerpts: pp. 37–8, 40, 41)

Dear Friend,

When I last addressed thee, I had not seen the Pastoral Letter of the General Association. It has since fallen into my hands, ...I am persuaded that when the minds of men and women become emancipated from the thralldom of superstition and "traditions of men," the sentiments contained in the Pastoral Letter will be recurred to with as much astonishment as the opinions of Catton Mather and other distinguished men of his day, on the subject of witchcraft...

But to the letter. It says, "We invite your attention to the dangers which at present seem to threaten the FEMALE CHARACTER with wide-spread and permanent injury." I rejoice that they have called the attention of my sex to this subject, because I believe if woman investigates it, she will soon discover that danger is impending, though from a totally different source from that which the Association apprehends, --danger from those who, having long held the reins of *usurped* authority, are unwilling to permit us to fill that sphere which God created us to move in, and who have entered into league to crush the immortal mind of woman. I rejoice, because I am persuaded that the rights of woman, like the rights of slaves, need only be examined to be understood and asserted, even by some of those, who are now endeavoring to smother the irrepressible desire for mental and spiritual freedom which glows in the breast of many, who hardly dare to speak their sentiments.

* * *

The Lord Jesus defines the duties of his followers in his Sermon on the Mount. he lays down grand principles by which they should be governed, without any reference to sex or condition....I follow him through all his precepts, and find him giving the same directions to women as to men, never even referring to the distinction now so strenuously insisted upon between masculine and feminine virtues: this is one of the anti-christian "traditions of men" which are taught instead of the "commandments of God." Men and women were CREATED EQUAL; they are both moral and accountable beings, and whatever is *right* for man to do, is *right* for woman."

..."Her influence is the source of mighty power." This has ever been the flattering language of man since he laid aside the whip as a means to keep woman in subjection. He spares her body; but the war he has waged against her mind, her heart, and her soul, has been no less destructive to her as a moral being. How monstrous, how anti-christian, is the doctrine that woman is to be dependent on man! Where, in all the sacred Scriptures, is this taught? Alas! she has too well learned the lesson, which MAN has labored to teach her. She has surrendered her dearest RIGHTS, and been satisfied with the privileges which man has assumed to grant her; she has been amused with the show of power, whilst man has absorbed all the reality into himself...

* * *

But we are told, "the power of woman is in her dependence, flowing from a consciousness of that weakness which God has given her for her protection." If physical weakness is alluded to, I cheerfully concede the superiority; if brute force is what my brethren are claiming, I am willing to let them have all the honor they desire; but if they mean to intimate, that mental or moral weakness belongs to woman, more than to man, I utterly disclaim the charge. Our powers of mind have been crushed, as far as man could do it, our sense of morality has been impaired by his interpretation of our duties; but no where does God say that he made any distinction between us, as moral and intelligent beings.

* * *

...Ah! how many of my sex feel in the dominion, thus unrighteously exercised over them, under the gentle appellation of protection, that what they have leaned upon has proved a broken reed at best, and oft a spear.

Elizabeth Cady Stanton (1815–1902)

Elizabeth Cady Stanton was one of the most important founders of the American feminist movement. In 1848, she helped organize the first women's rights convention in Seneca Falls, New York where she issued the "Declaration of Sentiments," an early manifesto of that movement. Stanton worked for women's rights with other great 19th century feminists such as Susan B. Anthony until her death in 1902. The selections below are from the "Declaration of Sentiments" and "Solitude of Self" (1892), a speech which describes the individualist view of human nature which shaped her approach to life.

Elizabeth Cady Stanton, "Declaration of Sentiments and Resolutions: Woman's Rights Convention Held at Seneca Falls, 19–20 July 1848," *The Elizabeth Cady Stanton & Susan B. Anthony Papers Project,* http://ecssba. rutgers.edu/docs/seneca.html, 1–6. (Excerpts: pp. 3–4)

* * *

Declaration of Sentiments

We hold these truths to be self-evident: that all men and women are created equal; that they are endowed by their Creator with certain inalienable rights; that among these are life, liberty, and the pursuit of happiness; that to secure these rights governments are instituted, deriving their just powers from the consent of the governed. Whenever any form of Government becomes destructive of these ends, it is the right of those who suffer from it to refuse allegiance to it, and to insist upon the institution of a new government, laying its foundation on such principles, and organizing its powers in such form as to them shall seem most likely to effect their safety and happiness....

The history of mankind is a history of repeated injuries and usurpations on the part of man toward woman, having in direct object the establishment of an absolute tyranny over her. To prove this, let facts be submitted to a candid world.

He has never permitted her to exercise her inalienable right to the elective franchise.

He has compelled her to submit to laws, in the formation of which she had no voice.

He has withheld from her rights which are given to the most ignorant and degraded men—both natives and foreigners.

Having deprived her of this first right of a citizen, the elective franchise, thereby leaving her without representation in the halls of legislation, he has oppressed her on all sides.

He has made her, if married, in the eye of the law, civilly dead.

He has taken from her all right in property, even to the wages she earns.

He has made her, morally, an irresponsible being, as she can commit many crimes with impunity, provided they be done in the presence of her husband. In the covenant of marriage, she is compelled to promise obedience to her husband, he becoming, to all intents and purposes, her master—the law giving him power to deprive her of her liberty, and to administer chastisement.

He has so framed the laws of divorce, as to what shall be the proper causes of divorce; in case of separation, to whom the guardianship of the children shall be given; as to be wholly regardless of the happiness of women—the law, in all cases, going upon the false supposition of the supremacy of man, and giving all power into his hands.

After depriving her of all rights as a married woman, if single and the owner of property, he has taxed her to support a government which recognizes her only when her property can be made profitable to it.

He has monopolized nearly all the profitable employments, and from those she is permitted to follow, she receives but a scanty remuneration.

He closes against her all the avenues to wealth and distinction, which he considers most honorable to himself. As a teacher of theology, medicine, or law, she is not known.

He has denied her the facilities for obtaining a thorough education—all colleges being closed against her.

He allows her in Church as well as State, but a subordinate position, claiming Apostolic authority for her exclusion from the ministry, and, with some exceptions from any public participation in the affairs of the Church.

He has created a false public sentiment, by giving to the world a different code of morals for men and women, by which moral delinquencies which exclude women from society, are not only tolerated but deemed of little account in man.

He has usurped the prerogative of Jehovah himself, claiming it as his right to assign for her a sphere of action, when that belongs to her conscience and her God.

He has endeavored, in every way that he could to destroy her confidence in her own powers, to lessen her self-respect, and to make her willing to lead a dependent and abject life.

Now, in view of this entire disfranchisement of one half the people of this country, their social and religious degradation,-in view of the unjust laws above mentioned, and because women do feel themselves aggrieved, oppressed, and fraudulently deprived of their most sacred rights, we insist that they have immediate admission to all the rights and privileges which belong to them as citizens of these United States.

* * *

Elizabeth Cady Stanton, "Solitude of Self" Address Delivered...before
the Committee of the Judiciary of the United States Congress, Monday,
January 18, 1892." http://www.wfu.edu/~zulick/340/solitude.html, 1–10
(Excerpts: pp. 1–2, 4, 6–7, 8, 10)

* * *

The point I wish plainly to bring before you on this occasion is the
individuality of each human soul; our Protestant idea, the right of individual
conscience and judgment-our republican idea, individual citizenship. In
discussing the rights of woman, we are to consider, first, what belongs to
her as an individual, in a world of her own, the arbiter of her own destiny...
Her rights under such circumstances are to use all her faculties for her own
safety and happiness.

Secondly, if we consider her as a citizen, as a member of a great nation,
she must have the same rights as all other members, according to the
fundamental principles of our Government.

Thirdly, viewed as a woman, an equal factor in civilization, her rights and
duties are still the same – individual happiness and development.

* * *

The strongest reason for giving woman all the opportunities for higher
education, for the full development of her faculties, forces of mind and
body; for giving her the most enlarged freedom of thought and action; a
complete emancipation from all forms of bondage, of custom, dependence,
superstition; from all the crippling influences of fear, is the solitude and
personal responsibility of her own individual life. The strongest reason why
we ask for woman a voice in the government under which she lives; in the
religion she is asked to believe; equality in social life, where she is a chief
factor; a place in the trades and professions, where she may earn her bread,
is because of her birthright to self-sovereignty; because, as an individual
she must rely on herself. No matter how much women prefer to lean, to be
protected and supported, nor how much men desire to have them do so,
they must make the voyage of life alone, and for safety in an emergency
they must know something of the laws of navigation....

* * *

...Seeing then that life must ever be a march and a battle, that each soldier
must be equipped for his own protection, it is the height of cruelty to rob
the individual of a single natural right.

To throw obstacles in the way of a complete education is like putting out the eyes; to deny the rights of property, like cutting off the hands. To deny political equality is to rob the ostracised of all self-respect; of credit in the market place; of recompense in the world of work; of a voice among those who make and administer the law; a choice in the jury before whom they are tried, and in the judge who decides their punishment. ...What a picture of woman's position! Robbed of her natural rights, handicapped by law and custom at every turn, yet compelled to fight her own battles, and in the emergencies of life to fall back on herself for protection.

* * *

Nothing strengthens the judgment and quickens the conscience like individual responsibility. Nothing adds such dignity to character as the recognition of one's self-sovereignty; the right to an equal place, everywhere conceded; a place earned by personal merit, not an artificial attainment, by inheritance, wealth, family, and position. Seeing, then, that the responsibilities of life rest equally on man and woman, that their destiny is the same, they need the same preparation for time and eternity; The talk of sheltering woman from the fierce storms of life is the sheerest mockery, for they beat on her from every point of the compass, just as they do on man, and with more fatal results, for he has been trained to protect himself, to resist, to conquer. Such are the facts in human experience, the responsibilities of individual sovereignty. Rich and poor, intelligent and ignorant, wise and foolish, virtuous and vicious, man and woman, it is ever the same, each soul must depend wholly on itself.

* * *

But when all artificial trammels are removed, and women are recognized as individuals, responsible for their own environments, thoroughly educated for all positions in life they may be called to fill; with all the resources in themselves that liberal thought and broad culture can give; guided by their own conscience and judgment; trained to self-protection by a healthy development of the muscular system and skill in the use of weapons of defense, and stimulated to self-support by a knowledge of the business world and the pleasure that pecuniary independence must ever give; when women are trained in this way they will, in a measure, be fitted for those hours of solitude that come alike to all, whether prepared or otherwise. As in our extremity we must depend on ourselves, the dictates of wisdom point to complete individual development.

* * *

Such is individual life. Who, I ask you, can take, dare take, on himself the rights, the duties, the responsibilities of another human soul?

Frederick Douglass (1818–95)

Frederick Douglass was perhaps the greatest African-American statesman of the 19th century. Born into slavery on a Maryland plantation in 1818, he fled North via the underground railroad in 1838 and began his career as an abolitionist in Massachusetts in 1841. He later wrote about his experiences as a slave in *The Narrative of the Life of Frederick Douglass* (1845), the first of several autobiographical works. In 1847–60 he published *The North Star* (later *Frederick Douglass's Paper*), an anti-slavery newspaper which he also used to champion the cause of women's rights. This selection below is taken from *The North Star*.

Frederick Douglass, "The Rights of Women," *The North Star*, July 28, 1848," *Uncle Tom's Cabin and American Culture*, http://utc.iath.virginia. edu/, 1–2.

One of the most interesting events of the past week, was the holding of what is technically styled a Woman's Rights Convention at Seneca Falls...Several interesting documents setting forth the rights as well as the grievances of women were read. Among these was a Declaration of Sentiments, to be regarded as the basis of a grand movement for attaining the civil, social, political, and religious rights of women. We should not do justice to our own convictions, or to the excellent persons connected with this infant movement, if we did not in this connection offer a few remarks on the general subject which the Convention met to consider and the objects they seek to attain. In doing so, we are not insensible that the bare mention of this truly important subject in any other than terms of contemptuous ridicule and scornful disfavor, is likely to excite against us the fury of bigotry and the folly of prejudice. A discussion of the rights of animals would be regarded with far more complacency by many of what are called the *wise* and the *good* of our land than would be a discussion of the rights of women. It is, in their estimation, to be guilty of evil thoughts, to think that a woman is entitled to equal rights with man. Many who have at last made the discovery that the negroes have some rights as well as other members of the human family, have yet to be convinced that women are entitled to any....Standing as we do upon the watch-tower of human freedom, we cannot be deterred from an expression of our approbation of any movement, however humble, to improve and elevate the character of any members of the human family. While it is impossible for us to go into this subject at length, and dispose of the various objections which are often urged against such a doctrine as that of female equality, we are free to say that in respect to political rights, we hold woman to be justly entitled to all we claim for man. We go farther, and express our conviction that all political rights that it is expedient for man to exercise, it is equally so for woman. All that distinguishes man as an intelligent and accountable being, is equally true of woman; and if that government only is just which governs by the free consent of the governed, there can be no reason in the world for denying to woman the exercise of the elective franchise, or a hand in making and administering the laws of the land. Our doctrine is that "right is of no sex." We therefore bid the women engaged in this movement our humble Godspeed.

Sojourner Truth (1797–1883)

Sojourner Truth was born into slavery in New York, but was freed by her master shortly before the state abolished slavery in 1827. In 1843, she began her long career as a preacher, an abolitionist, and a feminist. "Ain't I a Woman," the selection below, is her best known speech on the subject of women's rights. Truth helped black soldiers and former slaves during the Civil War and was received at the White House by President Abraham Lincoln.

Sojourner Truth, Ain't I A Woman? Delivered 1851 at the Women's Convention in Akron, Ohio." *feminist.com,* http://www.feminist.com/resources/artspeech/genwom/sojour.htm, 1–2.

Well, children, where there is so much racket there must be something out of kilter. I think that 'twixt the negroes of the South and the women at the North, all talking about rights, the white men will be in a fix pretty soon. But what's all this here talking about?

That man over there says that women need to be helped into carriages, and lifted over ditches, and to have the best place everywhere. Nobody ever helps me into carriages, or over mud-puddles, or gives me any best place! And ain't I a woman? Look at me! Look at my arm! I have ploughed and planted, and gathered into barns, and no man could head me! And ain't I a woman? I could work as much and eat as much as a man—when I could get it—and bear the lash as well! And ain't I a woman? I have borne thirteen children, and seen most all sold off to slavery, and when I cried out with my mother's grief, none but Jesus heard me! And ain't I a woman?

Then they talk about this thing in the head; what's this they call it? [member of audience whispers, "intellect"] That's it, honey. What's that got to do with women's rights or negroes' rights? If my cup won't hold but a pint, and yours holds a quart, wouldn't you be mean not to let me have my little half measure full?

Then that little man in black there, he says women can't have as much rights as men, 'cause Christ wasn't a woman! Where did your Christ come from? Where did your Christ come from? From God and a woman! Man had nothing to do with Him.

If the first woman God ever made was strong enough to turn the world upside down all alone, these women together ought to be able to turn it back, and get it right side up again! And now they is asking to do it, the men better let them.

Obliged to you for hearing me, and now old Sojourner ain't got nothing more to say.

Questions

1 Why was the "doctrine of separate spheres" so widely accepted at the time of the American Founding? Has this doctrine survived in any form today?

2 What is the relationship between civil rights and natural rights? If women are denied civil rights, is it plausible to believe, as the American Founders did, that the relevant men in their lives can or will secure their natural rights?

3 What distinguishes the early traditionalists from the early reformers with respect to their understanding of the biological differences between the sexes?

4 Compare the African–American struggle for freedom prior to the Civil War with the early American feminist struggle for civil rights. In what respects are these struggles similar and in what respects different?

5 Why is the American feminist movement considered one of the most highly successful social movements in American history? What accounts for the ability of this movement to change American law and public opinion so dramatically over time?

Suggested Reading

West, Thomas G. *Vindicating the Founders: Race, Sex, Class, and Justice in the Origins of America.* Lanham, MD: Rowman and Littlefield, 1997.

Degler, Carl. *At Odds: Women and the Family in America from the Revolution to the Present.* New York: Oxford University Press, 1981.

Tocqueville, Alexis de. *Democracy in America*, trans. Stephen D. Grant, ed. Sanford Kessler. Indianapolis: Hackett Press, 2000.

Grimké, Sarah. *Letters on the Equality of the Sexes and Other Essays*, ed. Elizabeth Ann Bartlett. New Haven and London: Yale University Press, 1988.

Stanton, Elizabeth Cady, and Anthony, Susan B. *The Elizabeth Cady Stanton–Susan B. Anthony Reader: Correspondence, Writings, Speeches,* ed. Ellen Carol Dubois. Boston: Northeastern University Press, 1992.

2

Sexual Equality:
A Constitutional Perspective

Introduction

The ratification of the United States Constitution and its Bill of Rights had little impact, if any, on the status of women in early American society. This document was directed at constraining federal power rather than changing the laws and practices of states. Thus, while the Constitution explicitly condoned, or at least permitted, the existence of slavery,[1] it was basically silent about the status of women, which was considered exclusively a matter of state concern. Early advocates for expanding opportunities for women, therefore, adopted political and social rather than constitutional strategies for change.

Equality under the Fourteenth Amendment

The ratification of the Fourteenth Amendment in 1868 changed the country's legal landscape because the Amendment's language suggested that it could be used to protect the rights of individuals against state action. Initially, the United States Supreme Court argued that the framers of the Fourteenth Amendment intended to protect former slaves from retaliatory state actions and to provide them with the means of becoming full and equal American citizens. Early feminists hoped, therefore, that the Privileges or Immunities Clause of the Fourteenth Amendment, which protects the "privileges or immunities of United States citizenship," could also advance their cause. They argued that women, as American citizens, were entitled to the same citizenship privileges as men which includes the right to vote and the right to pursue careers.[2]

The US Supreme Court's interpretation of the Privileges or Immunities Clause in the late nineteenth century, however, had little effect on expanding opportunities for women outside of the home. The Court ruled that "privileges or immunities" of American citizenship included using the nation's waterways and petitioning the federal government,[3] and thus, left undisturbed the existing moral and legal supports for the separate spheres doctrine. In an often quoted opinion in the case of *Bradwell v. Illinois* (1873),[4] Justice Joseph Bradley argued that women, regardless of their citizenship status, were naturally suited for their traditional roles of wives and mothers and, therefore, should not be allowed to become licensed attorneys. "The natural and proper timidity and delicacy which belongs to the female sex evidently," Justice Bradley explained, "unfits it for many of the occupations of civil life. The constitution of the family organization, which is founded in the divine ordinance, as well as in the nature of things, indicates the domestic sphere as that which properly belongs to the domain and functions of womanhood."[5]

Equal Protection and the Court's Two-Tiered Approach

After the Supreme Court rendered the Privileges or Immunities Clause of the Fourteenth Amendment useless with respect to promoting equality, reformers turned to the Amendment's Equal Protection Clause to achieve this end. The Court initially held that the Equal Protection Clause challenged discriminatory acts directed at African-Americans. However, in 1886, the justices ruled in a case involving a Chinese owner of a laundry that it could also challenge racially discriminatory laws, regardless of whether or not the aggrieved person was a former slave.[6] In 1938, Justice Harlan Fiske Stone's famous "Footnote Four" appended to his opinion in *United States v. Carolene Products*[7] argued that "insular and discrete minorities" (racial and ethnic minorities) deserved special judicial protection from discriminatory state action. Justice Stone's argument in Footnote Four became the philosophical foundation for what has come to be known as the Court's two-tiered approach to constitutional equality.

The two-tiered approach was based on two principles. The first holds that groups which are alike or "similarly situated" must be treated equally under the law. The second holds that policy choices resulting in unequal or discriminatory treatment must be reasonable rather than arbitrary.

According to these principles, "suspect classes"[8] or, "insular and discrete minorities," as Stone put it, comprised one tier or category. Racial and ethnic minorities, the Court argued, deserved special constitutional protection from discriminatory laws because they experienced discrimination historically, because they are all more alike than different, and because discrimination based on race or ethnicity is presumptively unreasonable. In several decisions after *Carolene Products*, the Court held that, absent a "compelling government interest," governments could not treat persons differently because of their race or ethnicity.

Until the 1970's, other, non-racial/ethnic groups were metaphorically placed in the Court's second tier. These groups included the old and young, the rich and the poor, the disabled and able-bodied, straights and gays, and men and women. The Court argued that, unlike suspect classes, these groups consisted of individuals who were sufficiently different or "differently situated" that governments could treat them differently or unequally as long as they showed a "rational basis" for their policy choices. The Court's two-tiered approach to constitutional equality remained in effect until the justices developed a new adjudicative strategy to respond to increasing demands for greater sexual equality.

Sexual Equality, Natural Differences, and the Constitution

Until the 1970s, Court majorities upheld sex-based policies using natural difference arguments to justify keeping women in the second tier. The case of *Goesaert v. Cleary*[9] is illustrative. The *Goesaert* case reached the Supreme Court in 1948 when a female bar owner challenged Michigan law prohibiting women who were not the wives or daughters of male bar owners from working as bartenders in licensed bars. Although the Court noted that many women worked outside of the home and at jobs traditionally held by men, a majority still upheld the restriction on the grounds that it was reasonable for the Michigan legislature to believe that bartending was an inappropriate job for most women.

By the 1970s, the Supreme Court, like other American institutions, reconsidered its approach to sexual equality as a result of the sweeping political and social changes that transformed America in the previous two decades. Perhaps the most dramatic of these changes resulted from the Civil Rights Movement. The achievements of this broad-based effort to protect the civil rights of African-Americans included the passage of federal civil rights legislation outlawing discriminatory state laws, and perhaps most important, the protection of minority voting rights.

Political and Social Changes

The struggle to achieve racial equality led reformers to re-energize efforts to add an amendment to the US Constitution which would establish legal equality for women in all spheres of life. This effort, which began shortly after the passage of the Nineteenth Amendment, failed to make headway until 1972 when Congress passed the Equal Rights Amendment by the constitutionally required two-thirds vote in both houses. The ERA was ultimately defeated, however, when reformers failed to secure its ratification by the constitutionally required three-fourths of the state legislatures. Traditionalists succeeded in defeating the ERA partly because many Americans—women as well as men—believed that women deserved special legal protection in areas such as employment, marriage and military service on natural difference grounds.

New Approach to Sexual Equality

During the struggle for the passage of the ERA, the Supreme Court began to re-examine how it adjudicated claims of sex discrimination. In the 1971 case of *Reed v. Reed*,[10] the Court signaled that it was no longer willing to be as deferential to policy makers as it had been in the past. The *Reed* case stemmed from a Utah law that established a preference for males when determining who would be the executor of an estate when the deceased died without a will. Striking down the law as unconstitutional, a unanimous Supreme Court maintained that it would continue to use the rational basis analysis for sex discrimination claims, but it would scrutinize future cases with less deference to legislators.

The unanimity in *Reed* soon dissolved when several sex discrimination cases reached the Court between 1971 and 1976.[11] The breakdown was most apparent when *Frontiero v. Richardson*[12] reached the Court in 1973. *Frontiero* involved a challenge to the Federal Government's benefits policy in which the dependents of female service members seeking benefits had to meet more stringent eligibility requirements than dependents of male service members. Eight justices ruled the sex-based policy unconstitutional, but evenly split over why the policy was unconstitutional and over how to adjudicate future sex discrimination cases.

Four justices argued that the rational basis test, as applied in *Reed v. Reed*, should continue to be used to adjudicate sexual equality claims. This test, they argued, provided the necessary flexibility to uphold policies that reasonably accounted for the natural differences between men and women and to invalidate policies that unreasonably discount the similarities between them.[13]

Four justices recommended a new approach to deciding sexual equality claims, however.[14] They argued that "sex" should be considered a suspect class and should have the same constitutional status as "race." Sex-based classifications (made on natural difference grounds) should be presumed to be unconstitutional because, in their view, men and women, like racial groups, were more alike than they were different. The practical effect of adopting this approach would have been to incorporate an "equal rights" mandate in the Constitution by judicial fiat.

The Court adopted a compromise between the two blocs in *Craig v. Boren* (1976)[15] established a new, middle (intermediate tier) approach to adjudicating sex discrimination cases. With varying levels of commitment, seven justices agreed both that sex and race were constitutionally distinct and that the rational basis standard was insufficiently stringent to advance a constitutionally required level of sexual equality. The intermediate tier approach, or what is known as "heightened scrutiny," treats each sex discrimination case individually.

Heightened judicial scrutiny represents a mid-point between the strict criteria used in deciding cases for "suspect classes" such as race, and the rational basis standard which defers to lawmakers. Under this approach, a sex-based classification must be based on an "important government objective" rather than just a legitimate government interest, and the classification must be "substantially related" to that objective rather than merely be a "reasonable" means to achieve it. Finally, the intermediate tier requires policy makers to show that the important government objective cannot be achieved by adopting gender-neutral policies.

In several subsequent decisions,[16] the Court added a yet more stringent test to the adjudicative approach developed in *Craig*. The Court ruled that "the burden remains on the party seeking to uphold a statute that expressly discriminates on the basis of sex to advance an 'exceedingly persuasive justification' for the challenged classification."[17] The Court explained that such a justification cannot be based on sex stereotypes and sex generalizations. In so doing, the Court seemed to indicate that only the most obvious natural differences between men and women provide constitutionally defensible grounds for treating the sexes unequally.

The 2001 case of *Nguyen and Boulais v. INS*[18] demonstrates that the justices' current approach to sexual equality has failed to unite the Court. Some justices have used natural difference arguments to defend policies that treat the sexes differently while other justices have argued that these arguments are no longer relevant in modern America. The issue in this case was whether the Federal Government can use a sex-based standard for bestowing citizenship on a child born out of wedlock to an American citizen and a non-citizen when the birth occurs outside the territory of the United States. The government policy imposes different requirements for children whose mothers are American citizens and for children whose fathers are American citizens. The central question in the *Nguyen* case was whether the biological differences between mothers and fathers justify treating their children differently for purposes of attaining American citizenship. A Court majority upheld the policy.

Conclusion

The United States Supreme Court still uses the intermediate scrutiny criterion developed in *Craig v. Boren* (1976) to adjudicate claims of sex discrimination. When the Court adopted the adjudicative principle that similarly situated groups and individuals must be treated similarly under the law, it placed natural difference arguments at the center of its efforts to define the scope of sexual equality under the Constitution. The justices incorporated the "exceedingly persuasive justification" standard in its analysis to insure that sex stereotypes would not be used as an excuse to defend traditional practices that fostered sexual inequality. Under the Court's current approach, the constitutionality of sex-based policies depends upon whether policy makers can convince a Court majority that the natural differences between the sexes justify treating men and women differently.

Notes

1 Three-fifths Clause (Art. I, Sec. 2, Cl. 3), the 1808 Clause (Art. I, Sec. 9, Cl. 1) and the Fugitive Slave Clause (Art. IV, Sec. 2, Cl. 3) are examples.

2 See *Minor v. Happersett*, 88 US 162 (1875) and *Bradwell v. Illinois*, 83 US 130 (1873).

3 See *The Slaughterhouse Cases*, 83 US 36 (1873).

4 83 US 130 (1873).

5 83 US 130, 141 (1873).

6 See *Yick Wo v. Hopkins*, 118 US 356 (1886).

7 See *United States v. Carolene Products Co.*, 304 US 144, 153 Footnote 4 (1938).

8 See *Korematsu v. United States*, 323 US 214 (1944).

9 335 US 464 (1948).

10 404 US 71 (1971).

11 Many of the sex discrimination cases that reached the Court during this period will be discussed later in this chapter and in subsequent chapters. Representative of these cases are *Weinberger v. Wisenfeld*, 420 US 636 (1975); *Stanley v. Illinois*, 405 US 645 (1972); and *Stanton v. Stanton*, 421 US 7 (1975).

12 411 US 677 (1973).

13 The four justices in the bloc were Chief Justice Warren Burger along with Justices Lewis Powell, Harry Blackmun and Potter Stewart. Justice William Rehnquist was the sole dissenter.

14 The four justices in this bloc were Justices William Brennan, William O. Douglas, Bryon White and Thurgood Marshall.

15 429 US 190 (1976).

16 See *Kirchberg v. Feenstra et al.*, 450 US 455 (1981); *Personnel Administrator of Massachusetts v. Feeney*, 442 US 256 (1979); *Mississippi University for Women v. Hogan*, 458 US 718 (1982).

17 See *Kirchberg v. Feenstra et al.*, 450 US 455, 461 (1981).

18 533 US 53 (2001).

READINGS

Goesaert et al. v. Cleary, et al., 335 US 464 (1948)

By the 1940's, women were no longer bound by the same restrictions that prevented early American women from pursuing jobs outside of the home. Under the Court's interpretation of the Equal Protection Clause, sex-based classifications had to have a rational basis to be constitutional. In assessing the reasonableness of the state policies that discriminated on the basis of sex, the Court adopted a deferential posture and was unwilling to conclude that state legislators acted unreasonably when the treating men and women differently.

The case of *Goesaert v. Cleary* illustrates how the Court used its traditional two-tiered approach to resolve sexual equality cases. Goesasert resulted from a challenge to a Michigan law regulating the licensing of bartenders in the state. Citing social and moral concerns, Michigan lawmakers prohibited women who were neither the wives nor daughters of male owners of licensed liquor establishments from working as bartenders. One of the litigants challenging the restriction was a female bar owner, who, under the Michigan act, was unable to tend bar in her own establishment.

The following excerpt from Justice Felix Frankfurter's majority opinion shows the Court's deference to state governments.

GOESAERT ET AL. v. CLEARY ET AL., MEMBERS OF THE LIQUOR CONTROL COMMISSION OF MICHIGAN

SUPREME COURT OF THE UNITED STATES

335 U.S. 464; 69 S. Ct. 198; 93 L. Ed. 163; 1948 U.S. LEXIS 2715

December 20, 1948, Decided

OPINION

[*465] [**199] [***165] MR. JUSTICE FELIX FRANKFURTER delivered the opinion of the Court.

*HN1*As part of the Michigan system for controlling the sale of liquor, bartenders are required to be licensed in all cities having a population of

50,000 or more, but no female may be so licensed unless she be "the wife or daughter of the male owner" of a licensed liquor establishment.

We are, to be sure, dealing with a historic calling. We meet the alewife, sprightly and ribald, in Shakespeare, but centuries before him she played a role in the social life of England. The *Fourteenth Amendment* did not tear history up by the roots, and the regulation of the liquor traffic is one of the oldest and most untrammeled of legislative powers. Michigan could, beyond question, forbid all women from working behind a bar. This is so despite the vast changes [*466] in the social and legal position of women. The fact that women may now have achieved the virtues that men have long claimed as their prerogatives and now indulge in vices that men have long practiced, does not preclude the States from drawing a sharp line between the sexes, certainly in such matters as the regulation of the liquor traffic. The Constitution does not require legislatures to reflect sociological insight, or shifting social standards, any more than it requires them to keep abreast of the latest scientific standards.

While Michigan may deny to all women opportunities for bartending, Michigan cannot play favorites among women without rhyme or reason. HN3The Constitution in enjoining the equal protection of the laws upon States precludes irrational discrimination as between persons or groups of persons in the incidence of a law. But the Constitution does not require situations "which are different in fact or opinion to be treated in law as though they [**200] were the same." *Tigner v. Texas,* [***166]

Since bartending by women may, in the allowable legislative judgment, give rise to moral and social problems against which it may devise preventive measures, the legislature need not go to the full length of prohibition if it believes that as to a defined group of females other factors are operating which either eliminate or reduce the moral and social problems otherwise calling for prohibition. Michigan evidently believes that the oversight assured through ownership of a bar by a barmaid's husband or father minimizes hazards that may confront a barmaid without such protecting oversight. This Court is certainly not in a position to gainsay such belief by the Michigan legislature. If it is entertainable, as we think it is, Michigan has not violated its duty to afford equal protection of its laws. We cannot cross-examine either actually or argumentatively the mind of Michigan legislators [*467] nor question their motives. Since the line they have drawn is not without a basis in reason, we cannot give ear to the suggestion that the real impulse behind this legislation was an unchivalrous desire of male bartenders to try to monopolize the calling.

Reed v. Reed 404 US 71 (1971)

In 1971, a unanimous United States Supreme Court intimated that it was changing the way in which it address sex discrimination claims. *Reed v. Reed* involved a challenge to Utah's policy for determining who will serve as executor/administrator of estates when the decedent died without a will or intestate. The law created classes of survivors (parents, spouses, siblings, children, etc.) to determine executor. Under Utah law, males would always be preferred over female in every class. For example, in deciding whether a daughter or son of a parent who dies intestate would be the estate's executor, Utah requires that, regardless of the skills, temperament or experiences of daughter, the son will be the executor.

Reed v. Reed stemmed from a dispute between a mother and father to become executor of the estate of their deceased child. Under the Utah statute, the father automatically was the executor. Ms. Reed challenged the statute as an unconstitutional form of sex discrimination.

The following is an excerpt of Chief Justice Warren Burger's unanimous opinion in *Reed v. Reed* (1971). Chief Justice Burger was appointed to the United States Supreme Court by President Richard Nixon. He was considered a conservative justice who was Chief Justice when the Court decided *Roe v. Wade* (1973), the decision that recognized a right to abortion.

REED v. REED, ADMINISTRATOR

SUPREME COURT OF THE UNITED STATES

404 U.S. 71; 92 S. Ct. 251; 30 L. Ed. 2d 225; 1971 U.S. LEXIS 8

November 22, 1971, Decided

OPINION BY: BURGER

MR. CHIEF JUSTICE WARREN BURGER delivered the opinion of the Court.

* * *

Section 15-312[2] designates the persons who are entitled to administer the estate of one who dies intestate. In making these designations, that section lists 11 classes [***228] of persons who are so entitled and provides, in substance, [*73] that the order in which those classes are listed in the section shall be determinative of the relative rights of competing applicants for letters of administration. One of the 11 classes so enumerated is "the father or mother" of the person dying intestate. Under this section, then, appellant and appellee, being members of the same entitlement class, would seem to have been equally entitled to administer their son's estate. Section 15-314 provides, however, that

"of several persons claiming and equally entitled [under § 15-312] to administer, males must be preferred to females, and relatives of the whole to those of the half blood."

* * *

In issuing its order, the probate court implicitly recognized the equality of entitlement of the two applicants under § 15-312 and noted that neither of the applicants was under any legal disability; the court ruled, however, that appellee, being a male, was to be preferred to the female appellant "by reason of Section 15-314 of the Idaho Code." In stating this conclusion, the probate judge gave no indication that he had attempted to determine the relative capabilities of the competing applicants to perform the functions incident to the administration of an estate. It seems clear the probate judge considered himself bound by statute to give preference to the male candidate over the female, each being otherwise "equally entitled."

* * *

Idaho does not, of course, deny letters of administration to women altogether. Indeed, under § 15-312, a woman whose spouse dies intestate has a preference over a son, father, brother, or any other male relative of the decedent. Moreover, we can judicially notice that in this country, presumably due to the greater longevity of women, a large proportion of estates, both intestate and under wills of decedents, are administered by surviving widows.

Section 15-314 is restricted in its operation to those situations where competing applications for letters of administration have been filed by both male and female members of the same entitlement class established by § 15-312. In such situations, § 15-314 provides that different treatment be accorded to the applicants on the basis of their sex; it thus establishes a classification subject to scrutiny under the Equal Protection Clause.

In applying that clause, this Court has consistently recognized that the Fourteenth Amendment does not deny to States the power to treat different classes of persons in different ways. The Equal Protection Clause of that amendment [**254] does, however, deny to States the power to legislate that different treatment be accorded to persons placed by a statute into [*76] different classes on the basis of criteria wholly unrelated to the objective of that statute. A classification "must be reasonable, not arbitrary, and must rest upon some ground of difference having a fair and substantial relation to the object of the legislation, so that all persons similarly circumstanced shall be treated alike." *Royster Guano Co. v. Virginia*, 253 U.S. 412, 415 (1920). The question presented by this case, then, is whether a difference in the sex of competing applicants for letters of administration bears a rational relationship to a state objective that is sought to be advanced by the operation of §§ 15-312 and 15-314.

* * *

...To give a mandatory preference to members of either sex over members of the other, merely to accomplish the elimination of hearings on the merits, is to make the very kind of arbitrary legislative choice forbidden by the Equal Protection Clause of the Fourteenth Amendment; and whatever may be [*77] said as to the positive values of avoiding intrafamily controversy, the choice in this context may not lawfully be mandated solely on the basis of sex.

The objective of § 15-312 clearly is to establish degrees of entitlement of various classes of persons in accordance with their varying degrees and kinds of relationship to the intestate. Regardless of their sex, persons within any one of the enumerated classes of that section are similarly situated with respect to that objective. By providing dissimilar treatment for men and women who are thus similarly situated, the challenged section violates the Equal Protection Clause.

The judgment of the Idaho Supreme Court is reversed and the case remanded for further proceedings not inconsistent with this opinion.

Reversed and remanded.

Frontiero v. Richardson, 411 US 677 (1973)

Four justices of the Supreme Court used *Frontiero v. Richardson* to propose a new approach for adjudicating sexual equality cases under the United States Constitution. The *Frontiero* case involved a challenge to the Federal Government's policy of providing benefits to dependents of military service members. Under the policy, wives of servicemen automatically received full spousal/dependency benefits while husbands of servicewomen had to demonstrate their actual dependency on their wives' incomes. Sharon Frontiero, a lieutenant in the United States Air Force, sought housing and medical benefits for her husband. Lieutenant Frontiero's husband had to demonstrate that he was, in fact, dependent on his wife for half of his support. When her husband was denied benefits, Frontiero charged that this spousal/dependency benefit system amounted to unconstitutional sex discrimination.

The following is an excerpt from Justice William Brennan's plurality opinion. Joined by Justices Douglas, White and Marshall, Justice Brennan argued for a new approach to adjudicate claims of sex discrimination. Justice William Brennan was appointed by Republican President Dwight Eisenhower, and Justice Brennan became one of the leading liberal justices on the Court.

FRONTIERO ET VIR v. RICHARDSON, SECRETARY OF DEFENSE, ET AL.

SUPREME COURT OF THE UNITED STATES

411 U.S. 677; 93 S. Ct. 1764; 36 L. Ed. 2d 583; 1973 U.S. LEXIS 153; 9 Fair Empl. Prac. Cas. (BNA) 1253; 5 Empl. Prac. Dec. (CCH) P8609

January 17, 1973, Argued
May 14, 1973, Decided

OPINION: BRENNAN

[*678] [***587] [**1766] MR. JUSTICE WILLIAM BRENNAN announced the judgment of the Court and an opinion in which MR. JUSTICE WILLIAM O. DOUGLAS, MR. JUSTICE BRYON WHITE, and MR. JUSTICE THURGOOD MARSHALL join.

The question before us concerns the right of a female member of the uniformed services[1] to claim her spouse as a "dependent" for the purposes of obtaining increased quarters allowances and medical and dental benefits under *37 U. S. C. §§ 401, 403,* and *10 U. S. C. §§ 1072, 1076,* on an equal footing with male members.

* * *

II

[***LEdHR4A] [LEdHN[4A]][4A]At the outset, appellants contend that classifications based upon sex, like classifications based upon race,[7] alienage,[8] and national origin,[9] are inherently suspect and must therefore be subjected to close judicial scrutiny. We agree and, indeed, find at least implicit support for such an approach in our unanimous decision only last Term in *Reed v. Reed, 404 U.S. 71 (1971)*.

.......This departure from "traditional" rational-basis analysis with respect to sex-based classifications is clearly justified.

There can be no doubt that our Nation has had a long and unfortunate history of sex discrimination.[13] Traditionally, such discrimination was rationalized by an attitude of "romantic paternalism" which, in practical effect, put women, not on a pedestal, but in a cage. Indeed, this paternalistic attitude became so firmly rooted in our national consciousness that, 100 years ago, a distinguished Member of this Court was able to proclaim:

"Man is, or should be, woman's protector and defender. The natural and proper timidity and delicacy which belongs to the female sex evidently unfits it for many of the occupations of civil life. The constitution of the family organization, which is founded in the divine ordinance, as well as in the nature of things, indicates the domestic sphere as that which properly belongs to the domain and functions of womanhood. The harmony, not to say identity, of interests and views which belong, or should belong, to the family institution is repugnant to the idea of a woman adopting a distinct and [*685] independent career from that of her husband. . . .

". . . [***591] The paramount destiny and mission of woman are to fulfil the noble and benign offices of wife and mother. This is the law of the Creator." *Bradwell v. State, 16 Wall. 130, 141 (1873)* (Bradley, J., concurring).

As a result of notions such as these, our statute books gradually became laden with gross, stereotyped distinctions between the sexes and, indeed, throughout much of the 19th century the position of women in our society was, in many respects, comparable to that of blacks under the pre-Civil War slave codes. ...

It is true, of course, that the position of women in America has improved markedly in recent decades.[15] [*686] Nevertheless, it can hardly be doubted that, in part because of the high visibility of the sex characteristic,[16] women still face pervasive, although at times more subtle, discrimination in our educational institutions, in the job market and, perhaps most conspicuously, in the political arena.

Moreover, since sex, like race and national origin, is an immutable characteristic determined solely by the accident of birth, the imposition of special disabilities upon the members of a particular sex because of their sex would seem to violate "the basic concept of our system that legal burdens should bear some relationship to individual responsibility . . . ." *Weber v. Aetna Casualty & Surety Co., 406 U.S. 164, 175* [***592] (1972). And what differentiates sex from such nonsuspect statuses as intelligence or physical disability, and aligns it with the recognized suspect criteria, is that the sex characteristic frequently bears no relation to ability to perform or contribute to society.[18] As a result, statutory distinctions [*687] between the sexes often have the effect of invidiously relegating the entire class of females to inferior legal status without regard to the actual capabilities of its individual members.

* * *

With these considerations in mind, we can only conclude that classifications based upon sex, like classifications based upon race, alienage, or national origin, are inherently suspect, and must therefore be subjected to strict judicial scrutiny. Applying the analysis mandated by that stricter standard of review, it is clear that the statutory scheme now before us is constitutionally invalid.

III

The sole basis of the classification established in the challenged statutes is the sex of the individuals involved. Thus, under *37 U. S. C. §§ 401, 403,* and *10 U. S. C.* [***593] §§ *1072, 1076,* a female member of the uniformed services seeking to obtain housing and medical benefits for her spouse must prove his dependency in fact, whereas no such burden is imposed upon male members. In addition, the statutes operate so as to deny benefits to a female member, such as appellant Sharron Frontiero, who provides less than one-half of her spouse's support, while at the same time granting such benefits to a male member who likewise provides less than one-half of his spouse's support. Thus, to this extent at least, it may fairly be said that these statutes command "dissimilar treatment for men and women who are . . . similarly situated." *Reed v. Reed, 404 U.S., at 77.*

Moreover, the Government concedes that the differential treatment accorded men and women under these statutes serves no purpose other than mere "administrative convenience." In essence, the Government maintains that, as an empirical matter, wives in our society frequently are dependent upon their husbands, while husbands [*689] rarely are dependent upon their wives. Thus, the Government argues that Congress might reasonably have concluded that it would be both cheaper and easier simply conclusively to presume that wives of male members are financially dependent upon their husbands, while burdening female members with the task of establishing dependency in fact.[22]

The Government offers no concrete evidence, however, tending to support its view that such differential treatment in [**1772] fact saves the Government any money. ...

....[A]ny statutory scheme which draws a sharp line between the sexes, solely for the purpose of achieving administrative convenience, necessarily commands "dissimilar treatment for men and women who are . . . similarly situated," and therefore involves the "very kind of arbitrary legislative choice forbidden by the [Constitution] . . . ." *Reed v. Reed, 404 U.S., at 77, 76.* We therefore conclude that, by according differential treatment to male and female members of the uniformed services for the sole purpose of achieving administrative [*691] convenience, the challenged statutes violate the *Due Process Clause of the Fifth Amendment* insofar as they require a female member to prove the dependency of her husband.[25]

* * *

Reversed.

Frontiero v. Richardson, 411 US 677 (1973)

The following excerpt is from the concurring opinion filed by Justice Lewis Powell. Joined by Chief Justice Warren Burger and Justice Harry Blackmun, Justice Powell urged his colleagues not to inject the Court prematurely into the ongoing debate over sexual equality and the ratification of the Equal Rights Amendment. Justice Powell was appointed by President Richard Nixon.

FRONTIERO v. RICHARDSON (1973)

MR. JUSTICE LEWIS POWELL, with whom THE CHIEF JUSTICE and MR. JUSTICE HARRY BLACKMUN join, concurring in the judgment.

I agree that the challenged statutes constitute an unconstitutional discrimination against servicewomen in violation of the Due Process Clause of the Fifth Amendment, but I cannot join the opinion of MR. JUSTICE BRENNAN, which would hold that all classifications based upon [***595] sex, "like classifications based upon race, alienage, and national origin," are "inherently suspect and must therefore be subjected to close judicial scrutiny." *Ante*, at 682. It is unnecessary for the Court in this case to [*692] characterize sex as a suspect classification, with all of the far-reaching implications of such a holding. *Reed* v. *Reed*, 404 U.S. 71 (1971), which abundantly supports our decision today, did not add sex to the narrowly limited group of classifications which are inherently suspect. In my view, we can and should decide this case on the authority of *Reed* and reserve for the future any expansion of its rationale.

There is another, and I find compelling, reason for deferring a general categorizing of sex classifications as invoking the strictest test of judicial scrutiny. The Equal Rights Amendment, which if adopted will resolve the substance of this precise question, has been approved by the Congress and submitted for ratification by the States. If this Amendment is duly adopted, it will represent the will of the people accomplished in the manner prescribed by the Constitution. By acting prematurely and unnecessarily, as I view it, the Court has assumed a decisional responsibility at the very time when state legislatures, functioning within the traditional democratic process, are debating the proposed Amendment. It seems to me that this reaching out to pre-empt by judicial action a major political decision which is currently in process of resolution does not reflect appropriate respect for duly prescribed legislative processes.

There are times when this Court, under our system, cannot avoid a constitutional decision on issues which normally should be resolved by the elected representatives of the people. But democratic institutions are weakened, and confidence in the restraint of the Court is impaired, when we appear unnecessarily to decide sensitive issues of broad social and political importance at the very time they are under consideration within the prescribed constitutional processes.

Craig v. Boren, 429 US 190 (1976)

Citing an increase in traffic accidents primarily resulting from young men driving under the influence of alcohol, the Oklahoma Legislature passed a statute prohibiting men under the age of 21 years old and women under the age of 18 years old from buying 3.2 beer. In effect, the state of Oklahoma created a sex-based classification in determining the legal age to buy 3.2 beer. Craig sued charging that, by denying men the same privileges the state extended to women, the state of Oklahoma was engaged in unconstitutional sex discrimination.

Three years after Justice Brennan argued that sex was the constitutional equivalent of race, he adopted a less radical position in *Craig*, which has become the Court's current criteria for adjudicating sex discrimination cases. The following excerpt highlights the major points of Justice Brennan's opinion along with Justice Stevens' concurring opinion.

CRAIG ET AL. v. BOREN, GOVERNOR OF OKLAHOMA, ET AL.

SUPREME COURT OF THE UNITED STATES

429 U.S. 190; 97 S. Ct. 451; 50 L. Ed. 2d 397; 1976 U.S. LEXIS 183

December 20, 1976

OPINION

[*191] [***403] [**454] MR. JUSTICE WILLIAM BRENNAN delivered the opinion of the Court.[HN1]

The interaction of two sections of an Oklahoma statute, *Okla. Stat., Tit. 37, §§ 241 and 245 (1958 and Supp. 1976)*,[1] [*192] prohibits the sale of "nonintoxicating" 3.2% beer to males under the age of 21 and to females under the age of 18. The question to be decided is whether such a gender-based differential constitutes a denial to males 18–20 years of age of the equal protection of the laws in violation of the *Fourteenth Amendment*.

* * *

[***LEdHR7] [LEdHN[7]][7] Analysis may appropriately begin with the reminder that Reed emphasized that statutory classifications that distinguish between males and females are "subject to scrutiny under the *Equal Protection Clause*." *404 U.S., at 75*. To withstand constitutional challenge, previous cases establish that classifications by gender must serve important governmental objectives and must be substantially related to achievement of those objectives. ...

Reed v. Reed has also provided the underpinning for decisions that have invalidated statutes employing gender as an inaccurate proxy for other, more germane bases of classification. Hence, "archaic and overbroad" generalizations, *Schlesinger v. Ballard, supra, at 508*, concerning the financial position of servicewomen, *Frontiero v. Richardson, supra, at 689 n. 23*, and working women, *Weinberger v. Wiesenfeld, 420 U.S. 636, 643 (1975)*, could not justify use of a gender line in determining eligibility for certain governmental entitlements. Similarly, increasingly outdated [*199] misconceptions concerning the [***408] role of females in the home [**458] rather than in the "marketplace and world of ideas" were rejected as loose-fitting characterizations incapable of supporting state statutory schemes that were premised upon their accuracy. *Stanton v. Stanton, supra*; *Taylor v. Louisiana, 419 U.S. 522, 535 n. 17 (1975)*. In light of the weak congruence between gender and the characteristic or trait that gender purported to represent, it was necessary that the legislatures choose either to realign their substantive laws in a gender-neutral fashion, or to adopt procedures for identifying those instances where the sex-centered generalization actually comported with fact. See, e.g., *Stanley v. Illinois, supra, at 658*; cf. *Cleveland Board of Education. v. LaFleur, 414 U.S. 632, 650 (1974)*.

[***LEdHR1B] *LEdHN[1B]*[1B] In this case, too, "Reed, we feel, is controlling...," *Stanton v. Stanton, supra, at 13*. We turn then to the question whether, under Reed, the difference between males and females with respect to the purchase of 3.2% beer warrants the differential in age drawn by the Oklahoma statute. We conclude that it does not.

* * *

It is so Ordered.

MR. JUSTICE STEVENS, concurring.

* * *

There is, of course, no way of knowing what actually motivated this discrimination, but I would not be surprised if it represented nothing more than the perpetuation of a stereotyped attitude about the relative maturity of the members of the two sexes in this age bracket. If so, the following comment is relevant:

"[A] traditional classification is more likely to be used without pausing to consider its justification than is a newly created classification. Habit, rather than analysis, makes it seem acceptable and natural to distinguish between male and female, alien and citizen, legitimate and illegitimate; for too much of our history there was the same inertia in distinguishing between black and white. But that sort of stereotyped reaction may have no rational relationship -- other than pure prejudicial discrimination -- to the stated purpose for which the classification is being made." *Mathews v. Lucas, 427 U.S. 495, 520–1* (STEVENS, J., dissenting

Craig v. Boren, 429 US 190 (1976)

Justice William Rehnquist, joined by Chief Justice Warren Burger, dissented in *Craig*. In his dissent, Justice Rehnquist was reluctant to embrace the majority's new approach to sexual equality. The following is an excerpt of Justice Rehnquist's dissenting opinion in *Craig v. Boren*. At the time that the Court heard the *Craig* case, Justice William Rehnquist was perhaps the most conservative justice on the Court. He was appointed by Republican President Richard Nixon, and he was later appointed as Chief Justice of the Supreme Court by President Ronald Reagan.

CRAIG ET AL. v. BOREN, GOVERNOR OF OKLAHOMA, ET AL.

SUPREME COURT OF THE UNITED STATES

429 U.S. 190; 97 S. Ct. 451; 50 L. Ed. 2d 397; 1976 U.S. LEXIS 183

Argued October 5, 1976
December 20, 1976

MR. JUSTICE WILLIAM REHNQUIST, dissenting.

The Court's disposition of this case is objectionable on two grounds. First is its conclusion that men challenging a gender-based statute which treats them less favorably than women may invoke a more stringent standard of judicial review than pertains to most other types of classifications. Second is the Court's enunciation of this standard, without citation to any source, as being that "classifications by gender must serve important governmental objectives and must be substantially related to achievement of those objectives." Ante, at 197 (emphasis added). The only redeeming feature of the Court's opinion, to my mind, is that it apparently signals a retreat by those who joined the plurality opinion in *Frontiero v. Richardson, 411 U.S. 677 (1973)*, from their view that sex is a "suspect" classification for purposes of equal protection analysis. I think the Oklahoma statute challenged here need pass only the "rational basis" equal [*218] protection analysis..., I believe that it is constitutional under that analysis.

I

In *Frontiero v. Richardson, supra*, the opinion for the plurality sets forth the reasons of four Justices for concluding that sex should be regarded as a suspect classification for purposes of equal protection analysis. These reasons center on our Nation's "long and unfortunate history of sex discrimination," *411 U.S., at 684*, which has been reflected in a whole range of restrictions on the legal rights of [**468] women, not the least of which have concerned the ownership of property and participation in the electoral process. Noting that the pervasive and persistent nature of the discrimination experienced by women is in part the result of their ready identifiability, the plurality rested its invocation of strict scrutiny largely upon the fact that "statutory distinctions between the sexes often have the effect of invidiously relegating the entire class of females to inferior legal status without regard to the actual capabilities of its individual members."

Subsequent to Frontiero, the Court has declined to hold that sex is a suspect class, *Stanton v. Stanton, supra, at 13,* and no such holding is imported by the Court's resolution of this case. However, the Court's application here of an elevated or "intermediate" level scrutiny, like that invoked in cases dealing with discrimination against females, raises the question of why the statute here should be treated any differently from countless legislative classifications unrelated to sex which have been upheld under a minimum rationality standard....

Most obviously unavailable to support any kind of special scrutiny in this case, is a history or pattern of past discrimination, such as was relied on by the plurality in Frontiero to support its invocation of strict scrutiny. There is no suggestion in the Court's opinion that males in this age group are in any way peculiarly disadvantaged, subject to systematic discriminatory treatment, or otherwise in need of special solicitude from the courts.

*   *   *

It is true that a number of our opinions contain broadly phrased dicta implying that the same test should be applied to all classifications based on sex, whether affecting females or males. However, before today, no decision of this Court has applied an elevated level of scrutiny to invalidate a statutory discrimination harmful to males, except where the statute impaired an important personal interest protected by the Constitution.[1] There being no such interest [*220] [**469] here, and there being no plausible argument that this is a discrimination against females,[2] the Court's reliance on our previous sex-discrimination cases is ill-founded. It treats gender classification as a talisman which -- without regard to the rights involved or the persons affected -- calls into effect a heavier burden of judicial review.

– – – – – – – – – – – – – Footnotes – – – – – – – – – – – – – –

2 I am not unaware of the argument from time to time advanced, that all discriminations between the sexes ultimately redound to the detriment of females, because they tend to reinforce "old notions" restricting the roles and opportunities of women. As a general proposition applying equally to

all sex categorizations, I believe that this argument was implicitly found to carry little weight in our decisions upholding genderbased differences.....

– – – – – – – – – – – End Footnotes- – – – – – – – – – – – -

The Court's conclusion that a law which treats males less favorably than females "must serve important governmental objectives and must be substantially related to achievement of those objectives" apparently comes out of thin air. The *Equal Protection Clause* contains no such language, and none of our previous cases adopt that standard

Tuan Anh Nguyen and Joseph Boulais v. Immigration and Naturalization Service, 533 US 53 (2001)

The *Nguyen* case shows how the "natural differences" argument continues to be a decisive factor in constitutional adjudication. The question asked whether the Federal Government can use a sex-based standard for bestowing citizenship on a child born out of wedlock to an American citizen parent and non-citizen parent when the birth occurs outside the territory of the United States. Under federal law, a child born to a female American citizen parent and a male non-citizen parent who are unmarried and if the child is born outside of the United States "...acquires at birth the nationality status of his mother." In other words, a child automatically is regarded as an American citizenship. This is not the case when, under the same circumstances (unmarried parents and child born outside of the United States), the child's father is an American citizen. Accordingly, "as to an individual born under the same circumstances, save that the parents are unwed, *§ 1409(a)* sets forth the following require-ments where the father is the citizen parent and the mother is an alien:

"(1) a blood relationship between the person and the father is established by clear and convincing evidence,
"(2) the father had the nationality of the United States at the time of the person's birth,
"(3) the father (unless deceased) has agreed in writing to provide financial support for the person until the person reaches the age of 18 years, and
"(4) while the person is under the age of 18 years –
    "(A) the person is legitimated under the law of the person's residence or domicile,
    "(B) the father acknowledges paternity of the person in writing under oath, or
    "(C) the paternity of the person is established by adjudication of a competent court."

In this case, Nguyen was born in Saigon, Vietnam; his father, an American citizen and his mother, a Vietnamese citizen, were never married. Nguyen came to live with his father when he was 6 years old. His father never filed the appropriate documentation for Nguyen to receive American citizenship. When Nguyen was facing deportation after being convicted of sexual assault, he challenged his deportation on the grounds that he should be considered an American citizen. While Nguyen's deportation was pending, his father sought to have him declared an American citizen. By this time, Nguyen was 28 years old, and, under United States law, he was ineligible to claim citizenship. Nguyen and his father challenged the policy as unconstitutional sex discrimination.

In his majority opinion, Justice Anthony Kennedy, who was appointed by President Ronald Reagan, upheld this immigration policy, citing the natural differences between men and women. The following is an excerpt from Justice Kennedy's 5-4 opinion.

TUAN ANH NGUYEN AND JOSEPH BOULAIS v. IMMIGRATION AND NATURALIZATION SERVICE

SUPREME COURT OF THE UNITED STATES

533 U.S. 53; 121 S. Ct. 2053; 150 L. Ed. 2d 115; 2001 U.S. LEXIS 4340; 69 U.S.L.W. 4438;

June 11, 2001, Decided

OPINION

JUSTICE KENNEDY delivered the opinion of the Court.

...Title *8 U.S.C. § 1409* governs the acquisition of United States citizenship by persons born to one United States citizen parent and one noncitizen parent when the parents are unmarried and the child is born outside of the United States or its possessions. The statute imposes different requirements for the child's acquisition of citizenship depending upon whether the citizen parent is [*57] the mother or the father. The question before us is whether the statutory distinction is consistent with the equal protection guarantee embedded in the *Due Process Clause of the Fifth Amendment.*

* * *

III

For a gender-based classification to withstand equal protection scrutiny, it must be established "'at least that the [challenged] classification serves "important governmental objectives and that the discriminatory means employed" are "substantially related to the achievement of those objectives."'

* * *

Before considering the important governmental interests advanced by the statute, two observations concerning the operation of the provision are in order. First, a citizen mother expecting a child and living abroad has the right to re-enter the United States so the child can be born here and be a *14th Amendment* citizen. From one perspective, then, the statute simply ensures equivalence between two expectant mothers who are citizens abroad if one chooses to reenter for the child's birth and the other chooses not to return, or does not have the means to do so. This equivalence is not a factor if the single citizen parent living abroad is the father. For, unlike the unmarried mother, the unmarried father as a general rule cannot control where the child will be born.

Second, although *§ 1409(a)(4)* requires certain conduct to occur before the child of a citizen father, born out of wedlock and [**2060] abroad, reaches 18 years of age, it imposes no limitations on when an individual who qualifies under the statute can claim citizenship.... And while the conditions necessary for a citizen mother to transmit citizenship under *§ 1409(c)* exist at birth, citizen fathers and/or their children have 18 years to satisfy [***127] the requirements of *§ 1409(a)(4)*. See *Miller, supra, at 435* (opinion of STEVENS, J.).

....Congress' decision to impose requirements on unmarried fathers that differ from those on unmarried mothers is based on the significant difference between their respective relationships to the potential citizen at the time of birth. Specifically, the imposition of the requirement for a paternal relationship, but not a maternal one, is justified by two important governmental objectives. We discuss each in turn.

A

The first governmental interest to be served is the importance of assuring that a biological parent-child relationship exists. In the case of the mother, the relation is verifiable from the birth itself. The mother's status is documented in most instances by the birth certificate or hospital records and the witnesses who attest to her having given birth.

In the case of the father, the uncontestable fact is that he need not be present at the birth. If he is present, furthermore, that circumstance is not incontrovertible proof of fatherhood....

Fathers and mothers are not similarly situated with regard to the proof of biological parenthood. The imposition of a different set of rules for making that legal determination with respect to fathers and mothers is neither surprising nor troublesome from a constitutional perspective....

Petitioners argue that the requirement of § 1409(a)(1), that a father provide clear and convincing evidence of parentage, is sufficient to achieve the end of establishing paternity, given the sophistication of modern DNA tests..... With respect to DNA testing, the expense, reliability, and availability of such testing in various parts of the world may have been of particular concern to Congress. ...Given the proof of motherhood that is inherent in birth itself, it is unremarkable that Congress did not require the same affirmative steps of mothers.

Finally, to require Congress to speak without reference to the gender of the parent with regard to its objective of ensuring a blood tie between parent and child would be to insist on a hollow neutrality. ..... Congress could have required both mothers and fathers to prove parenthood within 30 days or, for that matter, 18 years, of the child's birth. 523 U.S. at 436. Given that the mother is always present at birth, but that the father need not be, the facially neutral rule would sometimes require fathers to take additional affirmative steps which would not be required of mothers, whose names will appear on the birth certificate as a result of their presence at the birth, and who will have the benefit of witnesses to the birth to call upon. The issue is not the use of gender specific terms instead of neutral ones. Just as neutral terms can mask discrimination that is unlawful, gender specific terms can mark a permissible distinction. The equal protection question is whether the distinction is lawful. Here, the use of gender specific terms takes into account a biological difference between the parents. The differential treatment is inherent in a sensible statutory scheme, given the unique relationship of the mother to the event of birth.

B

1

[***LEdHR1I] LEdHN[1I][1I]The second important governmental interest furthered in a substantial manner by § 1409(a)(4) is the determination to ensure that the child and the citizen parent have some demonstrated opportunity or potential to develop not just a [*65] relationship that is recognized, as a formal matter, by the law, but one that consists of the real, everyday ties that provide a connection between child and citizen parent and, in turn, the United States. See *id. at 438–40* (opinion of STEVENS, J.). In the case of a citizen mother and a child born overseas, the opportunity for a meaningful relationship between citizen parent and child inheres in the very event of birth, an event so often critical to our constitutional and statutory understandings of citizenship. The mother knows that the child is in being and is hers [***129] and has an initial point of contact with him. There is at least an opportunity for mother and child to develop a real, meaningful relationship.

The same opportunity does not result from the event of birth, as a matter of biological inevitability, in the case of the unwed father. Given the 9-month interval between conception and birth, it is not always certain that a father will know that a child was conceived, nor is it always clear that even the mother will be sure of the father's identity. This fact takes on particular significance in the case of a child born overseas and out of wedlock. One concern in this context has always been with young people, men for the most part, who are on duty with the Armed Forces in foreign countries....

...The ease of travel and the willingness of Americans to visit foreign countries have resulted in numbers of trips abroad that must be of real concern when we contemplate the prospect of accepting petitioners' argument, which would mandate, contrary to Congress' wishes, citizenship by male parentage subject to no condition save the father's previous length of residence in this country. In 1999 alone, Americans made almost 25 million trips abroad, excluding trips to Canada and Mexico. ...

Principles of equal protection do not require Congress to ignore this reality. To the contrary, these facts demonstrate the critical importance of the Government's interest in ensuring some opportunity for a tie between citizen father and foreign born child which is a reasonable substitute for the opportunity manifest between mother and child at the time of birth. Indeed, especially in light of the number of Americans who take short sojourns abroad, the prospect that a father might not even know of the conception is a realistic possibility. See *Miller, supra, at 439* (opinion of STEVENS, J.). Even if a father knows of the fact of conception, moreover, it does not follow that he will be present at the birth of the child. Thus, unlike the case of the mother, there [***130] is no assurance that the father and his biological child will meet. Without an initial point of contact with the child by a father who knows the child is his own, there is no opportunity for father and child to begin a relationship. *Section 1409* takes the unremarkable step of ensuring that such an opportunity, inherent in the event of birth as to the [*67] mother-child relationship, exists between father and child before citizenship is conferred upon the latter.

The importance of the governmental interest at issue here is too profound to be satisfied merely by conducting a DNA test. The fact of paternity can be established even without the father's knowledge, not to say his presence. Paternity can be established by taking DNA samples even from a few strands of hair, years after the birth. Yet scientific proof of biological paternity does nothing, by itself, to ensure contact between father and child during the child's minority.

Congress is well within its authority in refusing, absent proof of at least the opportunity for the development of a relationship between citizen parent and child, to commit this country to embracing a child as a citizen entitled as of birth to the full protection of the United States, to the absolute right to enter its borders, and to full participation in the political process. ...Congress has not taken that path but has instead chosen, by means of § 1409, to ensure in the case of father and child the opportunity for a relationship to develop, an opportunity which the event of birth itself provides for the mother and child. It should be unobjectionable for Congress to require some evidence of a minimal opportunity for the development of a relationship with the child in terms the male can fulfill.

* * *

[***LEdHR1J] [1J]Petitioners and their amici argue in addition that, rather than fulfilling an important governmental interest, § 1409 merely embodies a gender-based stereotype. .....There is nothing irrational or improper in the recognition that at the moment of birth -- a critical event in the statutory scheme and in the whole tradition of citizenship law -- the mother's knowledge of the child and the fact of parenthood have been established in a way not guaranteed in the case of the unwed father. This is not a [***131] stereotype. See Virginia, 518 U.S. at 533 ("The heightened review standard our precedent establishes does not make sex a proscribed classification . . . . Physical differences between men and women . . . are enduring").

* * *

To fail to acknowledge even our most basic biological differences -- such as the fact that a mother must be present at birth but the father need not be -- risks making the guarantee of equal protection superficial, and so disserving it. Mechanistic classification of all our differences as stereotypes would operate to obscure those misconceptions and prejudices that are real. The distinction embodied in the statutory scheme here at issue is not marked by misconception and prejudice, nor does it show disrespect for either class. The difference between men and women in relation to the birth process is a real one, and the principle of equal protection does not forbid Congress to address the problem at hand in a manner specific to each gender.

The judgment of the Court of Appeals is

Affirmed.

Tuan Anh Nguyen and Joseph Boulais v. Immigration and Naturalization Service, 533 US 53 (2001)

In her dissenting opinion, Justice Sandra D. O'Connor charged Justice Kennedy with using sex generalizations and sex stereotypes in his majority opinion. Joined by Justices David Souter, Ruth Bader Ginsburg and Stephen Breyer, Justice O'Connor argued that the Federal Government could adopt a gender-neutral policy to achieve its important government objectives. Justice O'Connor was appointed by President Ronald Reagan, and she was the first woman appointed to the United States Supreme Court. During her tenure on the Court, Justice O'Connor was considered a centrist who became a pivotal vote in determining the outcome of cases.

Her dissent is excerpted below.

TUAN ANH NGUYEN AND JOSEPH BOULAIS v. IMMIGRATION AND NATURALIZATION SERVICE

SUPREME COURT OF THE UNITED STATES

533 U.S. 53; 121 S. Ct. 2053; 150 L. Ed. 2d 115; 2001 U.S. LEXIS 4340; 69 U.S.L.W. 4438;

June 11, 2001, Decided

DISSENT

JUSTICE O'CONNOR, with whom JUSTICE SOUTER, JUSTICE GINSBURG, and JUSTICE BREYER join, dissenting.

In a long line of cases spanning nearly three decades, this Court has applied heightened scrutiny to legislative classifications based on sex. The Court today confronts another statute that classifies individuals on the basis of their sex. While the Court invokes heightened scrutiny, the manner in which it explains and applies this standard is a stranger to our precedents. Because the Immigration and Naturalization Service (INS) has not shown an exceedingly persuasive justification for the sex-based classification embodied in *8 U.S.C. § 1409(a)(4)* -- i.e., because it has failed to establish at least that the classification substantially relates to the achievement of important governmental objectives -- I would reverse [***135] the judgment of the Court of Appeals.

I

Sex-based statutes, even when accurately reflecting the way most men or women behave, deny individuals opportunity. Such generalizations must be viewed not in isolation, but in the context of our Nation's "long and unfortunate history of sex discrimination." Sex-based generalizations both reflect and reinforce "fixed notions concerning the roles and abilities of males and females." *Mississippi Univ. for Women v. Hogan, 458 U.S. 718, 725, 73 L. Ed. 2d 1090, 102 S. Ct. 3331 (1982).*

For these reasons, a party who seeks to defend a statute that classifies individuals on the basis of sex "must carry the burden of showing an 'exceedingly persuasive justification' for the classification." *Id. at 724* (quoting *Kirchberg v.* [*75] *Feenstra, 450 U.S. 455, 461, 67 L. Ed. 2d 428, 101 S. Ct. 1195 (1981)*); see also *United States v. Virginia, 518 U.S. 515, 531, 135 L. Ed. 2d 735*, [**2067] *116 S. Ct. 2264 (1996)*. The defender of the classification meets this burden "only by showing at least that the classification serves 'important governmental objectives and that the discriminatory means employed' are 'substantially related to the achievement of those objectives.'"

* * *

Heightened scrutiny does not countenance justifications that "rely on overbroad generalizations about the different talents, capacities, or preferences of males and females." *Virginia, supra, at 533*. Rational basis review, by contrast, is much more tolerant of the use of broad generalizations about different classes of individuals, so long as the classification is not arbitrary or irrational. See, e.g., *Kimel v. Florida Bd. of Regents, 528 U.S. 62, 84, 145 L. Ed. 2d 522, 120 S. Ct. 631 (2000)*; *Fritz, supra, at 177*.

Moreover, overbroad sex-based generalizations are impermissible even when they enjoy empirical support. See, e.g., *J. E. B., supra, at 139, n. 11*; *Craig v. Boren, 429 U.S. 190, 199, 50 L. Ed. 2d 397, 97 S. Ct. 451 (1976)*; *Wiesenfeld, supra, at 645*. Under rational basis scrutiny, however, empirical support is not even necessary to sustain a classification.

* * *

The most important difference between heightened scrutiny and rational basis review, of course, is the required fit between the means employed and the ends served. Under heightened scrutiny, the discriminatory means must be "substantially related" to an actual and important governmental interest. See, e.g., *Virginia, supra, at 533*. Under rational basis scrutiny, the means need only be "rationally related" to a conceivable and legitimate state end. See, e.g., *Cleburne v. Cleburne Living Center, Inc., 473 U.S. 432, 440, 87 L. Ed. 2d 313, 105 S. Ct. 3249 (1985)*.

The fact that other means are better suited to the achievement of governmental ends therefore is of no moment under rational basis review..... But because we require a much tighter fit between means and ends under heightened scrutiny, the availability of sex-neutral alternatives to a sex-based classification is often highly probative of the validity of the classification....

II

A

* * *

The majority concedes that Congress could achieve the goal of assuring a biological parent-child relationship in a sex-neutral fashion, but then, in a surprising turn, dismisses the availability of sex-neutral alternatives as irrelevant. As the Court suggests, "Congress could have required both mothers and fathers to prove parenthood within 30 days or, for that matter, 18 years, of the child's birth." Ante, at 9 (citing *Miller, supra, at 436* (opinion of STEVENS, J.)). Indeed, whether one conceives the majority's asserted interest as assuring the existence of a biological parent-child relationship, ante, at 7, or as ensuring acceptable documentation of that relationship, ante, at 8, a number of sex-neutral arrangements -- including the one that the majority offers -- would better serve that end. As the majority seems implicitly to acknowledge at one point, ante, at 7, a mother will not always have formal legal documentation of birth because a birth certificate may not issue or may subsequently be lost. Conversely, a father's name may well appear on a birth certificate. While it [***140] is doubtless true that a mother's blood relation [*82] to a child is uniquely "verifiable from the birth itself" to those present at birth, ante, at 7, the majority has not shown that a mother's birth relation is uniquely verifiable by the INS, much less that any greater verifiability warrants a sex-based, rather than a sex-neutral, statute.

* * *

B

The Court states that "the second important governmental interest furthered in a substantial manner by § *1409(a)(4)* is the determination to ensure that the child and the citizen parent have some demonstrated opportunity or potential to develop not just a relationship that is recognized, as a formal matter, by the law, but one that consists of the real, [*84] everyday ties that provide a connection between child and citizen parent and, in turn, the United States." ...

* * *

...As the facts of this case demonstrate, ante, at 2, it is entirely possible that a father and child will have the opportunity to develop a relationship and in fact will develop a relationship without obtaining the proof of the opportunity during the child's minority. After his parents' relationship had ended, petitioner Nguyen lived with the family of his father's new girlfriend. In 1975, before his sixth birthday, Nguyen came to the United States, where he was reared by his father, petitioner Boulais. In 1997, a DNA test showed a 99.98% probability of paternity, and, in 1998, Boulais obtained an order of parentage from a Texas court.

* * *

Moreover, available sex-neutral alternatives would at least replicate, and could easily exceed, ...Congress could at least allow proof of such presence or knowledge to be one way of demonstrating an opportunity for a relationship. Under the present law, the statute on its face accords different treatment to a mother who is by nature present at birth and a father who is by choice present at birth even though those two individuals are similarly situated with respect to the "opportunity" for a relationship. The mother can transmit her citizenship at birth, but the father cannot do so in the absence of at least one other affirmative act. The different statutory treatment is solely on account of the sex of the similarly situated individuals. This type of treatment is patently inconsistent with the promise of equal protection of the laws.

Indeed, the idea that a mother's presence at birth supplies adequate assurance of an opportunity to develop a relationship while a father's presence at birth does not would appear to rest only on an overbroad sex-based generalization. A mother may not have an opportunity for a relationship if the child is removed from his or her mother on account of alleged abuse or neglect, or if the child and mother are separated by tragedy, such as disaster or war, [*87] of the sort apparently present in this case. There is no reason, other than stereotype, to say that fathers who are present at birth lack an opportunity for a relationship on similar terms. The "physical differences between men and women," *Virginia, 518 U.S. at 533,* therefore do not justify § *1409(a)(4)*'s discrimination.

* * *

The claim that § *1409(a)(4)* substantially relates to the achievement of the goal of a "real, practical relationship" [*89] thus finds support not in biological differences but instead in a stereotype -- i.e., "the generalization that mothers are significantly more likely than fathers . . . to develop caring relationships with their children." *Miller, supra, at 482–3* (BREYER, J., dissenting). Such a claim relies on "the very stereotype the law condemns," *J. E. B., 511 U.S. at 138* (internal quotation marks omitted), "lends credibility" to the generalization, *Mississippi Univ. for Women, 458 U.S. at 730,* and helps to convert that "assumption" into "a self-fulfilling prophecy," ....Indeed, contrary to this stereotype, Boulais has reared Nguyen, while Nguyen apparently has lacked a relationship with his mother.

* * *

In denying petitioner's claim that § *1409(a)(4)* rests on stereotypes, the majority articulates a misshapen notion of "stereotype" and its significance in our equal protection jurisprudence. The majority asserts that a "stereotype" is "defined as a frame of mind resulting from irrational or uncritical analysis." Ante, at 13. This Court has long recognized, however, that an impermissible stereotype may enjoy empirical support and thus be in a sense "rational." ....Indeed, the stereotypes that underlie a sex-based classification "may hold true for many, even most, individuals." *Miller, 523 U.S. at 460* (GINSBURG, J., dissenting). But in numerous cases where a measure of truth has inhered in the generalization, "the Court has rejected official actions that classify unnecessarily and overbroadly by gender when more accurate and impartial functional lines can be drawn." Ibid.

Nor do stereotypes consist only of those overbroad generalizations that the reviewing court considers to "show disrespect" for a class, ante, at 18. Compare, e.g., *Craig, supra, at 198–201.* The hallmark of a stereotypical sex-based classification under this Court's precedents is not whether the classification is insulting, but whether it "relies upon the simplistic, outdated assumption that gender could be used as a 'proxy for other, more germane bases of classification.'" *Mississippi Univ. for Women, supra, at 726* (quoting *Craig, supra, at 198*).

* * *

Section 1409(a)(4) is thus paradigmatic of a historic regime that left women with responsibility, and freed men from responsibility, for nonmarital children. Under this law, as one advocate explained to Congress in a 1932 plea for a sex-neutral citizenship law, "when it comes to the illegitimate child, which is a great burden, then the mother is the only recognized parent, and the father is put safely in the background." ...The majority, however, rather than confronting the stereotypical notion that mothers must care for these children and [***147] fathers may ignore them, quietly condones the "very stereotype the law condemns," *J. E. B., 511 U.S. at 138* (internal quotation marks omitted).

* * *

Finally, while the recitation of statistics concerning military personnel and overseas travel highlights the opportunities for United States citizens to interact with citizens of foreign countries, it bears little on the question whether *§ 1409(a)(4)*'s discriminatory means are a permissible governmental response to those circumstances. Indeed, the majority's discussion may itself simply reflect the stereotype of male irresponsibility that is [***148] no more a basis for the validity of the classification than are stereotypes about the "traditional" behavior patterns of women.

It is, of course, true that the failure to recognize relevant differences is out of line with the command of equal protection. See ante, at 18. But so too do we undermine the promise of equal protection when we try to make our differences carry weight they simply cannot bear. This promise informs the proper application of heightened scrutiny to sex-based classifications and demands our scrupulous adherence to that test.

III

* * *

No one should mistake the majority's analysis for a careful application of this Court's equal protection jurisprudence concerning sex-based classifications. Today's decision instead represents a deviation from a line of cases in which we have vigilantly applied heightened scrutiny to such classifications to determine whether a constitutional violation has occurred.

I trust that the depth and vitality of these precedents will ensure that today's error [**2079] remains an aberration. I respectfully dissent.

Questions

1 Is there a need today for an Equal Rights Amendment in the US Constitution?

2 In *Frontiero*, four justices wanted to incorporate an "equal rights" mandate into the Fourteenth Amendment via judicial fiat. What was the reaction by the other justices to this strategy? What are the advantages and disadvantages of having the Supreme Court, in effect, establish a constitutional guarantee of sexual equality?

3 What is the difference between a sex stereotype and a natural difference between men and women?

4 Do women need special protection from the courts in contemporary American society? Why or why not?

Suggested Reading

Adler, Libby S. et al. *Women and the Law*. New York: Foundation Press, 2008.

Berry, Mary Francis. *Why ERA Failed: Politics, Women's Rights and the Amending Process of the Constitution*. Bloomington: Indiana University Press, 1988.

Freeman, Jo. *The Politics of Women's Liberation: A Case Study of an Emerging Social Movement and Its Relation to the Policy Process*. New York: Longman, 1975.

Kirchberg v. Feenstra et al., 450 US 455 (1981).

Personnel Administrator of Massachusetts v. Feeney, 442 US 256 (1979)

Schlafly, Phyllis. *The Phyllis Schlafly Report*: 1986. http://www.eagleforum.org/psr/1986/sept86/psrsep86.hetml#.UDu6P2Ymwdg.email

Slaughterhouse Cases, 83 US 36 (1873).

Stanley v. Illinois, 405 US 645 (1972).

Stanton v. Stanton, 421 US 7 (1975).

3

Rights and Duties of Citizenship

Introduction

Although American citizenship is conferred automatically at birth on both men and women, the specific rights and duties that accompany American citizenship have been different for each. Until recently, the doctrine of separate spheres, which was based on the natural difference doctrine, provided a template for the civic responsibilities that men and women were expected to fulfill. Women were expected to serve American society chiefly by managing their households, rearing children, and shaping the mores of their families. Men had broad civic responsibilities which encompassed all aspects of public life. The readings in this chapter highlight how natural difference arguments shaped the debates over expanding the rights and duties of women. The focus here will be on the rights of suffrage and the duties of jury and military service.

Suffrage

While the US Constitution did not prohibit female suffrage in 1787, it gave the individual states the power to establish voting qualifications for citizens. Until the latter part of the nineteenth century very few women demanded the right to vote and only one state, New Jersey, granted them that right for a very short period of time. Early Americans of both sexes believed, as we have seen, that God endowed women as well as men with natural rights, but did not believe that this set of rights included the right to vote. Most early Americans held that voting was a civil right which should be limited to individuals who were economically independent, that is, who owned property. Such was not the case for most women who relied on the relevant men in their lives for sustenance as well as protection because of their natural vulnerabilities. Early Americans also believed that politics in general was an inherently male activity not suitable for the gentler sex.[1] Later opponents of women's suffrage like Horace Bushnell used arguments such as these when claiming that women's suffrage was a "reform against nature."[2]

The women's suffrage movement began in earnest shortly after the Seneca Falls Convention of 1848 which, as we have seen, gave birth to the modern American feminist movement. While this movement floundered until after African–Americans obtained the right to vote under the Fourteenth and Fifteenth Amendments, it then gradually grew in strength until it helped secure the passage of the Nineteenth Amendment in 1919. Historians generally credit Susan B. Anthony with being one of the most important moving forces behind this accomplishment. Anthony considered the right to vote an implied natural right calling it the only constitutional means by which citizens can peacefully alter or abolish unjust governments. She also argued that women needed the ballot to protect themselves against male hegemony, thereby rejecting the traditional view that women's interests were subsumed under the interests of their brothers, fathers, and husbands.[3]

Jury Service

Given the central role of the jury trial in the American justice system, jury service is an essential duty for American citizens. Yet, a citizen's sex has had a significant impact on who will actually sit on a jury. The debate over allowing women to sit on juries covered much of the same ground as the debate over female suffrage. Jury service was considered to be inappropriate for women because it was inconsistent with their delicate nature and their natural responsibilities as wives and mothers. Interestingly, proponents of jury service for women chiefly used natural difference arguments to make their case. Elizabeth Cady Stanton argued, for example, that the right to have a jury of one's peers required female representation on juries for female litigants because women were better suited than men to understand the nature of women and issues pertaining to families and the home.[4]

The ratification of the Nineteenth Amendment virtually ended the practice of excluding women from jury service because jury duty was based on the right to vote. While women, as new voters, could no longer be denied the right or privilege of sitting on juries,[5] their selection to actually serve on juries was not guaranteed. Interestingly, state courts used natural difference arguments to justify both including and excluding women from jury duty.[6] In *Bailey v. State* (Ark. 1949), the Arkansas Supreme Court defended Arkansas's policy of exclusion by noting that a criminal trial was an inappropriate venue for a "lady."[7] In contrast, the State of Oregon required that at least half of the jurors in cases involving minor defendants or minor complaining witnesses be women. The Oregon Supreme Court upheld this female quota, explaining that women's nurturing presence was comforting to minors and, in turn, insured the fair adjudication of their cases.[8]

By the mid-twentieth century, the debates over female representation on juries were often framed in terms of justice rather than equality. This occurred, for example, when convicted criminal defendants charged that the absence of women from their trial juries violated their Sixth Amendment fair trial right. The Sixth Amendment requires trial juries to reflect a cross-section of the community where the trial takes place so that the fates of criminal and civil defendants are determined by individuals who have different backgrounds, experiences and sensibilities. Reformers emphasized the different outlooks men and women bring to the task of deciding cases when arguing for increased female participation on juries. Women perform distinctive roles in society, they maintained, and thus, offered unique and valuable perspectives in some cases.[9] Traditionalists were more concerned with ensuring that women fulfill their responsibilities as homemakers than with having women leave the home to serve on juries. They argued that men from different backgrounds, classes and professions adequately represented the diversity of the community.

Two U.S. Supreme Court decisions illustrate both points of view. In *Hoyt v. Florida* (1961), a woman appealed her conviction for the murder of her husband on the grounds that having an all-male jury deprived her of a fair trial.[10] Hoyt claimed that an all-male jury could not fairly assess her guilt or innocence because men were not sufficiently capable of understanding or empathizing with women in her position. The Court upheld Hoyt's conviction on the grounds that Florida reasonably determined that women's family responsibilities were more important than their duties as jurors.

In 1975, however, the United States Supreme Court struck down state policies that automatically exempted women from jury service in *Taylor v. Louisiana*.[11] Taylor challenged an exemption policy that was similar to the one the Court had earlier upheld in *Hoyt v. Florida*. The Court argued that while family responsibilities were legitimate grounds for exempting women from jury duty, states were constitutionally prohibited from exempting all women on the presumption or "stereotype" that women's lives revolved around the home.

Eighteen years after its *Taylor* decision, the Court was asked to determine whether attorneys should be allowed to impanel an all-male or all-female jury by systematically excusing members of the opposite sex from the jury pool. The case of *JEB v. Alabama* (1994)[12] involved a child paternity and support dispute in which Alabama's state attorney, acting on behalf of the mother, removed all males from the jury pool, thus insuring that an all-female jury would determine the outcome of this dispute.

The case divided the Court. Four justices argued that gender differences within the jury do influence jury verdicts. Thus they concluded that sex could be a legitimate reason for excusing a prospective juror from deciding the case.[13] They noted, for example, that an attorney representing a female plaintiff in a sexual harassment case could legitimately try to impanel a jury composed of all women or a majority of women. The majority, however, argued that a person's sex should not be a factor in determining a civil duty as important as jury duty. Permitting attorneys to excuse or approve of jurors based on the sex of the prospective juror, it concluded, fostered unconstitutional sex stereotypes.

The debate continues today over whether the gender composition of juries affects jury verdicts because the empirical evidence is inconclusive.[14] However, the anecdotal evidence suggests that perceived or presumed differences between men and women are still relevant in jury selection.

Military Service

Natural difference arguments frame the closely-related debates over whether women should be subject to the draft and whether women soldiers should be assigned to combat duty. Fighting for one's country is perhaps the most important duty of citizenship. Yet while women have volunteered for military service and have fought beside their male counterparts,[15] they have never been drafted even during wartime and are currently exempt from the registration requirements of the Selective Service Law.

These debates focus on the appropriateness of compelling women to serve in the military and on the impact of women fighters on military readiness. Traditionalists argue that women are ill-suited for combat because of their physical and emotional vulnerabilities. In contrast, reformers charge that some men are also physically and psychologically ill-suited for military duty, while some women are perfectly capable of serving with men in a wide range of units, including those slated for combat.

In *Rostker v. Goldberg* (1981),[16] the U.S. Supreme Court ruled that the purpose of the Selective Service Act was not to discriminate against either sex, nor to undervalue women's service to the county, but to identify men who could be drafted for combat duty. The dissenters disagreed, arguing that restricting draft registration to men unfairly prevented women from serving their country in times of national crisis.

The most controversial issue involving women in the military today is whether women should be assigned to combat duty. Natural difference arguments play an important role in this debate which centers on the fitness of women for combat and on the impact that women fighters would have on military readiness. As we shall see, the Military Leadership Diversity Commission and Kingsley R. Browne disagree regarding both these issues. The Diversity Commission argues that giving women service members the same combat responsibilities as their male counterparts will establish a level playing field for career advancement without compromising military effectiveness. Browne believes, however, that the integration of women in combat units would jeopardize military missions by undermining military effectiveness.

Conclusion

For much of American history, the natural differences between men and women shaped American expectations regarding their respective civic rights and duties. The authors of the separate spheres doctrine never intended to undervalue women's contribution to the United States, but sought to align their civic duties with what were thought to be their natural strengths as homemakers and mothers. They believed that, in comparison with female citizens, male citizens were more capable of participating in electoral politics, more emotionally suited for serving on juries, and more able to withstand the rigors of combat and military service. Thus, women were not allowed to vote or serve on juries, but were expected to maintain strong and stable families and homes. Interestingly, when women did gain these rights, it was largely because their distinctive roles and experiences were believed to improve this country's political and judicial processes.

Although the Pentagon has recently removed restrictions on assigning women to units engaged in close physical fighting with the enemy, many Americans still remain ambivalent about whether women should engage in combat and whether they should be drafted (if the draft is reinstated).

Notes

1 See, in general, Thomas G. West, *Vindicating the Founders: Race, Sex, Class, and Justice in the Origins of America.* Lanham, MD: Rowman & Littlefield, 1997, 71–83.

2 Horace Bushnell, "Women's Suffrage: The Reform Against Nature (Selections)," in *The Struggle for Women's Rights: Theoretical and Historical Sources*, eds George and Margaret G. Klosko. Upper Saddle River, NJ: Prentice-Hall, 1999, 195–204.

3 Susan B. Anthony, "Constitutional Argument, 1872," in *The Elizabeth Cady*

Stanton—Susan B. Anthony Reader: Correspondence, Writings, Speeches, ed. Ellen Carol Dubois. Boston: Northeastern University Press, 1992, 152–65.

4 Elizabeth Cady Stanton, "Address to the New York Legislature (1854)." Found in Stanton, Susan B. Anthony and Matilda Joslyn Gage. *History of Woman Suffrage*, vol. 1. New York: Fowler and Wells, 1881, 595–606.

5 See, *State of New Jersey v. James*, 114 A 553 (NJ 1921).

6 For a very good historical examination of women and jury service, see Gretchen Ritter, "Jury Service and Women's Citizenship Before and After the Nineteenth Amendment". *Law and History Review* 20, 2002, 1–77.

7 215 Ark. 53, 61 (1949).

8 *State v. Chase*, 106 Ore. 263 (1922).

9 See *Ballard v. United States*, 329 US 187, 193 (1946).

10 368 US 57 (1961). It is important to note that Hoyt argued that the impaneled all-male jury violated the Equal Protection Clause, and the Sixth Amendment's right to a fair jury trial.

11 419 US 522 (1975). It is important to note that, unlike Hoyt in *Hoyt v. Florida*, Taylor based his challenge on the Sixth Amendment right to trial by jury.

12 511 US 127 (1994).

13 The actual vote count was 6-3 against the state of Alabama. However, Justice Sandra Day O'Connor wrote a concurring opinion that argued that the restriction on peremptory challenges should apply only to government litigants, not private attorneys. Her concurring argument supported the positions taken by the dissenters in this case. That is why O'Connor is listed as one of the four justices who disagreed with the majority opinion.

14 For a good discussion of empirical studies of the impact of gender in jury decision making, see Deborah L. Forman, "What Difference Does It Make? Gender and Jury Selection." *University of California at Los Angeles Women's Law Journal* 2, 1992, 35–83; Susan Hightower, "Sex and the Peremptory Strike: An Empirical Analysis of J. E. B. v. Alabama's First Five Years". *Stanford Law Review* 52, 2000, 895–928

15 See Mattie E. Treadwell. "The Women's Army Corps", 1954. www.history.army.mil/books/wwii/Wac/ch01.htm. Also, see "United States Army in World War II". United States Army Center of Military History, 1991. www.history.army.mil/books/wwii/Wach/index.htm

16 453 US 57 (1981).

READINGS

Suffrage

Horace Bushnell (1802–76)

Horace Bushnell was a prominent, controversial American theologian who is sometimes referred to as a founder of American religious liberalism. Although considered a religious reformer, his views on sexual equality were clearly traditionalist. His book, *Woman's Suffrage: The Reform against Nature,* from which the following selections are taken, denies that men and women are equal and that women have a natural right to vote.

Bushnell, Horace. "Women's Suffrage: The Reform Against Nature (Selections)". In *The Struggle for Women's Rights: Theoretical & Historical Sources,* edited by George and Margaret G Klosko. Upper Saddle River New Jersey:, Prentice-Hall, 1999. 195–204. (Excerpts: pp. 196–8).

Chapter II

The short argument, as it is commonly put, runs thus: women are the equals of men, and have therefore an equal right to vote. In which very brief and very simple form of deduction, there are, if we are not willing to be taken by the shallowest possible fallacies, two quite plainly untrue conclusions. First, it is not certainly true that women are equal to men. They are equally women as men are men; they are equally human as men; they are so far equally entitled to protection as men, but it does not hence appear that they are equal to men. They may be superior to men; they may be inferior to men; but what is a great deal closer probably to the truth, they may be very unlike in kind to men; so unlike that in the civil state they had best for their own sake and for the public good, stand back from any claim of right, in the public administration of the laws. How far this unlikeness extends is not here the question. ...for the present I cannot forbear citing from the *Nation,* a very short but excellently vigorous statement of the fact itself. "The unlikeness between men and women is radical and essential. It runs through all the spheres. Distinct as they are in bodily form and features, they are quite as distinct in mental and moral characteristics. They neither think, feel, wish, purpose, will, nor act alike. They take the same views of nothing. The old statements that one is passive, the other active; one emotional, the other moral, one affectionate, the other rational; one sentimental, the other intellectual, are likely to be more than verified by science. Of course, these statements, whether verified or not, do not justify the imposition of arbitrary limits on opportunity or enterprise. It still remains to determine what place each can fill, what work each can do, what standard each can reach; and these nature should be left to determine. But that both can not occupy the same place, do the same work, or reach the same standard, ought, we think, to be assumed. Nature has decreed it so." Accordingly, if the two sexes are so very unlike in *kind*, there can, so far, be no predication of equality between them. And then, just so far, the argument for a right in women to vote, in consideration of their equality, is inconclusive....

* * *

The second fallacy above referred to is built on an argument equally baseless; it is that, being equal to men, women have a right to vote because men have a right to vote. Here the meaning is, if there is any, that men have a natural right to vote, or a right to vote that is grounded in nature. The words *man* and *suffrage* have, in this view, a fixed relation; a universal and permanent relation; such that suffrage never was or can be denied them, save by a public wrong; for every right is a something never to be stripped away, except by a wrong. Since, then, prior to the arrival of our own American republic, there had never been more than two or three small peoples in the world that acknowledged any right to vote at all, and these no equal right, but only rights so unequal that a very few men of grade, as in Rome, counted more than a whole bottom tier of rabble that composed the chief population of the city,... Besides, we had not then, and never since have had, ourselves, any equal right of voting as being men, saying nothing of women, under our own constitutions and liberties. Some of us have been voting on the score of our property; some on the right we have bought by military service; some on the ground of qualifications imparted by our education; some on the count of our slaves. Doubtless we that are males are all so far equal, but we never to this day have been allowed to vote on our naked equality, except in here and there a single State. How then does it fare with the argument that women have a right, on the score of their equality with men, when men themselves can not vote on the score of their own equality with one another?....

Susan B. Anthony (1820–1906)

Susan B. Anthony, one of the greatest American reformers and suffragists, helped secure the passage of the Nineteeth Amendment to the Constitution which granted women the right to vote in 1920. Anthony was arrested in Rochester, New York for illegally voting in the presidential election of 1872. Although she was tried, convicted, and fined for her alleged offense, her case was dropped after she refused to pay the fine. The selection below is taken from a speech she delivered to lecture audiences in New York prior to her trial.

Anthony, Susan B. "Constitutional Argument, 1872". In *The Elizabeth Cady Stanton-Susan B. Anthony Reader: Correspondence, Writings, Speeches,* edited by Ellen Carol Dubois, 152–65. Boston: Northeastern University Press, 1992. (Excerpts: pp. 152–4)

Friends and Fellow-citizens: I stand before you to-night, under indictment for the alleged crime of having voted at the last Presidential election, without having a lawful right to vote. It shall be my work this evening to prove to you that in thus doing, I not only committed no crime, but, instead, simply exercised my citizen's right, guaranteed to me and all United States citizens by the National Constitution beyond the power of any State to deny.

Our democratic-republican government is based on the idea of the natural right of every individual member thereof to a voice and a vote in making and executing the laws. We assert the province of government to be to secure the people in the enjoyment of their inalienable rights. We throw to the winds the old dogma that government can give rights. No one denies that before governments were organized each individual possessed the right to protect his own life, liberty and property. When 100 to 1,000,000 people enter into a free government, they do not barter away their natural rights; they simply pledge themselves to protect each other in the enjoyment of them, through prescribed judicial and legislative tribunals. They agree to abandon the methods of brute force in the adjustment of their differences, and adopt those of civilization....The Declaration of Independence, the United States Constitution, the constitutions of the several States and the organic laws of the Territories, all alike propose to *protect* the people in the exercise of their God-given rights. Not one of them pretends to bestow rights.

All men are created equal, and endowed by their Creator with certain inalienable rights. Among these are life, liberty and the pursuit of happiness. To secure these, governments are instituted among men, deriving their just powers from the consent of the governed."

Here is no shadow of government authority over rights, or exclusion of any from their full and equal enjoyment. Here is pronounced the right of all men, and "consequently," as the Quaker preacher said, "of all women," to a voice in the government. And here, in this first paragraph of the Declaration, is the assertion of the natural right of all to the ballot; for, how can the "consent of the governed" be given, if the right to vote be denied?... The women, dissatisfied as they are with this form of government, that enforces taxation without representation-- that compels them to obey laws to which they have never given their consent---that imprisons and hangs them without a trial by a jury of their peers-- that robs them, in marriage of the custody of their own persons, wages and children--are this half of the people left wholly at the mercy of the other half, in direct violation of the spirit and letter of the declarations of the framers of this government, every one of which was based on the immutable principle of equal rights to all. By these declarations, kings, popes, priests, aristocrats, all were alike dethroned and placed on a common level, politically, with the lowliest born subject or serf. By them, too, men, as such, were deprived of their divine right to rule and placed on a political level with women. By the practice of these declarations all class and caste distinctions would be abolished, and slave, serf, plebeian, wife, woman, all arise from their subject position to the broader platform of equality.

The preamble to the Federal Constitution says:

We, the people of the United States, in order to form a more perfect union, establish justice, insure domestic tranquility, provide for the common defence, promote the general welfare and secure the blessings of liberty to ourselves and our posterity, do ordain and establish this Constitution for the United States of America.

It was we, the people, not we, the white male citizens, nor we, the male citizens; but we, the whole people, who formed this Union. We formed it, not to give the blessings of liberty but to secure them; not to the half of ourselves and the half of our posterity, but to the whole people-women as well as men. It is downright mockery to talk to women of their enjoyment of the blessings of liberty while they are denied the use of the only means of securing them provided by this democratic-republican government-the ballot.

* * *

Jury Service

Bailey v. State, 219 S.W.2d 424 (Ark. 1949)

The exclusion of women from serving on juries was challenged by criminal defendants as a violation of their due process (fair trial) rights. In *Bailey v. State*, Bailey cited the exclusion of women from his rape trial as grounds for reversing his conviction and sentence of life imprisonment. Interestingly, women were not automatically excluded from serving of state juries in

Arkansas, but there was no requirement that women be included in or excluded from the selection process. Therefore, a woman could be called for jury duty but would be excused if she chose not to serve. Mr. Bailey's appeal argued that jury commissioners had abused their discretion in impaneling juries by failing to summon women for jury duty for more than a decade.

Below are excerpts from the Arkansas Supreme Court's decision to uphold Bailey's conviction and sentence.

BAILEY V. STATE

SUPREME COURT OF ARKANSAS

215 Ark. 53; 219 S.W.2d 424; 1949 Ark. LEXIS 690; 9 A.L.R.2d 653

April 11, 1949, Opinion delivered

OPINION BY: Chief Justice Griffin Smith

OPINION

[*54] [**424] The verdict was: "We, the jury, find . . . John Bailey guilty of rape . . . and assess his punishment at life imprisonment in the penitentiary."

* * *

Fourth -- Systematic Exclusion of Women From Jury Panels. -- It was stipulated that in respect of the First Division of Pulaski Circuit Court, no woman had been selected by the Commissioners since 1925.

By Amendment No. 8 to the Constitution of Arkansas qualifications of electors were fixed and equal suffrage conferred, but "women shall not be compelled to serve on juries." See Act 402 of 1921; Pope's Digest, §§ 8302-3-4; Ark. Stats. (1947), § 39-112, 113, 114. The Constitutional proviso and statute sections have been [*61] construed as a privilege women may claim [***15] -- declarations of public policy pursuant to which it has not been thought that jury commissioners abused their discretion when there was failure to include women on the lists of those summoned.

Criminal court trials often involve testimony of the foulest kind, and they sometimes require consideration of indecent conduct, the use of filthy and loathsome words, references to intimate sex relationships, and other elements that would prove humiliating, embarrassing and degrading to a lady.

Under recognized requirements in this State, racial distinctions are disregarded in jury service. More often than not the fact-finders are not permitted to separate after a case has been submitted. Standards of deportment between men and women, and individual conceptions of personal propriety enter into the transactions; and while of course the State possesses power and could through an all-inclusive constitutional mandate say that in jury service there shall be no distinction between sexes, and while the *right* of Commissioners to call women unquestionably exists, it has not been thought that the policy .... was of a character depriving Commissioners of the discretion [***16] exercised in cases such as that with which we are dealing.

* * *

We think the inference deducible from the Fay [v. *New York,* 332 U.S. 261], case is that where a State does not impose upon women as a class the inescapable duty of jury service, a defendant who complains that due process was denied, or that he was not afforded the equal protection contemplated by the Fourteenth Amendment, must show something more than continuing failure of jury commissioners to call women for services in a division of the Court where the innate refinement peculiar to women would be assailed with verbal expressions, gestures, conversations and demonstrations from which most would recoil.

Attention is called [***20] to the fact that the stipulation upon which appellant relies does not say that women have been systematically excluded from jury service. The court, seeking to express what it thought was intended, remarked that "The stipulation relates to defendant's motion to quash the panel because the jury commissioners have habitually excluded women from jury service solely because they are women".

The motion did not allege they had been *"systematically"* excluded. Our decision, however, does not rest upon this technical refinement; but rather upon the substantial ground that the record does not show that [*64] the defendant failed to receive a fair trial at the hands of a competent jury.

State v. Chase, 211 P. 920 (Ore. 1922)

This case involved a challenge to Oregon's law that mandated that women must comprise half of trial juries in cases involving minor defendants or minor complaining witnesses.

Since Chase was on trial for the rape of a 9 year old girl, his trial jury was required to be comprised of 6 women and 6 men. The trial jury was randomly selected by pulling the names of individuals summoned for jury duty from a jury box. After 6 men and 5 women had been seated for Chase's jury, one more woman was needed to impanel the jury. But, the next person called was a male. Although this male would have ordinarily been eligible to serve on the trial jury, he was disqualified because of the statutory requirement of having women comprise half of the jury. The next person called was a woman, but she was excused for cause. Afterwards, several men were called, and all were disqualified. Defense counsel objected to the disqualification of all of the men and objected to seating a woman. When informed by the clerk that no females remained in the jury pool, the trial judge ordered the clerk to summon 10 more women and rescheduled the jury selection proceeding for a later date.

When the proceeding reconvened, the defense counsel repeated his objection to the disqualification of the male jurors. The trial judge informed the defendant that 6 women would sit on the jury and, if necessary, the Court would sit the 6th woman after the defendant had exhausted all of his challenges. With that pronouncement, the defendant decided not to challenge any more women.

Chase was convicted of statutory rape and appealed his conviction on the grounds that the trial court should not have disqualified male jurors in order to sit a female juror.

Below is an excerpt from the Oregon Supreme Court's decision that upheld the law and the actions of the trial judge.

STATE v. CHASE.

SUPREME COURT OF OREGON

106 Ore. 263; 211 P. 920; 1922 Ore. LEXIS 122

December 19, 1922, Decided

OPINION:

In Banc.

* * *

... The Constitution guarantees to a [*268] defendant the right of trial by an impartial jury, leaving the legislature to provide the method of securing such a jury. So long as it is a jury of his peers, that is, of qualified citizens impartial between the state and himself, the defendant has no right to complain because a particular class of persons is included or excluded. The law exempts from jury duty several classes of people: [***6] ministers, school-teachers, attorneys, civil officers, firemen, and many others, and excuses from such service jurors who have served for a period of four weeks or who for family reasons are unable to attend. Many of those in the exempt class would make ideal jurors, but reasons of public policy and convenience justify their exemption. The reason for requiring cases of the character of the present to be tried before a jury composed partly of women rests upon the highest considerations of public policy and humanity. Anyone who has occupied the circuit bench and seen a poor, frightened girl, a stranger to a courtroom, forced to detail the facts in regard to her injury or shame to a jury composed of strange men, has felt that the presence of a few of the mothers of children in the jury-box would be more in accordance with humanity and justice. The intention of the legislature in enacting Section 10, *supra*, is plain, and even if to give it effect one should hold that it works an implied amendment of Section 116, we should so hold rather than declare the law void for uncertainty. ...

* * *

3. The claim that the statute is in violation of the Constitution is not predicated upon the argument that it is unconstitutional to permit women to sit upon juries, a practice not now unusual in several of the [**923] states, but it is claimed that [***8] by allowing women summoned to serve upon the panel to decline such service, making it thereby optional with the person served to attend or not, the enactment of 1921 destroys the compulsory nature of jury duty and in some way not clearly explained by counsel deprives a party of a fair and impartial jury. While in the opinion of the writer it would have been better policy if the statute had specified the grounds upon which a woman could be excused from jury duty, such as necessity of caring for her family or the like, we think [HN4] there is no invasion of the constitutional rights of a defendant in permitting the service upon a jury by women to be largely voluntary. The right of a defendant is to have a fair and impartial jury, and if the statute gives him this, he has no reason to complain if it permits women to excuse themselves from service. From their physical constitution as well as from the nature of their duties and occupations, [*270] women have many reasons for not wishing to serve or being required to serve upon juries, which do not apply to male jurors, and some of these are such as a delicate woman would hesitate to specify in court or even to a judge.

* * *

Hoyt v. Florida, 368 US 57 (1961)

Rather than absolutely prohibiting women from participating on state juries, states like Florida exempted women from jury duty. This exemption meant that women would not be placed on the list from where prospective jurors were randomly chosen. In Florida, women who wanted to be jurors (or at least wanted to have the chance of being summoned for jury duty) could waive the exemption by requesting the clerk of the court to add their names to jury lists. Men received no automatic exemption and, therefore, were subject to be summoned for jury service. Men could be exempt based upon their age, their physical condition and specific occupational demands. Given this jury selection method, it is unsurprising that jury trials in Florida tended to have all-male or predominately male juries.

Hoyt v. Florida involved a challenge to the state's jury selection system when a female defendant appealed her murder conviction on the grounds that all-male jury denied her the equal protection of the laws. The defendant, Ms. Hoyt, apparently killed her husband in the midst of a fight over his infidelity. Ms. Hoyt claimed that women would be more sympathetic to and understanding of her decision to kill her husband than the men on her jury. She appealed her conviction on the grounds that the all-male jury, which resulted from Florida's jury selection system, constituted unconstitutional sex discrimination under the Fourteenth Amendment Equal Protection Clause.

Below is an excerpt from the United States Supreme Court's decision in *Hoyt v. Florida* (1961). In a unanimous decision, the Court defended Florida's jury selection system.

HOYT v. FLORIDA

SUPREME COURT OF THE UNITED STATES

368 U.S. 57; 82 S. Ct. 159; 7 L. Ed. 2d 118; 1961 U.S. LEXIS 136

November 20, 1961, Decided

OPINION BY: Justice John Harlan

OPINION

[*58] [***120] [**160] MR. JUSTICE JOHN HARLAN delivered the opinion of the Court.

Appellant, a woman, has been convicted in Hillsborough County, Florida, of second degree murder of her husband. ...[W]e noted probable jurisdiction, 364 U.S. 930, to consider appellant's claim that her trial before an all-male jury violated rights assured by the Fourteenth Amendment. The claim is that such jury was the product of a state jury statute which works an unconstitutional exclusion of women from jury service.

* * *

Manifestly, Florida's § 40.01 (1) does not purport to exclude women from state jury service. Rather, the statute "gives to women the privilege to serve but does not impose service as a duty." *Fay* v. *New York, supra*, at 277. It accords women an absolute exemption from jury service unless they expressly waive that privilege. ...

In the selection of jurors Florida has differentiated between men and women in two respects. It has given women an absolute exemption from jury duty based solely on their sex, no similar exemption obtaining as to men.[3] And it has provided for its effectuation in a manner less onerous than that governing exemptions exercisable by men: women are not to be put on the jury list unless they have voluntarily registered for such service; men, on the other hand, even if entitled to an exemption, are to be included on the list unless they have filed a written claim of exemption as provided by law.[4] Fla. Stat., 1959, § 40.10.

In neither respect can we conclude that Florida's statute is not "based on some reasonable classification," and that it is thus infected with unconstitutionality. Despite the enlightened emancipation of women from the restrictions [*62] and protections of bygone years, and their entry into many parts of community life formerly considered to be reserved to men, woman is still regarded as the center of home and family life. We cannot say that it is constitutionally impermissible for a [**163] State, acting in pursuit of the general welfare, to conclude that a woman should be relieved from the civic duty of jury service unless she herself determines that such service is consistent with her own special responsibilities.

...It is true, of course, that Florida could have limited the exemption, as some other States have done, only to women who have family responsibilities.[8] But [HN7] we cannot regard it as irrational for a state legislature to consider preferable a broad exemption, whether born of the State's historic public policy or of a determination [**164] that it would not be administratively feasible to decide in each individual instance whether the family responsibilities of a prospective female juror were serious enough to warrant an exemption.

Taylor v. Louisiana, 419 US 522 (1975)

Taylor v. Louisiana involved a challenge to Louisiana's jury selection statute that mirrored the system the United States Supreme Court upheld in *Hoyt v. Florida*. Like the Florida system, women were automatically exempt from jury service. Women could waive the exemption by formally declaring in writing to the clerk of court their desire to be summoned for jury duty. In 1961, the Court declared that the automatic exemption of women constituted a reasonable public policy choice; women's family responsibilities would be undermined if they were as susceptible to jury service as men.

Fourteen years later, Billy Taylor challenged his conviction of aggravated kidnapping on the grounds that the all-male jury violated his Sixth Amendment right to trial by jury. Taylor argued that the Louisiana jury selection system excluded women from jury service which had the effect of excluding over 50% of the parish's population. The policy of automatically exempting women from jury service prevented criminal defendants from having juries that are comprised of a cross-section of the community.

A Court majority distinguished its decision in *Taylor* from its ruling in *Hoyt*. Justice Bryon White, the author of the majority opinion, was appointed to the Supreme Court by Democratic President John F. Kennedy.

TAYLOR v. LOUISIANA

SUPREME COURT OF THE UNITED STATES

419 U.S. 522; 95 S. Ct. 692; 42 L. Ed. 2d 690; 1975 U.S. LEXIS 2

January 21, 1975, Decided

OPINION BY: Justice Bryon White

[*523] [***694] [**694] MR. JUSTICE BRYON WHITE delivered the opinion of the Court.

When this case was tried, Art. VII, § 41,[1] of the Louisiana Constitution, and Art. 402 of the Louisiana Code of Criminal Procedure[2] provided that a woman should not be selected for jury service unless she had previously filed a written declaration of her desire to be subject to jury service.....

* * *

II

The Louisiana jury-selection system does not disqualify women from jury service, but in operation its conceded systematic impact is that only a very few women, grossly disproportionate to the number of eligible women in the community, are called for jury service. In this case, no women were on the venire from which the petit jury was drawn. The issue we have, therefore, is whether a jury-selection system which operates to exclude from jury service an identifiable class of citizens constituting 53% [*526] of eligible jurors in the community comports with the Sixth and Fourteenth Amendments.

[***LEdHR2] [2]The State first insists that Taylor, a male, has no standing to object to the exclusion of women from his jury. But Taylor's claim is that he was constitutionally entitled to a jury drawn from a venire constituting a fair cross section of the community and that the jury that tried him was not such a jury by reason of the exclusion of women. Taylor was not a member of the excluded class; but there is no rule that claims such as Taylor presents may be made only by those defendants who are members of the group excluded from jury service....

* * *

The unmistakable import of this Court's opinions, ...is that [HN5] the selection of a petit jury from a representative cross section of the community is an essential component of the Sixth Amendment right to a jury trial. ...[T]he jury plays a political function in the administration of the law and [*530] that the requirement of a jury's being chosen from a fair cross section of the community is fundamental to the American system of justice. ...

We accept the fair-cross-section requirement as fundamental to the jury trial guaranteed by the Sixth [**698] Amendment and are convinced that the requirement has solid foundation. The purpose of a jury is to guard against the exercise of arbitrary power -- to make available the commonsense judgment of the community as a hedge against the overzealous or mistaken prosecutor and in preference to the professional or perhaps overconditioned or biased response of a judge. *Duncan* v. *Louisiana*, 391 U.S., at 155–6.... Restricting jury service to only special groups or excluding identifiable segments playing major roles in the community cannot be squared with the constitutional concept of jury trial. "Trial by jury presupposes a jury drawn from a pool broadly representative of the community as well as impartial in a specific case. . . . [The] broad representative character of the jury should be maintained, partly as assurance of a diffused impartiality and partly [*531] because sharing in the administration of justice is a phase of civic responsibility." *Thiel* v. *Southern Pacific Co.*, 328 U.S. 217, 227 (1946) (Frankfurter, J., dissenting).

IV

[***LEdHR5] [5]We are also persuaded that [HN6] the fair-cross-section requirement is violated by the systematic exclusion of women, who in the judicial district involved here amounted to 53% of the citizens eligible for jury service. This conclusion necessarily entails the judgment that women are sufficiently numerous and distinct from men and that if they are systematically eliminated from jury panels, the Sixth Amendment's fair-cross-section requirement cannot be satisfied....

* * *

V

There remains the argument that women as a class serve a distinctive role in society and that jury service would so substantially interfere with that function that the State has ample justification for excluding women from service unless they volunteer, even though the result is that almost all jurors are men. It is true that *Hoyt* v. *Florida*, 368 U.S. 57 (1961), held that such a system[14] did not deny due process of law or equal protection [*534] of the laws because there was a sufficiently rational basis for such an exemption.[15] But *Hoyt* did not involve a defendant's Sixth Amendment right to a jury drawn from a fair cross section of the community and the prospect of depriving him of that right if women as a class are systematically excluded. The right to a proper jury cannot be overcome on [**700] merely rational grounds.[16] There must be weightier reasons if a distinctive class representing 53% of the eligible jurors is for all practical purposes to be excluded from jury service. No such basis has been tendered here.

The States are free to grant exemptions from jury service to individuals in case of special hardship or incapacity and to those engaged in particular occupations the uninterrupted performance of which is critical to the community's welfare. *Rawlins* v. *Georgia*, 201 U.S. 638 (1906). It would not appear that such exemptions would pose substantial threats that the remaining pool of jurors would not be representative of the community. A system excluding all women, however, is a wholly different matter. It is untenable to suggest these days that it would be a special hardship for each and every woman to [***701] perform jury service or that society cannot [*535] spare *any* women from their present duties.[17] This may be the case with many, and it may be burdensome to sort out those who should be exempted from those who should serve. But that task is performed in the case of men, and the administrative convenience in dealing with women as a class is insufficient justification for diluting the quality of community judgment represented by the jury in criminal trials.

* * *

Accepting as we do, however, the view that the Sixth Amendment affords the defendant in a criminal trial the opportunity to have the jury drawn from venires representative of the community, we think it is no longer tenable to hold that women as a class may be excluded or given automatic exemptions based solely on sex if the consequence is that criminal jury venires are almost totally male. To this extent we cannot follow the contrary implications of the prior cases, including *Hoyt* v. *Florida*. If it was ever the case that women were unqualified to sit on juries or were so situated that none of them should be required to perform jury service, that time has long since passed. If at one time it could be held that Sixth Amendment juries must be drawn from a fair cross section of the community but that this requirement permitted the almost total exclusion of women, this is not the case today. Communities differ at different times and places. What is a fair cross section at one time or place is not necessarily a fair cross section at another time or a different place. Nothing persuasive has been presented to us in this case suggesting that all-male venires in the parishes involved here are fairly representative of the local population otherwise eligible for jury service.

* * *

...Louisiana's special exemption [**702] for women operates to exclude them from petit juries, which in our view is contrary to the command of the Sixth and Fourteenth Amendments.

J.E.B. v. Alabama, 511 US 127 (1994)

In this case, the United States Supreme Court addressed the constitutionality of using sex-based peremptory challenges to impanel trial juries. *JEB v. Alabama* involved a child paternity and child support dispute in which the state of Alabama, acting on behalf of the mother, was suing the alleged father for support. The state's attorney used his peremptory challenges to impanel an all-female jury. Ironically, the attorney for the alleged father used his peremptory challenges to remove as many women from the jury as possible. Specifically, JEB asked the Court to decide whether the state attorney could use his peremptory challenges to impanel all-female jury by excusing all of the men from the jury pool.

In siding for JEB, a majority of the Court expressed its concern that this use of peremptory challenges produced troubling discrimination and undermined the legitimacy of the jury process.

Justice Harry Blackmun wrote the majority opinion. Justice Blackmun, the author of *Roe v. Wade* (1973), was appointed to the Supreme Court by Republican President Richard Nixon.

J. E. B., PETITIONER v. ALABAMA EX REL. T. B.

SUPREME COURT OF THE UNITED STATES

511 U.S. 127; 114 S. Ct. 1419; 128 L. Ed. 2d 89; 1994 U.S. LEXIS

April 19, 1994, Decided

OPINION

JUSTICE HARRY BLACKMUN delivered the opinion of the Court.

I

* * *

[***LEdHR1B] [1B]We granted certiorari, 508 U.S. 905 (1993), to resolve a question that has created a conflict of authority -- whether the Equal Protection Clause forbids peremptory challenges on the basis of gender as well as on the basis of race.[1] Today we reaffirm what, by now, should be axiomatic: Intentional discrimination on the basis of gender by state actors violates [*131] the Equal Protection Clause, particularly where, as here, the discrimination serves to ratify and perpetuate invidious, archaic, and overbroad stereotypes about the relative abilities of men and women.

II

Discrimination on the basis of gender in the exercise of peremptory challenges is a relatively recent phenomenon. Gender-based peremptory strikes were hardly practicable during most of our country's existence, since, until the 20th century, women were completely excluded from jury service.[2] So [**1423] well entrenched was this exclusion of women that in 1880 this Court, while finding that the exclusion of African-American men from juries violated the Fourteenth Amendment, expressed no doubt that a State "may confine the selection [of jurors] to males." *Strauder* v. *West*

Virginia, 100 U.S. at 310; see also *Fay* v. *New York*, 332 U.S. 261, 289–90, 91 L. Ed. 2043, 67 S. Ct. 1613 (1947).

* * *

Despite the heightened scrutiny afforded distinctions based on gender, respondent argues that gender discrimination in the selection of the petit jury should be permitted, though discrimination on the basis of race is not. Respondent suggests that "gender discrimination in this country . . . has never reached the level of discrimination" against African-Americans, and therefore gender discrimination, unlike racial discrimination, is tolerable in the courtroom. Brief for Respondent 9.

While the prejudicial attitudes toward women in this country have not been identical to those held toward racial minorities, the similarities between the experiences of racial minorities and women, in some contexts, "overpower those differences."...

* * *

...Thus, the only question is whether discrimination on the basis of gender in jury selection substantially furthers the State's legitimate interest in achieving a fair and impartial [*137] trial.[6] In making this assessment, we do not weigh the value of peremptory challenges as an institution against our asserted commitment to eradicate invidious [**1426] discrimination from the courtroom.[7] Instead, we consider whether peremptory challenges based on gender stereotypes provide substantial aid to a litigant's effort to secure a fair and impartial jury.[8]

Far from proffering an exceptionally persuasive justification for its gender-based peremptory challenges, respondent maintains that its decision to strike virtually all the males from the jury in this case "may reasonably have been based upon the perception, supported by history, that men otherwise totally qualified to serve upon a jury in any case might [*138] be more sympathetic and receptive to the arguments of a man alleged in a paternity action to be the father of an out-of-wedlock child, while women equally qualified to serve upon a jury might be more sympathetic and receptive to the arguments of the complaining witness who bore the child."

We shall not accept as a defense to gender-based peremptory challenges "the very stereotype the [***103] law condemns." *Powers* v. *Ohio*, 499 U.S. at 410. Respondent's rationale, not unlike those regularly expressed for gender-based strikes, is reminiscent of the arguments advanced to justify the total exclusion of women from juries.[10] Respondent offers [*139] virtually no [**1427] support for the conclusion that gender alone is an accurate predictor of juror's attitudes; yet it urges this Court to condone the same stereotypes that justified the wholesale exclusion of women from juries and the ballot box.[11] Respondent seems to assume that gross generalizations that would be deemed impermissible if made on [***104] the [*140] basis of race are somehow permissible when made on the basis of gender.

Discrimination in jury selection, whether based on race or on gender, causes harm to the litigants, the community, and the individual jurors who are wrongfully excluded from participation in the judicial process. The litigants are harmed by the risk that the prejudice that motivated the discriminatory selection of the jury will infect the entire proceedings. See *Edmonson*, 500 U.S. at 628 (discrimination in the courtroom "raises serious questions as to the fairness of the proceedings conducted there"). The community is harmed by the State's participation in the perpetuation of invidious group stereotypes and the inevitable loss of confidence in our judicial system that state-sanctioned discrimination in the courtroom engenders.

When state actors exercise peremptory challenges in reliance on gender stereotypes, they ratify and reinforce prejudicial views of the relative abilities of men and women. Because these stereotypes have wreaked injustice in so many other spheres of our country's public life, active discrimination by litigants on the basis of gender during jury selection "invites cynicism respecting the jury's neutrality and its obligation to adhere to the law." *Powers* v. *Ohio*, 499 U.S. at 412. The potential for cynicism is particularly acute in cases where gender-related issues are prominent, such as cases involving rape, sexual harassment, or paternity. Discriminatory use of peremptory challenges may create the impression that the judicial system has acquiesced in suppressing full participation by one gender or that the "deck has been stacked" in favor of one side.

...Striking individual jurors on the assumption that they hold particular views simply because of their gender is "practically a brand upon them, affixed by the law, an assertion of their inferiority." *Strauder* v. *West Virginia*, 100 U.S. at 308. It denigrates the dignity of the excluded juror, and, for a woman, reinvokes a history of exclusion from political participation.[14] The message it sends to all those in the courtroom, and all those who may later learn of the discriminatory act, is that certain individuals, for no reason other than gender, are presumed unqualified by state actors to decide important questions upon which reasonable persons could disagree.[15]

* * *

Our conclusion that litigants [***106] may not strike potential jurors solely on the basis of gender does not imply the elimination of all peremptory challenges. Neither does it conflict with a State's legitimate interest in using such challenges in its effort to secure a fair and impartial jury. [HN12] Parties still may remove jurors who they feel might be less acceptable than others on the panel; gender simply may not serve as a proxy for bias. Parties may also exercise their peremptory challenges to remove from the venire any group or class of individuals normally subject to "rational basis" review. See *Cleburne v. Cleburne Living Center, Inc.*, 473 U.S. at 439–42; *Clark v. Jeter*, 486 U.S. 456, 461, 100 L. Ed. 2d 465, 108 S. Ct. 1910 (1988). Even strikes based on characteristics that are disproportionately associated with one gender could be appropriate, absent a showing of pretext.[16]

If conducted properly, *voir dire* can inform litigants about potential jurors, making reliance upon stereotypical and pejorative notions about a particular gender or race both unnecessary and unwise. *Voir dire* provides a means of discovering actual or implied bias and a firmer basis upon which the [*144] parties may exercise their peremptory challenges intelligently.

* * *

V

Equal opportunity to participate in the fair administration of justice is fundamental to our democratic system.[19] It not [*146] only furthers the goals of the jury system. It reaffirms the promise of equality under the law -- that all citizens, regardless of race, ethnicity, or gender, have the chance to take part directly in our democracy. *Powers v. Ohio*, 499 U.S. at 407 ("Indeed, with the exception of voting, for most citizens the honor and privilege of jury duty is their most significant opportunity to participate in the democratic process"). When persons are excluded from participation in our democratic processes solely because of race or gender, this promise of equality dims, and the integrity of our judicial system is jeopardized.

In view of these concerns, [HN17] the Equal Protection Clause prohibits discrimination in jury selection on the basis of gender, or on the assumption that an individual will be biased in a particular case for no reason other than the fact that the person happens to be a woman or happens to be a man. As with race, the "core guarantee of equal protection, ensuring citizens that their State will not discriminate . . ., would be meaningless were we to approve the exclusion [***108] of jurors on the basis of such assumptions, which arise solely from the jurors' [gender]."

It is so ordered.

J.E.B. v. Alabama, 511 US 127 (1994)

Four justices questioned the majority opinion. Justice O'Connor, who concurred with the majority along with 3 dissenting justices, focused on the importance of allowing attorneys' wide discretion in using peremptory challenges in jury selection. O'Connor concurred because she believed that government attorneys should not engage in actions that could be conceived as discriminating against protected groups. However, she sided with the dissenters in protecting the freedom of private attorneys to use their peremptory challenges as they see fit.

Below are excerpts from Justice O'Connor's concurring opinion, Chief Justice Rehnquist's dissent and Antonin Scalia's dissent, which was joined by Chief Justice William Rehnquist and Justice Clarence Thomas. Justice Scalia has become one of the most conservative justices on the Court, and he was appointed by Republican President Ronald Reagan.

J. E. B., PETITIONER v. ALABAMA EX REL. T. B.

SUPREME COURT OF THE UNITED STATES

511 U.S. 127; 114 S. Ct. 1419; 128 L. Ed. 2d 89; 1994 U.S. LEXIS 3121; 62 U.S.L.W. 4219

April 19, 1994, Decided

CONCUR

JUSTICE SANDRA DAY O'CONNOR, concurring.

* * *

Moreover, "the essential nature of the peremptory challenge is that it is one exercised without a reason stated, without [*148] inquiry and without being subject to the court's control." *Swain*, 380 U.S. at 220. Indeed, often a reason for it cannot be stated, for a trial [***109] lawyer's judgments about a juror's sympathies are sometimes based on experienced hunches and educated guesses, derived from a juror's responses at voir dire or a juror's "'bare looks and gestures.'" ...Our belief that experienced lawyers will often correctly intuit which jurors are likely to be the least sympathetic, and our understanding that the lawyer will often be unable to explain the intuition, are the very reason we cherish the peremptory challenge. But, as we add, layer by layer, additional constitutional restraints on the use of the peremptory, we force lawyers to articulate what we know is often inarticulable.

* * *

Nor is the value of the peremptory challenge to the litigant diminished when the [**1432] peremptory is exercised in a gender-based manner. We know that like race, gender matters. A [*149] plethora of studies make clear that in rape cases, for example, female jurors are somewhat more likely to vote to convict than male jurors. Moreover, though there have been no similarly definitive studies regarding, for example, sexual harassment, child custody, or spousal or child abuse, one need not be a sexist to share the intuition that in certain cases a person's gender and resulting life experience will be relevant to his or her view of the case. "'Jurors are not expected to come into the jury box and leave behind all that their human experience has taught them.'" *Beck* v. *Alabama*, 447 U.S. 625, 642, 65 L. Ed. 2d 392, 100 S. Ct. 2382 (1980). Individuals are not expected to ignore as jurors what they know as men -- or women.

Today's decision severely limits a litigant's ability to act on this intuition, for the import of our holding is that any correlation between a juror's gender and attitudes is irrelevant as a matter of constitutional law. But to say that gender makes no difference as a matter of law is not to say that gender makes no difference as a matter of fact. I previously have said with regard to *Batson*: "That the Court will not tolerate prosecutors' racially discriminatory use of the peremptory challenge, in effect, is a special rule of relevance, a statement about what this Nation stands for, rather than a statement of fact." *Brown* v. *North Carolina*, 479 U.S. 940, 941–2, 93 L. Ed. 2d 373, 107 S. Ct. 423 (1986) (opinion concurring in [***110] denial of certiorari). Today's decision is a statement that, in an effort to eliminate the potential discriminatory use of the peremptory, see *Batson*, 476 U.S. at 102 (Marshall, J., concurring), gender is now governed by the special rule of relevance formerly reserved for race. Though we gain much from this statement, we cannot ignore what we lose. In extending *Batson* to gender we have added an additional burden to the state and federal trial process, taken a step closer to eliminating the peremptory challenge, and diminished the ability of litigants [*150] to act on sometimes accurate gender-based assumptions about juror attitudes.

These concerns reinforce my conviction that today's decision should be limited to a prohibition on the government's use of gender-based peremptory challenges. The Equal Protection Clause prohibits only discrimination by state actors.

DISSENT

CHIEF JUSTICE WILLIAM REHNQUIST, dissenting.

* * *

...Unlike the [*156] Court, I think the State has shown that jury strikes on the basis of gender "substantially further" the State's legitimate interest in achieving a fair and impartial trial through the venerable practice of peremptory challenges. The two sexes differ, both biologically and, to a diminishing extent, in experience. It is not merely "stereotyping" to say that these differences may produce a difference in outlook which is brought to the jury room. Accordingly, use of peremptory challenges on the basis of sex is generally not the sort of derogatory and invidious act which peremptory challenges directed at black jurors may be.

* * *

JUSTICE ANTONIN SCALIA, with whom THE CHIEF JUSTICE and JUSTICE CLARENCE THOMAS join, dissenting.

Today's opinion is an inspiring demonstration of how thoroughly up-to-date and right-thinking we Justices are in matters pertaining to the sexes (or as the Court would have it, the genders), and how sternly we disapprove the male chauvinist attitudes of our predecessors. The price to be paid for this display -- a modest price, surely -- is that most of the opinion is quite irrelevant to the case at hand. The hasty reader will be surprised to learn, for example, that this lawsuit involves a complaint about the use of peremptory challenges to exclude *men* from a petit jury. To be sure, [*157] petitioner, a man, used all but one of *his* peremptory strikes to remove *women* from the jury (he used his last challenge to strike the sole remaining male from the pool), but the validity of *his* strikes is not before us. ...

The Court also spends time establishing that the use of sex as a proxy for particular views or sympathies is unwise and perhaps irrational. The opinion stresses the lack of statistical evidence to support the widely held belief that, at least in certain types of cases, a juror's sex has some statistically significant predictive value as to how the juror will behave. See *ante*, at 137–9, and n. 9. This assertion seems to place the Court in opposition to its earlier Sixth Amendment "fair cross-section" cases... But times and trends do change, and unisex is unquestionably in fashion. Personally, I am less inclined to demand statistics, and more inclined to credit the perceptions of experienced litigators who have had money on the line. But it does not matter. The Court's fervent defense of the proposition *il n'y a pas de différence entre les hommes et les femmes* (it stereotypes the opposite view as hateful "stereotyping") turns out to be, like its recounting of the history of sex discrimination against women, utterly irrelevant. Even if sex was a remarkably good predictor in certain cases, the Court would find its use in peremptories unconstitutional. See *ante*, at 139, n. 11; cf. *ante*, at 148–9 (O'CONNOR, J., concurring).

* * *

...This case is a perfect example of how the system as a whole is evenhanded. While the only claim before the Court is petitioner's complaint that the prosecutor struck male jurors, for every man [*160] struck by the government petitioner's own lawyer struck a woman. To say that men were singled out for discriminatory treatment in this process is preposterous. The situation would be different if both sides systematically struck individuals of one group, so that the strikes evinced group-based animus and served as a proxy for segregated venire lists. See *Swain* v. *Alabama*, 380 U.S. 202, 223–4, 13 L. Ed. 2d 759, 85 S. Ct. 824 (1965). The pattern here, however, displays not a systemic sex-based animus but each side's desire to get a jury favorably disposed to its case. That is why the Court's characterization of respondent's argument as "reminiscent of the arguments advanced to justify the total exclusion of women from juries," *ante*, at 138, is patently false. Women were categorically excluded from juries because of doubt that they were competent; women are stricken from juries by peremptory challenge because of doubt that they are well disposed to the striking party's case. See *Powers, supra*, at 424 (SCALIA, J., dissenting). There is discrimination and dishonor in the former, and not in the latter -- which explains the 106-year interlude [**1438] between our holding that exclusion from juries on the basis of race was unconstitutional, *Strauder* v. *West Virginia*, 100 U.S. 303, 25 L. Ed. 664 (1880), and our holding that peremptory challenges on the basis of race were unconstitutional, *Batson* v. *Kentucky, supra*.

* * *

The irrationality of today's strike-by-strike approach to equal protection is evident from the consequences of extending it to its logical conclusion. If a fair and impartial trial is a prosecutor's only legitimate goal; if adversarial trial stratagems must be tested against that goal in abstraction from their role within the system as a whole; and if, so tested, sex-based stratagems do not survive heightened scrutiny -- then the prosecutor presumably violates the Constitution when he selects a male or female police officer to testify because he believes one or the other sex might be more convincing in the context of the particular case, or because he believes one or the other might be more appealing to a predominantly male or female jury. A decision to stress one line of argument or present certain witnesses before a mostly female jury -- for example, to stress that the defendant victimized women -- becomes, under the Court's reasoning, intentional discrimination by a state actor on the basis of gender.

* * *

In order, it seems to me, not to eliminate any real denial of equal protection, but simply to pay conspicuous obeisance to the equality of the sexes, the Court imperils a practice that has been considered an essential part of fair jury trial since the dawn of the common law. The Constitution of the United States neither requires nor permits this vandalizing of our people's traditions.

For these reasons, I dissent.

Military Service

Rostker v. Goldberg, 453 US 57 (1981)

This case illustrates how the natural difference principle affects the duty of citizens in protecting the nation's defense. The issue in *Rostker* involves whether women should be required to register for military duty in the case of a national emergency or a war. The ending of the draft did not void the Federal Government's requirement that every male citizen and resident register at the Division of Military Registration when they reached 18 years old. The purpose of male registration is to provide the Federal Government with a list of eligible recruits in the event that a draft is needed.

The *Rostker* case was initiated by a man who argued that the existing policy unfairly and unconstitutionally placed the burden of registration and possible conscription on men. His argument was that since conscription does not automatically mean that the drafted person will engage in direct combat, women should be required to register in case their services are needed in the event of war or national emergency.

Justice William Rehnquist's majority opinion is excerpted below.

ROSTKER, DIRECTOR OF SELECTIVE SERVICE v. GOLDBERG ET AL.

SUPREME COURT OF THE UNITED STATES

453 U.S. 57; 101 S. Ct. 2646; 69 L. Ed. 2d 478; 1981 U.S. LEXIS 126; 49 U.S.L.W. 4798

June 25, 1981, Decided

JUSTICE WILLIAM REHNQUIST delivered the opinion of the Court.

The question presented is whether the Military Selective Service violates the Fifth Amendment to the United States Constitution in authorizing the President to require the registration of males and not females.

I

...The purpose of this registration is to facilitate any eventual conscription: pursuant to § 4 (a) of the Act, 62 Stat. 605, as amended, 50 U. S. C. App. § 454 (a), those persons required to register under § 3 are liable for [*60] training and service in the Armed Forces. The MSSA registration provision serves no other purpose beyond providing a pool for subsequent induction.

...[The President] ... recommended that Congress take action to amend the MSSA to permit the registration and conscription of women as well as men. See House Committee on Armed Services, Presidential Recommendations [*61] for Selective Service Reform -- [***484] A Report to Congress Prepared Pursuant to Pub. L. 96–107, 96th Cong., 2d Sess., 20–3 (Comm. Print No. 19, 1980) (hereinafter Presidential Recommendations), App. 57–61.

...Although Congress considered the question at great length, see *infra*, at 72–4, it declined to amend the MSSA to permit the registration of women.

* * *

[*63] [**2651] On Friday, July 18, 1980, three days before registration was to commence, the District Court issued an opinion finding that the Act violated the Due Process Clause of the Fifth Amendment and permanently enjoined the Government from requiring registration under the Act. .... Applying the "important government interest" test articulated in *Craig* v. *Boren*, 429 U.S. 190 (1976), the court struck down the MSSA. The court stressed that it was not deciding whether or to what extent women should

serve in combat, but only the issue of registration, and felt that this "should dispel any concern that we are injecting ourselves in an inappropriate manner into military affairs." 509 F.Supp., at 597. See also id., at 599, nn. 17 and 18. The court then proceeded to examine the testimony and hearing evidence presented to Congress by representatives of the military and the Executive Branch, and concluded on the basis of this testimony that "military opinion, backed by extensive study, is that the availability of women registrants would materially increase flexibility, not hamper it." Id., at 603. It rejected Congress' contrary determination in part because of what it viewed as Congress' "inconsistent positions" in declining to register women yet spending funds to recruit them and expand their opportunities in the military. Ibid.

* * *

This Court has consistently recognized Congress' "broad constitutional power" to raise and regulate armies and navies, ...

"[It] is difficult to conceive of an area of governmental activity in which the courts have less competence. The complex, subtle, and professional decisions as to the composition, training, equipping, and control of a military force are essentially professional military judgments, [*66] subject *always* to civilian control of the Legislative and Executive Branches."

* * *

...In light of the floor debate and the Report of the Senate Armed Services Committee hereinafter discussed, it is apparent that Congress was fully aware not merely of the many facts and figures presented to it by witnesses who testified before its Committees, but of the current thinking as to the place of women in the Armed Services. In such a case, we cannot ignore Congress' broad authority conferred by the Constitution to raise and support armies when we are urged to declare [*72] unconstitutional its studied choice of one alternative in preference to another for furthering that goal.

[***491] III

...[T]he decision to exempt women from registration was not the "'accidental by-product of a traditional way of thinking about females.'" *Califano* v. *Webster*, 430 U.S. 313, 320 (1977) (quoting *Califano* v. *Goldfarb*, 430 U.S. 199, 223 (1977) (STEVENS, J., concurring in judgment)).

* * *

...The purpose of registration, therefore, was to prepare for a draft *of combat troops.*

[HN13] Women as a group, however, unlike men as a group, are not eligible for combat. The restrictions on the participation of women in combat in the Navy and Air Force are statutory. Under 10 U. S. C. § 6015 (1976 ed., Supp. III), "women may not be assigned to duty on vessels or in aircraft that are engaged in combat missions," and under 10 U. S. C. § 8549 female members of the Air Force "may not be assigned to duty in aircraft engaged in combat missions." The Army and Marine Corps [***494] preclude the use of women in combat as a matter of established policy. See App. 86, 34, 58. Congress specifically recognized and endorsed the exclusion of women from [*77] combat in exempting women from registration. In the words of the Senate Report:

"The principle that women should not intentionally and routinely engage in combat is fundamental, and enjoys wide support among our people. It is universally supported by military leaders who have testified before the Committee . . . . Current law and policy exclude women from being assigned to combat in our military forces, and the Committee reaffirms this policy." S. Rep. No. 96-826, *supra,* at 157.

* * *

The existence of the combat restrictions clearly indicates the basis for Congress' decision to exempt women from registration. The purpose of registration was to prepare for a draft of combat troops. Since women are excluded from combat, Congress concluded that they would not be needed in the event of a draft, and therefore decided not to register them....

* * *

... The reason women are exempt from registration is not because military needs can be met by drafting men. This is not a case of Congress arbitrarily choosing to burden one of two similarly situated groups, such as would be the case with an all-black or all-white, or an all-Catholic or all-Lutheran, or an all-Republican or all-Democratic registration. [HN14] Men and women, because of the combat restrictions on women, are simply not similarly situated for purposes of a draft or registration for a draft.

[***LEdHR9] [9] [HN15] Congress' decision to authorize the registration of only men, [*79] therefore, does not violate the Due Process Clause. The exemption of women from registration is not only sufficiently but also closely related to Congress' purpose in authorizing registration....

...The Senate Report, evaluating the testimony before the Committee, recognized that "[the] argument for registration and induction of women . . . is not based on military [*80] necessity, but on considerations of equity." S. Rep. No. 96-826, p. 158 (1980). Congress was certainly entitled, in the exercise of its constitutional powers to raise and regulate armies and navies, to focus on the question of military need rather than "equity."[15] As Senator [***496] Nunn of the Senate Armed Services Committee put it:

"Our committee went into very great detail. We found that there was no military necessity cited by any witnesses for the registration of females.

"The main point that those who favored the registration of females made was that they were in favor of this because of the equality issue, which is, of course, a legitimate view. But as far as [**2660] military necessity, and that is what we are primarily, I hope, considering in the overall registration bill, there is no military necessity for this." 126 Cong. Rec. 13893 (1980).

* * *

In light of the foregoing, we conclude that Congress acted well within its constitutional authority when it authorized the registration of men, and not women, under the Military Selective Service Act. The decision of the District Court holding otherwise is accordingly

Reversed.

Rostker v. Goldberg, 453 US 57 (1981)

The dissenters, Justices William Brennan, Thurgood Marshall and Bryon White, argued for a gender-neutral registration policy because they contended that, as citizens, men and women are similarly situated. Furthermore, it is interesting to note that the *Rostker* case shows the limited impact of Brennan's *Frontiero* argument. The Brennan plurality was no longer advocating making sex a suspect class, nor were they adopting a reasonableness standard. These Justices settled for the intermediate approach announced in *Craig v. Boren* (1976).

Excerpts from the dissent filed by Justice Marshall follow. Justice Marshall was the first African-American appointed to the United States Supreme Court. He was nominated by Democratic President Lyndon B. Johnson.

ROSTKER, DIRECTOR OF SELECTIVE SERVICE v. GOLDBERG ET AL.

SUPREME COURT OF THE UNITED STATES

453 U.S. 57; 101 S. Ct. 2646; 69 L. Ed. 2d 478; 1981 U.S. LEXIS 126; 49 U.S.L.W. 4798

June 25, 1981, Decided

JUSTICE THURGOOD MARSHALL, with whom JUSTICE WILLIAM BRENNAN joins, dissenting.

The Court today places its imprimatur on one of the most potent remaining public expressions of "ancient canards about the proper role of women," *Phillips* v. *Martin Marietta Corp.*, 400 U.S. 542, 545 (1971) (MARSHALL, J., concurring). It upholds a statute that requires males but not females to register for the draft, and which thereby categorically excludes women from a fundamental civic obligation. Because I believe the Court's decision is inconsistent with the Constitution's guarantee of equal protection of the laws, I dissent.

* * *

When, as here, a federal law that classifies on the basis of gender is challenged as violating this constitutional guarantee, it is ultimately for this Court, not Congress, to decide whether there exists the constitutionally required "close and [*90] substantial relationship" between the discriminatory means employed and the asserted governmental objective. See *Powell* v. *McCormack*, 395 U.S. 486, 549 (1969); *Baker* v. *Carr*, 369 U.S. 186, 211 (1962). In my judgment, there simply is no basis for concluding in this case that excluding women from registration is substantially related to the achievement of a concededly important governmental interest in maintaining an effective defense. The Court reaches a contrary conclusion only by using an "[announced degree] of 'deference' to legislative [judgment]" as a "facile [abstraction] . . . [**2665] to justify a result." *Ante*, at 69, 70.

* * *

...Congress has never disagreed with the judgment of the military experts that women have made significant contributions to the effectiveness of the military. On the [***503] contrary, Congress has repeatedly praised the performance of female members of the Armed Forces, and has approved efforts by the Armed Services to expand their role. Just last year, the Senate Armed Services Committee declared:

"Women now volunteer for military service and are assigned to most military specialties. These volunteers now make an important contribution to our Armed Forces. The number of women in the military has increased significantly in the past few years and is expected to continue to increase." S. Rep. No. 96-826, p. 157 (1980).

* * *

...Thus, the Government's task in this case is to demonstrate that excluding women from registration substantially furthers the goal of preparing for a draft of combat troops. Or to put it another way, the Government must show that registering women would substantially impede its efforts to prepare for such a draft. Under our precedents, the Government cannot meet this burden without showing that a gender-neutral statute would be a less effective means of attaining this end. See *Wengler v. Druggists Mutual Ins. Co.*, 446 U.S., at 151. As the Court explained in *Orr v. Orr*, 440 U.S., at 283 (emphasis added):

"Legislative classifications which distribute benefits and burdens on the basis of gender *carry the inherent risk of* [*95] *reinforcing sexual stereotypes about the 'proper place' of women and their need for special protection. . . .* Where, as here, the [Government's] . . . purposes are as well served by a gender-neutral classification as one that gender classifies and therefore carries with it the baggage of sexual stereotypes, the [Government] cannot be permitted to classify on the basis of sex."

In this case, the Government makes no claim that preparing for a draft of combat troops cannot be accomplished just as effectively by *registering* both men and women but *drafting* only men if only men turn out to be needed.[11] Nor can the Government argue that this alternative entails the additional cost and administrative inconvenience of registering women

* * *

By "considerations of equity," the military experts acknowledged that female conscripts can perform as well as male conscripts [*103] in certain positions, and that there is therefore no reason why one group should be totally excluded from registration and a draft. Thus, what the majority so blithely dismisses as "equity" is nothing less than the Fifth Amendment's guarantee of equal protection of the laws which "requires that Congress treat similarly situated persons similarly," *ante*, at 79.

Military Leadership Diversity Commission

Congress established the Military Leadership Diversity Commission in 2009 to analyze and assess policies and practices that shape diversity within the leadership cadre of the United States military. Its final report "From Representation to Inclusion: Diversity Leadership for the 21st Century Military," contains twenty recommendations for improving demographic representation among military leaders including the recommendation in the selection below that combat exclusion policies for women be eliminated.

Military Leadership Diversity Commission, From Representation to Inclusion: Diversity Leadership for the 21st Century Military: Final Report (Arlington, Virginia: Military Leadership Diversity Commission, 2011) 1–140 (Excerpts: pp. 71–4)

DoD and the Services Should eliminate Combat Exclusion Policies for Women

Recommendation 9—

DoD and the Services should eliminate the "combat exclusion policies" for women, including the removal of barriers and inconsistencies, to create a level playing field for all qualified servicemembers. The Commission recommends a time-phased approach:

* * *

The Commission recommends that DoD and the Services eliminate the combat exclusion policies that have barred women from direct ground combat fields and assignments since the early 1990s. As previously described, these policies constitute a structural barrier that prevents women from entering the tactical/operational career fields associated with promotion to flag/general officer grades and from serving in career-enhancing assignments. The Commission is *not* advocating a lowering of standards with the elimination of the combat exlusion policy. Qualification standards for combat arms positions should remain in place.

The Commission considered four strands of argument related to rescinding the policies. First, the Commission addressed arguments related to readiness and mission capability. One frequently cited argument in favor of the current policies is that having women serving in direct combat will hamper mission effectiveness by hurting unit morale and cohesion. Comparable arguments were made with respect to racial integration but were ultimately never borne out. Similarly, to date, there has been little evidence that the intergration of women into previously closed units or occupations has had a negative effect on important mission-related performance factors, such as unit cohesion.... A study by the Defense Department Advisory Committee on Women in the Services (2009) actually found that a majority of focus group participants felt that women serving in combat in Iraq and Afghanistan have had a positive effect on mission accomplishment. Additionally, panel members discussing this topic...cited the need to bring to bear all talent: The blanket restriction for women limits the ability of commanders in theater to pick the most capable person for the job. For example, Colonel Martha McSally noted,

> If you want to have the best fighting force, why would you exclude 51 percent of your population from even being considered for any particular job? I've seen recent statistics that say 75 percent of our nation's youth between the ages of 17 and 25 are not even eligible to be in the military based on whether its mental, medical, or other—criminal issues or whatever. So we just have a very small pool to pick from. So if we're trying to have the most ready force, why would we just exclude 51 percent of the population from even competing?...

Second, and relatedly, the Commission considered whether the policies are still approapriate given the changes in warfare and doctrine that have occurred over the last decade. DoD and Service policies that bar women from certain combat-related career fields, specialities, units, and assignments are based on standards associated with conventional warfare and well-defined, linear battlefields. However, the current conflicts in Iraq and Afghanistan have been anything but conventional. As a result, some of the female servicemembers deployed to Iraq and Afghanistan have already been engaged in activities that would be considered combat related, including being collocated with combat units and engaging in direct combat for self-defense....Thus, the combat exclusion policies do not reflect the current operational environment.

Third, the Commission addressed arguments related to discrimination and fairness. Many Commissioners consider the policies fundamentally discriminatory because they stipulate that assignment decisions should be based solely on gender, without regard to capability or qualifications.

Finally, the Commission considered whether there might be unanticipated effects from rescinding the combat exclusion policies, especially with regard to opening career fields. In particular, the type of effect such a policy change would have on enlisted recruiting is unknown. If young women perceive the opening of combat career fields to mean that they will be *required* to enter these occupations rather than being *allowed* to volunteer for them, female propensity to enlist may drop, and the Services may find it difficult to achieve their recruiting missions.

Based on these considerations, the Commission recommends that DoD and the Services eliminate their combat exclusion policies for women, including the removal of barriers and inconsistencies, to create a level playing field for all qualified servicemembers. This should be done using a phased approach so that all potential issues, including how to best implement new policies, can be thought through... .

Women in Career Fields/Specialties Currently Open to Them Should Be Immediately Able to Be Assigned to Any Unit That Requires that Career Field/Specialty, Consistent with the Current Operational Environment

As previously discussed, current DoD and Service assignment policies prohibit women from being assigned to units that may be involved in direct ground combat. Again, this means that, for a given occupation, the policies determine to which units a female servicemember may be assigned to do the job for which she has been trained. However, given the nature of the wars in Iraq and Afghanistan, women are currently engaged in direct combat, even when it is not part of their formally assigned role. Two key features of the policies have created the disconnect between the roles women may be formally assigned (policy) and the roles they may fill while deployed (practice).

First, many of the terms used in the policies have either lost or changed meaning: Such concepts as "enemy," "exposed to hostile fire," "forward," and "well forward" are no longer useful when determining which units should be closed to women. The enemy is no longer clearly and consistently identifiable, and all units are essentially exposed to hostile fire. Additionally, the spatial concepts of "forward" and "well forward" are inadequate to convey the complexity of such operations as those in Iraq and Afghanistan.

Second, once a female servicemember has been assigned to a unit, the assignment policy prescribes neither what duties she can do nor with which other units she may interact. As a result women are performing in combat roles. Indeed, local commanders have the authority to use their personnel as they see fit to fulfill the unit mission. Harrell et al. (2007) found examples of female servicemembers who had been trained as cooks having received the Combat Action Badge in Iraq, likely because contractor cooks obviated the need for U.S. servicemembers to cook. Instead these women, along with their male colleagues trained as cooks, were performing other duties, such as guard duty, that placed them in greater danger.

The Commissioners were in near-unanimous agreement that this aspect of the combat exclusion policies should be eliminated immediately because, given current practices for employing women in the wars in Iraq and Afghanistan, it seems obsolete.

Kingsley R. Browne

Kingsley R. Browne teaches law at Wayne State University Law School. His publications deal primarily with various aspects of discrimination law and with the legal implications of the natural differences between the sexes. The following selection is part of Browne's response to the Military Leadership Diversity Commission report.

Browne, Kingsley R. *The Report of the Military Leadership Diversity Commission: An Inadequate Basis for Lifting the Exclusion of Women from Direct Ground Combat.* (April, 2012). Wayne State University Law School Research Paper No. 2012–13. Available at SSRN: http://ssrn.com/abstract=2151965. (Excerpts: pp. 1, 10, 19, 21, 22, 23, 24, 25, 28, 29, 30, 31.)

Introduction

* * *

Elimination of age-old restrictions barring women is a serious step that should be taken only with a high degree of confidence that it would not degrade the military's capacity to perform its mission. Unfortunately, the MLDC (Military Leadership Diversity Commission – eds.) failed to give the question the serious attention it deserved. The Commission's failure to focus clearly on combat effectiveness is understandable in light of its charter, which was directed toward diversity and not toward military effectiveness. Had its charge been to study battlefield effectiveness and to suggest means by which to enhance it, the composition of the Commission would have been very different—putting a premium on combat experience rather than diversity experience—and the Commission would have had to collect and examine a very different kind of data. If a "Battlefield Effectiveness Commission" were to reach the same conclusions as the MLDC actually did, one can only imagine that it would have done a better job of justifying them.

* * *

II. THE COMMISSION'S TREATMENT OF MANY ISSUES IS SERIOUSLY DEFICIENT

Those raising concern about sexual integration have identified a large number of problems that MLDC gave scant, if any, attention. Three of these are:

*Women's relatively lesser strength

*Pregnancy and motherhood, especially single motherhood

*The effect of the introduction of women on cohesion of formerly all-male groups

A. Strength and Physical Capacity

The Commission's treatment of the physical capacity issue is incomplete and misleading in a number of respects. First, although it acknowledges that "*sometimes* the physical requirements differ" between the sexes, it gives no clue about just how great these differences are. In fact, they are huge. The table below shows the difference between the requirements for men and those for women in order to score 100 points on the Physical Fitness Test:

Standards for U.S. Army Physical Fitness Test

Activity	Age									
	17-21		27-31		37-41		47-51		52-56	
	M	F	M	F	M	F	M	F	M	F
Sit-ups	78	78	82	82	76	76	66	66	66	66
Push-ups	71	42	77	50	73	40	59	34	56	31
2-Mile Run (min:sec)	13:00	15:36	13:18	15:48	13:36	17:00	14:24	17:36	14:42	19:00

As can be seen from the table, men and women are, as the Commission notes, required to do the same number of sit-ups. However, the requirements for other tasks are substantially different by sex. The average male requirement for push-ups across age groups is 72 percent higher than it is for females. As for running, a 20-year-old woman is given almost a full minute more to run two miles than a 56-year-old man is, and a 56-year-old woman is given over four minutes longer than a man of the same age. These differences in standards are unsurprising, given the fact that empirical data clearly reveal (also unsurprisingly) that men are substantially stronger than women. In fact, there is less overlap in strength between the sexes than there is in height. Indeed, the probability that a man selected at random from the population will have greater upper-body strength than a randomly selected woman is somewhere between 95 and 99%. (If there were no overlap at all between the groups, of course, then the probability would be 100%).

The Commission further suggests that "inability may be more a function of size than gender," and that "the capabilities of smaller men and larger women overlap." Significantly, the authority for that proposition is merely to note that "some argue," without providing any source for the assertion in order to determine whether there is actually any empirical basis for the argument. At a trivial level, the statement is true: the smallest, weakest men are weaker than the largest strongest women, although the smallest, weakest men are unlikely to volunteer for the military. The extent of overlap, however, is fairly small, with perhaps the strongest ten percent of women being stronger than the weakest ten percent of men. So, one question is simply whether there is enough overlap in strength to make a policy change worthwhile.

* * *

....[T]he Commission's Issue Paper #56 reported that "there is not much direct evidence to support claims that *all women* lack the physical ability to perform in combat roles." As is so frequent in the Commission's work, it is setting up a straw man. It does not cite any source for these claims, and it is extremely unlikely that any responsible person has ever made the absolute claim the Commission labors to reject. Contrary to the implication of the Commission, however, there is much evidence to support claims that *almost* all women lack the physical ability to perform ground-combat roles, although there is no indication in any of the Commission's documents that it made any effort to find such evidence. The Commission could have consulted, for example, an extensive study conducted by the British Ministry of Defence in 2002. That study made findings that were quite relevant to the Commission's analysis. It concluded:

The overwhelming majority of females applying to the Army or currently serving in the Army would be physically incapable of performing many of the tasks required by the Infantry and RAC [Royal Armoured Corps]. Among the remainder who might achieve the required standards, the risk of injury will be higher than among their male counterparts, as these individuals will be working at a higher percentage of their maximum capability, and their reserve capacity will be less.

However, there remains a *tiny minority of women estimated at 0.1 percent of recruits and 1 percent of trained soldiers* who could probably achieve the required standards and perform the job effectively without sustaining higher rates of injury.

* * *

There we have it. One out of one thousand British female recruits were estimated to have the potential to achieve the standards required for ground combat and to perform without sustaining higher rates of injury. Thus, when the Commission complains about the combat exclusion's elimination of half the recruiting pool for the military, its claims bears little relationship to reality. Of course, there is no indication that the Commission even considered any of this data, anyway.

* * *

B. Pregnancy

Many who have raised questions about women's participation in combat have argued that pregnancy presents a substantial readiness challenge.... Yet, the words "pregnant" and "pregnancy" do not appear in the Commission's report, nor can they be found in the documentation supporting the recommendation to drop the combat exclusion. The Decision Paper dealing with retention does acknowledge that one of the reasons for women's greater first-term attrition is pregnancy, but the Commission does not connect that fact to military readiness. Nonetheless, the Commission casually recommends eliminating the combat restriction, apparently oblivious to the detrimental effects of pregnancy on the readiness of combat units.

Reliable statistics on military pregnancies are not easy to get, but a reasonable estimate is that around ten percent of military women are pregnant at any one time, differing somewhat by branch and rank...

There is good reason to believe that pregnancy does have a negative effect on readiness, and that effect is likely substantial. As a nation, we are fortunate that when duty calls for the troops, it usually calls overseas. But when overseas deployment is required, the non-deployability rate for women is three to four times the rate for men, the difference being largely due to pregnancy. Once a soldier is confirmed to be pregnant she becomes 'non-deployable' and will remain so for up to a year....

* * *

C. The Effect of Integration on Cohesion

The MLDC gave only cursory treatment to the issue of sexual integration on cohesion, stating in its Branching and Assignments Decision Paper that "[t]o date, there has been little evidence that the integration of women into previously closed units or occupations has had a negative impact on important mission-related performance factors, such as cohesion."....

One way that sexual integration can diminish cohesion is by reducing discipline. It was precisely this effect that led the Federal Advisory Committee on Gender-Integrated Training and Related Issues (Kassebaum Baker Committee) to unanimously recommend the elimination of sexually integrated basic training in 1997 (although the Secretary of Defense rejected the recommendation). That body found that integration led to "less discipline, less unit cohesion, and more distraction from the training programs." More recent anecdotal reports support the lack of discipline within sexually integrated units. There is no indication that the MLDC considered any of these sources.

* * *

Studies conducted by psychologist Leora Rosen have similarly found that inclusion of women in army units can reduce cohesion, reporting that "overall patterns indicate a consistent negative relationship" between the percentage of women and unit cohesion. Of particular significance to the question of women in ground-combat units is the finding that the negative impact of women increases as the extent of physical danger increases.

Rosen and colleagues found that the dynamics of cohesion differ between the field and garrison. They found that increased time in the field was positively correlated with "group hypermasculinity"—defined as "expressions of extreme, exaggerated, or stereotypic masculine attributes and behaviors"—in both all male groups and mixed-sex groups. In mixed-sex groups, field duty time was associated with *decreased* acceptance of women. The researchers attributed this association to the fact that the field environment "is likely to emphasize 'warrior' values of toughness, independence, and aggression."....

Caution should be exercised in making important policy decisions based upon an assumed lack of relationship between sexual integration and cohesion. One problem with laboratory measures of cohesion is that they may not be capturing the aspect of cohesion that is militarily important. Cohesion is viewed by the military as a "performance enabler" rather than a "performance enhancer." It correlates with military performance "by maintaining the organized group at its tasks in the face of severe stresses of battle." Because sociological studies of cohesion generally do not take place in particularly stressful conditions, their results may substantially underestimate the importance of cohesion in the primary circumstances in which it matters most.

III. MISCELLANEOUS ISSUES IGNORED BY THE COMMISSION

There are a number of other issues that were apparently completely ignored by the MLDC, and they will not be explored at length here, but they should be considered by any serious study of sexual integration. These include:

*The impact on mission achievement caused by male protectiveness toward women

*The impact of female prisoners of war, especially those who are kept for a substantial period of time

*The impact of sexual and romantic relationships within combat units, including jealousy, favoritism, and frustration, in addition to the seemingly perpetual sex scandals that the military has endured

*The adverse effects of double standards on morale

*The question whether women can effectively lead men in the crucible of active ground combat

*The question whether men find it difficult to trust women in dangerous circumstances

*Single parenthood, which is much more of a problem for female soldiers than for males

*Hygiene issues, a concern that is sometimes ridiculed but is nonetheless serious

*Potential recruitment and retention issues for women, as women learn that they can be involuntarily assigned to combat duties, including potential exposure of women to the draft should a draft be reinstated

*Potential recruitment and retention issues for men, as many, if not most, men in combat arms oppose inclusion of women. Many feel betrayed by their leaders, as they believe that equal opportunity is "trumping" military effectiveness, which, for many, means that equal opportunity is viewed by the leadership as more important than their lives.

All of these are serious issues that should be considered before embarking on the policy change advocated by the MLDC.

＊ ＊ ＊

Questions

1 Political scientists have found a "gender gap" when examining the voting patterns of men and women. On average, women tend to support the Democratic Party and liberal candidates more than men, who tend to support the Republican Party and conservative candidates. To what extent, if any, do natural differences between men and women explain this "gender gap"?

2 Are there advantages to having an equal number of men and women on trial juries? Are there disadvantages?

3 Men have a civic obligation to defend this country from a threat or an attack. What comparable civic duty do women have?

4 Since an increasing number of women are currently serving in the military, should women be required to register for a draft?

5 Should women in the military be held to exactly the same physical requirements as men?

Suggested Reading

Burrelli, David. "Women in Combat: Issues for Congress." Congressional Research Service, 2012.

Department of Defense. *Report to Congress on the Review of Laws, Policies and Regulations Restricting the Service of Female Members in the United States Armed Forces*, 2012.

Forman, Deborah L. "What Difference Does It Make? Gender and Jury Selection." *University of California at Los Angeles Women's Law Journal* 2, 1992, 35–83.

Hightower, Susan. "Sex and the Peremptory Strike: An Empirical Analysis of J. E. B. v. Alabama's First Five Years." *Stanford Law Review* 52, 2000, 895–928.

Minor v. Happersett, 88 US 162 (1875).

Ritter, Gretchen. "Jury Service and Women's Citizenship Before and After the Nineteenth Amendment." *Law and History Review* 20, 2002, 1–77.

Stanton, Elizabeth Cady. Address to the New York Legislature, 1854. Found in *History of Woman Suffrage*, vol. 1. Stanton, Susan B. Anthony and Matilda Joslyn Gage. New York: Fowler and Wells, 1881.

4

Equality of Opportunity in American Society

Introduction

This chapter examines how natural difference arguments have been used by reformers and, surprisingly, by traditionalists to expand educational and employment opportunities for women. Although the separate spheres doctrine is less prominent in modern America than it once was, sex-based differences continue to affect the educational choices and employment options available to men and women. For example, most women still have to balance their career responsibilities with their traditional family obligations. Also, some traditionalists contend that policies intended to expand educational opportunities for women often, in fact, reduce educational choices available to men. As the selected readings for this chapter show, natural difference arguments have been cited by reformers to expand equality of opportunity in American society and by traditionalists to limit the scope of this principle.

Education

Contemporary debates about sexual equality in public education concern the desirability of single-sex public schools[1] and the demand for equity in college athletics. Title IX of the 1972 Education Amendments to the Civil Rights Act required that women and girls have exactly the same educational opportunities that men and boys have.[2] Virtually no one now objects to providing women and girls with a wide array of educational opportunities and encouraging them to study in traditionally male dominated disciplines. However, traditionalists and reformers still differ regarding whether mandating full legal equality in education downplays the important sex differences that shape how young men and young women develop.

Single-sex schools

Traditionalists and reformers also are divided over the constitutionality of single-sex public schools. Traditionalists defend single-sex schools on the grounds that they expand rather than limit educational opportunities, especially for those students who believe that they learn best with other students of their own sex.[3] However, reformers question the benefits of single-sex education. They argue that single-sex public schools foster sex stereotypes that exclude both men and women from professions traditionally dominated by one sex.[4]

The case of Virginia Military Institute (hereafter referred to as "VMI") illustrates both sides of the argument. When VMI's all-male admissions policy was found to be unconstitutional sex discrimination, the state of Virginia responded to this ruling by defending VMI's exclusion of women, by creating a female version of VMI (the Virginia Women's Institute for Leadership), and by justifying these actions on natural difference grounds. The admission of girls to VMI, they feared, would require the school to soften its demanding standards for physical training and to adopt a more cooperative and less confrontational and competitive instructional method. In *United States v. Virginia* (1996), Justice Ruth Bader Ginsburg, writing for a 6-2 majority,[5] argued that Virginia's actions unconstitutionally discriminated against women and fostered indefensible sex stereotypes. Justice Antonin Scalia dissented, lamenting the loss of single-sex public education and what he believed were the educational and personal benefits that students of both sexes derived from it.

Athletics

Title IX's requirement that colleges and universities allocate their athletic resources to insure that their female students have equal athletic opportunities has been the focus of much litigation and political debate. The chief disagreement centers on determining what constitutes compliance with this provision of the law.[6] Reformers support the First Circuit Court of Appeals' decision in *Cohen v. Brown University* (1st Cir. 1996)[7] that required colleges and universities, or institutions of higher learning, to expand their women's athletics programs in order to achieve statistical parity between the percentage of athletic resources (money, positions, teams) allocated to female sports and the percentage of females in the student body. Constantly expanding athletic offerings for women, they argued, will encourage greater female participation in college sports.[8] Traditionalist critics such as Jessica Gavora charge, however, that the allocation of athletic resources on this basis results in unfair and unwise sex quotas and ignores the actual needs and interests of both male and female students.[9]

Employment

Perhaps the most important question concerning sexual equality in the workplace is whether natural differences between men and women should determine or influence their employment opportunities. For some reformers, gender neutral workplaces are needed to ensure that working men and women be treated exactly alike with respect to jobs, promotions, and other employment benefits.[10] However, traditionalists deny the wisdom of striving for gender neutrality at work largely on the grounds that women do not live gender neutral lives. Nature hampers women from pursuing job opportunities and career advancement, they argue, because women bear children and tend to be the primary caretakers in families.[11]

Title VII of the Civil Rights Act of 1964: Background and Issues

While women in early America were encouraged to be wives and mothers, women who worked outside of the home were restricted to types of work, such as being governesses and maids, that emphasized feminine sensibilities.[12] As increasing numbers of women took more physically taxing jobs in the late nineteenth century, supporters of workers' rights pushed for "protectionist" legislation for female workers. Oregon lawmakers, for example, mandated a maximum hour work week for women employed in jobs they believed impaired women's childbearing capability. However, the Supreme Court, in *Lochner v. New York* (1905), invalidated a similar maximum hour law for male bakers in New York, citing the constitutional right of employers and employees to enter into employment contracts.[13]

Shortly thereafter, a laundry owner challenged the constitutionality of Oregon's maximum hour law, citing the Court's decision in *Lochner*. One of the key issues raised in what became the case of *Muller v. Oregon* (1908)[14] was whether women had the same right to enter into work contracts as men, or whether they required special government protection. Despite the *Lochner* precedent, a unanimous Court ruled that the health needs of women trumped the same constitutional "right to contract" the justices had granted to men three years earlier.

As women entered the workforce in growing numbers in post-World War II America, their opportunities for employment and career advancement were still limited by policies based on natural differences arguments. Title VII of the Civil Rights Act of 1964 sought to remedy this situation by making an individual's sex an irrelevant factor with respect to these matters.[15] Furthermore, employers were forbidden to base their decisions regarding such matters on sex stereotypes that reflected traditional ideals of femininity or masculinity.[16] Gender neutrality also became the standard 'for policing interactions and exchanges between co-workers and between subordinates and supervisors. Some employers, fearing sexual harassment lawsuits, created worker codes of conduct that restrict the "normal" inter-actions and exchanges between men and women.[17] Yet, Title VII allows sex-based decisions in some areas. Sex is determinative, for example, when an employer can demonstrate that being either a woman or a man is both a qualification for the job and necessary for the success of his or her business. The relevant legal term is a "bona fide occupational qualification" ("bfoq") for the job.[18]

There are several obvious jobs for which a worker's sex has been judged to be a legitimate "bfoq" or permissible job qualification. The classic examples are the all-female wait staff at the restaurant "Hooters," the all-male Chippendale dancers, and the men and women who act as male and female characters in dramatic productions. In each of these examples, the person's sex is necessary for the authenticity of the characters and/or, in the case of Hooters, essential to the business's success. Yet, several courts have rejected efforts by the airline industry to hire only women as flight attendants, holding that male and female flight attendants are equally able to help the industry perform its primary task, which is the safe conveyance of passengers.[19]

Prison Guards

The job of being a prison guard highlights the potential relevance of natural difference arguments in employment. Prison guards work in an environment in which physical strength is sometimes necessary and in which close personal contact with members of one sex is required. Their duties include conducting body searches, observing prisoners engage in very private, personal conduct, and maintaining prison safety and security. Should women work as guards in men's prisons and/or should men work as guards in women's prisons? Although courts and government agencies have addressed these questions on a case-by-case basis, two lawsuits that appear in the readings highlight the role natural difference arguments play in resolving these disputes. In these lawsuits, the courts allowed prison authorities to hire only male guards and female guards in a men's maximum security prison and a women's prison respectively.[20]

Pensions

Several work-related benefits affect men and women differently thereby raising concerns about how to balance the natural differences between the sexes with Title VII's mandate of fostering gender neutrality in the workplace. A challenge to the City of Los Angeles pension fund policy led the United States Supreme Court to consider these concerns. Women as a group live longer than men do. Thus, female workers of the same age, the same salary and the same years of service as male workers will tend to receive more money in retirement than their male counterparts. Taking this fact into account, the City of Los Angeles required its female workers to contribute a higher percentage of their salaries to the pension fund than its male workers. As a result, women took home less money than their male counterparts, even when both earned the same salary. The U.S. Supreme Court ruled that this policy discriminated against women in the case of *Los Angeles Department of Water and Power v. Manhart* (1978).[21]

Pay Equity

Despite the passage of the Equal Pay Act (1963), which required "equal pay for equal work," pay equity between men and women remains a contentious issue.[22] All parties agree that women and men with similar credentials who perform the same job should be paid basically the same salary or wage. All also agree that the data show the existence of a pronounced wage disparity between men and women in comparable jobs. Yet, reformers and traditionalists disagree regarding the causes of most sex disparities in wages and the need for new policy reforms to address them. Traditionalists tend to downplay the importance of wage disparities between men and women because they believe that they result from women's decisions to spend less time at work and more time with their families. Some reformers concede that women are more likely to have family–work conflicts than men, but they also contend that wage discrimination even under these circumstances is unjustified.

Pregnancy

The biological fact that women bear children raises concerns about the impact of Title VII's mandate for gender neutral employment policies on women's employment opportunities and career choices. Pregnancy is a physical condition experienced only by women, albeit not every woman, and all but a few pregnant women take time off from work at some point before and after giving birth. Furthermore, the physical effects of childbirth extend beyond the end of pregnancy because women nourish and nurture their young.

Should employment policies be gender neutral with respect to pregnancy, or should these policies accommodate the special needs of pregnant women? Some reformers argue that employers must provide benefits on a gender neutral basis and that pregnancy should not affect employment decisions at all. Traditionalists point out that women, as a group, will never be able to attain equality in employment unless employers accommodate their pregnant employees by allowing them to balance their role as mothers with their role as workers.[23]

The U.S. Supreme Court has addressed several aspects of this issue, including challenges to mandatory maternity leave policies and challenges to policies excluding pregnancy from employer insurance coverage. The Court struck down the Cleveland Board of Education's requirement that pregnant public schoolteachers take unpaid maternity leave starting five months before giving birth. The justices ruled that women had a constitutional right to decide when they were physically unable to teach their classes.[24] In two separate cases, women employed by the state of California and by General Electric Co. argued that excluding pregnancy from their medical/disability insurance plans constituted invidious sex discrimination because it required them to bear the full costs of giving birth. Employers countered that such exclusions are legitimate because pregnancy is optional for women and because pregnancy coverage is too costly. A divided Supreme Court ruled in favor of the employers in these cases.[25]

In 1978, Congress overturned the Supreme Court's interpretation of Title VII by passing the Pregnancy Discrimination Act, which sought to equalize employment opportunities for pregnant women. Unlike the protectionist legislation upheld in *Muller*, the PDA does not require employers to accommodate their pregnant workers. Instead, the law promotes gender neutrality by requiring employers to treat pregnant and non-pregnant workers alike. Thus businesses which provide health care benefits must include pregnancy care among these benefits. Businesses which provide no health care benefits for their employees, however, are under no legal obligation to assist pregnant workers.[26]

Fetal Protection Policies

Fetal protection policies present courts with different equality challenges because they exclude women from jobs which pose a danger to the health and wellbeing of fetuses. These include jobs which require workers to use toxic materials that can damage the fetuses of pregnant and potentially pregnant women. The equality problem arises because these dangerous jobs tend to have relatively high salaries. Hiring policies that exclude women applicants from such jobs deny them the opportunity to earn high wages and thus create a sex disparity. These exclusions also deny women the right to decide for themselves whether or not to work in hazardous conditions.

Family and Medical Leave Act of 1993

Congress passed the Family and Medical Leave Act in 1993 to mitigate the conflict many workers experience when dealing with family emergencies. The FMLA requires employers with at least 50 employees to provide 12 weeks of unpaid leave to both men and women for family concerns. Congress passed this act to overcome sex stereotypes that led employers to discriminate against women on the grounds that their familial duties make them less reliable employees than men and to encourage men to assume more of these duties.

Traditionalists criticize Congress for passing and the Supreme Court for upholding the FMLA while reformers tend to laud these actions.

Conclusion

Natural difference arguments affect sexual equality in education and employment. In education, as the case of VMI shows, the arguments addressed the question of whether sex-based differences require sex-based pedagogies. Similarly, Title IX requirements that women have equal educational opportunities when applied to college classrooms are relatively non-controversial but very contentious when applied to college athletics. Arguments about employment opportunities also demonstrate the current relevance of natural difference arguments. Controversies regarding pensions, pregnancy, and family leave policies illustrate how sex-based differences can affect the type of work benefits granted to male and female employees. Although American legislators, judges, and scholars may all say that they support sexual equality in education and employment, they differ with respect to how much the natural differences between the sexes should affect the means used to achieve this goal.

Notes

1 The discussion focuses upon single-sex education in higher education. The effects of single-sex education on the academic achievement and personal development of girls and boys is inconclusive.

2 It should be noted that the Fourteenth Amendment Equal Protection Clause has been used to challenge single-sex public schools.

3 See Justice Lewis Powell's dissent in *Mississippi University for Women v. Hogan*, 458 US 718 (1982).

4 See Justice Sandra Day O'Connor's majority opinion in *Mississippi University for Women v. Hogan*, 458 US 718 (1982).

5 Justice Clarence Thomas recused himself because his son attended VMI.

6 Compliance with Title IX is very important for any college receiving federal funds. Under the statute, colleges that fail to comply with Title IX risk losing their federal funding.

7 *Cohen v. Brown University*, 101 F 3d 155 (1st Cir. 1996).

8 See National Coalition for Women and Girls in Education, "Title IX Athletics Policies: Issues and Data for Education Decision Makers." May, 2007.

9 Jessica Gavora, *Tilting the Playing Field: Schools, Sports, Sex and Title IX*. San Francisco: Encounter Books, 2002. Also see Allison Kasic and Kimberly Schuld, "Title IX and Athletics: A Primer." Independent Women's Forum, Position Paper #610, September, 2008.

10 For a discussion of feminist thought, see Rosemarie Tong's *Feminist Thought: A Comprehensive Introduction*. Boulder: Westview Press, 1989.

11 See Julie C. Suk, "Are Gender Stereotypes Bad for Women? Rethinking Antidiscrimination Law and Work–Family Conflict." *Columbia Law Review* 110, 2010, 1–69; Jennifer Yue, "The Flood of Pregnancy Discrimination Cases: Balancing the Interests of Pregnant Women and Their Employers." *Kentucky Law Journal* 6, 2007/2008, 487–504; Heather Bennett Stanford, "Do You Want to Be an Attorney or a Mother? Arguing for the Feminist Solution to the Problem of Double Binds in Employment and Family Responsibilities Discrimination." *American University Journal of Gender, Social Policy and the Law* 17, 2009, 627–57.

12 For example, in rejecting a woman's petition to become licensed attorney, the Wisconsin Supreme Court explained that women were naturally ill-suited for the practice of law. The Court argued: "Nature has tempered woman as little for the juridical conflicts of the court room, as for the physical conflicts of the battle field. Womanhood is molded for gentler and better things ... Reverence for all womanhood would suffer in the public spectacle of woman so instructed and so engaged ... Discussions are habitually necessary in courts of justice, which are unfit for female ears." See, *In re Goodell*, 39 Wis. 232, 245–6, 1875.

13 See *Lochner v. New York*, 198 US 45 (1905).

14 See *Muller v. Oregon*, 208 US 412 (1908).

15 Title VII states: "It shall be an unlawful employment practice for an employer (1) to fail or refuse to hire or to discharge any individual, or otherwise discriminate against any individual with respect to his compensation, terms, conditions, or privileges of employment, because of such individual's race, color, religion, sex, or national origin ..."

16 See *Price Waterhouse v. Hopkins*, 490 US 228 (1989).

17 See Katherine M. Franke, "What's Wrong With Sexual Harassment?" *Stanford Law Review* 49, 1997, 691–772; 746. Also see, Eugene Volokh, "Freedom of Speech and Workplace Harassment." *University of California as Los Angeles* 39, 1992, 1791–872.

18 In *Phillips v. Martin Marietta Corp.*, 400 US 542 (1971), the United States Supreme Court ruled that Martin Marietta could not exclude women with young children from certain jobs unless it could show that these women could not adequately perform the job's duties.

19 See *Diaz v. Pan Am World Airlines, Inc.*, 442 F 2d 385 (5th Cir. 1971).

20 See *Dothard v. Rawlinson*, 433 US 321 (1977); *Torres v. Wisconsin Department of Health and Social Services*, 859 F. 2d 1523 (7th Cir. 1988).

21 435 US 702 (1978).

22 The recent political debate involved the adjudicative process for individuals to sue their employers when they believe they were the victims of pay inequality. The *Lilly Ledbetter* case stemmed from the United States Supreme Court's interpretation of the Equal Pay Act regarding the time allotted for suing companies for paying women less than their comparable male co-workers. (See *Ledbetter v. Goodyear Tire and Rubber Co.*, 550 US 618 (2007)). President Barack Obama signed into law the Ledbetter Fair Pay Act in 2009. This law overturned the Supreme Court's interpretation of the Equal Pay Act. The Paycheck Fairness Act, which was never passed by Congress, was intended to make the adjudicative process, according to Democrats, more accommodating for female plaintiffs and, according to Republicans, more difficult for defendant companies.

23 The dispute is over whether maternity or family leave should be provided for women only or be equally available to men.

24 *Cleveland Board of Education v. LaFleur*, 414 US 632 (1974).

25 See *Geldudig v. Aiello*, 417 US 484 (1974) and *General Electric Co. v. Gilbert*, 429 US 125 (1976).

26 In *California Federal Savings and Loan Association v. Guerra*, 479 US 272 (1987), the Court ruled that the PDA was not violated if employers provided pregnancy benefits for female workers without providing their male workers disability benefits or insurance coverage.

READINGS

Education

United States v. Virginia, 518 US 515 (1996)

Single sex education has been especially controversial when all-male military schools were asked to admit women. The decision to maintain VMI's all-male status and to create a female version of VMI was based on a natural difference argument. VMI's "adversative" method of pedagogy was central to maintaining its single sex status. According to VMI's defenders, educational diversity within Virginia's higher education system justified the creation of an all-female alternative to VMI. According to experts cited by Virginia, the adversative method is incompatible with the way girls develop and learn. With the support of VMI's politically powerful alumni, the state of Virginia founded the Virginia Women's Institute for Leadership. The Virginia Women's Leadership Institute was intended to adopt a pedagogy that was designed for young women.

By the time *United States v. Virginia* reached the United States Supreme Court in 1996, the issues had expanded beyond whether women should be admitted to VMI. The Court had to address a wide range of interrelated issues: whether VMI's adversative method was sufficient grounds to deny women admission; whether the different learning styles of men and women also justified not only maintaining VMI's all-male status but also establishing all-female VWIL; and whether the plan offered by Virginia was based on sex stereotypes and sex generalizations that constituted unconstitutional sex discrimination.

In her opinion for the Court majority, Justice Ruth B. Ginsburg addressed all of these questions. Justice Ginsburg, as an attorney, was a leading supporter of women's equality. She was appointed to the Supreme Court by Democratic President Bill Clinton. The excerpt below highlights the major points of her opinion.

UNITED STATES, PETITIONER 94-1941 v. VIRGINIA ET AL.
VIRGINIA, ET AL., PETITIONERS 94-2107 v. UNITED STATES

SUPREME COURT OF THE UNITED STATES

518 U.S. 515; 116 S. Ct. 2264; 135 L. Ed. 2d 735; 1996 U.S. LEXIS
4259; 64 U.S.L.W. 4638;

June 26, 1996, Decided *

OPINION

JUSTICE RUTH BADER GINSBURG delivered the opinion of the Court.

Virginia's public institutions of higher learning include an incomparable
military college, Virginia Military Institute (VMI). The United States
maintains that [HN1] the Constitution's equal protection guarantee
precludes Virginia from reserving exclusively to men the unique educational
opportunities VMI affords. We agree.

* * *

III

...[T]his case present two ultimate issues. First, does Virginia's exclusion of
women from the educational opportunities provided by VMI -- extraordinary
opportunities for military training and civilian leadership development --
deny to women "capable of all of the individual activities required of VMI
cadets," 766 F. Supp., at 1412, the equal protection of the laws guaranteed
by the Fourteenth Amendment? Second, if VMI's "unique" situation, id.,
at 1413 -- as Virginia's sole single-sex public institution of [*531] higher
education -- offends the Constitution's equal protection principle, what is
the remedial requirement?

IV

...[T]he Court has repeatedly recognized that neither federal nor state
government acts compatibly with the equal protection principle when a
law or official policy denies to women, simply because they are women,
full citizenship stature -- equal opportunity to aspire, achieve, participate in
and contribute to society based on their individual talents and capacities. ...

...To summarize the Court's current directions [HN4] for cases of official
classification based on gender: Focusing on the differential [*533] treatment

or denial of opportunity for which relief is sought, the reviewing court must determine whether the proffered justification is "exceedingly persuasive." ...The justification must be genuine, not hypothesized or invented *post hoc* in response to litigation. And it must not rely on overbroad generalizations about the different talents, capacities, or preferences of males and females. ...

...Supposed "inherent differences" are no longer accepted as a ground for race or national origin classifications. See *Loving* v. *Virginia*, 388 U.S. 1, 18 L. Ed. 2d 1010, 87 S. Ct. 1817 (1967). Physical differences between men and women, however, are enduring: "The two sexes are not fungible; a community made up exclusively of one [sex] is different from a community composed of both." *Ballard* v. *United States*, 329 U.S. 187, 193, 91 L. Ed. 181, 67 S. Ct. 261 (1946).

"Inherent differences" between men and women, we have come to appreciate, remain cause for celebration, but not for denigration of the members of either sex or for artificial constraints on an individual's opportunity....

Measuring the record in this case against the review standard just described, we conclude that Virginia has shown no "exceedingly persuasive justification" for excluding all women from the citizen-soldier training afforded by VMI. ...Because the remedy proffered by Virginia -- the Mary Baldwin VWIL program -- does not cure the constitutional violation, *i.e.*, it does not provide equal opportunity, we reverse the Fourth Circuit's final judgment in this case.

V

Virginia ...asserts two justifications in defense of VMI's exclusion of [*535] women. First, the Commonwealth contends, "single-sex education provides important [***753] educational benefits," Brief for Cross-Petitioners 20, and the option of single-sex education contributes to "diversity in educational approaches," *id.*, at 25. Second, the Commonwealth argues, "the unique VMI method of character development and leadership training," the school's adversative approach, would have to be modified were VMI to admit women. *Id.*, at 33–6 (internal quotation marks omitted). We consider these two justifications in turn.

A

Single-sex education affords pedagogical benefits to at least some students, [**2277] Virginia emphasizes, and that reality is uncontested in this litigation.[8] Similarly, it is not disputed that diversity among public educational institutions can serve the public good. But Virginia has not shown that VMI was established, or has been maintained, with a view to diversifying, by its categorical exclusion of women, educational opportunities within the Commonwealth.

* * *

Neither recent nor distant history bears out Virginia's alleged pursuit of diversity through single-sex educational options....

* * *

In sum, we find no persuasive evidence in this record that VMI's male-only admission policy "is in furtherance of a state policy of 'diversity.'" ...A purpose genuinely to advance an array of educational [*540] options, ..., is not served by VMI's historic and constant plan -- a plan to "afford a unique educational benefit only to males." *Ibid.* However "liberally" this plan serves the Commonwealth's sons, it makes no provision whatever for her daughters. That is not *equal* protection.

B

Virginia next argues that VMI's adversative method of training provides educational benefits that cannot be made available, unmodified, to women. Alterations to accommodate women would necessarily be "radical," so "drastic," Virginia asserts, as to transform, indeed "destroy," VMI's program. See Brief for Cross-Petitioners 34–6. Neither sex would be favored by the transformation, Virginia maintains: Men would be deprived of the unique opportunity currently available to them; women would not gain that opportunity because their participation would "eliminate the very aspects of [the] program that distinguish [VMI] from . . . other institutions of higher education in Virginia." *Id.*, at 34.

The District Court forecast from expert witness testimony, and the Court of Appeals accepted, that coeducation would materially affect "at least these three aspects of VMI's program -- physical training, the absence of privacy, and the adversative approach." 976 F.2d, at 896–7. And it is uncontested that women's admission would require accommodations, primarily in arranging housing assignments and physical training programs for female cadets. See Brief for Cross-Respondent 11, 29–30. It is also undisputed, however, that "the VMI methodology could be used to educate women." ...In sum, as the Court of Appeals stated, "neither the goal of producing citizen soldiers," VMI's *raison d'etre*, "nor VMI's implementing methodology is inherently unsuitable to women." *Id.*, at 899.

...[T]he District Court made "findings" on "gender-based developmental differences." 766 F. Supp., at 1434–5. These "findings" restate the opinions of Virginia's expert witnesses, opinions about typically male or typically female "tendencies." *Id.*, at 1434. For example, "males tend to need an atmosphere of adversativeness," while "females tend to thrive in a cooperative atmosphere." *Ibid.* "I'm not saying that some women don't do well under [the] adversative model," VMI's expert on educational institutions testified, "undoubtedly there are some [women] who do"; but educational experiences must be designed "around the rule," this expert maintained, and not "around the exception." *Ibid.* (internal quotation marks omitted).

[However,] State actors controlling gates to opportunity, we have instructed, may not exclude qualified individuals based on "fixed notions concerning the roles and abilities of males and females."

It may be assumed, for purposes of this decision, that most women would not choose VMI's adversative method. ...[I]t is also probable that "many men would not want to be educated in such an environment." 52 F.3d, at 93. (On that point, even our dissenting colleague might agree.) Education, to be sure, is not a "one size fits all" business. The issue, however, is not whether "women -- or men -- should be forced to attend VMI"; rather, the question is whether the Commonwealth can constitutionally deny to women who have the will and capacity, the training and attendant opportunities that VMI uniquely affords. *Ibid.*

The notion that admission of women would downgrade VMI's stature, destroy the adversative system and, with it, even the school,[11] is a judgment hardly proved,[12] a prediction [*543] hardly different from other "self-fulfilling prophec[ies]," see *Mississippi Univ. for Women*, 458 U.S. at 730, once routinely used to deny rights or [***758] opportunities. ....

*********(Justice Ginsburg discusses how professions in law, medicine, law enforcement, etc. have historically been denied to women.)*********

...The Commonwealth's justification for excluding all women from "citizen-soldier" training for which some are qualified, in any event, cannot rank as "exceedingly persuasive," as we have explained and applied that standard.

* * *

The Commonwealth's misunderstanding and, in turn, the District Court's, is apparent from VMI's mission: to produce "citizen-soldiers," individuals "'imbued with love of learning, confident in the functions and attitudes of leadership, possessing a high sense of public service, advocates of the American democracy and free enterprise system, and ready [**2282] . . . to defend their country in time of national peril.'" 766 F. Supp., at 1425 (quoting Mission Study Committee of the VMI Board of Visitors, Report, May 16, 1986).

Surely that goal is great enough to accommodate women, who today count as citizens in our American democracy equal in stature to men. Just as surely, the Commonwealth's [*546] great goal is not substantially advanced by women's categorical exclusion, in total disregard of their individual merit, from the Commonwealth's premier "citizen-soldier" corps.[16] Virginia, in sum, "has fallen far short of establishing the 'exceedingly persuasive justification,'" *Mississippi Univ. for Women,* 458 U.S. at 731, that must be the solid base for any gender-defined classification.

VI

In the second phase of the litigation, Virginia presented its remedial plan -- maintain VMI as a male-only college and create VWIL as a separate program for women....

[*547] A

* * *

Virginia chose not to eliminate, but to leave untouched, VMI's exclusionary policy. ...Virginia described VWIL as a "parallel program," and asserted that VWIL shares VMI's mission of producing "citizen-soldiers" and VMI's goals of providing "education, military training, mental and physical discipline, character . . . and leadership development." ...A comparison of the programs said to be "parallel" informs our answer. In exposing the character of, and differences in, the VMI and VWIL programs, we recapitulate facts earlier presented.

VWIL affords women no opportunity to experience the rigorous military training for which VMI is famed. See 766 F. Supp., at 1413–4 ("No other school in Virginia or in the United States, public or private, offers the same kind of rigorous military training as is available at VMI."); *id.,* at 1421 (VMI "is known to be the most challenging military school in the United States"). Instead, the VWIL program "deemphasize[s]" military education, 44 F.3d, at 1234, and uses a "cooperative method" of education "which reinforces self-esteem," 852 F. Supp., at 476.

* * *

Virginia maintains that these methodological differences are "justified pedagogically," based on "important differences between men and women in learning and developmental needs," "psychological and sociological differences" Virginia describes as "real" and "not stereotypes." ...

[G]eneralizations about "the way women are," estimates of what is appropriate for *most women*, no longer justify denying opportunity to women whose talent and capacity place them outside the average description. Notably, Virginia never asserted that VMI's method of education suits *most men*. It is also revealing that Virginia accounted for its failure to make the VWIL experience "the entirely militaristic experience of VMI" on the ground that VWIL "is planned for women who do not necessarily expect to pursue military careers." 852 F. Supp., at 478. By that reasoning, VMI's "entirely militaristic" program would be inappropriate for men in general or *as a group*, for "only about 15% of VMI cadets enter career military service." See 766 F. Supp., at 1432.

In contrast to the generalizations about women on which Virginia rests, we note again these dispositive realities: VMI's "implementing methodology" is not "inherently unsuitable to women," 976 F.2d, at 899; "some women . . . do well under [the] adversative model," 766 F. Supp., at 1434 (internal quotation marks omitted); "some women, at least, would want to attend [VMI] if they had the opportunity," *id.*, at 1414; "some women are capable of all of the individual activities required of VMI cadets," *id.*, at 1412, and "can meet the physical standards [VMI] now impose[s] on men," 976 F.2d, at 896. It is on behalf of these women that the United States has instituted this suit, and it is for them that a remedy must be crafted,[19] a remedy that will end their [*551] exclusion from a state-supplied educational opportunity for which they are fit, a decree that will "bar like discrimination in the future." *Louisiana*, 380 U.S. at 154.

B

In myriad respects other than military training, VWIL does not qualify as VMI's equal. VWIL's student body, faculty, course offerings, and facilities hardly match VMI's. Nor can the VWIL graduate anticipate the benefits associated with VMI's 157-year history, the school's prestige, and its influential alumni network.

* * *

Virginia, in sum, while maintaining VMI for men only, has failed to provide any "comparable single-gender women's institution." *Id.*, at 1241. Instead, the Commonwealth has created a VWIL program fairly appraised as a "pale shadow" of VMI in terms of the range of curricular choices and faculty stature, funding, prestige, alumni support and influence. See *id.*, at 1250 (Phillips, J., dissenting).

* * *

...In sum, Virginia's [*556] remedy does not match the constitutional violation; the Commonwealth has shown no "exceedingly persuasive justification" for withholding from women qualified for the experience premier training of the kind VMI affords.

* * *

United States v. Virginia, 518 US 515 (1996)

Writing in dissent, Justice Antonin Scalia, who was joined by Chief Justice William Rehnquist, lamented the end of single sex education and the educational and personal benefits accrued to men and women who wanted to have this particular educational experience.

UNITED STATES, PETITIONER 94-1941 v. VIRGINIA ET AL. VIRGINIA, ET AL., PETITIONERS 94-2107 v. UNITED STATES

SUPREME COURT OF THE UNITED STATES

518 U.S. 515; 116 S. Ct. 2264; 135 L. Ed. 2d 735; 1996 U.S. LEXIS 4259; 64 U.S.L.W. 4638

June 26, 1996, Decided*

DISSENT

JUSTICE ANTONIN SCALIA, dissenting.

Today the Court shuts down an institution that has served the people [***772] of the Commonwealth of Virginia with pride and distinction for over a century and a half. To achieve that desired result, it rejects (contrary to our established practice) the factual findings of two courts below, sweeps aside the precedents of this Court, and ignores the history of our people. As to facts: It explicitly rejects the finding that there exist "gender-based developmental differences" supporting Virginia's restriction of the "adversative" method to only a men's institution, and the finding that the all-male composition of the Virginia Military Institute (VMI) is essential to that institution's character. As to precedent: It drastically revises our established standards for reviewing sex-based classifications. And as to history: It counts for nothing the long tradition, enduring down to the present, of men's military colleges supported by both States and the Federal Government.

Much of the Court's opinion is devoted to deprecating the closed-mindedness of our forebears with regard to women's education, and even with regard to the treatment of women in areas that have nothing to do with education. ...So to counterbalance the Court's criticism of our ancestors, let me say a word in their praise: They left us free to change. The same cannot be said of this most illiberal Court, which has embarked on a course of inscribing one after another of the current preferences of the society (and in some cases only the counter majoritarian preferences of the society's law-trained elite) into our Basic Law. Today it enshrines the notion that no substantial educational value is to be served by an all-men's military academy -- so that the decision by the people of Virginia to maintain such an institution denies equal protection to women who cannot attend that institution but can attend others. Since it is entirely clear that the Constitution of the United States -- the old one -- takes no sides in this educational debate, I dissent.

* * *

III

* * *

A

It is beyond question that Virginia has an important state interest in providing effective college education for its citizens. That single-sex instruction is an approach substantially related to that interest should be evident enough from the long and continuing history in this country of men's and women's colleges. But beyond that, as the Court of Appeals here stated: "That single-gender education at the college level is beneficial to both sexes is a *fact established in this case*." 44 F.3d 1229, 1238 (CA4 1995) (emphasis added).

* * *

But besides its single-sex constitution, VMI is different from other colleges in another way. It employs a "distinctive educational method," sometimes referred to as the "adversative, or doubting, model of education." 766 F. Supp., at 1413, 1421. "Physical rigor, mental stress, absolute equality of treatment, absence of privacy, minute regulation of behavior, and indoctrination in desirable values are the salient attributes of the VMI educational experience." *Id.*, at 1421. No one contends that this method is appropriate for all individuals; education is not a "one size fits all" business. Just as a State may wish to support junior colleges, vocational institutes, or a law school that emphasizes case [*578] practice instead of classroom study, so too a State's decision to maintain within its system one school that provides the adversative method is "substantially related" to its goal of good education. Moreover, it was uncontested that "if the state were to establish a women's VMI-type [*i. e.*, adversative] program, the program would attract an insufficient number of participants to make the program work," 44 F.3d, at 1241; and it was found by the District Court that if Virginia were to include women in VMI, the school "would eventually find it necessary to drop the adversative system altogether," 766 F. Supp., at 1413. Thus, Virginia's options were an adversative method that excludes women or no adversative method at all.

There can be no serious dispute that, as the District Court found, single-sex education and a distinctive educational method "represent legitimate contributions to diversity in the Virginia higher education system." ...

* * *

3. In addition to disparaging Virginia's claim that VMI's single-sex status serves a state interest in diversity, the Court finds fault with Virginia's failure to offer education based on the adversative training method to women. It dismisses the District Court's "'findings' on 'gender-based developmental differences'" on the ground that "these 'findings' restate the opinions of Virginia's expert witnesses, opinions about typically male or typically female 'tendencies.'" *Ante*, at 541 (quoting 766 F. Supp., at 1434–5). ...

* * *

.... Not a single witness contested, for example, Virginia's "substantial body of 'exceedingly persuasive' evidence . . . that some students, both male and female, benefit from attending a single-sex college" and "[that] for those students, the opportunity to attend a single-sex college is a valuable one, likely to lead to better academic and professional achievement." 766 F. Supp., at 1411–12. Even the United States' expert witness "called himself a 'believer in single-sex education,'" although it was his "personal, philosophical preference," not one "born of educational-benefit considerations," "that single-sex education should be provided only by the private sector." *Id.*, at 1412.

* * *

5. The Court argues that VMI would not have to change very much if it were to admit women....

....[However,] [t]he District Court found as follows: "The evidence establishes that key elements of the adversative VMI educational system, with its focus on barracks life, would be fundamentally altered, and the distinctive ends of the system would be thwarted, if VMI were forced to admit females and to make changes necessary to accommodate their needs and interests." 766 F. Supp., at 1411. Changes that the District Court's detailed analysis found would be required include new allowances for personal privacy in the barracks, such as locked doors and coverings on windows, which would detract from VMI's approach of regulating minute details of student behavior, "contradict the principle that everyone is constantly subject to scrutiny by everyone else," and impair VMI's "total egalitarian approach" under which every student must be "treated alike"; changes in the physical training program, which would reduce "the intensity and aggressiveness of the current program"; and various modifications in other respects of the adversative training program that permeates student life. See *id.*, at 1412–13, 1435–43. As the Court of Appeals summarized it, "the record supports the district court's findings that at least these three aspects of VMI's program -- physical training, the absence of privacy, and the adversative approach -- would be materially affected by coeducation, leading to a substantial change in the egalitarian ethos that is a critical aspect of VMI's training." 976 F.2d, at 896–7.

....It sufficed to establish, as the District Court stated, that VMI would be "significantly different" upon the admission of women, 766 F. Supp., at 1412, and "would eventually find it necessary to drop the adversative system altogether," *id.*, at 1413.[5]

6. Finally, the absence of a precise "all-women's analogue" to VMI is irrelevant.

* * *

IV

* * *

A

Under the constitutional principles announced and applied today, single-sex public education is unconstitutional....

* * *

This is especially regrettable because, as the District Court here determined, educational experts in recent years have increasingly come to "support [the] view that substantial educational benefits flow from a single-gender environment, be it male or female, *that cannot be replicated in a coeducational setting.*"

* * *

Cohen v. Brown University, 101 F3d. 155 (1st Cir. 1992)

The passage of Title IX of the Education Amendments to the Civil Rights Act was intended to insure that women and girls have the same educational opportunities that men and boys have. One area where Title IX has sparked a great deal of controversy is the distribution of resources between male and female sports in colleges and universities. Title IX requires all colleges and universities receiving federal funds to insure that its female students have access to college sports and have equal opportunities to participate in college athletics. Determining exactly what colleges must do to comply with Title IX has been the focus of much litigation, political debates and social discussion. Some college administrators argued that Title IX requires them to meet the needs and interests of the women in the student body. Under this interpretation, colleges are in compliance with Title IX if they can demonstrate that their female students are satisfied with the sports and athletic opportunities available to them and that their female students' interests in participating in sports are continually being met. An alternative interpretation of Title IX argues that the federal statute imposes an equity standard on collegiate athletics. Under this interpretation, intercollegiate athletics must be structured and financed to insure that women's sports are on an equal footing as men's sports. This interpretation means that athletic resources (funds, teams, positions, etc.) must be allocated so that the percentage of resources given to women's sports must be commensurate to the percentage of female students in the student body.

The case of *Cohen v. Brown University* resulted when a group of female students enrolled at Brown University challenged its administrators' decision to end university funding for two women's sports teams in 1993–94. Brown University had a two- tiered athletics program in which varsity sports received university funding and donor-funded sports received little or no university funding. Citing a cost-cutting plan, Brown University defunded four varsity sports teams by demoting them to donor status. The demoted teams were two women's teams (volleyball, gymnastics) and two men's teams (water polo, golf). Brown University defended its decision by citing that an equal number of women's teams and men's teams lost university funding.

When *Cohen v. Brown University* reached the First Circuit Court of Appeals, the two sides used different interpretations of Title IX to support their positions. Brown University noted the equitable way the cost-cutting program had been implemented and, despite the demotion of women's volleyball and gymnastics, the university was still meeting their female students' interests in sports. Cohen argued that Brown University allocated athletic resources in an inequitable way. She noted that, in the 1993–94 academic year, Brown's student body was comprised of 51% women, yet only 38% of the Brown's athletic resources were allocated for women's athletics. This disparity indicated to Cohen that Brown was not providing the appropriate athletic opportunities to its female students. The excerpt below shows why the First Circuit Court adopted Cohen's interpretation of Title IX.

AMY COHEN, ET AL., Plaintiffs – Appellees, v. BROWN UNIVERSITY, ET AL., Defendants – Appellants.

UNITED STATES COURT OF APPEALS FOR THE FIRST CIRCUIT

101 F.3d 155; 1996 U.S. App. LEXIS 30192

November 21, 1996, Decided

OPINION: SENIOR CIRCUIT JUDGE BOWNES

[*161]

* * *

F.

Brown has contended throughout this litigation that the significant disparity in athletics opportunities for men and women at Brown is the result of a gender-based differential in the level of interest in sports and that the district court's application of the three-part test requires universities to provide athletics opportunities for women to an [**66] extent that exceeds their relative interests and abilities in sports. Thus, at the heart of this litigation is the question whether Title IX permits Brown to deny its female students equal opportunity to participate in sports, based upon its unproven assertion that the district court's finding of a significant disparity in athletics opportunities for male and female students reflects, not discrimination in

Brown's intercollegiate athletics program, but a lack of interest on the part of its female students that is unrelated to a lack of opportunities.

We view Brown's argument that women are less interested than men in participating in intercollegiate athletics, as well as its conclusion that institutions should be required to accommodate the interests and abilities of its female students only to the extent that it accommodates the interests and abilities of its male students, with great suspicion. To assert that Title IX permits institutions to provide fewer athletics participation opportunities for women than for men, based upon the premise that women are [*179] less interested in sports than are men, is (among other things) to ignore the fact that Title IX was enacted in order to remedy [**67] discrimination that results from stereotyped notions of women's interests and abilities.

Interest and ability rarely develop in a vacuum; they evolve as a function of opportunity and experience. The Policy Interpretation recognizes that women's lower rate of participation in athletics reflects women's historical lack of opportunities to participate in sports. *See* 44 Fed. Reg. at 71,419 ("Participation in intercollegiate sports has historically been emphasized for men but not women. Partially as a consequence of this, participation rates of women are far below those of men.").

Moreover, the Supreme Court has repeatedly condemned gender-based discrimination based upon "archaic and overbroad generalizations" about women. *Schlesinger v. Ballard*, 419 U.S. 498, 508, 42 L. Ed. 2d 610, 95 S. Ct. 572 (1975). *See, e.g., Mississippi Univ. for Women v. Hogan*, 458 U.S. 718, 725, 73 L. Ed. 2d 1090, 102 S. Ct. 3331 (1982); *Califano v. Webster*, 430 U.S. 313, 317, 51 L. Ed. 2d 360, 97 S. Ct. 1192 (1977); *Frontiero v. Richardson*, 411 U.S. 677, 684–6, 36 L. Ed. 2d 583, 93 S. Ct. 1764 (1973). The Court has been especially critical of the use of statistical evidence offered to prove generalized, stereotypical notions about men and women. For example, in holding that Oklahoma's 3.2% beer statute [**68] invidiously discriminated against males 18–20 years of age, the Court in *Craig v. Boren*, 429 U.S. 190, 208–9, 50 L. Ed. 2d 397, 97 S. Ct. 451 (1976), stressed that "the principles embodied in the Equal Protection Clause are not to be rendered inapplicable by statistically measured but loose-fitting generalities."

Thus, there exists the danger that, rather than providing a true measure of women's interest in sports, statistical evidence purporting to reflect women's interest instead provides only a measure of [**69] the very discrimination that is and has been the basis for women's lack of opportunity to participate in sports. Prong three requires some kind of evidence of interest in athletics, and the Title IX framework permits the use of statistical evidence in assessing the level of interest in sports.[15] Nevertheless, to allow a numbers-based [*180] lack-of-interest defense to become the instrument of further discrimination against the underrepresented gender would pervert the remedial purpose of Title IX. We conclude that, [HN34] even if it can be empirically demonstrated that, at a particular time, women have less interest in sports than do men, such evidence, standing alone, cannot justify providing fewer athletics opportunities for women than for men. Furthermore, such evidence is completely irrelevant where, as here, viable and successful women's varsity teams have been demoted or eliminated. We emphasize that, on the facts of this case, Brown's lack-of-interest arguments are of no consequence. As the prior panel recognized, while the question of full and effective accommodation of athletics interests and abilities is potentially a complicated issue where plaintiffs seek to create a new team or to [**70] elevate to varsity status a team that has never competed in varsity competition, no such difficulty is presented here, where plaintiffs seek to reinstate what were successful university-funded teams right up until the moment the teams were demoted.[16] *Cohen II*, 991 F.2d at 904; *see also Cohen I*, 809 F. Supp. at 992 ("Brown is cutting off varsity opportunities where there is great interest and talent, *and* where Brown still has an imbalance between men and women varsity athletes in relation to their undergraduate enrollments.").

On these facts, Brown's failure to accommodate fully and effectively the interests and abilities of the underrepresented gender is clearly established...Under these circumstances, the district court's finding that there are interested women able to compete at the university-funded varsity level, *Cohen III*, 879 F. Supp. at 212, is clearly correct. Finally, the tremendous growth in women's participation in sports since Title IX was enacted disproves Brown's argument that women are less interested in sports for reasons unrelated to lack of opportunity. *See, e.g.*, Mike Tharp et al., *Sports crazy! Ready, set, go. Why we love our games*, U.S. News & World Report, July 15, 1996, at 33–4 (attributing to Title IX the explosive growth of women's participation in sports and the debunking of "the traditional myth that women aren't interested in sports").

Brown's relative interests approach is not a reasonable interpretation of the three-part test. This approach contravenes the [**73] purpose of the statute and the regulation because it does not permit an institution or a district court to remedy a gender-based disparity in athletics participation opportunities. Instead, this approach freezes that disparity by law, thereby disadvantaging further the underrepresented gender. Had Congress intended to entrench, rather than change, the status quo -- with its historical emphasis on men's participation opportunities to the detriment of women's opportunities -- it need not [*181] have gone to all the trouble of enacting Title IX.

* * *

VIII.

There can be no doubt that Title IX has changed the face of women's sports as well as our society's interest in and attitude toward women athletes and women's sports. *See, e.g.,* Frank DeFord, *The Women of Atlanta,* Newsweek, June 10, 1996, at 62–71; Tharp, *supra,* at 33; Robert Kuttner, *Vicious Circle of Exclusion,* Washington Post, September 4, 1996, at A15. In addition, there is ample evidence that increased athletics participation opportunities for women and young girls, available as a result of Title IX enforcement, have had salutary effects in other areas of societal concern. *See* DeFord, *supra,* at 66.

One need look no further than the impressive performances of our country's women athletes in the 1996 Olympic Summer Games to see that Title IX has had a dramatic and positive impact on the capabilities of our women athletes, particularly in team sports. These Olympians represent [**98] the first full generation of women to grow up under the aegis of Title IX. The unprecedented success of these athletes is due, in no small measure, to Title IX's beneficent effects on women's sports, as the athletes themselves have acknowledged time and again. What stimulated this remarkable change in the quality of women's athletic competition was not a sudden, anomalous upsurge in women's interest in sports, but the enforcement of Title IX's mandate of gender equity in sports. Kuttner, *supra,* at A15.

Affirmed in part, reversed in part, and remanded for further proceedings. No costs on appeal to either party.

Jessica Gavora

Jessica Gavora is a writer currently living in Washington, D.C. She is the author of *Tilting the Playing Field: Schools, Sports, Sex and Title IX,* a critical analysis of the effect that gender equity policies have had on male and female school sports in the United States. The following selection is taken from this work.

Gavora, Jessica. *Tilting the Playing Field: Schools, Sports, Sex and Title IX.* San Francisco: Encounter Books, 2002. 1–181. (Excerpts: pp. 5, 6, 7, 9, 133, 134, 140, 141, 142.)

Introduction: The Stronger Women Get, the More They Hate Feminism

* * *

Title IX has acquired sweeping jurisdiction over all aspects of education, from kindergarten to graduate school, including test scoring, housing facilities, sexual harassment and teenage pregnancy. When the law was passed, few people—least of all the original congressional sponsors –were concerned about increasing opportunities for women to row crew and play basketball. They had in mind more prosaic educational benefits like admission to schools and programs, access to financial aid and career opportunities.

Nonetheless, it has been in sports---intercollegiate sports in particular---that Title IX has won its greatest notoriety. Here too is where the law has been molded into something quite different from what its congressional sponsors intended.

Sports, of course, are unique in the American educational experience: while coeducation has become the norm in the classroom, sexual segregation still reigns on the playing field. Educational institutions routinely and without controversy set up separate programs, provide separate facilities and in some cases hire separate administrative staff for girls and boys and men and women in athletics. Doing the same thing for, say, an English department or a drama or dance program would be unthinkable. In fact, it would be illegal.

It could be argued that Congress contradicted the very principle of nondiscrimination it was trying to promote when it allowed for separate athletic teams for men and women under Title IX. Moreover, applying a law that outlaws discrimination on the basis of sex to an activity that accepts discrimination on the basis of sex has cast the most difficult issues of "gender equity" in stark relief. How can the law guarantee that men and women receive the "same opportunity" when they compete on different teams and even in different sports? How can fairness be measured? Are men and women different when it comes to sports? Do they have different levels of interest? Of ability? Do they share the same zeal for competition? The same need for hierarchy and organized, team activity?

Feminist supporters of Title IX have answered these difficult questions by trying to have it both ways: separate and equal—or, as I will argue, more than equal. In this respect, they have committed themselves to a great compromise of their own. Whereas in every other area of life, from the military to the boardroom to the bedroom, women's rights activists have insisted that women be allowed to compete in the same arena with men, Title IX activists have worked in athletics to protect women's special status. They implicitly acknowledge that if women were forced to compete with men for positions on the playing field, very few would make the cut. On this narrow score, difference is accepted. But on every other count, sameness is insisted upon, and it is from this dubious premise that Title IX has come to have such an unsettling impact on athletics.

The gender-quota logic of Title IX is inexorable. It begins with the presumption that men and women, boys and girls are identical in their athletic interests, equally eager to kick a soccer ball or wield an oar. And if interests are equal, then "equity" between men and women dictates that actual participation must also be equal. There must be just as many girl athletes per capita at any given school as there are boy athletes. Anything less is prima facie proof that someone is being discriminated against.

* * *

.....As might be expected, Title IX activists have taken the presumption of sameness that holds for sports and applied it to math and science and other traditionally male-dominated fields. Here, as in sports, the definition of "equity" promoted under Title IX is not equal opportunity but equal outcomes. And here, as in sports, what feminists seek is not expanded opportunities for females to prove their mettle vis-a-vis males, but preferences for girls and women in an educational system they continue to view as dominated by "patriarchal oppression."

* * *

.....Do the activists who are leading the fight for Title IX quotas really represent the grievances, wishes and aspirations of the majority of American women? Are girls and women really, as the law has been twisted to assume, identical in their interests and abilities to boys and men? Are we as likely to want to kick a ball or take a physics class? Should the law penalize men if we are not?

..... What should be of greater concern to those who care about equal opportunity for girls and women is the implicit message of Title IX today: that young girls aren't worthy of respect and admiration unless and until they act like young boys. Playing sports and studying the hard sciences, those who enforce the law tell us, are worthier than the interests women have traditionally pursued. And to make sure no one misses the point, this message is backed up by real advantages in funding and resource allocation for girls and women who act accordingly—and by just as real penalties for boys and men. The losers aren't just males but also the millions of females whose talents and interests lie outside those dictated by the affirmative androgyny of the law.

Chapter Six: Why Can't a Woman Be More Like a Man

* * *

....Title IX is increasingly committed to equality of results. The question that is never confronted is whether this process is driven by a scientific understanding of how men and women would behave in a world without sex discrimination, or rather by politics.

...Feminists don't even speak in terms of "sex" when discussing females and males; "gender" is now the default term. Why? Because unlike "sex," which connotes immutable differences between men and women, "gender"can be said to be "socially constructed." That is, the differences we observe between little boys and little girls are inculcated in them by social prejudices and power relationships. Girls are not by their nature more inclined toward Barbie dolls and tea parties than little boys are; they are taught by their perhaps unconsciously phallocentric parents and a culture saturated by male primacy that this is how they should behave. The same is true for little boys, who would be less prone to reenact WWF wrestling matches in their back yards if they weren't schooled by society in the violence and insensitivity of "masculinity." More recently, feminists and other progressive thinkers have advocated that gender roles be jettisoned altogether, arguing that designating people as "male" and "female" places arbitrary limitations on their freedom and creativity.

But for serious social scientists, as opposed to feminists and other political activists, the reasons for the differences between the sexes we observe every day are considerably more complex. Social scientists don't discount the role of environmental factors or socialization in producing girls who would rather play with dolls and boys who would rather play with guns; they simply discount these factors as *the* explanation of sex differences. Recent years have brought great advances in genetics, the understanding of male and female sex hormones, and evolutionary psychology. All of these have important things to say, not just about how men and women are different, but *why* they are different.

No one theory, it is true, fully explains why girls and boys and men and women behave the way they do, and in any case it is beyond the scope of this book to undertake a comprehensive review of the literature on the science of sex difference. What is pertinent to a discussion of Title IX is whether sex differences, as feminists claim, are "constructed" by the malign influence of a patriarchal society. If such differences are "socially constructed," we can deconstruct them through enlightened public policy.

But if boys and girls are in some general way hardwired to pursue different interests and excel in different subjects, then it is time to take a serious look at federal anti-discrimination law that has come to assume exactly the opposite.

* * *

The most recent rebuttal of the theory of inherent sex sameness that underlies Title IX quotas comes in a vial marked "T." Testosterone, scientists are beginning to discover, is an important factor in the way physical and behavioral differences between men and women that have evolved over the eons are transmitted to us today.

* * *

The New York Times called testosterone the "he hormone," but in fact, males and females both produce it. It's just that men have, on average, ten to twenty times as much as women.

* * *

What about the differences that testosterone creates between the sexes? It is not an exaggeration to say that testosterone makes *the* difference between males and females. Testosterone first appears in the second trimester of pregnancy, flooding the womb and turning the developing sexually neutral fetus into a male. This *in utero* exposure to T influences later behavior.

* * *

It is important to emphasize that all these social scientists warn that in the sex differences they have observed there is an overlap in the distribution of abilities in males and females. That is, within both sexes there is a range of ability and interest. Some girls are better than some boys in math and science, and some girls are more likely than their male classmates to turn out for the lacrosse team. The upshot is that none of the findings presented here can be used to make judgments about any individual man or woman. Yes, boys in general show a greater propensity toward team athletic competition than girls; but this doesn't mean we should conclude that any individual girl is less willing and able to compete than any individual boy.

Such an appreciation for the variety and subtlety of human nature is, however, not part of the worldview of those who enforce Title IX today. Instead of judging men and women by their individual interests and abilities,

Title IX regulators direct their sweeping mandate on the sexes as groups. They prejudge the sexes to have identical interests and abilities. What's worse, they trample on the individual preferences of boys and girls and men and women by mandating outcomes so as to verify this prejudgment.

Employment

Muller v. Oregon (Plaintiff's Brief), 208 US 412 (1908)

This excerpt is from the brief filed by Muller (a factory owner) opposing the Oregon law that mandated that women employed in his factory could work no more than ten hours a day. Muller's brief challenged the legality of protection legislation for women on the grounds that it fostered inequality between men and women.

MULLER, PLAINTIFF IN ERROR, v. THE STATE OF OREGON.

SUPREME COURT OF THE UNITED STATES

208 U.S. 412; 28 S. Ct. 324; 52 L. Ed. 551; 1908 U.S. LEXIS 1452

February 24, 1908, Decided

COUNSEL: Mr. William D. Fenton, with whom Mr. Henry H. Gilfry was on the brief, for plaintiff in error:

Women, within the meaning of both the state and Federal constitutions, are persons and citizens, and as such are entitled to all the privileges and immunities therein provided, and are as competent to contract with reference to their labor as are men.

The right to labor or employ labor and to make contracts in respect thereto upon such terms as may be agreed upon, is both a liberty and a property right, included in the constitutional guarantee that no person shall be deprived of life, liberty or property without due process of law.

The law operates unequally and unjustly, and does not affect equally and impartially all persons similarly situated, and is therefore class legislation...

* * *

Women, equally with men, are endowed with the fundamental and inalienable rights of liberty and property, and these rights cannot be impaired or destroyed by legislative action under the pretense of exercising the police power of the State. Difference in sex alone does not justify the destruction or impairment of these rights. Where, under the exercise of the police power, such rights are sought to be restricted, impaired or denied, it must clearly appear that the public health, safety or welfare is involved. This statute is not declared to be a health measure. The employments forbidden and restricted are not bin fact or declared to be, dangerous to health or morals.

Muller v. Oregon, 208 US 412 (1908)

The *Muller* case is one of the few historical examples in which natural differences were cited to expand employment opportunities for women. In this case, the United States Supreme Court had to decide whether the precedent established three years earlier in *Lochner v. New York*[1] applied. In *Lochner*, the Court, in a 8-1 decision, invalidated a New York law mandating maximum hours work requirement for male bakers as being inconsistent with an individual's right to contract that was protected by the Fourteenth Amendment Due Process Clause.

Below is an excerpt from Justice David Brewer's opinion for the Court

MULLER, PLAINTIFF IN ERROR, v. THE STATE OF OREGON.

SUPREME COURT OF THE UNITED STATES

208 U.S. 412; 28 S. Ct. 324; 52 L. Ed. 551; 1908 U.S. LEXIS 1452

February 24, 1908, Decided

OPINION

[*416] [**324] MR. JUSTICE DAVID BREWER delivered the opinion of the court.

On February 19, 1903, the legislature of the State of Oregon passed an act (Session [***9] Laws, 1903, p. 148), the first section of which is in these words:

"SEC. 1. That no female (shall) be employed in any mechanical establishment, or factory, or laundry in this State more than ten hours during any one day. The hours of work may be so arranged as to permit the employment of females [*417] at any time so that they shall not work more than ten hours during the twenty-four hours of any one day."

* * *

The single question is the constitutionality of the statute under which the defendant was convicted so far as it affects the work of a female in a laundry. ...

* * *

It is the law of Oregon that women, whether married or single, have equal contractual and personal rights with men. ...

It thus appears that, putting to one side the elective franchise, in the matter of personal and contractual rights they stand on the same plane as the other sex. Their rights in these respects can no more be infringed than the equal rights of their brothers. ...But this assumes that the difference between the sexes does not justify a different rule respecting a restriction of the hours of labor.

* * *

That woman's physical structure and the performance of maternal functions place her at a disadvantage [***16] in the struggle for subsistence is obvious. This is especially true when the burdens of motherhood are upon her. Even when they are not, by abundant testimony of the medical fraternity continuance for a long time on her feet at work, repeating this from day to day, tends to injurious effects upon the body, and as healthy mothers are essential to vigorous offspring, the physical well-being of woman becomes an object of public interest and care in order to preserve the strength and vigor of the race.

Still again, history discloses the fact that woman has always been dependent upon man. He established his control at the outset by superior physical strength, [**327] and this control in various forms, with diminishing intensity, has continued to the present. As minors, though not to the same extent, she has been looked upon in the courts as needing especial care that her rights may be preserved. Education was long denied her, and while now the doors of the school room are opened and her opportunities for acquiring knowledge are great, yet even with that and the [*422] consequent increase of capacity for business affairs it is still true that in the struggle for subsistence [***17] she is not an equal competitor with her brother. Though limitations upon personal and contractual rights may be removed by legislation, there is that in her disposition and habits of life which will operate against a full assertion of those rights. She will still be where some legislation to protect her seems necessary to secure a real equality of right. Doubtless there are individual exceptions, and there are many respects in which she has an advantage over him; but looking at it from the viewpoint of the effort to maintain an independent position in life, she is not upon an equality. Differentiated by these matters from the other sex, she is properly placed in a class by herself, and legislation designed for her protection may be sustained, even when like legislation is not necessary for men and could not be sustained. It is impossible to close one's eyes to the fact that she still looks to her brother and depends upon him. Even though all restrictions on political, personal and contractual rights were taken away, and she stood, so far as statutes are concerned, upon an absolutely equal plane with him, it would still be true that she is so constituted that she will rest upon [***18] and look to him for protection; that her physical structure and a proper discharge of her maternal functions -- having in view not merely her own health, but the well-being of the race -- justify legislation to protect her from the greed as well as the passion of man. The limitations which this statute places upon her contractual powers, upon her right to agree with her employer as to the time she shall labor, are not imposed solely for her benefit, but also largely for the benefit of all. Many words cannot make this plainer. The two sexes differ in structure of body, in the functions to be performed by each, in the amount of physical strength, in the capacity for long-continued labor, particularly when done standing, the influence of vigorous health upon the future well-being of the race, the self-reliance which enables one to assert full rights, and in the capacity to maintain the struggle for subsistence. This difference [*423] justifies a difference in legislation and upholds that which is designed to compensate for some of the burdens which rest upon her.

...The reason runs deeper, and rests in the inherent difference between the two sexes, and in the different functions in life which they perform.

For these reasons, ...it cannot be adjudged that the act in question is in conflict with the Federal Constitution, so far as it respects the work of a female in a laundry, and the judgment of the Supreme Court of Oregon is

Affirmed.

Dothard v. Rawlinson, 433 US 321 (1977)

The *Dothard* case involved the decision of the state of Alabama to restrict the job of prison guard in its men's maximum security prison to men only. Rawlinson, a female applicant for the guard position, sued the state on the grounds that Alabama's policy was an illegal form of sex discrimination under Title VII. The state of Alabama argued that uncontrollable conditions within the men's maximum security prison and the dangerousness of the inmate population posed a grave danger to any female. Having a female guard in that prison would endanger male guards and threatened the security and administration of the prison. In other words, Alabama argued that being a man was a legitimate job qualification or a bona fide occupational qualification for working as a guard in the state men's maximum security prison.

The following excerpts are taken from the majority opinion.

DOTHARD, DIRECTOR, DEPARTMENT OF PUBLIC SAFETY OF ALABAMA, ET AL. *v.* RAWLINSON ET AL.

SUPREME COURT OF THE UNITED STATES

433 U.S. 321; 97 S. Ct. 2720; 53 L. Ed. 2d 786; 1977 U.S. LEXIS 143;

June 27, 1977; as amended

OPINION

MR. JUSTICE POTTER STEWART delivered the opinion of the Court.

* * *

III

Unlike the statutory height and weight requirements, Regulation 204 explicitly discriminates against women on the basis of their sex.[16] In defense of this overt discrimination, [*333] the appellants rely on [HN11] § 703 (e) of Title VII, 42 U.S.C.§ 2000e-2 (e), which permits sex-based discrimination "in those certain instances where... sex... is a bona fide occupational qualification reasonably necessary to the normal operation of that particular business or enterprise."

* * *

But... the federal courts have agreed that [HN12] it is impermissible under Title VII to refuse to hire an individual woman or man on the basis of stereotyped characterizations of the sexes,[17] and the District [*334] Court in the present case held in effect that Regulation 204 is based on just such stereotypical assumptions.

....In the particular factual circumstances of this case, however, we conclude that the District Court erred in rejecting the State's contention that Regulation 204 falls within the narrow ambit of the bfoq exception.

The environment in Alabama's penitentiaries is a peculiarly inhospitable one for human beings of whatever sex. Indeed, a Federal District Court has held that the conditions of confinement in the prisons of the State, characterized by "rampant violence" and a "jungle atmosphere," are constitutionally intolerable. *Pugh v. Locke,* 406 F.Supp. 318, 325 [***801] (MD Ala.). The record in the present case shows that [*335] because of inadequate staff and facilities, no attempt is made in the four maximum-security male penitentiaries to classify or segregate inmates according to their offense or level of dangerousness – a procedure that, according to expert testimony, is essential to effective penological administration. Consequently, the estimated 20% of the male prisoners who are sex offenders are scattered throughout the penitentiaries' dormitory facilities.

In this environment of violence and disorganization, it would be an oversimplification to characterize Regulation 204 as an exercise in "romantic paternalism. " Cf. *Frontiero v. Richardson,* 411 U.S. 677, 684. [**2730] [HN16] In the usual case, the argument that a particular job is too dangerous for women may appropriately be met by the rejoinder that it is the purpose of Title VII to allow the individual woman to make that choice for herself.[21] More is at stake in this case, however, than an individual woman's decision to weigh and accept the risks of employment in a "contact" position in a maximum-security male prison.

The essence of a correctional counselor's job is to maintain prison security. A woman's relative ability to maintain order in a male, maximum-security, unclassified penitentiary of the type Alabama now runs could be directly reduced by her womanhood. There is a basis in fact for expecting that sex offenders who have criminally assaulted women in the past would be moved to do so again if access to women were established within the prison. There would also be a real risk that other inmates, deprived of a normal heterosexual environment, would assault women guards because they were women.[22] In a prison system where violence is the order [*336] of the day, where inmate access to guards is facilitated by dormitory living arrangements, where every institution is understaffed, and where a substantial portion of the inmate population is composed of sex offenders mixed at random with other prisoners, there are few visible deterrents to inmate assaults on women custodians.

Appellee Rawlinson's own expert testified that dormitory housing for aggressive inmates poses a greater security problem than single-cell lockups, and further testified that it would be unwise to use women as guards in a prison where even 10% of the inmates had been convicted of sex crimes and were not segregated from the other prisoners.[23] The likelihood that inmates would assault a woman because she was a woman [***802] would pose a real threat not only to the victim of the assault but also to the basic control of the penitentiary and protection of its inmates and the other security personnel. The employee's very womanhood would thus directly undermine her capacity to provide the security that is the essence of a correctional counselor's responsibility.

There was substantial testimony from experts on both sides of this litigation that the use of women as guards in "contact" positions under the existing conditions in Alabama maximum-security male penitentiaries would pose a substantial security problem, directly linked to the sex of the prison guard. On the basis of that evidence, we conclude that the District Court was in error in ruling that being male is not a bona fide occupational qualification for the job of [*337] correctional counselor in a "contact" position in an Alabama male maximum-security penitentiary.[24]

It is so ordered.

Dothard v. Rawlinson, 433 US 321 (1977)

The following excerpt is from the dissenting opinion filed by Justice Thurgood Marshall. Joined by Justice William Brennan, Justice Marshall was concerned that the majority opinion would become a justification for limiting employment opportunities for women.

DOTHARD, DIRECTOR, DEPARTMENT OF PUBLIC SAFETY OF ALABAMA, ET AL. *v.* RAWLINSON ET AL.

SUPREME COURT OF THE UNITED STATES

433 U.S. 321; 97 S. Ct. 2720; 53 L. Ed. 2d 786; 1977 U.S. LEXIS 143;

June 27, 1977; as amended

DISSENT: JUSTICE THURGOOD MARSHALL

MR. JUSTICE THURGOOD MARSHALL, with whom MR. JUSTICE BRENNAN joins, concurring in part and dissenting in part.

* * *

The Court properly rejects two proffered justifications for denying women jobs as prison guards. It is simply irrelevant here that a guard's occupation is dangerous and that some women might be unable to protect themselves adequately. Those themes permeate the testimony of the state officials below, but as the Court holds, "the argument that a particular job is too dangerous for women" is refuted by the "purpose of Title VII to allow the individual woman to make that choice for herself." *Ante,* at 335. Some women, like some men, undoubtedly are not qualified and do not wish to serve as prison guards, but that does not justify the exclusion of all women from this employment opportunity. ...

What would otherwise be considered unlawful discrimination against women is justified by the Court, however, on the [*342] basis of the "barbaric and inhumane" conditions in Alabama prisons, conditions so bad that state officials have conceded that they violate the Constitution....

The Court's error in statutory construction is less objectionable, however, than the attitude it displays [***806] toward women. Though the Court recognizes that possible harm to women guards is an unacceptable reason for disqualifying women, it relies instead on an equally speculative threat to prison discipline supposedly generated by the sexuality of female guards. There is simply no evidence in the record to show that women guards would create any danger to security in Alabama prisons significantly greater than that which already exists. All of the dangers – with one exception discussed below – are inherent in a prison setting, whatever the gender of the guards.

[*343] The Court first sees women guards as a threat to security because "there are few visible deterrents to inmate assaults on women custodians." *Ante,* at 336. In fact, any prison guard is constantly subject to the threat of attack by inmates, and "invisible" deterrents are the guard's only real protection. No prison guard relies primarily on his or her ability to ward off an inmate attack to maintain order. Guards are typically unarmed and sheer numbers of inmates could overcome the normal complement. Rather, like all other law enforcement officers, prison guards must rely primarily [**2734] on the moral authority of their office and the threat of future punishment for miscreants. As one expert testified below, common sense, fairness, and mental and emotional stability are the qualities a guard needs to cope with the dangers of the job. App. 81. Well qualified and properly trained women, no less than men, have these psychological weapons at their disposal.

The particular severity of discipline problems in the Alabama maximum-security prisons is also no justification for the discrimination sanctioned by the Court. The District Court found in *Pugh* v. *Locke, supra,* that guards "must spend all their time attempting to maintain control or to protect themselves." 406 F.Supp., at 325. If male guards face an impossible situation, it is difficult to see how women could make the problem worse, unless one relies on precisely the type of generalized bias against women that the Court agrees Title VII was intended to outlaw. For example, much of the testimony of appellants' witnesses ignores individual differences among members of each sex and reads like "ancient canards about the proper role of women." *Phillips* v. *Martin Marietta Corp.*, 400 U.S., at 545. The witnesses claimed that women guards are not strict disciplinarians; that they are physically less capable of protecting themselves and subduing unruly inmates; that inmates take advantage of them as they did their mothers, while male guards are strong father figures [*344] who easily maintain discipline, and so on.[2] Yet [***807] the record shows that the presence of women guards has not led to a single incident amounting to a serious breach of security in any Alabama institution.[3] And, in any event, "[g]uards rarely enter the cell blocks and dormitories," *Pugh* v. *Locke*, 406 F.Supp., at 325, where the danger of inmate attacks is the greatest.

It appears that the real disqualifying factor in the Court's view is "[t]he employee's very womanhood." *Ante*, at 336. The Court refers to the large number of sex offenders in Alabama prisons, and to "[the] likelihood that inmates would assault a woman because she was a woman." *Ibid.* In short, the fundamental justification for the decision is that women as guards will generate sexual assaults. With all respect, this rationale regrettably perpetuates one of the most insidious of the old myths about women – that women, wittingly or not, are seductive sexual objects. The effect of the decision, made I am sure with the best of [**2735] intentions, is to punish women because their very presence might provoke sexual assaults. It is women who are made to pay the price in lost job opportunities for the threat of depraved conduct by prison inmates. Once again, "[t]he pedestal upon which women have been placed has..., upon closer inspection, been revealed as a cage." *Sail'er Inn, Inc.* v. *Kirby*, 5 Cal. 3d 1, 20, 485 P. 2d 529, 541 (1971). It is particularly ironic that the case is erected here in response to feared misbehavior by imprisoned criminals.[4]

The Court points to no evidence in the record to support the asserted "likelihood that inmates would assault a woman because she was a woman." *Ante*, at 336. Perhaps the Court relies upon common sense, or "innate recognition," Brief for Appellants 51. But the danger in this emotionally laden context is that common sense will be used to mask the "'romantic paternalism'" and persisting discriminatory attitudes [*346] that the Court properly eschews. *Ante*, at 335. To me, the only matter of innate recognition is that the incidence of sexually motivated attacks on guards will be minute compared [***808] to the "likelihood that inmates will assault" a *guard* because he or she is a guard.

The proper response to inevitable attacks on both female and male guards is not to limit the employment opportunities of law-abiding women who wish to contribute to their community, but to take swift and sure punitive action against the inmate offenders. Presumably, one of the goals of the Alabama prison system is the eradication of inmates' antisocial behavior patterns so that prisoners will be able to live one day in free society. Sex offenders can begin this process by learning to relate to women guards in a socially acceptable manner. To deprive women of job opportunities because of the threatened behavior of convicted criminals is to turn our social priorities upside down.[5]

Although I do not countenance the sex discrimination [*347] condoned by the majority, it is fortunate that the Court's decision is carefully limited to the facts before it. I trust the lower courts will recognize that the decision was impelled by the shockingly inhuman conditions in Alabama prisons, and thus that the "extremely narrow [bfoq] exception" recognized here, *ante*, at 334, will not be allowed "to swallow the rule" against sex discrimination. See *Phillips* v. *Martin Marietta Corp.*, 400 U.S., at 545. Expansion of today's decision beyond its narrow factual basis would erect a serious roadblock to economic equality for women.

Torres v. Wisconsin Department of Health and Social Services, 838 F.2d 944 (7th Cir. 1988)

The Torres case asks the question of whether male guards should work in the living quarters in a women's prison. The case stemmed from a lawsuit filed by male prison guards working in a female prison who were demoted because of a new policy requiring that only female prison guards could be assigned in buildings where female inmates lived. The demoted male guard charged that the new policy violated Title VII's mandate that employment decisions could not be based on sex. The warden argued that being female was a necessary job requirement for these guards in order to achieve the prison's objective of rehabilitating female inmates.

The facts of the case along with the three-judge panel's decision are excerpted here.

RAYMOND J. TORRES, FRANKLIN J. UTZ, and GERALD F.
SCHMIT, Plaintiffs-Appellees, v. WISCONSIN DEPARTMENT OF
HEALTH & SOCIAL SERVICES, et al., Defendants-Appellants.

UNITED STATES COURT OF APPEALS FOR THE SEVENTH
CIRCUIT

838 F.2d 944; 1988 U.S. App. LEXIS 19472;

January 29, 1988, Decided

JUDGES: Before CUDAHY and RIPPLE, Circuit Judges, and WILL, Senior
District Judge.*

OPINION BY: JUDGE CUDAHY

OPINION

CUDAHY, *Circuit Judge.* The plaintiffs in this suit are three men who are
employed as correctional officers at a prison for women. They were demoted
pursuant to the creation and implementation of a policy that designated
certain correctional officer positions (including those formerly held by the
plaintiffs) as open to women only. The plaintiffs sued, challenging this
policy as violative of their right to be free from employment discrimination
on the basis of sex, as guaranteed by Title VII of the Civil Rights Act of
1964, 42 U.S.C. §§ 2000e to 2000e-17 (1982). The defendants responded
that sex is a "bona fide occupational qualification" ("bfoq"), 42 U.S.C. §
2000e-2(e)(1), for the positions at issue because that distinction on the basis
of sex is necessary [*2] to protect the privacy rights of the inmates and to
promote the prison's purposes of security and rehabilitation....

* * *

The defendant Taycheedah Correctional Institution ("TCI") is the only
women's maximum security prison in Wisconsin. TCI is operated by the
Wisconsin Department of Health and Social Services ("DHSS"), which
is also a defendant in this action. The final named defendant is Nona J.
Switala who is the Superintendent of TCI, a position she has held since
September 1978.

Prior to 1975, TCI was a prison for women. In 1975, DHSS designated
TCI a co-correctional institution and transferred male inmates and male
correctional officers to TCI. TCI again became a prison for women only
in February 1978 and currently continues to be a women's prison. When

the male inmates were transferred out of TCI, however, male correctional officers remained employed at TCI.

TCI includes three buildings in which inmates are regularly housed; each building has three residence floors. The inmates live in single, double and multiple occupancy rooms. Each room contains a bed for each inmate, a desk, chair, light, toilet and wash basin. In two of the three residence buildings, privacy curtains have been installed around the toilets. When an inmate is behind the curtain, only her feet are visible. Privacy [*5] curtains will soon be installed in the rooms in the remaining residence building.

The inmates' rooms have solid doors that contain, at eye level, a clear glass window that measures approximately four inches by six inches. During the hours of 6 a.m. to 9 p.m., the inmates are permitted to cover that window from the inside with a piece of cardboard known as a "privacy card" for a maximum of ten minutes while they are using the toilet or changing their clothing. During the hours 9 p.m. to 6 a.m., the privacy card is placed over the window on the outside of the door which enables the correctional officers to lift the card to see into the room in order, for example, to perform body counts. During these nighttime hours, the inmates apparently are not permitted to place the card over the window on the inside of the door for the ten-minute intervals.[2]

[*6] The correctional officers perform body counts each day at 7:30 a.m., 12:30 p.m., 5:30 p.m., 9:30 p.m., and once an hour between 10 p.m. and 6 a.m. The inmates are aware of this schedule. The officers perform the counts at night by looking in the windows in the doors to the inmates' rooms. The inmates are provided appropriate sleepwear from TCI but are not required to wear it.

Shower rooms are located on each floor of the residence halls. The doors to the shower rooms are solid; some contain windows, but the windows have been rendered opaque. Each shower room has one to three shower stalls, one to three toilet stalls, and some have one or more bathtubs. Each shower and toilet stall has a curtain or door which shields the inmate from view from the rest of the shower room. In all but the maximum security residence hall, only one inmate may occupy the shower room at a time, except that roommates may use the shower room together. Inmates are allowed fifteen minutes in the shower room.

Absent an emergency or rule violation, no correctional officer would see an inmate in any state of undress. In order to use the shower room, an inmate must sign up with the floor officers. The [*7] inmate must wear at least a robe or housecoat while traveling to and from the shower room.

Correctional officers do not routinely enter the shower rooms while they are occupied.

Correctional officers at TCI perform three types of searches of inmates, all of which are authorized by the Wisconsin Administrative Code. Pat searches are the least intrusive and may be performed at any time, subject to certain restrictions and requirements. The inmate remains fully clothed during a pat search; she empties her pockets and then the searching officer runs his or her hands over the inmate's entire body. Although the Wisconsin Administrative Code provides that correctional officers may perform pat searches on inmates of the opposite sex, there is an unwritten rule at TCI that only female officers may perform pat searches. Strip searches, the second type of search used at TCI, must be authorized by a "lieutenant" and are performed in private, and, except in emergencies, only by officers of the same sex as the inmate. Body cavity searches, the most invasive of the searches, are performed only by medical personnel. Searches of the inmates' rooms are performed when the inmates are out of the [*8] rooms.

DHSS ranks its correctional officers as follows (in ascending order): correctional officer 1 ("CO-1"), correctional officer 2 ("CO-2") and correctional officer 3 ("CO-3"). TCI employs officers from all three classifications in its living units. The CO-3 in charge of a living unit is known as a "sergeant."

Prior to the implementation in 1980 of the plan that designated specified positions as available only to women, all correctional officer positions were open to all qualified officers without any restrictions based on sex. In August 1978, DHSS authorized correctional institution superintendents to submit requests for restricting certain correctional officer positions to women only where those positions involved performing strip searches or supervising the showers or living units. TCI's then-acting superintendent responded by proposing that five positions, including one CO-3 post, be limited to female officers. This plan was never formally adopted.

In June 1980, DHSS approved a different plan (the "Plan") which was based on a proposal by defendant TCI superintendent Switala. The Plan provided that nineteen of the twenty-seven correctional officer posts in the residence [*9] halls would be limited to women. This number included all of the CO-3 posts in the residence halls as well as all CO-1 and CO-2 "single coverage" posts, that is, posts where only one officer was assigned to a floor. Beginning on September 1, 1980, all vacancies for these posts were to be filled with female officers. If any of these posts were still held by men as of September 1, 1982, the male officers were to be replaced by female officers. With the full implementation of the Plan, fifteen of the eighteen CO-3 positions at TCI were restricted to women.

* * *

C.

The defendants' ... rationale for the Plan is that restricting the CO-3 positions in the living units to women furthers the rehabilitation needs of the inmates. They argue that "normalization" of the prison environment is desirable and necessary for rehabilitation to take place and that "such normalization cannot be rationally furthered by subjecting inmates in the showers or toilets to scrutiny by the opposite gender officers." Defendants' [*28] Brief at 18. The defendants also claim that among female inmates there has been a history of a "high incidence of physical, sexual, and psychological abuse and domination by men." This pattern of male domination, according to the defendants, would be reinforced by allowing male correctional officers to work in the living units, which in turn would be "destructive to a female inmate's development of an independent self-image." Id. at 20–1.

The defendants have not proven the asserted factual bases for their rehabilitation rationale. The district court found, and we have found no basis in the record for disagreeing, that correctional officers at TCI do not and need not view inmates in the showers or toilets or in any state of undress, absent an emergency. Further, the defendants have not shown that female inmates assigned to TCI have experienced more severe abuse and domination by men than have women in our society as a whole. The defendants' own expert witness, psychologist Dr. Henry Musk, testified that "the rate of abuse, physical or sexual of women in the general population apparently is about the same of women in prison." Trial transcript, Volume 10, at 76 (Aug. 6, 1985).

[*29] Defendants did represent that many female inmates have been unusually scarred by male abuse and that the peculiar power relationship between male guards and female prisoners makes male guards an obstacle to rehabilitation. E.g., Trial transcript, Volume 10, at 33–7 (Aug. 6, 1985) (testimony of Joanne M. Brown). If demonstrated, this proposition might justify excluding males from the staff even if female inmates have not suffered unusually severe male abuse. The district court, however, found:

Defendants offered only a *theory* of rehabilitation as a justification for the BFOQ Plan. They offered no objective evidence, either from empirical studies or otherwise, displaying the validity of their theory. Indeed, Superintendent Switala testified that there had been no change in the recidivism rate at TCI from 1980 to the present. The Court refuses to find the Plan valid based strictly on the unproven rehabilitation theory presented by defendants at trial.

639 F. Supp. at 280 (emphasis in original). The court also noted that the plaintiffs had presented expert testimony that directly contradicted the defendants' theory; the plaintiffs' experts [*30] testified that the presence of male correctional officers in the living units would contribute to the normalization of the prison environment and therefore have a beneficial effect on inmate rehabilitation. *E.g.*, Trial transcript, Volume 6, at 14–15 (July 30, 1985) (testimony of Dr. Frederick Forsdal). We agree with the district court that the defendants have not met their heavy burden of proving that their rehabilitation theory satisfied the requirements of the very narrow bfoq exception to Title VII.

III.

In upholding the district court's judgment for the plaintiffs in this Title VII claim, we are not holding that a state could never establish a valid sex bfoq for a correctional officer position in a women's prison. Specifically, we do not hold that the state would have to dispel all reasonable doubts about its theory of female inmate rehabilitation before it could exclude male correctional officers. It is even conceivable that the rehabilitation theories and privacy concerns asserted by the defendants in the present case could be shown to justify the Plan instituted by the state.[7] The defendants, however, did not prove this.....

* * *

Torres v. Wisconsin Department of Health and Social Services, 859 F.2d 1523 (7th Cir. 1988 en banc)

The Wisconsin Department of Health and Social Services petitioned the entire 7th Circuit Court to rehear the Torres case. With all circuit judges participating, the 7th Circuit Court, sitting en banc, reversed the decision of the three-judge panel. The highlights of this court's ruling are excerpted below.

RAYMOND J. TORRES, FRANKLIN J. UTZ, and GERALD F. SCHMIT, Plaintiffs-Appellees, v. WISCONSIN DEPARTMENT OF HEALTH AND SOCIAL SERVICES, et al., Defendants-Appellants

UNITED STATES COURT OF APPEALS FOR THE SEVENTH CIRCUIT

859 F.2d 1523; 1988 U.S. App. LEXIS 14478;

January 29, 1988, Decided

OPINION BY: CIRCUIT COURT JUDGE RIPPLE

[*1524] *****

III

Analysis

A. *Title VII and the BFOQ*

* * *

This case involves overt sex discrimination. It presents one issue--whether the district court correctly determined that sex was not a BFOQ for correctional officer positions at TCI. [HN3] Section 703(e) of Title VII only permits classifications based on sex "where . . . sex . . . is a bona fide occupational qualification *reasonably necessary* to the normal operation of that particular business or enterprise." 42 U.S.C. § 2000e-2(e)(1) (emphasis supplied). It is universally recognized that this exception to Title VII was "meant to be an extremely narrow exception to the general prohibition of discrimination. . . ." ...[I]t has been held that [HN5] "an employer could rely on the BFOQ exception only by proving 'that he had reasonable cause to believe, that is, a factual basis for believing, that all or substantially all women would be unable to perform safely and efficiently the duties of the job involved.'"

It is also well established that a BFOQ may not be based on "stereotyped characterizations of the sexes." *Dothard*, 433 U.S. at 333. "Myths and purely habitual assumptions about a woman's [or a man's] inability to perform certain kinds of work are no longer acceptable reasons for refusing to employ qualified individuals, or for paying them less." *City of Los Angeles Dep't of Water & Power v. Manhart*, 435 U.S. 702, 707, 55 L. Ed. 2d 657, 98 S. Ct. 1370 (1978). On the other hand, there are real as well as fictional differences between men and women. *Id*. For instance, the Supreme Court has never hesitated to recognize sex-based differences, particularly in cases involving physiology, marriage, child-birth, or sexuality....

Nevertheless, while recognizing that sex-based differences may justify a limited number of distinctions between men and women, we must discipline our inquiry to ensure that our tolerance for such distinctions is not widened artificially by--as the district court aptly put it--our "own culturally induced proclivities." *Torres*, 639 F. Supp. at 278. Nor, of course, can we tolerate the same preconceptions or predilections on the part of employers. Rather, we must ask whether, given the reasonable objectives of the employer, the very womanhood or very manhood of the employee undermines his or her capacity to perform a job satisfactorily. *Dothard*, 433 U.S. at 336.

* * *

B. *The "Business" of the Employer*

* * *

[HN7] The validity of a BFOQ can only be ascertained when it is assessed in relationship to the business of the employer....

.....A more precise definition of the "business" of the defendants is to recognize that they are in the business of administering a penal institution. Few tasks are more challenging. ...

Those who assume the responsibility of administering any prison must grapple with the "perplexing sociological problems of how best to achieve the goals of the penal function in the criminal justice system: to punish justly, to deter future crime, and to return imprisoned persons to society with an improved chance of being useful, law-abiding citizens. In fulfilling these responsibilities, prison administrators always have been expected [**21] to innovate and experiment. *See Turner v. Safley*, 482 U.S. 78, 107 S. Ct. 2254, 2262, 96 L. Ed. 2d 64 (1987) (prison administrators must be allowed "to adopt innovative solutions to the intractable problems of prison administration"). Unless prison administrators try new approaches, the "intractable problems" will remain and the lot of the incarcerated individual will not improve. Indeed, it probably will deteriorate.

This general description of the task of prison administrators is still too general to permit us to assess accurately the claims of the parties... The defendants here are charged with the administration of a distinct type of penal institution--a women's maximum security facility. As the district court and one of the plaintiffs' own witnesses quite candidly acknowledged,[2] the same [**22] historical and empirical evidence that might guide the administrator of a similar institution for males simply is not available with respect to this environment. Therefore, the administrators of TCI were obliged, to a greater degree than their counterparts in male institutions, to innovate in achieving one of the tasks mandated by the Wisconsin legislature--rehabilitation. [*1530] The defendants' "business" explicitly included--by legislative mandate--the task of rehabilitation....

[**23] C. *Rehabilitation: The TCI Approach*

Ms. Switala, the superintendent of TCI, made a professional judgment that giving women prisoners a living environment free from the presence of males in a position of authority was necessary to foster the goal of rehabilitation. This decision was based on Ms. Switala's professional expertise and on her interviews and daily contact with female prisoners. Tr. 10 at 110–11. She also based her decision on the fact that a high percentage of female inmates has been physically and sexually abused by males. Indeed, she noted that sixty percent of TCI's inmates have been so abused. Tr. 9 at 39.

1.

There can be no question that the proposed BFOQ is directly related to the "essence" of the "business"--the rehabilitation of females incarcerated in a maximum security institution. As we already have noted, the Wisconsin legislature has mandated that rehabilitation is one of the objectives of that state's prison system....

2.

The more difficult question is whether the proposed BFOQ was "reasonably necessary" to furthering the objective of rehabilitation. The defendants can establish that the BFOQ was reasonably necessary only if they "had reasonable cause to believe, that is, a factual basis for believing, that all or substantially all [men] would be unable to perform safely and efficiently the duties of the job involved."...

* * *

Certainly, it is hardly a "myth or purely habitual assumption," *Los Angeles Dep't of Water & Power v. Manhart*, 435 U.S. 702, 707, 55 L. Ed. 2d 657, 98 S. Ct. 1370 (1978), that the presence of unrelated males in living spaces where intimate bodily functions take place is a cause of stress to females. ...

* * *

[**31] We believe, therefore, that the defendants were required to meet an unrealistic, and therefore unfair, burden when they were required to produce "objective evidence, either from empirical studies or otherwise, displaying the validity of their theory." *Torres*, 639 F. Supp. at 280. Given the nature of their "business"--administering a prison for female felons--the defendants, of necessity, had to innovate. Therefore, their efforts ought to be evaluated on the basis of the totality of the circumstances as contained in the entire record. In the Title VII context, the decision of penal administrators need not be given as much deference as accorded their decisions in constitutional cases. *Whitley v. Albers*, 475 U.S. 312, 321–2, 89 L. Ed. 2d 251, 106 S. Ct. 1078 (1986); *Rhodes v. Chapman*, 452 U.S. 337, 351–2, 69 L. Ed. 2d 59, 101 S. Ct. 2392 (1981); *Bell v. Wolfish*, 441 U.S. 520, 547, 60 L. Ed. 2d 447, 99 S. Ct. 1861 (1979). However, their judgments still are entitled to substantial weight when they are the product of a reasoned decision-making process, based on available information and experience. The fact that [**32] the program is considered a reasonable approach by other professional penologists also is a factor to be given significant consideration. In an area where the questions are so many and the answers so few, the range of reasonable options must necessarily be more extensive. Certainly, the court ought not require unanimity of opinion and ought not to substitute completely its own judgment for that of the administration.[5]

Conclusion

* * *

Finally, we emphasize that it would be a mistake to read our decision today as a signal that we are willing to allow employers to elude Title VII's requirements simply by arguing that they were "innovating." Rare is the employment situation in which an employer could argue that gender-based distinctions are a "reasonably [*1533] necessary" approach to innovation in one's business. We hold only that, given the very special responsibilities of these defendants and the obvious lack of guideposts for them to follow, it was error to require that they adopt only a course that was subject to objective validation. Accordingly, the judgment of the district court is reversed and the case is remanded for proceedings consistent with this opinion.

REVERSED and REMANDED

City of Los Angeles Department of Water and Power et al. v. Manhart et al., 435 US 702 (1978)

There is a series of work-related benefits that affect men and women differently. One benefit that raises sexual equality concerns involves how companies fund their pensions. Most pensions are based on a funding strategy that requires workers to contribute a portion of their salary to a retirement fund that will, in turn, provide them with a pension when they retire. The longer a retired worker lives, the more he or she takes out of the pension fund. The Title VII issue arose because women, as a group, live longer than men, as a group. Female retirees will take more out of the pension fund than men. The question is whether employers should require that their female workers to contribute a higher percentage of their salaries to the pension fund than what is required of their male workers.

The Department of Water and Power in Los Angeles adopted this pension funding plan. Two thousand female workers at the Department of Water and Power would have higher retirement or pension costs than the 10,000 male workers. To address the costs incurred from their female workers, the Department required women to contribute more of their pay to the pension fund than men.

This case required the United States Supreme Court to determine whether real differences between men and women justified this disparate treatment in pension funding. Here, the longevity data showed that men and women were physically different and their different lifespans were based on fact, and not on sex stereotypes. The Court had to decide whether documented biological differences between men and women allow employers like the Los Angeles Department of Water and Power to take their employee's sex into account in determining worker contributions to the company's pension fund.

Below is an excerpt from the Court's majority opinion that was written by Justice John Stevens.

CITY OF LOS ANGELES DEPARTMENT OF WATER AND POWER ET AL. v. MANHART ET AL.

SUPREME COURT OF THE UNITED STATES

435 U.S. 702; 98 S. Ct. 1370; 55 L. Ed. 2d 657; 1978 U.S. LEXIS 23;

April 25, 1978, Decided 1403 words

OPINION BY: STEVENS

MR. JUSTICE JOHN STEVENS delivered the opinion of the Court.

As a class, women live longer than men. For this reason, the Los Angeles Department of Water and Power required its female employees to make larger contributions to its pension fund than its male employees. We granted certiorari to decide whether this practice discriminated against individual female employees because of their sex in violation of § 703 (a) (1) of the Civil Rights Act of 1964, as amended.[1]

* * *

I

There are both real and fictional differences between women and men. It is true that the average man is taller than the average woman; it is not true that the average woman driver is more accident [**1375] prone than the average man.[12] Before the Civil Rights Act of 1964 was enacted, an employer could fashion his personnel policies on the basis of assumptions about the differences between men and women, whether or not the assumptions were valid.

It is now well recognized that employment decisions cannot be predicated on mere "stereotyped" impressions about the characteristics [***665] of males or females.[13] Myths and purely habitual assumptions about a woman's inability to perform certain kinds of work are no longer acceptable reasons for refusing to employ qualified individuals, or for paying them less. This case does not, however, involve a fictional difference between men and women. It involves a generalization that the parties accept as unquestionably true: Women, as a class, do live longer than men. The Department treated its women employees differently from its men employees because the two [*708] classes are in fact different. It is equally true, however, that all individuals in the respective classes do not share the characteristic that differentiates the average class representatives.

Many women do not live as long as the average man and many men outlive the average woman. The question, therefore, is whether the existence or nonexistence of "discrimination" is to be determined by comparison of class characteristics or individual characteristics. A "stereotyped" answer to that question may not be the same as the answer that the language and purpose of the statute command.

The statute makes it unlawful "to discriminate against any *individual* with respect to his compensation, terms, conditions, or privileges of employment, because of such *individual's* race, color, religion, sex, or national origin." 42 U. S. C. § 2000e-2 (a)(1) (emphasis added). The statute's focus on the individual is unambiguous. It precludes treatment of individuals as simply components of a racial, religious, sexual, or national class. If height is required for a job, a tall woman may not be refused employment merely because, on the average, women are too short. Even a true generalization about the class is an insufficient reason for disqualifying an individual to whom the generalization does not apply.

That proposition is of critical importance in this case because there is no assurance that any individual woman working for the Department will actually fit the generalization on which the Department's policy is based. Many of those individuals will not live as long as the average man. While they were working, those individuals received smaller paychecks because of their sex, but they will receive no compensating advantage when they retire.

It is true, of course, that while contributions are being collected from the employees, the Department cannot know which individuals will predecease the average woman. Therefore, unless women as a class are assessed an extra charge, they will be subsidized, to some extent, by the class of male [*709] employees.[14] It follows, according to the Department, that fairness to its class of male [***666] employees justifies the extra assessment against all of its female employees.

But the question of fairness to various classes affected by the statute is essentially [**1376] a matter of policy for the legislature to address. Congress has decided that classifications based on sex, like those based on national origin or race, are unlawful. Actuarial studies could unquestionably identify differences in life expectancy based on race or national origin, as well as sex.[15] But a statute that was designed to make race irrelevant in the employment market, see *Griggs* v. *Duke Power Co.*, 401 U.S. 424, 436, could not reasonably be construed to permit a take-home-pay differential based on a racial classification.[16]

Even if the statutory language were less clear, the basic policy of the statute requires that we focus on fairness to individuals rather than fairness to classes. Practices that classify employees in terms of religion, race, or sex tend to preserve traditional assumptions about groups rather than thoughtful scrutiny of individuals. The generalization involved in this case illustrates the point. Separate mortality tables are easily interpreted as reflecting innate differences between the sexes; but a significant part of the longevity [*710] differential may be explained by the social fact that men are heavier smokers than women.[17]

Finally, there is no reason to believe that Congress intended a special definition of discrimination in the context of employee group insurance coverage. It is true that insurance is concerned with events that are individually unpredictable, but that is characteristic of many employment decisions. Individual risks, like individual performance, may not be predicted by resort to classifications proscribed by Title VII. Indeed, the fact that this case involves a group insurance program highlights a basic flaw in the Department's fairness argument. For when insurance risks are grouped, the better risks always subsidize the poorer risks. Healthy persons subsidize medical benefits for the less healthy; unmarried workers subsidize the pensions of married workers;[18] persons who eat, drink, or smoke to excess may subsidize pension benefits for persons whose habits are more temperate. Treating different classes of risks as though they were the same for purposes of group insurance is a common practice that has never been considered [***667] inherently unfair. To insure the flabby and the fit as though they were equivalent risks may be more common than treating men and women alike;[19] but nothing more than habit makes one "subsidy" seem less fair than the other.[20]

II

* * *

III

* * *

In this case, however, the Department argues that the absence of a discriminatory effect on women as a class justifies an employment practice which, on its face, discriminated against individual employees because of their sex. But even if the Department's actuarial evidence is sufficient to prevent plaintiffs from establishing a prima facie case on the theory that the effect of the practice on women as a class was discriminatory, that evidence does not defeat the claim that the practice, on its face, discriminated against every individual woman employed by the Department.[30]

In essence, the Department is arguing that the prima facie showing of discrimination based on evidence of different contributions for the respective sexes is rebutted by its demonstration that there is a like difference in the cost of providing benefits for the respective classes. That argument might prevail if Title VII contained a cost-justification defense comparable to the affirmative defense available in a price discrimination [*717] suit.[31] But neither Congress nor [**1380] the courts have recognized such a defense under Title VII.[32]

...[W]e conclude that the Department's practice violated Title VII

It is so ordered.

City of Los Angeles Department of Water and Power et al. v. Manhart et al., 435 US 702 (1978)

Chief Justice Warren Burger, joined by Justice William Rehnquist, dissented from the majority's interpretation of Title VII and argued that statistical evidence had to be considered in determining whether or not employers engage in illegal sex discrimination.

Excerpts from Chief Justice Burger's dissenting opinion follow.

CITY OF LOS ANGELES DEPARTMENT OF WATER AND POWER ET AL. v. MANHART ET AL.

SUPREME COURT OF THE UNITED STATES

435 U.S. 702; 98 S. Ct. 1370; 55 L. Ed. 2d 657; 1978 U.S. LEXIS 23

April 25, 1978, Decided

DISSENT

MR. CHIEF JUSTICE WARREN BURGER, with whom MR. JUSTICE REHNQUIST joins, concurring in part and dissenting in part.

Gender-based actuarial tables have been in use since at least [*726] 1843,[1] and their statistical validity has been repeatedly verified.[2] The vast life insurance, annuity, and pension plan industry is based on these tables. As the Court recognizes, *ante*, at 707, it is a fact that "women, as a class, do live longer than men." It is equally true that employers cannot know in advance when individual members of the classes will die. *Ante*, at 708. Yet, if they are to operate economically workable group pension programs, it is only rational to permit them to rely on statistically sound and proved disparities in longevity between men and women. Indeed, it seems to me irrational to assume Congress intended to outlaw use of the fact that, for whatever reasons or combination of reasons, women as a class outlive men.

The Court's conclusion that the language of the civil rights statute is clear, admitting of no advertence to the legislative history, such as there was, is not soundly based. An effect upon pension plans so revolutionary and discriminatory -- this time favorable to women at the expense of men -- should not be read into the statute without either a clear statement of that intent in the statute, or some reliable indication in the legislative history that this was Congress' purpose. ... It is reasonably clear there was no intention to abrogate an employer's right, in this narrow and limited context, to treat women differently from men in the [**1385] face of historical reliance on mortality experience statistics. Cf. *ante*, at 713 n. 25.

The reality of differences in human mortality is what mortality experience tables reflect. The difference is the added [*727] longevity of women. All the reasons why women statistically outlive men are not clear. But categorizing people on the basis of sex, the one acknowledged immutable difference between men and women, is to take into account all of the unknown reasons, whether biologically or culturally based, or both, which give women a significantly greater life expectancy than men. ...

Here, of course, petitioners are discriminating in take-home pay between men and women. Cf. *General Electric Co.* v. *Gilbert*, 429 U.S. 125 (1976); *Nashville Gas Co.* v. *Satty*, 434 U.S. 136 (1977). The practice of petitioners, however, falls squarely under the exemption provided by the Equal Pay Act of 1963, 29 U. S. C. § 206 (d), incorporated into Title VII by the so-called Bennett Amendment, 78 Stat. 257, now 42 U. S. C. § 2000e-2 (h). That exemption tells us that an employer may not discriminate between employees on the basis of sex by paying one sex lesser compensation than the other "except where such payment is made pursuant to . . . a differential based on any other factor other than sex . . . ." The "other factor other than sex" is longevity; sex is the umbrella-constant under which all of the elements leading to differences in longevity are grouped and assimilated, and the only objective feature upon which an employer -- or anyone else, including insurance companies -- may reliably base a cost differential for the "risk" being insured.

This is in no sense a failure to treat women as "individuals" in violation of the statute, as the Court holds. It is to treat [*728] them as individually as it is possible to do in the face of the unknowable length of each individual life. Individually, every woman has the same statistical possibility of outliving men. This is the essence of basing decisions on reliable statistics when individual determinations are infeasible or, as here, impossible.

Of course, women cannot be disqualified from, for example, heavy labor just because the generality of women are thought not as strong as men -- a proposition which perhaps may sometime be statistically demonstrable, but will remain individually refutable. When, however, it is impossible to tailor a program such as a pension plan to the individual, nothing should prevent application [***678] of reliable statistical facts to the individual, for whom the facts cannot be disproved until long after planning, funding, and operating the program have been undertaken.

I find it anomalous, if not contradictory, that the Court's opinion tells us, in effect, *ante*, at 717–8, and n. 33, that the holding is not really a barrier to responding to the complaints of men employees, as a group. The Court states that employers may give their employees precisely the same dollar amount and require them to secure their own annuities directly from an insurer, who, of course, is under no compulsion to ignore 135 years of accumulated, recorded longevity experience.[3]

Pay Equity

Republican Minority in House of Representatives on Wage Gap

In a Minority Report to the Report of Paycheck Fairness, sponsored by the House Committee from Education and Labor, the Republican members challenged the view that the wage gap resulted from discriminatory practices used by employers against female workers. The Minority Report was intended to argue against federal legislation designed to encourage female workers to challenge what they perceive to be pay inequity in their workplaces.

Minority Views, Report on Paycheck Fairness Act, Committee from Education and Labor, 110th Congress, 2d Session, Report 110-783, July 28, 2008: p1–54 (Excerpt: p. 48–50)

The Flawed "Wage Gap" Theory

Equal pay advocates claim that despite federal law prohibiting discrimination in pay on the basis of gender, female workers are still, paid considerably less than male workers, and thus a "wage gap" exists. Advocates commonly support this claim with reference to the most recent census data available, which indicated that in 2005,the average median income for women was $31,858, roughly 77 percent of the median income for men, which was $41,386....

Pay equity advocates argue that the root cause of pay inequity is the fact that "many women and people of color are still segregated into a few low-paying occupations. More than half of all women workers hold sales, clerical and service jobs. Studies show that the more an occupation is dominated by women or people of color, the less it pays....In other words, certain jobs pay less because they are held by women and people of color." Supporters thus appear to argue that differences in wages between men and women (or minorities) are not caused by intentional discrimination, or the fact that these workers are paid less because of the nature of the jobs they hold, but rather because certain jobs are held predominantly by women or minorities, employers systematically undervalue the job and thus "underpay" these workers.

The logic of this assertion is readily discredited. Critics of the wage gap theory note that the "77 percent" figure most frequently cited as evidence of wage discrimination derived by comparing the 2005 full-time (defined as working 35 hours per week or more) median annual earnings of women with men, as compiled by the Census Bureau. If the comparison is men and women who work 40 hours weekly, this data shows women's earning at 88 percent of men's. Moreover, these statistics do not necessarily take into account education, job title, responsibility, regional labor markets, work experience, occupation, and time in the work force. Critics of the "wage gap" theory note that when economic studies include these major determinants of income, rather than simple averages of all men and women's salaries, the pay gap shrinks considerably.

GAO (Government Accountability Office) has reached similar conclusions. In October 2003, GAO released a report entitled "Women's Earnings: Work Patterns Partially Explain Difference between Men's and Women's Earnings." GAO's report found that a number of factors are critical to resolving the issue of whether a "pay gap" exists, and notably explained that the agency could not concluded that the "wage gap" was simply a function of wage or sex discrimination. As GAO summarized (emphasis added):

"Of the many factors that account for differences in earnings between men and women, our model indicated that work patterns are key. *Specifically, women have fewer years of work experience, work fewer hours per year, are less likely to work a full-time schedule, and leave the labor force for longer periods of time than men. Other factors that account for earnings differences include industry, occupation, race, marital status, and job tenure.* When we account for differences between male and female work patterns as well as other key factors, women earned, on average, 80 percent of what men earned in 2000. While the difference fluctuated in each year we studied, there was a small but statistically significant decline in the earnings difference over the time period.

Even after accounting for key factors that affect earnings, our model could not explain all of the differences in earnings between men and women. Due to inherent limitations in the survey data an in statistical analysis, *we cannot determine whether this remaining difference is due to discrimination or other factors that may affect earnings. For example, some experts said that some women trade off career advancement or higher earnings for a job that offers flexibility to manage work and family responsibilities.*

In conclusion, while we were able to account for much of the difference in earnings between men and women, we were not able to explain the remaining earnings difference. It is difficult to evaluate this remaining portion without a full understanding of what contributes to this difference. *Specifically, an earnings difference that results from individuals' decisions about how to manage work and family responsibilities may not necessarily indicate a problem unless these decisions are not freely made.* On the other hand, an earnings difference may result from discrimination in the workplace or subtler discrimination about what types of career or job choices women can make. Nonetheless, it is difficult, and in some cases, may be impossible, to precisely measure and quantify individual decisions and possible discrimination. *Because these factors are not readily measurable, interpreting any remaining earnings difference is problematic."*

Given the flaws in its advocates' logic, and the absolute lack of definitive evidence that a "wage gap" counsels enactment of sweeping reforms to the Equal Pay Act and other federal laws, Committee Republicans question the premise upon which [Paycheck Fairness Act] H.R. 1338 is founded.

Michelle J. Budig

In her testimony before the United States Congressional Joint Economic Committee, Professor Michelle Budig, a sociologist at the University of Massachusetts at Amherst, summarized her research on pay equity in the workplace. Professor Budig argued that workplace reforms were needed to minimize the wage gap between men and women and to address the discrimination that mothers experience in the work place.

Michelle J. Budig "New Evidence on the Gender Pay Gap for Women and Mothers in Management" Testimony before the US Congressional Joint Economic Committee Hearing, September 28, 2010: p.1–10. (Excerpts: p.2, 4, 4–5, 6, 6–7)

Today I will testify that a significant portion of the persistent gender gap in earnings, among workers with equivalent qualifications and in similar jobs, is attributable to parenthood. Specifically, to the systematically lower earnings of mothers and higher earnings of fathers, among comparable workers. Thus, public policies that target the difficulties families face in balancing work and family responsibilities, as well as discrimination by employers by workers' parental status, may be the most effective at reducing the gender pay gap.

* * *

My research and others demonstrate that a significant portion of gender-based differences in employment, earnings, and experiences of discrimination are increasingly related to parenthood, and the greater struggles of mothers to balance careers and family demands.

* * *

In the GAO report, among the mothers who persist in management, their gender pay gap relative to fathers is far larger (ranging from 21% to 34%) than the gender pay gap among childless managers (17% to 24%).

The shrinking gender gap among young childless workers has captured national attention....Moreover, in multiple instances in this unencumbered group, women out-earn men....[T]hese women are also largely unmarried.

...Whereas childless women earn 94 cents of a childless man's dollar, mothers earn only 60 cents of a father's dollar.

* * *

The finding that having children reduces women's earnings, even among workers with comparable qualifications, experience, work hours, and jobs, is now well established in the social science literature.....All women experience reduced earnings for each additional child they have. This penalty ranges in size from -15% per child among low-wage workers to about 4% per child among high-wage workers.

That mothers work less and may accept lower earnings for more family-friendly jobs explains part of the penalty experienced by low-wage workers, and that mothers have less experience, due to interruptions for childbearing, explains a part of the penalty for high-wage workers.

But a significant motherhood penalty persists even in estimates that account for these differences, such that the size of the wage penalty after all factors are controlled is roughly 3% per child. This means we could expect the typical full-time female worker in 2009 to earn roughly $1,100 less per child in annual wages, all else equal.

* * *

What lies behind this motherhood penalty that is unexplained by measurable characteristics of workers and jobs? One factor may be employer discrimination against mothers. It is difficult to obtain data on discrimination and virtually impossible to match it to outcomes in large-scale national surveys. However, evidence from experimental and audit studies support arguments of employer discrimination against mothers in callbacks for job applications, hiring decisions, wage offer, and promotions. Stanford sociologist Shelley Correll's experimental research shows that, after reviewing resumes that differed only in noting parental status, subjects in an experiment systematically rated childless women and fathers significantly higher than mothers on competency, work commitment, promotability, and recommendations for hire. Most telling,...raters gave mothers the lowest wage offers, averaging $13,000 lower than wage offers for fathers.

* * *

The motherhood penalty compares women against women to see how children depress their wages. While it is known that fathers earn more than mothers, new research is highlighting the importance of fatherhood among men in enhancing their wages. A portion of fathers' higher earnings can be explained by the facts fathers tend to work more hours, have more experiences, and have higher ranking occupations, relative to childless men. But after we adjust for these differences, we still find a bonus for fatherhood, and one that increases with educational attainment. ...

Putting these sets of finding together, we see that parenthood exacerbates gender inequality in American workplaces. Mothers lose while fathers gain from parenthood, and these penalties and bonuses are found beyond the differences between parents and childless persons in terms of hours worked, job experiences, seniority, and a wide host of other relevant labor marker characteristics.

Pregnancy

General Electric v. Gilbert, 429 US 125 (1976)

Like many companies, General Electric Co. provided its workers with disability coverage for non-work related injuries and illnesses. General Electric's plan was designed to be financially viable. General Electric's plan excluded pregnancy from its coverage. When the exclusion was challenged by a group of female workers, General Electric argued that the financial viability of the disability plan would be undermined if all possible disabilities were covered, that men and women had equal coverage under the existing plan, and that the exclusion of pregnancy was not gender-based discrimination because all women were not affected.

After losing in the lower federal courts, General Electric Co. appealed to the United States Supreme Court. Two years earlier, a Court majority had ruled that the exclusion of pregnancy coverage from an insurance plan of the state of California did not violate the Fourteenth Amendment's Equal Protection Clause.[2] In *General Electric v. Gilbert*, the Court had to determine whether a similar policy by a private employer violated Title VII of the Civil Rights Act of 1964.

Justice William Rehnquist wrote the Court's opinion for five of his colleague.

GENERAL ELECTRIC CO. v. GILBERT ET AL.

SUPREME COURT OF THE UNITED STATES

429 U.S. 125; 97 S. Ct. 401; 50 L. Ed. 2d 343; 1976 U.S. LEXIS 178

December 7, 1976*

OPINION

MR. JUSTICE WILLIAM REHNQUIST delivered the opinion of the Court.

* * *

There is no ... showing in this case ... that the exclusion of pregnancy benefits is a mere "pretex[t] designed to effect an invidious discrimination against the members of one sex or the other."].... As we noted in that opinion, a distinction which on its face is not sex related might nonetheless violate the Equal Protection Clause if it were in fact a subterfuge to accomplish a forbidden discrimination. But we have here no question of excluding a disease or disability comparable in all other respects to covered diseases or disabilities and yet confined to the members of one race or sex. Pregnancy is, of course, confined to women, but it is in other ways significantly different from the typical covered disease or disability. The District Court found that it is not a "disease" at all, and is often a voluntarily undertaken and desired condition, 375 F. Supp., at 375, 377. We do not therefore infer that the exclusion of pregnancy disability benefits from petitioner's plan is a simple pretext for discriminating against women. ...

* * *

...[W]e start from the indisputable baseline that "[t]he fiscal and actuarial benefits of the program... accrue to members of both sexes," 417 U.S., at 497 n. 20. We need not disturb the findings of the District Court to note that neither is there a finding, nor was there any evidence which would support a finding, that the financial benefits of the Plan "worked to discriminate against any definable group or class in terms of the aggregate risk protection derived by that group or class from the program," id., at 496. The Plan, in effect (and for all that appears), is nothing more than an insurance package, which covers some risks, but excludes others, see id., at 494, 496–7.[16] The "package" going to relevant identifiable groups we are presently concerned with – General Electric's [***356] male and female employees – covers exactly the same categories of risk, and is facially nondiscriminatory in the sense that "[t]here is no risk from which men are protected and women are not. Likewise, there is no risk from which women are protected and men are not." Id., at 496–7. As there is no proof that the package is in fact worth more to men than to women, it is impossible to find any gender-based discriminatory effect in this scheme simply because women disabled as a result of pregnancy do not receive benefits; that is to say, gender-based discrimination does not result simply because an employer's disability-benefits plan is less [*139] than all-inclusive.[17] [**410] For all that appears, pregnancy-related disabilities constitute an additional risk, unique to women, and the failure to compensate them for this risk does not destroy the presumed parity of the benefits, accruing to men and women alike, which results from the facially evenhanded inclusion of risks. To hold otherwise would endanger the commonsense notion that an employer who has no disability benefits program at all does not violate Title VII even though the "underinclusion" of risks impacts, as a result [*140] of pregnancy-related disabilities, more heavily upon one gender than upon the other.[18] Just as there is no facial [***357] genderbased discrimination in that case, so, too, there is none here.

* * *

We therefore agree with petitioner that its disability-benefits plan does not violate Title VII because of its failure [*146] to cover pregnancy-related disabilities. The judgment of the Court of Appeals is

Reversed.

General Electric v. Gilbert, 429 US 125 (1976)

Justice Brennan disagreed with the majority decision. His dissent is excerpted below.

GENERAL ELECTRIC CO. v. GILBERT ET AL.

SUPREME COURT OF THE UNITED STATES

429 U.S. 125; 97 S. Ct. 401; 50 L. Ed. 2d 343; 1976 U.S. LEXIS 178

December 7, 1976*

DISSENT: MR. JUSTICE WILLIAM BRENNAN, with whom MR. JUSTICE MARSHALL concurs, dissenting.

The Court holds today that without violating Title VII of the Civil Rights Act of 1964, 42 U.S.C. § 2000e et seq., a private employer [***361] may adopt a disability plan that compensates employees for all temporary disabilities except one affecting exclusively women, pregnancy. I respectfully dissent....

* * *

II

* * *

Plainly then, ...[t]he Court, ..., proceeds to a discussion of purported neutral criteria that suffice to explain the lone exclusion of pregnancy from the program. The Court argues that pregnancy is not "comparable" to other disabilities since it is a "voluntary" condition rather than a "disease." Ibid. The fallacy of this argument is that even if "non-voluntariness" and "disease" are to be construed as the operational criteria for inclusion of a disability in General Electric's program, application of these criteria is inconsistent with the Court's gender-neutral interpretation of the company's policy.

For example, the characterization of pregnancy as "voluntary"[3] is not a persuasive factor, for as the Court of Appeals correctly noted, "other than for childbirth disability, [General [***364] Electric] had never construed its plan as eliminating all so-called 'voluntary' disabilities," including sport injuries, attempted suicides, venereal disease, disabilities incurred in the commission of a crime or during a fight, and elective cosmetic surgery. 519 F. 2d, at 665. Similarly, the label "disease" rather than "disability" cannot be deemed determinative since General [**416] Electric's pregnancy disqualification also excludes the 10% of pregnancies that end in debilitating miscarriages, 375 F. Supp., at 377, the 10% of cases where pregnancies are complicated by "diseases" in the intuitive sense of the word, ibid., and cases where women recovering from childbirth are stricken by severe diseases unrelated to pregnancy.[4]

Moreover, even the Court's principal argument for the plan's supposed gender neutrality cannot withstand analysis. The central analytical framework relied upon to demonstrate the absence of discrimination is the principle described in Geduldig: "There is no risk from which men are protected and women are not... [and] no risk from which women are protected and men are not." 417 U.S., at 496–7, quoted, ante, at 138. In fostering the impression that it is faced with a mere underinclusive assignment of risks in a gender-neutral fashion – that is, all other disabilities are insured irrespective of gender – the Court's analysis proves to be simplistic and misleading. For although all mutually contractible risks are covered irrespective of gender, but see n. 4 supra, [the plan also insures risks such as prostatectomies, vasectomies, and circumcisions that are specific to the reproductive system of men and for which there exist no female counterparts covered by the plan.] Again, pregnancy affords the only disability, sex-specific or otherwise, that is excluded from coverage. ...

* * *

III

* * *

General Electric's disability program has three divisible sets of effects. First, the plan covers all disabilities that mutually afflict both sexes. But see n. 4, supra. Second, the plan insures against all disabilities that are male-specific or have a predominant impact on males. Finally, all female-specific and female-impacted disabilities are covered, except for the most prevalent, pregnancy. The Court focuses on the first factor – the equal inclusion of mutual risks – and therefore understandably can identify no discriminatory effect arising from the plan. In contrast, the EEOC and plaintiffs rely upon the unequal exclusion manifested in effects two and three to pinpoint an adverse impact on women. However [**418] one defines the profile of risks protected by General Electric, the determinative question must be whether the social policies and aims to be furthered by Title VII and filtered through the phrase "to discriminate" contained in § 703(a)(1) fairly forbid an ultimate pattern of coverage that insures all risks except a commonplace one that is applicable to women but not to men.

* * *

These policy formulations are reasonable responses to the uniform testimony of governmental investigations which show that pregnancy exclusions built into disability programs both financially burden women workers and act to break down the continuity of the employment relationship, thereby exacerbating women's comparatively transient role in the labor force....

...A realistic understanding [**420] of [***369] conditions found in today's labor environment warrants taking pregnancy into account in fashioning disability policies. Unlike the hypothetical situations conjectured by the Court, ante, at 139–40, and n. 17, contemporary disability [*160] programs are not creatures of a social or cultural vacuum devoid of stereotypes and signals concerning the pregnant woman employee. Indeed, no one seriously contends that General Electric or other companies actually conceptualized or developed their comprehensive insurance programs disability-by-disability in a strictly sex-neutral fashion.[10] Instead, the company has devised a policy that, but for pregnancy, offers protection for all risks, even those that are "unique to" men or heavily male dominated. In light of this social experience, the history of General Electric's employment practices, the otherwise all-inclusive design of its disability program, and the burdened role of the contemporary working woman, the EEOC's construction of sex discrimination under § 703(a)(1) is fully consonant with the ultimate objective of Title VII, "to assure equality of employment opportunities and to eliminate those discriminatory practices and devices which have fostered [sexually] stratified job environments to the disadvantage of [women]." McDonnell Douglas Corp. v.. Green, 411 U.S., at 800.

I would affirm the judgment of the Court of Appeals.

Hall v. Nalco Co., 2006 US Dist. LEXIS 68482 (ND Ill.2006)

The PDA (Pregnancy Discrimination Act) covers pregnancy, childbirth and "related medical conditions". Is infertility, which conceivably may affect men and women, covered as a "related medical condition" under PDA? The principal issue in *Hall v. Nalco Co.* is whether a female worker who has taken a number of days away from work to pursue infertility treatments protected from termination or other employment sanction by the PDA.

Cheryl Hall's request for a leave of absence to undergo in vitro fertilization treatments was granted. She was away from her job as a sales secretary from March 24, 2003 to April 21, 2003. Because these treatments were unsuccessful, Hall asked for another leave for a second round on fertility treatments in July. During the time of her leave, Nalco Co. underwent a significant reorganization that led to the merger of 2 offices and the elimination of 1 of 2 sales secretary positions. Hall asked about the status of her leave application in August. In responding to her request, Hall's supervisor informed her that she would be terminated effective the end of August. Hall assumed that she was going to be fired because of her ongoing fertility treatment, and she sued Nalco Co., citing the PDA.

The official reason Nalco Co. gave for Hall's termination was "absenteeism." The company claimed that she had "missed a lot of work due to health" and that her termination "was in [her] best interest due to [her] health condition." The secretary who kept her job was a woman who apparently was incapable of becoming pregnant.

The District Court ruled that Hall was not protected by the PDA because the Act did not cover fertility treatments.

CHERYL HALL, Plaintiff, v. NALCO COMPANY, F/BA ONDEO NALCO COMPANY, A Delaware corporation, Defendant.

UNITED STATES DISTRICT COURT FOR THE NORTHERN DISTRICT OF ILLINOIS, EASTERN DIVISION

2006 U.S. Dist. LEXIS 68482

September 12, 2006, Decided

JUDGES: JUDGE DAVID H. COAR, United States District Judge.

OPINION

* * *

III. ANALYSIS

The Plaintiff's discrimination claim is pursuant to Title VII of the Civil Rights Act of 1964, 42 U.S.C. § 2000e-2, as amended by the Pregnancy

Discrimination Act (PDA), 42 U.S.C. § 2000e(k). Title VII requires the plaintiff to show that the employer would not have taken the alleged adverse employment action against the plaintiff but for plaintiff's membership in a protected class. *Cerutti v. BASF Corp.*, 349 F.3d 1055, 1060, 1061 n.4 (7th Cir. 2003). The burden lies with the plaintiff to demonstrate that she is within the protected class. *Id.*

Title VII discrimination [*5] "on the basis of sex" was amended by the PDA to include discrimination "because of or on the basis of pregnancy, childbirth, or related medical conditions." 42 U.S.C. § 2000e(k) (1994). Plaintiff states that she "is a member of a protected class, female with a pregnancy related condition, infertility." (Comal. P 21). At issue is whether a reasonable jury could find that infertility is included in the meaning of the phrase "related medical conditions" of the PDA, such that the Plaintiff falls within the protected class of those discriminated against on the basis of sex.

The PDA protects women from pregnancy discrimination, where the discriminatory condition is "unique to women." *Saks v. Franklin Covey Co.*, 316 F.3d 337, 346 (2d Cir. 2003). Only when there is some disparity in treatment on account of an individual's sex does Title VII protection become properly invoked. Infertility is a "medical condition that afflicts men and women with equal frequency." *Id.* The Second Circuit has found that "including infertility within the PDA's protection as a 'related medical condition' would result in the anomaly of defining a class that simultaneously [*6] includes equal numbers of both sexes and yet is somehow vulnerable to sex discrimination." *Id.* This is "incompatible with the PDA's purpose of clarifying the definition of 'because of sex'." *Id.* See also *Int'l Union, United Auto., etc. v. Johnson Controls*, 499 U.S. 187, 198, 111 S. Ct. 1196, 113 L. Ed. 2d 158 (U.S. 1991). Further, neither the legislative history nor the EEOC guidelines reference infertility treatments or suggest that infertility should fall within the scope of the PDA. *Krauel v. Iowa Methodist Medical Ctr.*, 95 F.3d 674, 679–80 (8th Cir. 1996). Thus, "infertility standing alone does not fall within the meaning of the phrase 'related medical conditions' under the PDA." *Saks v. Franklin Covey Co.*, 316 F.3d 337, 346 (2d Cir. 2003); *Krauel v. Iowa Methodist Medical Ctr.*, 95 F.3d 674, 679–80 (8th Cir. 1996)....

... The Plaintiff alleges that she was terminated because she was undergoing infertility treatments. As stated above, infertility alone does not fall within "related medical conditions" of the PDA, and seeking infertility treatment does not give rise to grounds for sex discrimination. The fact that the Plaintiff happens to be a woman in the present case does not qualify her for protection under Title VII. Thus, the plaintiff does not fall within a protected class.

Summary judgment for the defendant is appropriate on the grounds that no reasonable jury could find that the Plaintiff falls within the protected class of those discriminated against on the basis of sex.

IV. CONCLUSION

For the foregoing reasons, summary judgment is granted to the Defendant. All other motions are moot and terminated. This case is closed.

Hall v. Nalco Co., 534 F 3d 644 (7th Cir. 2008)

The 7th Circuit argued that Ms. Hall's infertility treatments were covered under PDA. The Court's reasoning is presented below.

CHERYL HALL, Plaintiff-Appellant, v. NALCO COMPANY, formerly known as ONDEO NALCO COMPANY, a Delaware corporation, Defendant-Appellee.

UNITED STATES COURT OF APPEALS FOR THE SEVENTH CIRCUIT

534 F.3d 644; 2008 U.S. App. LEXIS 15106

July 16, 2008, Decided

OPINION: CIRCUIT COURT JUDGE SYKES

[*645] SYKES, *Circuit Judge.* Cheryl Hall maintains she was fired by Nalco Company for taking time off from work to undergo in vitro fertilization after being diagnosed with infertility. She filed this suit under Title VII of the Civil Rights Act of 1964, as amended by the Pregnancy Discrimination Act ("PDA"), alleging her termination constituted discrimination on the basis of sex. Without reaching the merits of her claim, the district court granted summary judgment for Nalco on the ground that Hall could not prove sex discrimination because infertility is a gender-neutral condition.

We reverse. [HN1] The focus of any Title VII sex-discrimination claim is whether the employer treated the employee differently because of the employee's sex. The PDA amended Title [**2] VII to provide that discrimination "because of" sex includes discrimination "because of or on the basis of pregnancy, childbirth, or related medical conditions." 42 U.S.C. § 2000e(k). Although infertility affects both men and women, Hall claims she was terminated for undergoing a medical procedure--a particular form of surgical impregnation--performed only on women on account of their childbearing capacity. Because adverse employment actions taken on account of childbearing capacity affect only women, Hall has stated a cognizable sex-discrimination claim under the language of the PDA.

* * *

II. Discussion

* * *

The PDA was enacted to overrule the Supreme Court's decision in *General Electric Co. v. Gilbert,* 429 U.S. 125, 97 S. Ct. 401, 50 L. Ed. 2d 343 (1976), which had held that excluding pregnancy from a list of nonoccupational disabilities covered by an employer's disability [**7] benefits plan did not amount to discrimination on the basis of sex. *See Newport News Shipbuilding & Dry Dock Co. v. EEOC,* 462 U.S. 669, 676–8, 103 S. Ct. 2622, 77 L. Ed. 2d 89 (1983).

[HN6] The PDA created no new rights or remedies, but clarified the scope of Title VII by recognizing certain inherently gender-specific characteristics that may not form the basis for disparate treatment of employees. *Id.* at 678–9. "[T]he simple test" in any Title VII sex-discrimination claim is whether the employer action in question treats an employee "in a manner which but for that person's sex would be different." *City of L.A., Dep't of Water & Power v. Manhart,* 435 U.S. 702, 711, 98 S. Ct. 1370, 55 L. Ed. 2d 657 (1978). The enactment of the PDA did not change this basic approach. *Newport News,* 462 U.S. at 683–5. [HN7] The PDA "made clear that, for all Title VII purposes, discrimination based on a woman's pregnancy is, on its face, discrimination because of her sex." *Id.* at 684. The same is true for disparate treatment based on childbirth and medical conditions related to pregnancy or childbirth. *See* 42 U.S.C. § 2000e(k) (discrimination "because of sex" includes discrimination "because of or on the basis of pregnancy, childbirth, or related medical conditions").

The district [**8] court concluded that Hall's allegations do not state a Title VII claim because infertility is a gender-neutral condition entitled to no protection under the language of the PDA. In reaching this conclusion, the court relied primarily on two cases from other circuits holding that the PDA does not require employer insurance policies to cover infertility treatment so long as both male and female treatments are excluded.

* * *

Nalco's conduct, viewed in the light most favorable to Hall, suffers from the same defect as the policy in *Johnson Controls*. Employees terminated for taking time off to undergo IVF--just like those terminated for taking time off to give birth or [*649] receive other pregnancy-related care--will always be women. This is necessarily so; IVF is one of several assisted reproductive technologies that involves a surgical impregnation procedure. *See The Merck Manual of Medical Information, supra* at 1418–19; *Mayo Clinic Family Health Book, supra* at 1069–70. Thus, contrary to the district court's conclusion, Hall was terminated not for the gender-neutral condition of infertility, but rather for the gender-specific quality of childbearing capacity.

Because [HN10] adverse employment action based on childbearing capacity will always result in "treatment of a person in a manner which but for that person's sex would be different," *Manhart*, 435 U.S. at 711, Hall's allegations present a cognizable claim of sex discrimination under Title [**13] VII.[3..]

* * *

REVERSED [**15] AND REMANDED.

Reeves v. Swift Transportation Co., 446 F 3d 637 (6th Cir. 2006)

This case involves the application of the PDA in the workplace. It asks whether the federal statute requires employers to provide pregnant workers with special accommodation or special protection when their pregnancy interferes with the execution of their job tasks. The PDA was enacted to insure that pregnancy would not limit the employment opportunities for women. Pregnancy is a physical condition that may prevent women from engaging in physically demanding jobs. Two contrasting arguments can be made. Providing pregnant workers with special duties may be viewed as a sex discrimination against men who will never receive similar dispensation. Conversely, terminating pregnant workers because their pregnancy (their health and health of their child) keeps from engaging in physically demanding work arguably is a form of pregnancy-based discrimination and restricts employment opportunities available to women.

Swift Transportation Co. allows workers injured on the job to engage in light duty work in lieu of the heavy lifting that was normally required of its workers. Reeves requested light duty work when her physician told her that heavy lifting during her pregnancy would be harmful to her and her unborn child. Her request was denied, and Reeves was subsequently fired. Reeves sued Swift Transportation Co. on the ground that its refusal to provide her with light duty work violated PDA.

The 6th Circuit Court of Appeals decision is excerpted below.

AMANDA REEVES, v. Plaintiff-Appellant, SWIFT TRANSPORTATION COMPANY, INC., also known as Swift Transportation Corporation, Defendant-Appellee.

UNITED STATES COURT OF APPEALS FOR THE SIXTH CIRCUIT

06a0163p.06; 446 F.3d 637; 2006 U.S. App. LEXIS 12046

May 16, 2006, Decided

OPINION BY: CIRCUIT JUDGE ROGERS

OPINION

[*638] [***1] ROGERS, Circuit Judge. This is an action for pregnancy discrimination, brought under 42 U.S.C. § 2000e(k), on a theory of disparate treatment. The plaintiff, Amanda Reeves, formerly worked for the defendant-employer as an over-the-road truck driver. She claims that her former employer, Swift Transportation Company, Inc., unlawfully terminated her when she became pregnant. Swift terminated Reeves pursuant to a pregnancy-blind policy denying light-duty work to employees who could not perform heavy lifting and also were not injured on the job....

* * *

At all times relevant to this lawsuit, Swift maintained a policy of providing light-duty work only to employees on workers' compensation leave, i.e., employees who had sustained on-the-job injuries. Such injured employees receive light-duty assignments that accommodate their injuries and Swift's work needs. Light-duty assignments include "basic office work such as answering phones for recruiting, entering orders, filing, handing out towels and the like."

Reeves stated in her deposition that she never sustained a job-related injury. She also stated that, to her knowledge, no Swift employee had been given a light work assignment who was not on workers' compensation leave. As of the time of Sally Redwine's deposition in 2004, all employees injured on the job who could not perform heavy lifting received [**5] light work if they sought it. Swift maintains that if Reeves had been injured on the job, she would have received light work through the workers' compensation system, her pregnant condition notwithstanding. Swift has made no exceptions to its light-duty policy.

* * *

Reeves says that the policy's terms are themselves discriminatory because they provide light-duty [**10] work to employees injured on the job who can perform no heavy lifting but not to pregnancy employees who can do no heavy lifting. This part of the policy, Reeves argues, violates the Act's provision that [HN4] pregnant employees "shall be treated the same for all employment-related purposes . . . as other persons not so affected but similar in their ability or inability to work . . . ." 42 U.S.C. § 2000e(k). A person injured on the job with the same work abilities as Reeves, the argument goes, receives light duty and therefore has been treated better than Reeves. This better treatment, in Reeves' view, violates the Act's plain language.

But Swift's policy cannot be viewed as direct evidence of discrimination because the Act merely requires employers to "ignore" employee pregnancies. *See Spivey v. Beverly Enters* ., 196 F.3d 1309, 1313 (11th Cir. 1999); *Urbano v. Cont'l Airlines*, 138 F.3d 204, 206 (5th Cir. 1998) ("An employer is obliged to ignore a woman's pregnancy . . ."); *Troupe v. May Dep't Stores Co.*, 20 F.3d 734, 738 (7th Cir. 1994).

Swift's light-duty policy is indisputably pregnancy-blind. It simply does [**11] not grant or deny light work on the basis of pregnancy, childbirth, or related medical conditions. It makes this determination on the nonpregnancy-related basis of whether there has been a work-related injury or condition. [HN5] Pregnancy-blind policies of course can be tools of discrimination. But challenging them as tools of discrimination requires evidence and inference beyond such policies' express terms.

Swift's pregnancy-blind policy, therefore, cannot serve as direct evidence of Swift's alleged discrimination against Reeves.

Equal Employment Opportunity Commission v. Horizon/CMS Healthcare Corporations, 220 F. 3d 1184 (10th Cir. 2000)

This case presents an alternative analysis in determining whether an employer's refusal to provide light duty work to pregnant workers violates the Pregnancy Discrimination Act. This case involves a suit brought by female workers who were denied light work when they became pregnant. The decision by the 10th Circuit Court illustrates how courts scrutinize employment policies and practices to determine whether pregnant workers are treated the same as other workers. It contrasts with the approach taken by the Sixth Circuit Court in *Reeves v. Swift Transportation Co.* (6th Cir.2006). The facts of this case are included in the excerpt.

EQUAL EMPLOYMENT OPPORTUNITY COMMISSION, Plaintiff-Appellant, v. HORIZON/CMS HEALTHCARE CORPORATION, Defendant-Appellee.

UNITED STATES COURT OF APPEALS FOR THE TENTH CIRCUIT

OPINION BY: CIRCUIT COURT JUDGE MURPHY

[*1188] .

Plaintiff-Appellant, the Equal Employment Opportunity Commission (the "Commission"), brought a public enforcement [*1189] action against Defendant, Horizon/CMS Healthcare Corporation. Seeking relief for four charging parties (the "Charging [**2] Parties") under the Pregnancy Discrimination Act, 42 U.S.C. § 2000e(k), the Commission filed a complaint with the United States District Court for the District of New Mexico alleging Defendant had unlawfully denied the Charging Parties and a group of similarly-situated pregnant employees the opportunity to work modified duty when they became temporarily unable to perform heavy lifting due to their pregnancies. Defendant purportedly based its decision on a company policy allowing modified duty only for those employees injured on the job.

* * *

I. BACKGROUND

A. Facts

The following facts are undisputed or, because the Commission is the party opposing summary judgment, construed in the Commission's favor. *See Curtis v. Oklahoma City Pub. Schs. Bd. of Educ.*, 147 F.3d 1200, 1214 (10th Cir. 1998). During the time period relevant to this lawsuit, Defendant owned and operated twenty-six, long-term care facilities in the state of New Mexico. The Charging Parties are former employees of Defendant. Three of the Charging Parties held the position of Certified Nursing Assistant ("CNA"). The job description for the position of CNA contained a requirement [**4] that the CNA be able to lift up to seventy-five pounds. The fourth Charging Party worked as an Activity Assistant. All four Charging Parties became pregnant during the term of their employment with Defendant. As a result of their pregnancies, the Charging Parties were placed under work restrictions by their respective physicians. The work restrictions included various limitations on the amount each Charging Party was allowed to lift. The work restrictions arose from the Charging Parties' pregnancies and not from any injury sustained by a Charging Party at work. Each Charging Party could have performed all of her job duties with the exception of the heavy-lifting.

Defendant had instituted and maintained a policy pursuant to which it allowed employees to work modified-duty positions consistent with any work restrictions imposed by the employee's physician (the "Modified Duty Policy" or the "Policy"). The terms of the Modified Duty Policy expressly limited its availability to those employees who had sustained "a work-related injury while working for Horizon Healthcare Corporation."[2] Pursuant to the terms of the Policy, Defendant had provided modified-duty assignments to employees who [**5] had suffered work-related injuries. Each Charging Party, however, applied for and was denied a modified-duty assignment. Because their work restrictions prevented them from performing all [*1190] of their job duties, the Charging Parties were terminated, laid off, or placed on an unpaid leave of absence by Defendant.

* * *

Unexplained or irrational differences in Defendant's treatment of pregnant and non-pregnant employees do not establish discrimination as a matter of law. Nevertheless, differential treatment of similarly-situated employees *may* support a finding of pretext.[11] *See McDonnell Douglas*, 411 U.S. at 804.

The Commission has also presented evidence that Defendant refused to provide modified-duty assignments to pregnant employees who were injured on the job during their pregnancies. The Commission contends that this evidence demonstrates an unlawful discriminatory bias against pregnant employees in Defendant's allocation of modified-duty assignments. [**38] The Commission's evidence on this point consists of affidavits from two pregnant employees who claim they were denied modified-duty assignments although they had suffered work-related injuries during their pregnancies. The Commission claims that a jury could conclude from this evidence that the real purpose behind the distinction made in the Modified Duty Policy between employees injured on the job and those injured off the job was not to limit workers' compensation costs but to unlawfully discriminate against pregnant workers.

The Commission then presented evidence which it claims shows that Defendant harbored a bias against employees who became pregnant. The Commission's evidence includes statements and comments made by managers employed by Defendant who were responsible for the implementation of the Modified Duty Policy.[12] When one of the Charging Parties informed her supervisor that she was pregnant and inquired into the availability of modified duty, she was told "[we] don't have any light duty for pregnant women." [*1200] Another Charging Party testified that she experienced a similar reaction when she informed her supervisor of her pregnancy and was told that there is no modified-duty [**39] work for "pregnant people." One affiant, who worked as a CNA, testified that when she discussed her pregnancy with a registered nurse employed by Defendant, she was told that she "should not have taken the job if [she] was going to get pregnant." Another affiant testified that at one point during her pregnancy, a supervisor told her that she was "too big to be working" and removed her from the schedule. After a careful review of the entire record, we conclude that these comments, read in context and construed in the light most favorable to the Commission, are not sufficient by themselves to support a finding of pretext.

[**40] None of the admissible, relevant evidence presented by the Commission, standing alone, is sufficient to raise a genuine issue of material fact on pretext. The Commission's proffered evidence viewed in the aggregate, however, is sufficient to raise a genuine doubt about Defendant's motivation for making a distinction in the Modified Duty Policy between employees injured on the job and those injured off the job. From the Commission's evidence, considered in the aggregate and construed in the light most favorable to the Commission, a reasonable jury could conclude that Defendant's proffered explanation for the distinction is pretextual. Thus, we hold that the Commission has produced sufficient evidence to preclude the entry of summary judgment in this case.

III. CONCLUSION

This court concludes that the Commission has presented a prima facie case of pregnancy discrimination and presented sufficient evidence for a jury to conclude Defendant's reason for denying modified duty to the Charging Parties was pretextual. The grant of summary judgment by the district court in favor of Defendant is **reversed** and this case is **remanded** to the district court for further proceedings [**41] consistent with this opinion.

Wallace v. Pyro Mining Co., 789 F.Supp. 867 (WD Ky. 1990)

The issue in *Wallace v. Pyro Mining Co.* is whether the PDA covers breast-feeding. This case arose when Wallace asked her employer Pyro Mining Co. to extend her pregnancy leave so she could engage in breast feeding for her baby who was refusing to take a bottle. Her employer denied her request because it did not have a policy of allowing personal leave or pregnancy leave for breast feeding. Wallace argued that breastfeeding was a "related medical condition" that should be covered under the Pregnancy Discrimination Act.

The United States District Court in Kentucky had to determine whether Wallace's interpretation of the PDA was correct. Its decision is excerpted below.

MARTHA R. WALLACE, PLAINTIFF, v. PYRO MINING COMPANY, DEFENDANT

UNITED STATES DISTRICT COURT FOR THE WESTERN DISTRICT OF KENTUCKY, AT OWENSBORO

789 F. Supp. 867; 1990 U.S. Dist. LEXIS 19935;

August 27, 1990, Decided

OPINION BY: JUDGE CHARLES R. SIMPSON III

OPINION

[*868] *MEMORANDUM OPINION AND ORDER* 833 words

* * *

Plaintiff contends that Pyro's refusal to extend her leave of absence constitutes discrimination on the basis of sex, pursuant to Title VII, 42 U.S.C. § 2000(e) *et seq.*

II

Although not specifically relied upon by plaintiff, it appears, from her memorandum opposing Pyro's summary judgment motion, that [**3] she intended to bring her claim under [HN1] 42 U.S.C. § 2000e-2(a)(1). That provision prohibits discrimination "against any individual with respect to . . . conditions of . . . employment . . . because of sex. . . ." Further, although she does not expressly say so, it appears that this is a "disparate impact" rather than a "disparate treatment" case. For example, in her opposing memorandum, plaintiff contends that "defendant's decision [to deny requests for personal leave for breast-feeding] has an *adverse impact* only on women and therefore is an employment decision based on sex." (Emphasis added)

...In *Gilbert*, the Court rejected the argument that it was impermissible sex discrimination for an employer to exclude pregnancy from those conditions for which disability benefits would be paid. Despite the fact that only women would be adversely affected by the exclusion, [**4] the Court found it "impossible to find any gender-based discriminatory effect" merely because the disability-benefits plan was less than all-inclusive. The Court reasoned that so long as men and women [*869] were treated the same for purposes of those benefits which the plan conferred, there was no actionable disparate impact claim under Title VII, even though a uniquely female condition, pregnancy, was excluded.

We see no significant difference between the situation in *Gilbert* and the case here. Pyro's decision does not deny anyone personal leave on the basis of sex -- it merely removes one situation, breast-feeding, from those for which personal leave will be granted. While breast-feeding, like pregnancy, is a uniquely female attribute, excluding breast-feeding from those circumstances for which Pyro will grant personal leave is not impermissible gender-based discrimination....

...The Pregnancy Discrimination Act ...expanded the definition of the Title VII phrases "because of sex" and "on the basis of sex" to include "because of or on the basis of pregnancy, childbirth or related medical conditions." Pursuant to the Act, women "affected by pregnancy, childbirth or related medical conditions shall be treated the same . . . as other persons not so affected but similar in their ability or inability to work. . . ." When read together with § 2000e-2(a)(1), the Pregnancy Discrimination Act makes it illegal to discriminate "against any individual with respect to . . . conditions of . . . employment . . . because of or on the basis of pregnancy, childbirth or related medical [**6] conditions."

Nothing in plaintiff's case states a claim under Title VII as amended by the Pregnancy Discrimination Act. Pyro's decision to deny her request for additional leave, assuming that such leave is a "condition of employment," was not because of her "pregnancy, childbirth or related medical conditions." It was based instead on Pyro's policy that breast-feeding would not be grounds for granting personal leave. This circumstance simply does not entitle plaintiff to the protections of the Pregnancy Discrimination Act.

Such a conclusion is mandated by the plain language of the act, and by its legislative history. While it may be that breast-feeding and weaning are natural concomitants of pregnancy and childbirth, they are not "medical conditions" related thereto. Admittedly, the act does not define what constitute "related medical conditions." However, the substantive references to "related medical conditions" within that legislative history are all in the context of the extent to which female employees can be denied medical benefits, such as sick leave and health insurance coverage, arising from pregnancy and childbirth. ...We believe these factors indicate Congress' intent that "related medical conditions" be limited to incapacitating conditions for which medical care or treatment is usual and normal. Neither breast-feeding and weaning, nor difficulties arising therefrom, constitute such conditions.

...Nothing in the Pregnancy Discrimination Act, or Title VII, obliges employers to accommodate the child-care concerns of breast-feeding female workers by providing additional breast-feeding leave not available to male workers. If Congress had wanted these sorts of child-care concerns to [**8] be covered by Title VII or the Pregnancy Discrimination Act, it could have included them in the plain language of the statutes. It did not. It is not the province of this court to add to the legislation by judicial fiat.

...Neither Title VII, nor the Pregnancy Discrimination Act intended to make it illegal for an employer to deny personal leave to a female worker who requests it to accommodate child-care concerns.

Christine Moore

In her law review, scholar Christine Moore provides a strong critique of the 6th Circuit Court's interpretation of the Pregnancy Discrimination Act in the case of *Wallace v. Pryo Mining Company* (6th Cir. 1990).

Christine Moore. "The PDA Fails to Deliver: Why Nalco and Wallace Cannot Coexist, and a New Standard for Defining 'Related Medical Condition'" *University of San Francisco Law Review* 44 (2010): 683–705. (Excerpts: p.698–701)

[*683]

* * *

The PDA used "the broad phrase 'women affected by pregnancy, childbirth and related medical conditions'" to extend it to "the whole range of matters concerning the child-bearing process."[n74] There is no doubt that Congress wanted the language interpreted broadly,[n75] and interpreting the term "medical" narrowly renders many matters concerning the childbearing process, like breastfeeding, improperly unprotected. A narrow interpretation of the term "medical" would contravene Congress's intended broad interpretation and unreasonably limit the "childbearing capacity" standard. A new definition of "medical" is needed to join the childbearing capacity standard in order to broaden the range of conditions covered and therefore comport with Congress's intentions.

Courts should adopt the broader "health and well-being" interpretation of "medical." Using the childbearing capacity standard [*699] alone to determine a related medical condition under the PDA led to the Wallace court's confusion regarding conditions that may be clearly "related" to childbearing capacity but are not overtly medical. The Wallace court failed to recognize Congress's intent to cover a "whole range of matters concerning the child-bearing process,"[n76] and a clarified definition of "medical," as encompassed in this new standard, would provide much needed guidance. Courts should therefore use the health and well-being definition of medical in order to comport with Congress's intent to make the PDA cover a range of pregnancy-related conditions.

B. Wallace's Definition of "Medical" Misinterprets the Intent of the PDA

The Wallace court held that breastfeeding is not a related medical condition under the PDA because it is not an "incapacitating condition for which medical care or treatment is usual and normal."[n77] Plaintiff Martha Wallace was employed by Pyro Mining Company as an accounting clerk and became pregnant in 1986.[n78] She took approximately one month of disability leave at the end of her pregnancy due to complications, and then requested an additional six-week leave of absence after her maternity leave because she had not yet weaned her child from breastfeeding.[n79] Wallace was informed before she was supposed to return to work that this leave would not be granted and failure to return would result in her termination.[n80] When Wallace did not return to work, she was terminated and replaced with another hire.[n81]

The Wallace court indicated that Congress wanted the term "related medical conditions" to cover disabilities caused by pregnancy,[n82] and therefore that related medical conditions should be limited to those that are "incapacitating ... [and] for which medical care or treatment is usual and normal."[n83] However, the Wallace court misinterprets Congress's intent in enacting the PDA. First, the court mistakenly believes that because Congress expressed a desire to treat [*700] disabilities caused by pregnancy, it intended to cover only those conditions that are "incapacitating." The court failed to recognize that pregnancy is not, in and of itself, incapacitating. Pregnant women remain employed and continue working often until they actually go into labor. Further, the court's aforementioned reasoning seems to indicate that disabilities are incapacitating, and such an interpretation renders a plain reading of the rest of the PDA impossible.

The PDA requires employers to treat pregnant women as they would other temporarily disabled workers (i.e., by providing alternative work tasks and schedules). According to the court's reasoning, however, all of these "disabled" workers are "incapacitated" and simply unable to work.[n84] Such a reading is clearly not what Congress intended by alluding to "temporary disabilities."

Second, the Wallace court failed to recognize that the PDA has been extended to other conditions that are not incapacitating. The Wallace court cites a House of Representative's Report as evidence that Congress intended to cover pregnancy-related disabilities but fails to mention the section explaining that the PDA is intended to apply to women who are terminated for having abortions.[n85] Here it is clear that Congress intended the PDA to protect abortion as a related medical condition, and women who undergo abortions are not incapacitated. While they may be temporarily unable to work full days or perform certain tasks, much like women who may be breastfeeding, these women are not incapacitated and under constant medical supervision.

Third, the Wallace court does not recognize that the PDA's protection is broad and open-ended to account for flexibility and special situations.[n86] The same House Report cited by the court actually explains the intent behind the general language: "In using the broad phrase 'women affected by pregnancy, childbirth and related medical conditions,' the bill makes clear that its protection extends to the whole range of matters concerning the childbearing process."[n87] Nowhere does the Report mention that a condition must be incapacitating in order to be protected as a related medical condition. In fact, it shows that Congress intended to extend coverage to a "whole range of matters concerning the childbearing process."[n88]

[*701] The Wallace court thus misinterprets the language and intent of the PDA in formulating its incapacitation standard. The Wallace decision does indicate that "breast-feeding and weaning are natural concomitants of pregnancy and childbirth" but concludes that they are not "medical conditions" because they are not incapacitating.[n89] The court recognizes the natural connection between breastfeeding and pregnancy but is limited by its incapacitation standard and cannot extend protection to this "natural" part of pregnancy. The court's error in interpreting congressional intent is clear,....

Fetal Protection Policies

International Union, United Automobile, Aerospace and Agricultural Implement Workers of America v. Johnson Controls, 886 F.2d 871 (7th Cir. 1989)

This case involves Johnson Controls' fetal protection policy. Johnson Controls manufactures lead-based batteries. Some workers are exposed to lead during the manufacturing process. Citing scientific evidence linking exposure to lead by women to fetal damage, Johnson Controls prohibited women of childbearing age from working in jobs where lead exposure was possible. Only women who could demonstrate that they were unable to have children were eligible to work in these high paying jobs. Some female workers were voluntarily sterilized in order to have access to these jobs. Another group of female workers sued Johnson Controls on the grounds that its fetal protection policy discriminated on the basis of pregnancy and prevented women from deciding whether they wanted to work in these jobs. Johnson Controls argued that its policy was an attempt to balance the health of women, the health of children, and its business interests.

The 7th Circuit Court of Appeals ruled in favor of Johnson Controls. Its decision is excerpted here.

INTERNATIONAL UNION, UNITED AUTOMOBILE, AEROSPACE AND AGRICULTURAL IMPLEMENT WORKERS OF AMERICA, UAW, et al., Plaintiffs-Appellants, and LOCAL 322, ALLIED INDUSTRIAL WORKERS OF AMERICA, AFL-CIO, Intervening Plaintiff-Appellant, v. JOHNSON CONTROLS, INC., Defendant-Appellee

UNITED STATES COURT OF APPEALS FOR THE SEVENTH CIRCUIT

886 F.2d 871; 1989 U.S. App. LEXIS 14812

September 26, 1989, Decided

OPINION: CIRCUIT COURT JUDGE OPICOFFEY

[*874]

* * *

A. *Substantial Risk of Harm to the Unborn Child*

Both the UAW and Johnson Controls agree on appeal that the significant evidence of risks to the health of the fetus contained in the record establishes a *substantial* health risk to the unborn child. The UAW in its brief admits that "it is clear that . . . substantial risk of harm to the fetus . . . has been established." UAW Brief at 33. Similarly, Johnson states that "the evidence in the record on [substantial risk of harm to the fetus] is overwhelming." Johnson Controls Brief at 22. In light of the parties' agreement on the question of substantial risk of harm to the unborn child, this issue is not before this court on appeal.

Although the parties do not contest this question on appeal, the evidence in the record ... conclusively supports the accepted medical and scientific finding that lead creates a substantial risk of harm to unborn children. In order to present the risk of harm necessary to sustain a fetal protection policy "it is not necessary to prove the existence of a general consensus on the [question of risk of harm to the unborn child] within the qualified scientific community. It suffices to show that within that community there is so considerable a body of opinion that significant risk exists . . . that an informed employer could not responsibly [*889] fail to act on the assumption that this opinion might be the accurate one." *Olin*, 697 F.2d at 1191. The overwhelming medical and scientific research data demonstrating a substantial risk to the unborn child from lead exposure,..., approaches a "general consensus within the qualified scientific community," and certainly "suffices to show that within that community there is [a] considerable body of opinion that significant risk exists."[27] Accordingly, we are convinced that there is no genuine issue of material [**53] fact with respect to this component of Johnson Controls' business necessity defense.[28]

* * *

...Unlike the recorded evidence of a substantial risk of harm resulting to an unborn child from exposure to lead through the mother's [**56] blood stream and placenta, the evidence of risk to the unborn child resulting from exposure of the father to the lead levels currently present in Johnson Controls' battery manufacturing factories is, at best, speculative and unconvincing....The facts the UAW posits do not negate the conclusions that the harm lead exposure causes to the unborn child is "substantially confined to female employees."

his recognition of the physical differences between the human sexes creates a distinction between men and women that accords with our previous recognition that Title VII permits distinctions based upon the real sex-based differences between men and women, especially those related to child birth....Because scientific data available as of this date reflects that the risk of transmission of harm to unborn children is confined to fertile female employees, the sex-based distinction present in Johnson Controls' fetal protection policy is based upon real physical differences between men and women relating to childbearing capacity and is consistent with Title VII.

* * *

The record also demonstrates [**66] that viable alternatives to the fetal protection program were not presented to the court that would equally effectively further Johnson's legitimate interests. As detailed in Section I, *supra*, Johnson Controls itself considered various possible less discriminatory alternatives prior to its adoption of the current fetal protection policy in 1982. In considering these alternatives, Johnson realized that lead could not be eliminated as a battery component. Furthermore, technically and economically feasible alternatives in the manufacturing process are incapable of reducing lead exposure to acceptable levels for pregnant women.[31] Limitation of the exclusion from high lead positions to women actually pregnant or planning pregnancy [*893] was inadequate because lead exposure frequently takes place during the time period before the woman or her doctor determine her pregnancy. In addition, reduction of blood lead levels following removal of a pregnant female employee from lead exposure requires a significant period of time that can extend well into the pregnancy term....

* * *

[**69] V.

Having just held that the business necessity defense shields an employer from liability for sex discrimination under Title VII in a fetal protection policy involving the type of facts present herein, we are also convinced that Johnson Controls' fetal protection policy could be upheld under the bona fide occupational qualification defense.

...The bona fide occupational qualification defense, like other Title VII defenses, must be construed in a manner which gives meaningful and thoughtful consideration [**70] to the *interests of all those affected by a company's policy, in this case the employer, the employee and the unborn child*....

In the context of the Pregnancy Discrimination Act,[36] application of the bona fide occupational qualification defense requires a court to consider the special concerns which pregnancy poses. A proposed BFOQ relating [**71] to capacity for pregnancy (or actual pregnancy) will exclude fewer employees than a BFOQ excluding all women. The court must also consider the physical changes caused by pregnancy, i.e., the presence of the unborn child, in determining whether the employee's continuance in a particular employment assignment [*894] will endanger the health of her unborn child....

*   *   *

...At a broad level, Johnson's business, insofar as relevant to this case, is the manufacture of batteries.[37] Johnson's business is "unique" because it requires the use of lead, an extremely toxic substance that has been scientifically established to pose very serious dangers to young children and, in particular, to the offspring of female employees. In order to respond to the problems accompanying its unique battery manufacturing operation, Johnson Controls has properly made it part of its business to attempt to manufacture batteries in as safe a manner as possible. Furthermore, ..., Johnson has found it necessary to "innovate" to achieve its essential goal of manufacturing batteries safely through the adoption of a fetal protection policy that would address the health/safety problems related to its female employees significantly more effectively than the alternative policies it had considered.

*   *   *

..."[M]ore is at stake in this case . . . than an individual woman's decision to weigh and accept the risks of employment." *Id.* at 335. A female's decision to work in a high lead exposure job risks the intellectual and physical development of the baby she may carry. The status of women in America has changed both in the family and in the economic system. Since they have become a force in the workplace as well as in the home because of their desire to better the family's station in life, it would not be improbable that a female employee might somehow rationally discount this clear risk in her hope and belief that her infant would not be adversely affected from lead exposure. The unborn child has no opportunity to avoid this grave danger, but bears the definite risk of suffering permanent consequences. [**85] This situation is much like that involved in blood transfusion cases. There courts have held that individuals may choose for themselves whether to refuse to personally acquiesce in a blood transfusion that had been established as medically necessary, but that parents may not always rely upon parental rights or religious liberty rights to similarly refuse to consent to such a medically necessary transfusion for their minor children.[38] The risks to the unborn child from lead are also shared by society in the form of government financed programs to train or maintain a handicapped child in non-institutional or institutional environments and to provide the [*898] child with the training necessary to overcome the mental and physical harm attributable to lead exposure.[39] Thus, since "more is at stake" than the individual woman's decision to risk her own safety,[;].... "given the reasonable objectives of the employer, the very womanhood . . . of the employee undermines . . . her capacity to perform a job satisfactorily....

* * *

[**87] Against this substantive background, we hold that Johnson has carried its burden of demonstrating that its fetal protection plan is reasonably necessary to further industrial safety, a matter we have determined to be part of the essence of Johnson Controls' business. Initially, there can be no doubt that the exclusion of women who are actually pregnant from positions involving high levels of lead exposure sets forth a bona fide occupational qualification. As established in section II, *supra*, there is clear and unrefuted evidence in the record of a substantial and irreversible risk to the unborn child's mental development from lead exposure in the womb. This danger is "hardly a 'myth or purely habitually assumption.'" The convincing scientific evidence of this risk and the very serious consequences of this danger combine to make this health risk quite different from the concerns in *Muller v. Oregon*, 208 U.S. 412, 421–2, 52 L. Ed. 551, 28 S. Ct. 324 (1908), which we would currently characterize [**88] as stereotypical rather than real.

We are also of the opinion that Johnson Controls' well reasoned and scientifically documented decision to apply this policy to all fertile women employed in high lead exposure positions constitutes a bona fide occupational qualification. The evidence presented concerning the lingering effects of lead in a woman's body, combined with the magnitude of medical difficulties in detecting and diagnosing early pregnancy, lead us to agree with Johnson Controls that there exists a reasonable basis in fact to conclude that an extension of this policy to all fertile women is proper and reasonably necessary to further the industrial safety [*899] concern of preventing the unborn child's exposure to lead.

International Union, United Automobile, Aerospace and Agricultural Implement Workers of America v. Johnson Controls, 499 US 187 (1991)

The decision of the 7th Circuit Court of Appeals was appealed to the United States Supreme Court. Its decision is excerpted below.

INTERNATIONAL UNION, UNITED AUTOMOBILE, AEROSPACE & AGRICULTURAL IMPLEMENT WORKERS OF AMERICA, UAW, et al., PETITIONERS v. JOHNSON CONTROLS, INC.

SUPREME COURT OF THE UNITED STATES

499 U.S. 187; 111 S. Ct. 1196; 113 L. Ed. 2d 158; 1991 U.S. LEXIS 1715; 59 U.S.L.W. 4209

March 20, 1991, Decided

OPINION: JUSTICE HARRY BLACKMUN

[*190] [***168] [**1199] JUSTICE BLACKMUN delivered the opinion of the Court.

[***LEdHR1A] [1A]In this case we are concerned with an employer's gender-based fetal-protection policy. May an employer exclude a fertile female employee from certain jobs because of its concern for the health of the fetus the woman might conceive?

I

Respondent Johnson Controls, Inc., manufactures batteries. In the manufacturing process, the element lead is a primary ingredient. Occupational exposure to lead entails health risks, including the risk of harm to any fetus carried by a female employee.

* * *

III

The bias in Johnson Controls' policy is obvious. Fertile men, but not fertile women, are given a choice as to whether they wish to risk their reproductive health for a particular job. [HN1] Section 703(a) of the Civil Rights Act of 1964, 78 Stat. 255, as amended, 42 U. S. C. § 2000e-2(a), prohibits sex-based classifications in terms and conditions of employment, in hiring and discharging decisions, and in other employment decisions that adversely affect an employee's status.[2] Respondent's fetal-protection policy explicitly discriminates against women on the basis of their sex. The policy excludes women with childbearing capacity from lead-exposed jobs and so creates a facial classification based on gender.

* * *

...The [Court of Appeals]... assumed that because the asserted reason for the [***173] sex-based exclusion (protecting women's unconceived offspring) was ostensibly benign, the policy was not sex-based discrimination. That assumption, however, was incorrect.

[***LEdHR1B] [1B]First, Johnson Controls' policy classifies on the basis of gender and childbearing capacity, rather than fertility alone. Respondent does not seek to protect the unconceived children of all its employees. Despite evidence in the record about the debilitating effect of lead exposure on the male reproductive system, Johnson Controls is concerned only with the harms that may befall the unborn offspring of its female employees. ...Johnson Controls' policy is facially discriminatory because it requires only a female employee to produce proof that she is not capable of reproducing.

[***LEdHR1C] [1C] [***LEdHR4] [4]Our conclusion is bolstered by the [HN3] Pregnancy Discrimination Act (PDA), 42 U. S. C. § 2000e(k), in which Congress explicitly provided that, for purposes of Title VII, discrimination "'on the basis of sex'" includes discrimination "because [*199] of or on the basis of pregnancy, childbirth, or related medical conditions."[3] "The Pregnancy Discrimination Act has now made clear that, for all Title VII purposes, discrimination based on a woman's pregnancy is, on its face, discrimination because of her sex." *Newport News Shipbuilding & Dry Dock Co. v. EEOC*, 462 U.S. 669, 684 (1983). In its use of the words "capable of bearing children" in the 1982 policy statement as the criterion for exclusion, Johnson Controls explicitly classifies on the basis of potential for pregnancy. Under the PDA, such a classification must be regarded, for Title VII purposes, in the same light as explicit sex discrimination. Respondent has chosen to treat all its female employees as potentially pregnant; that choice evinces discrimination on the basis of sex.

We concluded above that Johnson Controls' policy is not neutral because it does not apply to the reproductive capacity of the company's male employees in the same way as it applies to that of the females. Moreover, the absence of a malevolent motive does [**1204] not convert a facially discriminatory policy into a neutral policy with a discriminatory effect. Whether an employment practice involves disparate treatment through explicit facial discrimination [***174] does not depend on why the employer discriminates but rather on the explicit terms of the discrimination. ...

* * *

The legislative history confirms what the language of the PDA compels. Both the House and Senate Reports accompanying the legislation indicate that this statutory standard was chosen to protect female workers from being treated differently from other employees simply because of their capacity to bear children. See Amending Title VII, Civil Rights Act of 1964, S. Rep. No. 95-331, pp. 4–6 (1977):

> "Under this bill, the treatment of pregnant women in covered employment must focus not on their condition alone but on the actual effects of that condition on their [**1207] ability to work. Pregnant women who are able to work must be permitted to work on the same conditions as other employees. . . .

> "Under this bill, employers will no longer be permitted to force women who become pregnant to stop working regardless of their ability to continue."

... The Senate Report quoted above states that employers may not require a pregnant woman to stop working at any time during her pregnancy unless she is unable to do her work. Employment late in pregnancy often imposes risks on the unborn child, see Chavkin, Walking a Tightrope: Pregnancy, Parenting, and Work, in Double Exposure 196, 196–202 (W. Chavkin ed. 1984), but Congress indicated that the employer may take into account [***178] only the woman's ability to get her job done. See Becker, From *Muller v. Oregon* to Fetal Vulnerability Policies, 53 U. Chi. [*206] L. Rev. 1219, 1255–6 (1986). With the PDA, Congress made clear that [HN12] the decision to become pregnant or to work while being either pregnant or capable of becoming pregnant was reserved for each individual woman to make for herself.

[***LEdHR6B] [6B] [***LEdHR7A] [7A]We conclude that [HN13] the language of ...the PDA ...prohibit an employer from discriminating against a woman because of her capacity to become pregnant unless her reproductive potential prevents her from performing the duties of her job.

* * *

Fertile women, as far as appears in the record, participate in the manufacture of batteries as efficiently as anyone else. Johnson Controls' professed moral and ethical concerns about the welfare of the next generation do not suffice to establish a BFOQ of female sterility. Decisions about the welfare of future children must be left to the parents who conceive, bear, support, and raise them rather than to the employers who hire those parents. Congress has mandated this choice through Title VII, as amended by the [*207] PDA. Johnson Controls has attempted to exclude women because of their reproductive capacity. Title VII and the PDA simply do not allow a woman's dismissal because of her failure to submit to sterilization.

Nor can concerns about the welfare of the next generation be considered a part of the "essence" of Johnson Controls' business.

* * *

VII

[***LEdHR1G] [1G]Our holding today that Title VII, as so amended, forbids sex-specific fetal-protection [**1210] policies is neither remarkable nor unprecedented. Concern for a woman's existing or potential offspring historically has been the excuse for denying women equal employment opportunities. See, e. g., *Muller* v. *Oregon*, 208 U.S. 412 (1908).Congress in the PDA prohibited discrimination on the basis of a woman's ability to become pregnant. We do no more than hold that the PDA means what it says.

It is no more appropriate for the courts than it is for individual employers to decide whether a woman's reproductive role is more important to herself and her family than her economic role. Congress has left this choice to the woman as hers to make.

The judgment of the Court of Appeals is reversed, and the case is remanded for further proceedings consistent with this opinion.

It is so ordered.

Family Leave

Nevada Department of Human Resources v. Hibbs, 538 US 721 (2003)

This case stemmed from a dispute between the Nevada Department of Human Resources and a male public employee regarding the requirements of the Family and Medical Leave Act. Mr. William Hibbs wanted to use all 12 weeks allotted to him under the FMLA to care for his wife who was recovering from a car accident. The Nevada Department of Human Resources granted Hibbs' request for 12 weeks of leave, but ordered him to take the leave intermittently over an approximately six-month period. Mr. Hibbs refused and was subsequently terminated. He sued, citing the FMLA. The state of Nevada argued that the Federal Government had no authority to require sovereign state governments to comply with the congressional act.

The issue before the United States Supreme Court involved the power relationship between the Federal Government and state governments. The Court ruled that Section 5 of the Fourteenth Amendment gave Congress the authority to enforce the equality mandate in Section 1 of the amendment. Finding that the FMLA was an appropriate use of congressional power to redress sex discrimination in private as well as public workplaces, the Court majority defended Congress's adoption of a gender neutral approach to deal with family leave.

The excerpts from the Court's decision pertain to its defense of having gender neutral family leave policy.

NEVADA DEPARTMENT OF HUMAN RESOURCES, et al., Petitioners v. WILLIAM HIBBS et al.

SUPREME COURT OF THE UNITED STATES

538 U.S. 721; 123 S. Ct. 1972; 155 L. Ed. 2d 953; 2003 U.S. LEXIS 4272; 71 U.S.L.W. 4375;

May 27, 2003, Decided

OPINION: CHIEF JUSTICE WILLIAM REHNQUIST

Chief Justice Rehnquist delivered the opinion of the Court.

The Family and Medical Leave Act of 1993 (FMLA or Act) entitles eligible employees to take up to 12 work weeks of unpaid leave annually for any of several reasons, including the onset of a "serious health condition" in an employee's spouse, child, or parent.

* * *

The FMLA aims to protect the right to be free from gender-based discrimination in the workplace.[2] We have held that [HN8]statutory classifications that distinguish between males and females are subject to heightened scrutiny. For a gender-based classification to withstand such scrutiny, it must "serve important governmental objectives," and "the discriminatory means employed [must be] substantially related to the achievement of those objectives." The State's justification for such a classification "must not rely on overbroad generalizations about the

different [***964] talents, capacities, or preferences of males and females."
Ibid. We now inquire whether Congress had evidence of a pattern of
constitutional violations on the part of the States in this area.

The history of the many state laws limiting women's employment
opportunities is chronicled in--and, until relatively recently, was sanctioned
by--this Court's own opinions. For example, in *Bradwell v. State, 16 Wall.*
130, 21 L Ed 442 (1873) (Illinois), and *Goesaert v. Cleary, 335 U.S.*
464, 466, 93 L. Ed. 163, 69 S. Ct. 198 (1948) (Michigan), the Court
upheld state laws prohibiting women from practicing law and tending
bar, respectively. State laws frequently subjected women to distinctive
restrictions, terms, conditions, and benefits for those jobs they could take.
In *Muller v. Oregon, 208 U.S. 412, 419, n. 1, 52 L. Ed. 551, 28 S. Ct. 324*
(1908), for example, this Court approved a state law limiting the hours that
women could work for wages, and observed that 19 States had such laws
at the time. Such laws were based on the related beliefs that (1) woman is,
and should remain, "the center of home and family life," *Hoyt v. Florida,*
368 U.S. 57, 62, 7 L. Ed. 2d 118, 82 S. Ct. 159 (1961), and (2) "a proper
discharge of [a woman's] maternal functions--having in view not merely her
own health, but the well-being of the race--justifies legislation to protect her
from the greed as well as the passion of man," *Muller, supra, at 422, 52 L*
Ed 551, 28 S Ct 324.. Until our decision in *Reed v. Reed, 404 U.S. 71, 30*
L. Ed. 2d 225, 92 S. Ct. 251 (1971), "it remained the prevailing doctrine
that government, both federal and state, could withhold from women
opportunities accorded men so long as any 'basis in reason'"--such as the
above beliefs--"could be conceived for the discrimination." *Virginia, supra,*
at 531, 135 L Ed 2d 735, 116 S Ct 2264 (quoting *Goesaert, supra, at 467,*
93 L Ed 163, 69 S Ct 198).

Congress responded to this history of discrimination by abrogating States'
sovereign immunity in *Title VII of the Civil Rights Act of 1964,* ....But
state gender discrimination did not cease. "It can hardly be doubted that . .
. women still face pervasive, although at times more subtle, discrimination
. . . in the job market." [**1979] *Frontiero v. Richardson, 411 U.S. 677,*
686, 36 L. Ed. 2d 583, 93 S. Ct. 1764 (1973). According to evidence that
was before Congress when it enacted the FMLA, States continue to rely
on invalid gender stereotypes in the employment context, specifically in
the administration of leave benefits. Reliance on such stereotypes cannot
justify the States' gender discrimination in this area. *Virginia, supra, at*
533, 135 L Ed 2d 735, 116 S Ct 2264. The long and extensive history of
sex discrimination prompted us to hold that measures that differentiate on
the basis of gender warrant heightened scrutiny; here, as in *Fitzpatrick*, the
persistence of such unconstitutional discrimination by the States justifies
Congress' passage of prophylactic § 5 legislation.

As the FMLA's legislative record reflects, a 1990 Bureau of Labor Statistics (BLS) survey stated that 37 percent of surveyed private-sector employees were covered by maternity leave policies, while only 18 percent were covered by paternity leave policies. [***965] S. Rep. No. 103-3, pp 14–15 (1993). The corresponding numbers from a similar BLS survey the previous year were 33 percent and 16 percent, respectively. Ibid. While these data show an increase in the percentage of employees eligible for such leave, they also show a widening of the gender gap during the same period. Thus, stereotype-based beliefs about the allocation of family duties remained firmly rooted, and employers' reliance on them in establishing discriminatory leave policies remained widespread.[3]

Congress also heard testimony that "parental leave for fathers . . . is rare. Even . . . where child-care leave policies do exist, men, both in the public and private sectors, receive notoriously discriminatory treatment in their requests for such leave." Many States offered women extended "maternity" leave that far exceeded the typical 4- to 8-week period of physical disability due to pregnancy and childbirth,[4] but very few States granted men a parallel benefit: Fifteen States provided women up to one year of extended maternity leave, while only four provided men with the same. This and other differential leave policies were not attributable to any differential physical needs of men and women, but rather to the pervasive sex-role stereotype that caring for family members is women's work.[5]

Finally, Congress had evidence that, even where state laws and policies were not facially discriminatory, they were applied in discriminatory ways. It was aware of the "serious problems with the discretionary nature of family leave," because when "the authority to grant leave and to arrange the length of that leave rests with individual supervisors," it leaves "employees open to discretionary and possibly unequal treatment." H. R. Rep. No. 103-8, pt. 2, pp 10–11 (1993). Testimony supported that conclusion, explaining that "the lack of uniform parental and medical leave policies in the work place has created an environment where [sex] discrimination is rampant."

* * *

Furthermore, the dissent's statement that some States "had adopted some form of family-care leave" before the FMLA's enactment, post, at 155 L Ed 2d, at 977, glosses over important shortcomings of some state policies. First, seven States had childcare leave provisions that applied to women only. Indeed, Massachusetts required that notice of its leave provisions be posted only in "establishments in which females are employed."[6] These laws reinforced the very stereotypes that Congress sought to remedy through the FMLA. Second, 12 States provided their employees no family leave, beyond an initial childbirth or adoption, to care for a seriously ill child [***967] or [**1981] family member.[7] Third, many States provided [*734] no statutorily guaranteed right to family leave, offering instead only voluntary or discretionary leave programs. Three States left the amount of leave time primarily in employers' hands.[8] Congress could reasonably conclude that such discretionary family-leave programs would do little to combat the stereotypes about the roles of male and female employees that Congress sought to eliminate. Finally, four States provided leave only through administrative regulations or personnel policies, which Congress could reasonably conclude offered significantly less firm protection than a federal law.[9] Against the above backdrop of limited state leave policies, no matter how generous petitioner's own may have been, see post, at *155 L Ed 2d, at 981* (the dissent), Congress was justified in enacting the FMLA as remedial legislation.[10]

In sum, the States' record of unconstitutional participation in, and fostering of, gender-based discrimination in the administration of leave benefits is weighty enough to justify the enactment of prophylactic § 5 legislation.[11]

* * *

Here, however, Congress directed its attention to state gender discrimination, which triggers a heightened level of scrutiny. See, e.g., *Craig, 429 U.S., at 197–9, 50 L Ed 2d 397, 97 S Ct 451.* Because [HN9]the standard for demonstrating the constitutionality of a gender-based classification is more difficult to meet than our rational-basis test--it must "serve important governmental objectives" and be "substantially related to the achievement of those objectives," *Virginia, 518 U.S., at 533, 135 L Ed 2d 735, 116 S Ct 2264*--it was easier for Congress to show a pattern of state constitutional violations. ....

The impact of the discrimination targeted by the FMLA is significant. Congress determined:

"Historically, denial or curtailment of women's employment opportunities has been traceable directly to the pervasive presumption that women are mothers first, and workers second. This prevailing ideology about women's roles has in turn justified discrimination against women when they are mothers or mothers-to-be." Joint Hearing 100.

Stereotypes about women's domestic roles are reinforced by parallel stereotypes presuming a lack of domestic responsibilities for men. Because employers continued to regard the family as the woman's domain, they often denied men similar accommodations or discouraged them from taking leave. These mutually reinforcing stereotypes created a self-fulfilling cycle of discrimination that forced women to continue to assume the role of primary family caregiver, and fostered employers' stereotypical views about women's commitment to work and their value as employees. Those perceptions, in turn, Congress reasoned, lead to subtle discrimination that may be [***969] difficult to detect on a case-by-case basis.

[*737] We believe that Congress' chosen remedy, the family-care leave provision of the FMLA, is "congruent and proportional to the targeted violation," *Garrett, supra, at 374, 148 L Ed 2d 866, 121 S Ct 955.* Congress had already tried unsuccessfully to address this problem through Title VII and the amendment of Title VII by the *Pregnancy Discrimination Act, 42 U.S.C. § 2000e(k) [42 USCS § 2000e(k)].*

By creating an across-the-board, routine employment benefit for all eligible employees, Congress sought to ensure that family-care leave would no longer be stigmatized as an inordinate drain on the workplace caused by female employees, and that employers could not evade leave obligations simply by hiring men. By setting a minimum standard of family leave for all eligible employees, irrespective of gender, the FMLA attacks the formerly [**1983] state-sanctioned stereotype that only women are responsible for family caregiving, thereby reducing employers' incentives to engage in discrimination by basing hiring and promotion decisions on stereotypes.

The dissent characterizes the FMLA as a "substantive entitlement program" rather than a remedial statute because it establishes a floor of 12 weeks' leave. *Post, at 155 L Ed 2d, at 980.* In the dissent's view, in the face of evidence of gender-based discrimination by the States in the provision of leave benefits, ...

Indeed, in light of the evidence before Congress, a statute mirroring Title VII, that simply mandated gender equality in the administration of leave benefits, would not have achieved Congress' remedial object. Such a law would allow States to provide for no family leave at all. Where "two-thirds of the nonprofessional caregivers for older, chronically ill, or disabled persons are working women," H. R. Rep. No. 103-8, pt. 1, p 24 (1993); S. Rep. No. 103-3, at 7, and state practices continue to reinforce the stereotype of women as caregivers, such a policy [***970] would exclude far more women than men from the workplace.

...[T]he FMLA is narrowly targeted at the fault line between work and family--precisely where sex-based overgeneralization has been and remains strongest--and affects only one aspect of the employment relationship...

* * *

The judgment of the Court of Appeals is therefore affirmed.

Julie C. Suk

In her law review article, this legal scholar questions the adoption of a gender neutral approach to family leave. She focuses on the United States Supreme Court's decision in *Nevada Department of Human Resources v. Hibbs* (2003). To Suk, this opinion validated the gender neutral Family and Medical Leave Act because of the concern that gender stereotypes closed or limited employment opportunities for women. In the following passage, Suk explained succinctly why she is so critical of the *Hibbs* decision. She writes:

"Thus, [Nevada Department of Human Resources v.]Hibbs suggests that ...any state action that helps women balance work and caregiving to the exclusion of men is likely based on stereotypes of women as caregivers, a motivation inconsistent with the antidiscrimination logic of equal protection." (p.45)

Julie C. Suk. "Are Gender Stereotypes Bad for Women? Rethinking Antidiscrimination Law and Work-Family Conflict" *Columbia Law Review* 110 (2010): 1- 69. (Excerpts: p.46–9, 51–4, 56–9, 66, 68–9)

* * *

[*46] Although Hibbs does not explicitly address the significance of the medical leave provisions of the FMLA, the Court's theory as to how the statute will deter discrimination against women depends on the amalgamation of family and medical leave. Congress's purpose, according to the Court, was to "ensure that family-care leave would no longer be stigmatized as an inordinate drain on the workplace caused by female employees."[n281] But making the leave available to both men and women will not eradicate employers' perception of family leave as a drain caused by women unless it leads employers to believe that men are just as likely to take leave as women. Given the Court's acknowledgement of the "pervasive sex-role stereotype that caring for family members is women's work"[n282] among employers, it is unlikely that making family leave gender neutral would deter employers' discrimination against women. Rather, the deterrence of sex discrimination becomes plausible because the statute creates a significant number of male leave-takers through the medical leave provision. This logic is assumed when FMLA leave is referred to as an "across-the-board, routine employment benefit for all eligible employees"[n283] that can reduce the incentive to discriminate against women. ... But today, it is clear that tying family leave to medical leave has introduced other risks that are detrimental to women's equal employment opportunities: the escalating costs of sick leave, which undermine the possibility of adequate parental leave.

* * *

[*47] Taken together, the PDA and the antidiscrimination framing of the FMLA tend to reinforce the analogy between pregnancy and sickness that was forged in the 1970s. This analogy was part of a legal strategy devised to advance women's interests under the constraints of historically specific background conditions where employers and states offered job security and/or wage replacement to workers who were temporarily disabled, but not explicitly to those who were pregnant or caring for a newborn. If new mothers wanted job-protected leave or wage replacement, temporary disability was the only game in town. Thus, pregnancy came to be framed as a medical condition requiring the same treatment as incapacitating illnesses and injuries.

The analogy between maternity and sickness is flawed. ...

But common sense should tell us that twelve weeks of paid leave every year for one's own serious medical condition seems excessive (assuming the application of FMLA definitions of "serious medical condition"), while twelve weeks of paid leave for maternity may seem a bit on the short side, ... This inefficient one-size-fits-all approach is a result of our legal culture's deep internalization of the antidiscrimination logic that permeates Hibbs. Grouping pregnant women with fathers and sick men and women is understood to be necessary to attack "the stereotype that only women are responsible for family caregiving."[n288]

The American legal culture treats the analogy between pregnancy and disability as a principle of equality rather than a legal strategy that was necessary to advance women's interests at a particular historical moment. ...

...United States law construed paternalistic protection of mothers as sex discrimination. The argument that pregnant women were "the same" as temporarily disabled men grew out of this legal trajectory, and ultimately prevailed in the passage of the PDA. The sameness proponents did not foresee the particular ways in which the costs of administering sick leave might begin to threaten the legitimacy of maternity and parental leave, perhaps because the legitimacy of women's participation in the labor market was not yet established.

Today, the analogy between pregnancy and sick leave has outlived its usefulness. In the 1970s, temporary disability leave programs were already established, during a time when few women were in the work force. Thus, temporary disability enjoyed more legitimacy than pregnancy or maternity leave. In order for pregnancy and maternity leave to become a possibility, advocates believed it needed to derive its legitimacy from that of disability leave. But today, the reverse is the case. Employers publicly affirm the legitimacy of family leave under the FMLA, but complain about the costs and illegitimate uses of medical leave.[n293] The pendulum [*49] has swung, and now, maternity leave enjoys far more legitimacy than medical leave. It is therefore time to extricate maternity and parental leave from the morass of medical leave. Such a step is necessary if the United States is to solve the work-family conflict.

* * *

B. Gender Paternalism

As the Supreme Court's language in Frontiero suggests, the American rejection of special protections for maternity was tied up with the rejection of paternalism.... It is assumed in U.S. law that state paternalism is an affront to women's equality, but...some forms of paternalism can strengthen the ability of employees to exercise their rights, which can strengthen women's cotinued participation in the labor market.

* * *

Thus, in the United States, the paternalistic treatment of pregnant women and mothers is no longer a legal possibility. ...

...In the United States, it is assumed that restricting women's choice about the [*53] length of maternity leave undermines their equality. But this may not necessarily be the case....

The same logic can be deployed to justify mandatory maternity leave. When maternity leave is optional, employers can pressure all women to take shorter leave, or hire only those women they believe will take shorter leave. With such dynamics at work, the legal right to choose sixteen weeks of maternity leave will become difficult to exercise. And, as the framers of the FMLA recognized, if women do not have a meaningful right to take adequate time off to recover from childbirth and care for a newborn, they will fare worse than men in the workplace.[n317] Understood in this light, the paternalism in compulsory maternity leave is not merely a manifestation of the "romantic paternalism" that is repudiated by American constitutional doctrine. Despite its origins, the paternalism in compulsory maternity leave can be justified as a necessary measure to offset the social and economic pressures that undermine women's ability to choose to do what is best for their own health and that of their children....

* * *

Does gender equality require the elimination of gender stereotypes above all? ...

In the United States, the law makes it problematic for employers to treat women differently based on the belief that women tend to have family responsibilities that conflict with their ability to meet the demands of the workplace. This is because such a belief is precisely the type of generalization that constitutes a gender stereotype.

* * *

...[T]he "essence of **Title VII**" is that generalizations should not be imposed on individuals, even if the generalizations are based on well-documented social realities. But this norm does nothing to help workers (often women) who experience difficulty balancing employment and family responsibilities. If it is "undoubtedly true" that an employer can adversely treat a worker whose work performance suffers due to childcare responsibilities without incurring **Title VII** liability,[n334] the antistereotyping doctrine does nothing to ease the actual conflicts that parents face between work and family. Women tend to face this conflict more acutely than men do in societies where the expectation that women engage in more caregiving than men is firmly entrenched.

...If an employer offers a lighter, lower-profile caseload to a female employee who is [*57] a new mom, without offering the same to a male employee, the employer can be liable for discrimination. In this legal landscape, the employer's best bet for avoiding liability is to apply the same standards to men and women.

But, since women tend to do more family caregiving than men, even in dual-career families,[n336] employers are left to apply the same standards to differently situated individuals. Therefore, when employers make the same demands on women and men, without regard for their caregiving responsibilities, people who are primary caregivers (usually women) will find it more difficult to meet the employer's expectations than people who are not primary caregivers (usually men).

Even in the face of these unfair outcomes, employers have an incentive to remain willfully blind to the caregiving responsibilities of their employees.... If employers are required to treat women the same as men, and to treat people with caregiving responsibilities no differently from all other workers, the easiest way for employers to comply with antidiscrimination law is to offer nothing to both men and women, especially in a tough economy.

* * *

...The EEOC tells employers not to "ask questions about the applicant's or employee's children, plans to start a family, pregnancy, or other caregiving-related issues during interviews or performance reviews,"[n344] or "assume that certain employees (for example, mothers of young children or single parents) will not be interested in positions that require significant travel or working long or unusual hours."[n345] But, when professional advancement depends on significant travel or working long or unusual hours, employees who are also primary caregivers will be conflicted and disadvantaged. These employees are more often than not women. Ultimately, employment discrimination law attempts to eliminate gender stereotypes for the purpose of increasing women's opportunities to "prove their mettle," while ignoring the gendered barriers to their ability to do so.

* * *

Despite the legal framework's stated goal of combating gender stereotypes, the framework does nothing to disrupt the underlying social reality upon which the gender stereotypes are based. The reality is that women do more caregiving than men, which makes it difficult for them to perform as ideal workers in a workplace designed around male norms. Unless the social reality of traditional gender roles is disrupted, women's disadvantage in the American workplace will persist, and may even reinforce women's tendency to do more caregiving than men.

* * *

...[T]he role of antidiscrimination law in addressing work-family conflict needs to be reconfigured. As Hibbs suggests, the Equal Protection Clause may constrain governments from adopting policies that protect mothers without offering the same protections to the temporarily disabled or to fathers because such policies would be based on gender stereotypes and thus violate equal protection. Yet, the legal regimes that protect maternity based on gender stereotypes produce higher levels of female labor market participation and a lower gender wage gap than a legal regime that combats gender stereotypes. This should lead us to be more precise about why American antidiscrimination doctrine is so preoccupied with combating gender stereotypes in the first place....

* * *

But, our legal rhetoric tends to oversimplify paternalism. Mandatory maternity leave does limit women's choice to resume work immediately following birth, but it protects women's ability to choose to exercise their right to an adequate maternity leave

* * *

It is time to rethink U.S. antidiscrimination law, particularly as it has shaped the way American lawyers and policymakers frame the work-family conflict. Two lessons can be drawn from the European experience. First, family and medical leave should be disaggregated. Second, gender stereotypes are not necessarily bad for women.

...[D]isaggregating family and medical leave in the United States will remove a significant barrier to the achievement of paid family leave. Paid medical leave should be pursued, but there is no reason [*69] to provide all American employees with twelve weeks of sick leave, paid or unpaid, per year. Disaggregating family leave from sick leave makes it possible to imagine longer paid leave for new parents.

But disaggregation will require abandoning at least some established antidiscrimination norms, including that of treating new mothers the same as temporarily disabled workers. Abandoning this notion does require a legal conception of pregnancy as a special category of work incapacity, which highlights the difference between men and women. Any advancement in work-family reconciliation will require the liberation of pregnancy, maternity, and parental leave from the costs, baggage, and illegitimacy associated with medical leave.

* * *

Both the disaggregation of family and medical leave and the loosening of antistereotyping doctrine require us to undo the received wisdom of American antidiscrimination law. ...

Notes

1 See *Lochner v. New York*, 198 US 45 (1905).

2 See *Geduldig v. Aiello*, 417 US 484 (1974).

Questions

1 What are the advantages and disadvantages of having single-sex schools?

2 If you need to hire a person to work at least 70 hours a week as well as to be "on call" on his or her days off, would you hire an unmarried woman with 3 small children? Why or why not?

3 Should employers be required to provide special accommodations for their pregnant workers?

4 Since women are still the primary caretakers in families, should the US adopt a mandatory family leave policy for women only?

5 Do you think that workplaces would become more "family friendly" if more women became business executives and business owners?

6 Are there circumstances which justify a company's policy of prohibiting women from working in jobs that cause fetal injury or death? If so, what are those circumstances?

Suggested Reading

Cleveland Board of Education v. LaFleur, 414 US 632 (1974).

Fineman, Martha Albertson. *The Neutered Mother, the Sexual Family and Other Twentieth Century Tragedies.* New York: Routledge, 1995.

Franke, Katherine M. "What's Wrong With Sexual Harassment?" *Stanford Law Review* 49, 1997, 691–772.

Geldudig v. Aiello, 417 US 484 (1974).

Kasic, Allison and Kimberly Schuld. "Title IX and Athletics: A Primer," Independent Women's Forum, Position Paper # 610, September 2008.

Ledbetter v. Goodyear Tire and Rubber Co, 550 US 618 (2007).

Mississippi University for Women v. Hogan, 458 US 718 (1982).

Moore, Christine. "The PDA Fails to Deliver: Why Nalco and Wallace Cannot Coexist, and a New Standard for Defining 'Related Medical Condition'." *University of San Francisco Law Review* 44, 2010, 683–705.

National Coalition for Women and Girls in Education. "Title IX Athletics Policies: Issues and Data for Education Decision Makers," 2007.

Price Waterhouse v. Hopkins, 490 US 228 (1989).

Stanford, Heather Bennett. "Do You Want to Be an Attorney or a Mother? Arguing for the Feminist Solution to the Problem of Double Binds in Employment and Family Responsibilities Discrimination." *American University Journal of Gender, Social Policy and the Law* 17, 2009, 627–57.

Suk, Julie C. "Are Gender Stereotypes Bad for Women? Rethinking

Antidiscrimination Law and Work–Family Conflict." *Columbia Law Review* 110, 2010, 1–69.

Yue, Jennifer. "The Flood of Pregnancy Discrimination Cases: Balancing the Interests of Pregnant Women and Their Employers." *Kentucky Law Journal* 6, 2007/2008, 487–504.

5

Violence

Introduction

Violence between men and women continues to be a major problem in the United States. While virtually all Americans want to stop domestic violence and sexual assault, considerable controversy exists regarding how best to deal with these evils. Should policies which strive to address crimes of sexual violence focus almost exclusively on the needs of women, or should these policies be gender neutral? In the readings for this chapter, traditionalists use natural difference arguments to support women-centered policies for dealing with these evils while reformers support a gender neutral approach.

Traditionalists favor women-centered policies because crimes of sexual violence largely involve male perpetrators abusing female victims. Women are particularly vulnerable to male sexual assault, they argue, because they are smaller in stature, weaker in physical strength and less aggressive sexually. Reformers criticize women-centered policies for ignoring or downplaying the sufferings of male victims of sexual assault and for fostering negative stereotypes about the capacity of women. They argue that gender neutral strategies can address the needs of all victims of such violence while respecting the autonomy and power of women.

Domestic Violence and the Battered Woman Syndrome

The current debate regarding how best to help battered women highlights the differences between the two approaches. Dr. Lenore Walker found in her seminal research on battered women,[1] that women who were subjected to prolonged and savage brutality by their male partners exhibited a new type of victimology that she referred to as "The Battered Woman's Syndrome."[2]

According to Walker, a "battered woman" suffers from a psychological condition called "learned helplessness,"[3] which results from physical abuse, psychological depression and "sex-role stereotyping." She also discovered that women with low self-esteem, who believe that their self-worth depends on being subservient to men, are particularly susceptible to entering into abusive relationships which they have difficulty ending. This difficulty leads to a "point of psychological paralysis," which lasts until some battered women lash out physically against their abusers.[4] The most controversial cases arise when a battered woman kills her abuser under circumstances which are inconsistent with traditional legal definitions of self-defense.

Traditionalists such as Kit Kinports[5] have made this condition the centerpiece of their approach to domestic violence. They argue that battered women are so psychologically traumatized and so susceptible to the wiles of their male abusers that only direct and, at times, forceful interventions from external actors can free them from their abusive relationships. They urge police, prosecutors, judges and jurors to provide special treatment for such women when they enter the criminal justice system either as crime victims or as criminal defendants.

Reformers like Anne Coughlin[6] reject this approach on the grounds that it demeans battered women by portraying them as weak, irrational and psychologically incompetent. They further charge that policies which focus on the needs of battered women ignore the plight of men who are abused by their male and female partners. These men, in contrast to their female counterparts, have little or no access to shelters, have limited protection from police and courts, and have virtually no social support and sympathy.

Battered Women and the Debate over Mandatory Prosecution

Traditionalists and reformers also view mandatory prosecution policy differently. In many domestic violence cases, efforts to prosecute and convict male abusers have been frustrated because abused women often fail to press charges, fail to attend court proceedings, and fail to testify against their abusive partners. Mandatory prosecution policies allow district attorneys to threaten battered women who refuse to cooperate with law enforcement authorities with criminal penalties.

The chief disagreement between traditionalists and reformers in this area, however, centers on the competency of battered women. Traditionalists believe that battered women are so psychologically traumatized and so afraid of their abusive partners that they are rationally unable to extricate themselves from their abusive relationships. Mandatory prosecution, they argue, protects these mentally fragile women by increasing the likelihood of sentencing the abuser to prison.[7]

Reformers argue, however, that battered women are often rational actors who understand their interests better than police officers, prosecutors and social workers. They charge that mandatory prosecution demeans women by re-enforcing old stereotypes that portray them as less able than men to make rational decisions.[8] Thus, they would empower women by respecting their choices to refrain from or assist in prosecuting their partners.

Battered Woman Syndrome and the Debate over Self-Defense

Finally, traditionalists and reformers differ regarding the merits of the battered woman's syndrome defense. This debate centers on whether battered women who kill their abusers in legally questionable circumstances should be allowed to use their battered state as a legal justification for their homicides. In other words, should the battered woman's syndrome defense be considered as legitimate in criminal cases? Traditionalists answer affirmatively because they believe that battered women are unlike most criminal defendants and thus should be treated differently from them. They argue that a battered woman's criminality is episodic, that it stems directly from experiencing sustained and brutal abuse by her male partner, and that it results from psychological trauma that led her to believe that death at the hands of her partner was imminent.[9]

Reformers reject the battered woman's syndrome defense on the grounds that it absolves criminal defendants of their responsibility for their criminal conduct. Battered women should be treated like other criminal defendants, they maintain, because women, like men, should be held accountable for their actions. To do otherwise would undermine feminist efforts to empower women by portraying them as irrational and irresponsible.[10]

The cases of *North Carolina v. Norman* (NC 1989)[11] and *Bechtel v. Oklahoma* (Okla.Ct.App. 1992)[12] illustrate the different ways in which state courts have responded to the battered woman's syndrome defense. Both cases involve a battered woman accused of murdering her husband after experiencing sustained and horrible psychological and physical abuse at his hands. Each woman killed her spouse when he was asleep or drunk and, under traditional self-defense law, did not pose an imminent physical threat to her. The North Carolina Supreme Court ruled that the battered woman's syndrome defense was inappropriate in a homicide prosecution because it did not meet the traditional definition of self-defense. Three years later in *Bechtel*, the Oklahoma Court of Criminal Appeals ruled that this defense was consistent with Oklahoma's self-defense statute.

Gender Neutral Laws and Rape

Should the law distinguish between male and female victims of rape and sexual assault? Traditionalists believe that rape statutes should only penalize men who assault women on the grounds that rape is by nature an almost exclusively male crime. Some scholars, like Catharine MacKinnon, also believe that rape is a weapon which men in patriarchal societies like the United States use systematically to subjugate and marginalize women. Thus, in her view, rape laws must address broad issues of sexual inequality in America as well as penalizing the criminal acts themselves.

Reformers, such as Elizabeth Kramer, argue that these laws should be gender neutral because male rape victims, who tend to be ignored because of false cultural stereotypes about male sexuality, also deserve sympathy and support and have a constitutional right to legal protection. Others further maintain that traditional rape statutes unfairly impose criminal liability on men only and therefore constitute unconstitutional sex discrimination.

California's old statutory rape law is illustrative. A generation ago, men in California were subject to criminal prosecution for engaging in sexual intercourse with a female minor between the ages of 14 and 18 years old, but women who engaged in sexual intercourse with minor males of a similar age cohort faced no criminal charges.[13] California defended its statute by citing the "immutable physiological fact that it is the female exclusively who can become pregnant."[14] The US Supreme Court upheld California's statutory rape law in the case of *Michael M. v. Sonoma County* (1981).[15] The Michael M. case resulted when Michael M., a 17 ½-year-old male, had sexual relations with a 16 ½-year-old girl. Although both parties had been drinking alcohol before the sexual encounter,[16] only Michael M. was arrested and subsequently convicted of statutory rape. While four justices defended the law's constitutionality, three justices were troubled by the fact that it imposed criminal liability on men only.

In the 1980s, New York and nine other state had rape statutes that similarly defined rape as "forcible compulsion" to engage in sexual intercourse. Three years after the *Michael M.* case was decided, a man challenged the constitutionality of New York's old rape law on the grounds that only men could be prosecuted for rape in the state of New York. Two courts heard this challenge and disagreed about the statute's constitutionality.[17] The New York Court of Appeals ruled in *New York v. Liberta* (NY1984)[18] that the law was unconstitutional on sex discrimination grounds, and the U. S. Second Circuit Court of Appeals in 1988, citing the *Michael M.* precedent, found that the same law was, in fact, constitutional.

Conclusion

The debates in this chapter turn on whether gender neutral policies favored by reformers, or women-centered policies supported by traditionalists, are most effective in combatting sexual and domestic violence. Most states have now adopted the gender neutral wording in their rape laws that reformers favor.[19] However, domestic violence policies continue to focus exclusively on battered women while male victims of domestic and sexual violence in the United States are largely unrecognized and unsupported.

Notes

1 See Lenore Walker, *The Battered Woman*. New York: Harper & Row, 1979.

2 Walker, *The Battered Woman Syndrome*. New York: Springer Publishing Company, 1984.

3 Walker, 1979, 43–53.

4 Ibid., 43–53, 51, 43.

5 See Kit Kinports, "Deconstructing the 'Image' of the Battered Woman: So Much Activity, So Little Change: A Reply to the Critics of Battered Women's Self-Defense." *St. Louis University Public Law Review* 23 (2004): 155–91.

6 See Anne M. Coughlin, "Excusing Women." *California Law Review* 82, 1984, 1–92.

7 Cheryl Hanna, "No Right to Choose: Mandated Victim Participation in Domestic Violence Prosecutions." *Harvard Law Review* 109, 1996, 1849–1910.

8 Leigh Goodmark, "Autonomy Feminism: An Anti-Essentialist Critique of Mandating Intervention in Domestic Violence Cases." *Florida State University Law Review* 37, 2009, 1–48.

9 See Kinports, 2004.

10 See Coughlin, 1994. Also for a critical analysis of these defenses, see Alan M. Dershowitz, *The Abuse Excuse*. New York: Little, Brown & Company, 1994.

11 378 SE 2d 8 (NC 1989).

12 840 P 2d 1 (Okla. Ct. Crim. App. 1992).

13 It should be noted that, under California law, "anyone, regardless of gender, can be guilty of engaging in lewd, lascivious acts including consensual sexual intercourse with a child under the age of 14 years. Also, any person can be criminally prosecuted for molesting, annoying or contributing to the delinquency of anyone under 18 years old."

14 450 US 464, 467 (1981).

15 450 US 464 (1981).

16 There was a dispute over whether the girl actually consented to the sexual intercourse. The United States Supreme Court focused on the constitutionality of the California statute that placed all criminal liability on the men, and none on women.

17 See *People of the State of New York v. Liberta*, 474 NE 2d 207 (NY 1984); *Liberta v. Kelly*, 839 F2d 77 (2nd Cir. 1988).

18 474 NE 2d 207 (NY 1984).

19 At the time of this writing, only two states did not have gender neutral rape statutes.

READINGS

Domestic Violence

Kit Kinports

Law Professor Kinports presents a defense of Lenore Walker's battered woman's syndrome as well as the accompanying battered woman's syndrome defense against criticism that they harm women.

Kit Kinports, "Deconstructing the 'Image' of the Battered Woman: So Much Activity, So Little Change: A Reply to the Critics of Battered Women's Self-Defense" *St. Louis University Public Law Review* 23 (2004): 155- 1991 (Excerpts: pp. 155, 168–9, 170–2, 177–8, 180–3, 190–1)

[*155]

Prior to 1970, the term "domestic violence" referred to ghetto riots and urban terrorism, not the abuse of women by their intimate partners.[n1] Today, of course, domestic violence is a household word. After all, it has now been ten years since the revelation of football star O.J. Simpson's history of battering purportedly sounded "a wake-up call for all of America";[n2] ten years since Congress enacted legislation haled as ""a milestone ... truly a turning point in the national effort to break the cycle'" of violence; [n3] and twenty years since Farrah Fawcett's portrayal of Francine Hughes in the movie The Burning Bed supposedly "left an indelible mark upon society's collective consciousness."[n4] Despite these and numerous other "milestones" and "wake-up calls," domestic violence continues to be a seemingly intractable problem in this country. Substantial numbers of women are still beaten by their husbands and boyfriends every day, and many of them die as a result.[n5] A much smaller number of women strike back and kill their abusers, but it is these cases – and [*156] the self-defense issues they raise – that seem to receive a disproportionate share of the attention.[n6]

The most troublesome self-defense questions arise, of course, in cases involving non-confrontational killings – where the woman struck back before or after a beating, or, most controversially, when her abuser was asleep. Although statistically most killings do not fall into this category,[n7] they raise the most difficult questions and have generated the most interest. Can a woman who kills under these circumstances legitimately argue that she acted in self-defense – that, pursuant to the prevailing definition of the defense, she honestly and reasonably believed she was in imminent danger of death or serious bodily harm?[n8] A number of critics contend that she cannot, and it is my purpose here to evaluate the various arguments they have advanced.

* * *

III

* * *

Psychologist Lenore Walker, one of the early pioneers in the field of domestic violence, coined the term "battered woman syndrome" to describe the effects of intimate-partner abuse.[n75] In her 1979 book, The Battered Woman, Walker observed that women who find themselves in abusive relationships tend to share certain characteristics, including low self-esteem, passivity, and traditional attitudes about male-female roles.[n76] Walker also found that many battering relationships are characterized by a cyclical pattern – the so-called "cycle of violence," consisting of a tension-building stage, an acute battering incident, and then a stage of loving contrition.[n77] The book also explained Walker's theory of "learned helplessness": once battered women learn that they cannot control or prevent the beatings, they come to feel that the violence is unavoidable and that there is no escape from the relationship.[n78] Walker used these findings to try to dispel the myth that battered women remain in abusive relationships because they are masochists.[n79] Instead, she pointed out that women stay for a number of reasons, which included not only their feelings of helplessness and the reinforcement they received during the third stage of the cycle, but also other factors – namely, fear, lack of resources, concern for children, love for their partner, shame, and lack of external support resulting from the batterer's efforts to isolate them from others.[n80]

* * *

IV. The Imminence Requirement

Focusing on self-defense's imminence requirement, some critics argue that a battered woman who kills under non-confrontational circumstances might reasonably fear future abuse,[n136] but she cannot honestly and reasonably believe she is in imminent danger of harm at the time she acts.[n137] There are four responses to this objection.

First, research shows that battered women tend to become hypersensitive to their abuser's behavior and to the signs that predict a beating.[n138] Many battered women who kill say that something in the abuser's behavior changed or signaled to them that this time he really was serious about carrying out his threats to kill.[n139] That experience may enable battered women to recognize the [*181] imminence of an attack at a time when others without their prior experience would not.

Second, given her history, a battered woman may reasonably come to believe that the only time she can realistically protect herself is when her abuser is, for example, asleep. She may have learned that trying to defend herself during a beating is futile and merely escalates the violence.[n140] She may have tried numerous other ways of protecting herself and escaping the relationship, only to find that the criminal justice system and social service agencies were unable or unwilling to help her and that her husband would find her, bring her back, and punish her with even more severe abuse for attempting to leave him.[n141] In fact, research shows that battered women are often attacked and even killed when they try to leave the relationship and the batterer fears that he is losing control.[n142]

[*182] Third, even though "inevitable future harm" may not be the same as "imminent harm,"[n143] imminence is in some sense a proxy for necessity.[n144] The battered woman who kills her sleeping husband arguably satisfies that notion of imminence, just like the hostage who is being slowly poisoned over a period of time, or who has been told to expect to die later in the week, and who suddenly has a window of opportunity to attack her kidnapper and save her life.[n145]

Finally, it is important to note that standard self-defense doctrine requires only a reasonable belief in the imminence of the threat, and not actual imminence. As the Oklahoma Court of Criminal Appeals observed, "the issue is not whether the danger was in fact imminent, but whether, given the [*183] circumstances as she perceived them, the defendant's belief was reasonable that the danger was imminent."[n146]

Nevertheless, some critics counter, the imminence requirement cannot be satisfied in non-confrontational cases because the woman always had the option of leaving before the abuser woke up.[n147] In addition to the difficulties that a battered woman faces in leaving the relationship or otherwise protecting herself from the abuse,[n148] other commentators have pointed out that "a rule that demands the defendant "avoid the confrontation'" by leaving the relationship is "a "pre-retreat' rule [that] ... has never been part of standard self-defense law."[n149] Just as "the man who goes for the fiftieth time to the violent gang-bar is not deprived of his self-defense claim because he "should have left' [*184] before the violence erupted," the law should likewise recognize that "there is no general duty to avoid violence before the confrontation" when battered women raise a claim of self-defense.[n150]

Once again, the battered woman is simply asking the courts to faithfully apply the standard self-defense doctrine to her case, something that the courts are seemingly reluctant to do. ...The real hurdle battered women faced was that their "cases are in general not seen as "real fights,'" so that "even when the cases are confrontational – when the gun is pointed at her – they still are not seen as confrontational,"....

* * *

V. Justification or Excuse?

Critics of battered women's self-defense claims also argue that women claiming self-defense in non-confrontational cases are really advancing an excuse for their conduct, rather than a justification,[n163] and therefore, presumably by definition, are not entitled to the justification of self-defense. ...

* * *

From the perspective of the individual defendant, presumably most people would be indifferent between a not guilty verdict based on a justification and one based on an excuse. ...Anne Coughlin rejects that assumption, however, arguing that battered women are in fact "harmed by the finding of irresponsibility that their successful excuse defenses incur" because "the dubious moral status occupied by the excused actor – that creature who is more like a "dog' or a "rock' than a human being" – reinforces gender stereotypes and thus "has profound implications for the construction of gender."[n170] Interestingly, Coughlin's description of defendants who raise a successful duress defense has very a different tone. ...Coughlin observes that the defendant who acts under duress is excused because "the alternatives open to him were so agonizing that we accept his claim that he was carrying out a course of conduct that he did not choose – and would not have chosen – for himself."[n172] Thus, in Coughlin's view, "the model of the responsible actor is heavily inscribed on the duress defense" even though, as she notes, duress is generally considered an excuse rather than a justification.[n173] Why don't those defendants suffer from the same "dubious moral status" as the battered woman Coughlin characterizes as "less than a full human being"?[n174] Why do we simply "withhold blame" from defendants excused by duress rather than "harm[] [them] by [a] finding of irresponsibility"?[n175] While Coughlin is certainly right to criticize the gender stereotypes that underlay the now-discarded doctrine of marital coercion,[n176] one wonders whether it is those same stereotypes – and the devaluation of women, their experiences, and their stories that they reflect – that lead her to describe a battered woman's self-defense claim so differently from that of the defendant who acted under duress.

VI. The Abuse Excuse

A related objection argues that battered women's self-defense claims fall prey to "the determinist reductio"[n177] or – in somewhat more colorful terms – that they are illustrative of the "abuse excuse" crisis sweeping through criminal law.... Alan Dershowitz argues that "the abuse excuse is a symptom of a general abdication of responsibility" that "is dangerous to the very tenets of democracy, which presuppose personal accountability for choices and actions."[n181] And, according to Dershowitz, "it all began with the so-called battered woman syndrome."[n182]

...[T]he law takes it for granted that reasonable people will use deadly force when confronted by an "uplifted knife,"[n186] that the man who finds his wife in bed with someone else will lose control and react with violence,[n187] and that no "manly" individual will retreat from home in order to escape an attacker.[n188] Why are those defendants not asked to take "personal responsibility" for their actions? Or, as Nourse puts it, "why not [*189] demand that those who act under duress or provocation also exercise self-control?"[n189]

Likewise, although Professor Dershowitz is certainly correct in pointing out that "the vast majority of people who have experienced abuse ... do not commit violent crimes,"[n190] the same can be said of defenses long accepted by the criminal law. Many people faced with an "uplifted knife" will not respond with defensive force,[n191] most people who find their partner in bed with another will not react violently,[n192] and some who are subjected to threats will not succumb and commit a crime.[n193] Nevertheless, the fact that many people are able to avoid violent or otherwise criminal behavior in these circumstances has not led to widespread outcry for the abolition of the defenses of duress, provocation, or self-defense.[n194] Nor has the fact that, to a large extent, these defenses, premised as they are on a male model of behavior, tend to be of greatest benefit to a subset of society – namely, men – who are more likely to [*190] act in ways that require that they avail themselves of the defenses.

VII. Conclusion

"Allowing victims of abuse to invoke an abuse excuse, while doing nothing to prevent the underlying abuse, is little more than symbolism on the cheap," Alan Dershowitz charges.[n196] In somewhat less provocative terms, Anne Coughlin urges that we "change our experiences, perhaps even eliminate domestic violence," by "persuading the community to change its assumptions about gender relationships."[n197] It is certainly important to remind ourselves to keep our eyes on the ball – not to allow the relatively small number of cases where battered women kill their abusers under non-confrontational circumstances to divert our attention from the plight of the much larger number of women victimized by domestic violence. But I know of no one who advocates "doing nothing" about these larger issues and simply focusing on self-defense as the solution to the problem of domestic violence.

* * *

In the longer term, the difficulty with the proposal that we simply end domestic violence is that it is much easier said than done. As our experience with thirty years of reform efforts has demonstrated, the gender bias that leads individual men to feel free to beat their partners – and that leads society to treat that violence more cavalierly than it treats stranger assaults – is so well [*191] entrenched that it has proven very resistant to change. In the meantime, and certainly while we continue our efforts to end violence against women, we should also recognize the gender bias so firmly embedded in our criminal laws and strive to give battered women's self-defense claims the same consideration we have traditionally afforded to defenses raised by male defendants.

The following two articles by Anne Coughlin and Alexander Detschelt offer a critical commentary to current policies and strategies intended to address domestic violence by focusing upon the victimization of women.

Anne Coughlin

Anne M. Coughlin is a professor at the University of Virginia School of Law and presents a very critical analysis of Lenore Walker's battered woman's syndrome. She argues that the syndrome along with the battered woman's syndrome defense in criminal cases are actually harming women rather than helping them. The following excerpt shows why Coughlin is critical of the battered woman's syndrome.

Anne M. Coughlin "Excusing Women" *California Law Review* 82 (1994): 1–92. (Excerpts: pp. 5–6, 7, 54, 57, 58–9, 62–3, 87)

* * *

...It is my thesis that the existing feminist critique of the battered woman syndrome defense is inadequate because the negative implications for women go far beyond the reinforcement of particular aspects of stereotyped gender roles that some of us may wish to shed. None of those who advocate, or, for that matter, criticize, adoption of the battered woman syndrome defense has noticed that, for many centuries, the criminal law has been content to excuse women for criminal misconduct on the ground that they cannot be expected to, and, indeed, should not, resist the influence exerted by their husbands. No similar excuse has ever been afforded to men; to the contrary, the criminal law consistently has demanded that men withstand any pressures in their lives that compel them to commit crimes, including pressures exerted by their spouses.... By construing wives as incapable of choosing lawful conduct when faced with unlawful influence from their spouses, the theory invests men with the authority to govern both themselves and their irresponsible wives.

The battered woman syndrome defense rests on and reaffirms this invidious understanding of women's incapacity for rational self-control. ...[I]t fails to hold women to the same demanding standard against which men are measured. ...[B]y denying that women are capable of abiding by criminal prohibitions, in circumstances said to afflict many women at some point during their lives,[n13] the defense denies that women have the same capacity for self-governance that is attributed to men, ...

...The defense itself defines the woman as a collection of mental symptoms, motivational deficits, and behavioral abnormalities; indeed, the fundamental premise of the defense is that women lack the psychological capacity to choose lawful means to extricate themselves from abusive mates.

* * *

II

* * *

...The heart of [battered woman]...defense is a psychological diagnosis of battered women that construes them as suffering from various emotional, cognitive, and behavioral deficits, which negatively influence [them] from leaving a relationship after the battering occurs.[n265] The central testimony for the defense is not provided by the accused woman, but by the expert witness, usually a psychologist, who claims that the battering caused the woman to succumb to a mental health disorder[] called learned helplessness,[n266] which made it impossible for her to contemplate leaving her violent mate even though other people perceived that she could, and should, have separated from him.[n267] She may have avenues of escape from the marriage, short of homicide, to which others would turn, but the battered woman's dysfunctional mental condition leaves her unable to act to take advantage of them.[n268]

...The strategy of the battered women's defenders has not been to [*55] ask the jurors to find, as under a self-defense claim, that the woman's act of killing was justified because the typical person also would have believed that deadly force was necessary under the circumstances.[n271] Rather, the defense concedes that the typical person would have chosen to terminate the relationship long before the battering escalated to the point where the use of deadly force became necessary.[n272] Then, carefully tracking the traditional requirements of excuse, the defense goes on to ask the jurors to determine that the accused woman suffered from cognitive and volitional disabilities that deprived her of the capacity to choose lawful conduct (that is, leaving her spouse).[n273]

* * *

...By proving that women suffer from special psychological deficits that make them incapable of resisting illegal pressures exerted by men, it explicitly locates the source of women's subjugation, not within legal or cultural convention, but within women themselves....

* * *

...Since women are, as Lenore Walker has assisted the courts in constructing us, more prone than men to succumbing to mental disorders[n308] that cause us helplessly to obey the commands of the males in our lives, then we must be provided supervision, at least in some contexts, even before we have violated any criminal prohibition.[n309] By securing leniency on the ground that we are predisposed to losing our power of rational choice, the battered woman syndrome excuse relinquishes to men, acting either individually as husbands or officially as representatives of the state, the authority to make, or, at least, superintend, our choices for us. The excuse thereby withholds from women the basic life satisfactions that the capacity for responsibility is said to secure. If our misconduct incurs not blame for our evil choices, but pity for our psychological infirmity, then our good works will be characterized, not as the product of our own achievements and willings, but as the successful work [*63] of the expert therapists whose cognitive restructuring procedures[n310] overcame the effects of our mental disabilities.

* * *

Conclusion

* * *

If the community holds powerful feelings of sympathy for women who offend under the pressure of domestic violence, (and the widespread recognition of the new defense certainly suggests that it does), then we must decide whether we can embody those feelings in a defense that does not effectively withhold from women the respect for their achievements and authority over their lives that the capacity for responsible conduct presently secures for men. For the reasons expressed in the preceding parts of this paper, I am persuaded that the battered woman syndrome defense, at least as it is presently constituted, is profoundly anti-feminist. ...

* * *

Alexander Detschelt

In his article on male victims of domestic violence, Alexander Detschelt, an attorney in private practice, challenges the assumption that domestic violence is exclusively a woman's issue.

Alexander Detschelt (2003) "Recognizing Domestic Violence Directed Towards Men: Overcoming Societal Perceptions, Conducting Accurate Studies, and Enacting Responsible Legislation" *Kansas Journal of Law and Public Policy* 12 (2003): 249–61. (Excerpts: pp. 249–50, 250–1, 252, 255–6, 258, 260–1

[*249]

I. INTRODUCTION

"I was hit in the head with a beer mug . . . requiring stitches."

". . . would throw hot scalding coffee in my face."

"I was slapped, punched, poked and kicked repeatedly."

"I suffered a broken leg, a broken ankle, and [a] broken wrist."

"I have been chased with a car and attacked with a chainsaw."

". . . sitting on my chest with a butcher knife in hand and the blade at my throat."

". . . attempted to smother [me] with a pillow while I slept."[n1]

In the public's mind, these true recollections of violence evoke the image of an abusive husband or boyfriend. In reality they were all perpetrated by a wife or girlfriend. The traditional societal view of domestic violence, as evidenced by legal, medical, and statistical data, involves the notion of men engaging in the domestic abuse of their female partner or spouse, hence making it very difficult to accept that male spousal abuse is a serious problem.[n2]

This note takes the position that domestic violence against men is in fact a serious social issue that must be fully addressed by overcoming societal perceptions, conducting accurate studies, and enacting responsible legislation.

Societal trends indicate that we are becoming more and more concerned with reducing all forms of abuse and violence that manifest themselves in domestic relations.[n3] Therefore, the next appropriate action would be to discard the long-held and stereotypical view that "violence is considered the province of the male," and accept the reality [*250] that women have the same capacity for violence.[n4] Not addressing this issue will result in serious ramifications, not just to the men who are abused, but also to society as a whole.[n5] In reducing domestic violence, it is therefore imperative to develop a societal approach, based on education and coordination of efforts between the legal and law enforcement communities, academics and statisticians, domestic violence support groups, and popular culture influences.

* * *

II. THE HIDDEN SIDE OF DOMESTIC VIOLENCE

* * *

Popular culture has had a great impact on minimizing the problem of domestic violence against men. Upon hearing about the topic of battered men, the public's first reaction is usually that of incredulity and amusement.[n7] Historically, battered husbands have been ignored, ridiculed, and chastised.[n8] Print media has also made battered men a topic for jokes, a common example being the stereotypical cartoon image of a woman chasing her husband while wielding a rolling pin above her head.[n9] A researcher has also noted that women are depicted as the perpetrators in seventy-three percent of newspaper comics addressing domestic violence situations.[n10] Furthermore, surveys regarding public attitudes about slapping have changed dramatically for men, but not for women.[n11] Movies and television have continually presented scenes in which women who, upon being subjected to emotionally upsetting circumstances, immediately slap the man who is the cause of them. The audience's reaction can range from that of laughter and cheer to even applause; however, were a man to do the same things, the reaction would be quite the opposite.

The media is also instrumental in perpetuating this stereotype, and in effect is detrimental to the recognition of domestic violence against men.[n12] News headlines regarding domestic violence against men have been phrased in such a way as to be sensational and evoke humor.[n13] ....[n15] These societal reactions and media perceptions are in keeping with the unfortunate, stereotypical view society holds of men as being sturdy and women being the weaker, more helpless sex.[n16]

* * *

[*252]

Due to gender stereotypes regarding domestic violence against men, social ridicule is the fear that confronts male spousal abuse victims.[n32] Men perceive society as expecting them to be the strong, dominant party in their intimate relationships, and therefore are less willing to report incidents of domestic violence.[n33] Men are less likely to call law enforcement, even when there is an injury, because they feel shame about disclosing family violence, especially since the police adhere to traditional gender role expectations.[n34] Hence, the stereotypical male feels shame and inadequacy when he realizes that he cannot keep his wife under control.[n35] The impact of domestic violence is also less apparent and less likely to come to the attention of others outside of law enforcement when a man is abused.[n36] For example, it is assumed that a man with a bruised or black eye was involved in a fight with another man, he was injured during employment, or was playing a contact sport. Society's disbelief and the humiliation directed towards abused men makes disclosure even more difficult.[n37] Since the general public refuses to confront the issue of domestic violence against men, one would assume that in the professional realm of shelters and counseling, there would be more recognition of this problem- unfortunately, this is not the case.

* * *

IV. THE NEED FOR REPONSIBLE LEGISLATION

Neither federal nor state legislative bodies have enacted explicit statutes and provisions dealing with domestic violence against men. Even those domestic violence laws that purport to be gender-neutral do not fully address the concerns of battered men.

The Violence Against Women Act (VAWA)[n83] is a primary example of what is wrong with the current state of domestic violence legislation. The very title of the VAWA and the congressional findings underlying its enactment indicate that it encompasses male offenders and female victims.[n84] Although it has been argued that the VAWA uses gender-neutral language when referring to substantive legal provisions,[n85] it would be intellectually dishonest to state that male victims of domestic violence were even remotely considered as the rationale used for enacting the VAWA.[n86] In fact, the VAWA is discriminatory as applied, in that it excludes men from some of the services and support offered to women by the Act. ...In terms of financial expenditures, the VAWA mandated the issuance of grants for objectives such as "strengthen[ing] effective law enforcement and prosecution strategies to combat violent crimes against women, and . . . develop[ing] and strengthen[ing] victim services in cases involving violent crimes against women."[n88] Funding was also allocated to "develop a research agenda to increase the understanding and control of violence against women,"[n89] and to overcome [*256] gender stereotypes against women.[n90] ...

* * *

Not only do such gender-specific statutes create a disparity in the protections afforded to male victims of domestic abuse as compared to female victims, but they also invoke constitutional issues of equal protection.[n101] The Equal Protection Clause of the Fourteenth Amendment provides in relevant part that "no State shall make or enforce any law which shall . . . deny to any person within its jurisdiction the equal protection of the laws."[n102] The United States Supreme Court has interpreted this clause to mean that persons who are similarly situated must be treated alike.[n103] Therefore, male victims of domestic violence, who suffered the same forms of abuse as women and wish to introduce battering syndrome self-defense evidence into court are being denied their constitutional rights.

* * *

VI. CONCLUSION

"Domestic violence against men is just not a social problem."[n144]

This statement was made by Ellen Pence, founder of the nationally acclaimed Domestic Abuse Intervention Project[n145] in Duluth, Minnesota, and a leader in the battered women's movement.[n146] Such statements are disheartening but are in a sense a wake-up call to how much more needs to be accomplished in order for society to fully realize and deal with the problem of domestic violence against men. ...

...The ultimate question, says one commentator, is whether society's perceptions of "masculinity will become more humane and less judgmental,"[n153] allowing society to acknowledge that women can be as abusive of their partners, as men can. Only by overcoming societal [*261] perceptions, conducting accurate studies, and enacting responsible legislation, will equal resources and protections be allocated and made available to all victims of domestic violence, women and men alike.

Cheryl Hanna

Cheryl Hanna, a law professor and a former prosecutor, argues in favor of requiring or, even, coercing women to participate in their abusers' criminal prosecution.

Cheryl Hanna, "No Right to Choose: Mandated Victim Participation in Domestic Violence Prosecutions" *Harvard Law Review* 109 (1996): 1849–1910. (Excerpts: pp. 1850–1, 1852, 1867–8, 1891, 1895, 1897, 1909–10)

If Nicole Brown Simpson had lived in Duluth, Minnesota, we might have seen a very different O.J. Simpson trial. For had she lived in Duluth in October 1993, when Mr. Simpson broke into her home and terrorized her, Mr. Simpson might have been tried much earlier – for domestic violence. The Los Angeles District Attorney's Office dropped the 1993 prosecution because Ms. Simpson did not want to press charges. In Duluth, she would not have had a choice.

One of the defining moments in the O.J. Simpson murder trial came when the prosecution introduced the 911 tape from October 1993 that vividly illustrated prior abuse in the Simpson marriage.[n1] On the tape, Ms. Simpson's terrified voice begs the operator to send the police, as Mr. Simpson had just smashed the door. She says she fears that he will "beat the shit" out of her.[n2] O.J. Simpson is heard screaming in the background – threatening her, taunting her. The operator's voice sounds surprised when she learns that the suspect is O.J. Simpson. "I think you know his record," Ms. Simpson tells the opera- [*1851] tor.[n3] Mr. Simpson was never arrested or prosecuted for the 1993 incident because Ms. Simpson did not want to press charges.[n4]

Under these same circumstances, the Duluth District Attorney would likely have initiated charges against Mr. Simpson, signing the complaint and requesting an arrest warrant.[n5] A proper investigation of the case would have been conducted and might have led to a wealth of physical evidence. Under established police protocols for handling domestic violence calls, the police could have photographed the door that Mr. Simpson allegedly broke.

They could also have photographed both Ms. Simpson and Mr. Simpson to document the physical condition of each of them....

In Duluth, Ms. Simpson would not have been asked if she wanted to proceed.[n6] She would not have had a choice. She would have been interviewed in the early stages of the case and subpoenaed to testify.[n7] If she refused after being counseled, she could have been held in contempt.[n8] If Ms. Simpson recanted at trial, prosecutors could have used statements that she made at the scene to police and to the 911 opera- [*1852] tor to impeach her testimony. ...

* * *

...What should prosecutors do when faced with cases in which the victim does not want to cooperate?

As a former assistant state's attorney in an urban domestic violence prosecution unit, I struggled daily with cases like Nicole Brown Simpson's. Abused women often will not cooperate and refuse to appear in court. Sometimes they change their stories to protect their batterers or to shield themselves and their families from outside intervention....

* * *

... I argue that jurisdictions can increase their commitment to holding men who batter criminally responsible by mandating participation as part of an overall prosecution strategy. Mandated participation is a better policy choice than dismissing cases when women refuse to participate. I acknowledge, however, that this solution is imperfect and entails some risks, particularly to women's sense of autonomy. Nevertheless, we must be willing to bear these costs if we are truly committed to ending violence against women.

* * *

D. Mandated Participation Defined

* * *

...Mandated participation may also involve forced testimony if the case proceeds to trial – although such extreme measures are unlikely given that 90% to 95% of all criminal cases end in plea bargains.[n85] Therefore, mandated participation may require the victim to play a much greater role in the early stages of the process in order to prevent the case from proceeding to trial. Nevertheless, there must be a consistent policy of requiring victim testimony if that testimony is necessary to prove the case.

... Decisions to prosecute are based on [*1868] the quality of the evidence and the seriousness of the case,[86] not the victim's reluctance or refusal to proceed. ...[T]this policy ultimately gives the woman no right to choose whether the state criminally prosecutes her partner.

* * *

... Aggressive prosecution offers at least some hope for controlling violence against women and for ultimately reducing the physical injury and related social, economic, and personal costs caused by domestic violence.[n167] Although most women may be powerless to stop the abuse on their own,[n168] evidence suggests that prosecution of batterers can deter future violence,[n169] especially when punishment includes incarceration.[n170] Indeed, incarceration may be the most effective re- [*1888] sponse because it completely incapacitates the batterer for a period of time.

* * *

...[P]rosecutors should develop strategies for domestic violence cases that address the victim's concerns,[n188] but should never allow the victim's level of cooperation to be the sole or primary factor in deciding whether to prosecute. This approach is consistent with the criminal justice system's approach in other areas and preserves the integrity of the state's response. It is also far less paternalistic and sexist than dismissing cases based on the victim's wishes in the domestic violence context while refusing to do so in other contexts. Requiring mandated participation places domestic violence on the same level as all violent crimes and ensures the equal protection of law enforcement for women who are victimized by their intimate partners as well as for women who are victimized by strangers.

* * *

C. Concerns About Revictimization

* * *

If the batterer is not held accountable for his actions, domestic violence generally increases in both severity and frequency.[n206] If a battered woman does not cooperate when there has been criminal intervention and the case results in dismissal, she is likely to be beaten again. If compelled to participate, she may experience a great deal of hardship, but the loss of control over criminal outcomes is not as harmful as physical violence and the risk of death. Also, if the prosecution is successful, she may never be victimized by anyone again, especially if she gains more confidence in herself and the system as a result of the criminal process.

Failure to prosecute because of lack of cooperation can also have consequences beyond the victim's own danger. Most batterers will continue to be abusive and will batter new partners until prevented. Thus, prosecution protects not only the victim, but also other women who might enter into a relationship with the abuser.

* * *

Indeed, we do more harm than good by trying to protect women from the criminal justice system. Domestic violence reflects not only a psychological problem in individual men or women, but also a deeper problem of state-condoned violence.[n212] Shielding women who do not want to proceed through the criminal system reinforces the idea that domestic violence is a private crime without social consequence[n213] and, ultimately, marginalizes and isolates women who are not expected to respond to the violence on a broader scale.

* * *

V. Conclusion

Clearly, there are risks to the aggressive approaches that I have described in this Article. Women who have been victims of domestic violence are likely to resist mandated participation in criminal prosecution, and there are no assurances that by pursuing these cases, individual women will be better off. Yet leaving the choice of prosecution to the victim – and rationalizing that decision on the basis of feminist theory – creates more problems than it solves. To condemn and control violence against women, we have to make some hard choices – choices that challenge some assumptions about the nature of family violence and the role of domestic violence victims in the criminal process.

The O.J. Simpson trial marks a critical point in history for these issues. We may have avoided the question of the proper relationship between crime and domestic violence in the past, but we can do so no longer. As pressure mounts on the criminal justice system to respond more effectively and responsibly to domestic violence, prosecutors have [*1910] to decide to mandate participation in certain cases and to accept the costs, as well as the benefits, of that decision. Otherwise, we will find ourselves looking back and asking, "What other choices could we have made?"

Leigh Goodmark

Law professor Leigh Goodmark argues against mandatory prosecution because it sends the wrong message to women and about women.

Leigh Goodmark (2009) "Autonomy Feminism: An Anti-Essentialist Critique of Mandatory Interventions in Domestic Violence Cases" *Florida State University Law Review* 37 (2009): 1–48. (Excerpts: pp. 25–6, 27, 28–9, 41, 45, 46, 48)

* * *

The question of whether women can act autonomously or with agency within a patriarchal system is complicated significantly by the presence of domestic violence. Some philosophers have questioned whether women who have been battered are ever capable of acting autonomously.[n144] They argue that battering is inherently coercive, creating a context that precludes women who have been battered from being able to exercise free will.[n145]

* * *

...While domestic violence can certainly involve coercion, these thinkers assume that the choice not to engage the legal system is always a coerced choice. Given how these mandatory policies operate to deprive a victim of choice, it is worth questioning whether a woman who has been battered is ever free of coercion, regardless of the measures she uses to address the violence she experiences.

Women who have been battered can exercise autonomy and/or agency. The exercise of autonomy does not require unfettered or entirely consistent choice.... Women who have been battered must be free to make choices that others disagree with or fail to understand.[n160] As Morwenna Griffiths writes, "Women want autonomy; they want to decide the course of their own lives-even though this may mean that they decide to continue with precisely the situations that others may define for them as ones in which they lack autonomy."[n161]

* * *

The arguments made by those who support mandatory interventions beg the conclusion that women who have been battered can rarely, if ever, act autonomously, a problematic assertion given the primacy of autonomy in the American political and legal systems. Accepting that women who have been battered are incapable of engaging in independent deliberation devalues these women as members of the political society and invites and justifies what some might characterize as paternalism on their behalf.[n165] Paternalism reflects a lack of respect for autonomy and for the individual as a person.[n166] A number of the policies adopted to address domestic violence-policies championed by many advocates for women who have been battered -are guided by what seems to be patently paternalistic views of these women as powerless, limited individuals incapable of acting on their own behalf. [n167]

A better way to characterize the spirit motivating these policy choices, at least on the part of advocates for women who have been battered, is that they exemplify maternalism. These policies come from a well-meaning place-the desire to protect women who have been battered from further intimidation and violence, from their own inability to invoke the legal system given their fear of retaliation [*29] from their abusers, from losing their children or economic benefits in unfair mediations. ...

But maternalism is no better than paternalism in that it assumes that women who have been battered are incapable of considering the full range of possibilities and deprives them of the ability to make choices for themselves, based on their own goals, values, beliefs, and understanding of their situations. Maternalism undermines the autonomy of women who have been battered. Exercises of maternalism to justify the implementation of mandatory policies are fundamentally at odds with one of the foundational goals of the battered women's movement-empowerment.

* * *

Mandatory policies are disempowering because they deprive women who have been battered of the ability to control their use of tools like arrest, prosecution, and mediation. Women who have been battered use the legal system to attempt to regain control from their abusers. [n239] Researcher David Ford has described how women who have been battered use the threat of prosecution as a "power resource," a tool that can be deployed to equalize the power imbalances within the relationship. [n240] Women call police not only because they want their partners arrested, but also to interrupt the battering incident or to show their partners that they are willing to reach out to others and to invoke the power of the state to stop the violence. [n241] Women participate in prosecutions against their partners not only because they want those partners punished, but also to teach them a lesson, to secure counseling for the battering partner, or to get support payments, for example. [n242] Similarly, women drop charges for a variety of reasons beyond intimidation by their partners: because the violence has stopped, he has agreed to counseling, or he has agreed to divorce. [n243] The instrumental use of arrest and prosecution empowers the woman who has been battered in the negotiation of the terms of her relationship with her partner. Ford warns, however, that "criminal justice options are victim power resources only if she can control the manner in which they are brought to bear on her mate." [n244]

* * *

VI. From Dominance to Anti-Essentialist Feminism

* * *

... Mandatory policies assume that all women who have been battered are "victims," stereotyping them as meek, afraid, and easily manipulated and controlled, rather than seeing the complexity of and differences among them. [n265] These policies deny women the ability to define themselves, distilling every woman down to the stereotypical victim in need of the system's protection, unable to make rational choices. Mandatory policies ignore that women experiencing violence may have multiple goals, assuming instead that all women prioritize safety and accountability.

Defining all women as victims allowed the legal system to narrow the available options, depriving women who had been battered of the ability to pursue possibilities beyond the range of those deemed acceptable by the legal system....[W]omen who have been battered should not be told by the state that they have no choice about arrest, prosecution, or mediation. [n266] Instead, domestic violence law and policy should respect the rights of individual women to choose whether and how to use the criminal and civil legal systems....

* * *

The choices made by women who have been battered will certainly have consequences, sometimes overwhelmingly negative consequences. [n269] Some women who choose not to have their partners arrested will be battered again; some will die. [n270] Some offenders will be free to abuse again as a result of dismissed prosecutions. Some women will strike bad deals in mediation or experience revictimization in the process. Creating space for individuals to exercise their ability to choose, regardless of the outcomes of those choices, is a hallmark of autonomy. But many other women will be empowered by the ability to make these choices for themselves in the contexts of their own lives, rather than having the legal system impose decisions upon them based on what they "should" want. If empowerment is still the goal of the battered women's movement, we must accept that women who have been battered have the right to make choices that we might disagree with, dislike, or fear. [n271]

* * *

VII. Conclusion

* * *

Agency is the power to make informed decisions and implement them without interference by the batterer. Agency is the power to organize one's life. Agency is the power to establish stable, nurturing homes for children. Agency is the power to participate, without batterer impediment, in work, education, faith, family and community . . . . Agency is the power to employ the legal options, community resources, economic remedies, housing opportunities, and educational programs available in order to escape the violence and achieve lives that are free of intimidation, degradation, and violation. [n279]

But agency is also the power to choose not to have an intimate partner arrested. Agency is the power to choose not to participate in a prosecution that could cause an intimate partner to go to jail or be deported or simply be removed from the family. Agency is the power to confront an intimate partner with his violence and advocate on one's own behalf for a mediated settlement to pending litigation. Agency is the power to see a physician to have injuries treated but choose to have that physician maintain confidentiality about the cause of those injuries. Agency is self-direction, self-determination, and the ability to identify, evaluate, and make decisions. Agency and autonomy are what women who have been battered are denied by mandatory policies in cases involving domestic violence.

North Carolina v. Norman, 378 S.E.2d 8 (1989)

The case of Judy Norman shows how the legal community is divided over the appropriateness of using Battered Woman's Syndrome as a defense for justifiable homicide. This excerpt from the North Carolina Supreme Court's opinion describes the abuse that led to Ms. Norman's decision to shoot and kill her sleeping husband. The Court majority rejected Ms. Norman's claim that killing her husband was justifiable because, as a battered woman suffering Battered Woman's Syndrome, she feared for her life and acted in self-defense.

STATE OF NORTH CAROLINA v. JUDY ANN LAWS NORMAN
SUPREME COURT OF NORTH CAROLINA

324 N.C. 253; 378 S.E.2d 8; 1989 N.C. LEXIS 158

April 5, 1989, Filed

OPINION: Chief Justice Mitchell

[*253] [**9] The defendant was tried at the 16 February 1987 Criminal Session of Superior Court for Rutherford County upon a proper indictment charging her with the first degree murder of her husband. [*254] The jury found the defendant guilty of voluntary manslaughter. The defendant appealed from the [***3] trial court's judgment sentencing her to six years imprisonment.

The Court of Appeals granted a new trial, citing as error the trial court's refusal to submit a possible verdict of acquittal by reason of perfect self-defense. Notwithstanding the uncontroverted evidence that the defendant shot her husband three times in the back of the head as he lay sleeping in his bed, the Court of Appeals held that the defendant's evidence that she exhibited what has come to be called "the battered wife syndrome" entitled her to have the jury consider whether the homicide was an act of perfect self-defense and, thus, not a legal wrong.

We conclude that the evidence introduced in this case would not support a finding that the defendant killed her husband due to a reasonable fear of imminent death or great bodily harm, as is required before a defendant is entitled to jury instructions concerning either perfect or imperfect self-defense. Therefore, the trial court properly declined to instruct the jury on the law relating to self-defense. Accordingly, we reverse the Court of Appeals.

At trial, the State presented the testimony of Deputy Sheriff R. H. Epley of the Rutherford County Sheriff's Department, [***4] who was called to the Norman residence on the night of 12 June 1985. Inside the home, Epley found the defendant's husband, John Thomas Norman, lying on a bed in a rear bedroom with his face toward the wall and his back toward the middle of the room. He was dead, but blood was still coming from wounds to the back of his head. A later autopsy revealed three gunshot wounds to the head, two of which caused fatal brain injury. The autopsy also revealed a. 12 percent blood alcohol level in the victim's body.

Later that night, the defendant related an account of the events leading to the killing, after Epley had advised her of her constitutional rights and she had waived her right to remain silent. The defendant told Epley that her husband had been beating her all day and had made her lie down on the floor while he slept on the bed. After her husband fell asleep, the defendant carried her grandchild to the defendant's mother's house. The defendant took a pistol from her mother's purse and walked the short distance back to her home. She pointed the pistol at the [*255] back of her sleeping husband's head, but it jammed the first time she tried to shoot him. She fixed the gun [***5] and then shot her husband in the back of the head as he lay sleeping. After one shot, she felt her husband's chest and determined that he was still breathing and making sounds. She then shot him twice more in the back of the head. The defendant told Epley that she killed her husband because "she took all she was going to take from him so she shot him."

The defendant presented evidence tending to show a long history of physical and mental abuse by her husband due to his [**10] alcoholism. At the time of the killing, the thirty-nine-year-old defendant and her husband had been married almost twenty-five years and had several children. The defendant testified that her husband had started drinking and abusing her about five years after they were married. His physical abuse of her consisted of frequent assaults that included slapping, punching and kicking her, striking her with various objects, and throwing glasses, beer bottles and other objects at her. The defendant described other specific incidents of abuse, such as her husband putting her cigarettes out on her, throwing hot coffee on her, breaking glass against her face and crushing food on her face. Although the defendant did not [***6] present evidence of ever having received medical treatment for any physical injuries inflicted by her husband, she displayed several scars about her face which she attributed to her husband's assaults.

The defendant's evidence also tended to show other indignities inflicted upon her by her husband. Her evidence tended to show that her husband did not work and forced her to make money by prostitution, and that he made humor of that fact to family and friends. He would beat her if she resisted going out to prostitute herself or if he was unsatisfied with the amounts of money she made. He routinely called the defendant "dog," "bitch" and "whore," and on a few occasions made her eat pet food out of the pets' bowls and bark like a dog. He often made her sleep on the floor. At times, he deprived her of food and refused to let her get food for the family. During those years of abuse, the defendant's husband threatened numerous times to kill her and to maim her in various ways.

[*256] The defendant said her husband's abuse occurred only when he was intoxicated, but that he would not give up drinking. She said she and her husband "got along very well when he was sober," and that [***7] he was

"a good guy" when he was not drunk. She had accompanied her husband to the local mental health center for sporadic counseling sessions for his problem, but he continued to drink.

In the early morning hours on the day before his death, the defendant's husband, who was intoxicated, went to a rest area off I-85 near Kings Mountain where the defendant was engaging in prostitution and assaulted her. While driving home, he was stopped by a patrolman and jailed on a charge of driving while impaired. After the defendant's mother got him out of jail at the defendant's request later that morning, he resumed his drinking and abuse of the defendant.

The defendant's evidence also tended to show that her husband seemed angrier than ever after he was released from jail and that his abuse of the defendant was more frequent. That evening, sheriff's deputies were called to the Norman residence, and the defendant complained that her husband had been beating her all day and she could not take it anymore. The defendant was advised to file a complaint, but she said she was afraid her husband would kill her if she had him arrested. The deputies told her they needed a warrant before they could [***8] arrest her husband, and they left the scene.

The deputies were called back less than an hour later after the defendant had taken a bottle of pills. The defendant's husband cursed her and called her names as she was attended by paramedics, and he told them to let her die. A sheriff's deputy finally chased him back into his house as the defendant was put into an ambulance. The defendant's stomach was pumped at the local hospital, and she was sent home with her mother.

While in the hospital, the defendant was visited by a therapist with whom she discussed filing charges against her husband and having him committed for treatment. Before the therapist left, the defendant agreed to go to the mental health center the next day to discuss those possibilities. The therapist testified at trial that the defendant seemed depressed in the hospital, and that she expressed considerable anger toward her husband. He [*257] testified that the defendant threatened a number of times that night to kill her husband and that she [**11] said she should kill him "because of the things he had done to her."

The next day, the day she shot her husband, the defendant went to the mental health center to talk [***9] about charges and possible commitment, and she confronted her husband with that possibility. She testified that she told her husband later that day: "J. T., straighten up. Quit drinking. I'm going to have you committed to help you." She said her husband then told her he would "see them coming" and would cut her throat before they got to him.

The defendant also went to the social services office that day to seek welfare benefits, but her husband followed her there, interrupted her interview and made her go home with him. He continued his abuse of her, threatening to kill and to maim her, slapping her, kicking her, and throwing objects at her. At one point, he took her cigarette and put it out on her, causing a small burn on her upper torso. He would not let her eat or bring food into the house for their children.

That evening, the defendant and her husband went into their bedroom to lie down, and he called her a "dog" and made her lie on the floor when he lay down on the bed. Their daughter brought in her baby to leave with the defendant, and the defendant's husband agreed to let her baby-sit. After the defendant's husband fell asleep, the baby started crying and the defendant [***10] took it to her mother's house so it would not wake up her husband. She returned shortly with the pistol and killed her husband.

The defendant testified at trial that she was too afraid of her husband to press charges against him or to leave him. She said that she had temporarily left their home on several previous occasions, but he had always found her, brought her home and beaten her. Asked why she killed her husband, the defendant replied: "Because I was scared of him and I knowed when he woke up, it was going to be the same thing, and I was scared when he took me to the truck stop that night it was going to be worse than he had ever been. I just couldn't take it no more. There ain't no way, even if it means going to prison. It's better than living in that. That's worse hell than anything."

[*258] The defendant and other witnesses testified that for years her husband had frequently threatened to kill her and to maim her. When asked if she believed those threats, the defendant replied: "Yes. I believed him; he would, he would kill me if he got a chance. If he thought he wouldn't a had to went to jail, he would a done it."

Two expert witnesses in forensic psychology [***11] and psychiatry who examined the defendant after the shooting, Dr. William Tyson and Dr. Robert Rollins, testified that the defendant fit the profile of battered wife syndrome. This condition, they testified, is characterized by such abuse and degradation that the battered wife comes to believe she is unable to help herself and cannot expect help from anyone else. She believes that she cannot escape the complete control of her husband and that he is invulnerable to law enforcement and other sources of help.

* * *

Based on the evidence that the defendant exhibited battered wife syndrome, that she believed she could not escape her husband nor expect help from others, that her husband had threatened [*259] her, and that her husband's abuse of her had worsened in the two days preceding his death, the Court of Appeals concluded that a jury reasonably could have found that her killing of her husband was justified as an act of perfect self-defense. The Court of Appeals reasoned that the nature of battered wife syndrome is such that a jury could not be precluded from finding the defendant killed her husband [***13] lawfully in perfect self-defense, even though he was asleep when she killed him. We disagree.

The right to kill in self-defense is based on the necessity, real or reasonably apparent, of killing an unlawful aggressor to save oneself from imminent death or great bodily harm at his hands. *State v. Gappins, 320 N.C. 64, 357 S.E. 2d 654 (1987).* Our law has recognized that self-preservation under such circumstances springs from a primal impulse and is an inherent right of natural law. *State v. Holland, 193 N.C. 713, 718, 138 S.E. 8, 10 (1927).*

In North Carolina, a defendant is entitled to have the jury consider acquittal by reason of perfect self-defense when the evidence, viewed in the light most favorable to the defendant, tends to show that at the time of the killing it appeared to the defendant and she believed it to be necessary to kill the decedent to save herself from imminent death or great bodily harm. *State v. Gappins, 320 N.C. at 71, 357 S.E. 2d at 659.* That belief must be reasonable, however, in that the circumstances as they appeared to the defendant would create [***14] such a belief in the mind of a person of ordinary firmness. Id. Further, the defendant must not have been the initial aggressor provoking the fatal confrontation. Id. A killing in the proper exercise of the right of perfect self-defense is always completely justified in law and constitutes no legal wrong.

Our law also recognizes an imperfect right of self-defense in certain circumstances, including, for example, when the defendant is the initial aggressor, but without intent to kill or to seriously injure the decedent, and the decedent escalates the confrontation to a point where it reasonably appears to the defendant to be necessary to kill the decedent to save herself from imminent death or great bodily harm. ...

The defendant in the present case was not entitled to a jury instruction on either perfect or imperfect self-defense. The trial court was not required to instruct on either form of self-defense unless evidence was introduced tending to show that at the time of the killing the defendant reasonably believed herself to be confronted by circumstances which necessitated her killing her husband to save herself from imminent death or great bodily harm. Id. No such evidence was introduced in this case, and it would have been error for the trial court to instruct the jury on either perfect or imperfect self-defense. See *State v. Gappins, 320 N.C. 64, 73, 357 S.E. 2d 654, 660 (1987); State v. Mize, 316 N.C. 48, 53, 340 S.E. 2d 439, 442 (1986); State v. Spaulding, 298 N.C. 149, 157, 257 S.E. 2d 391, 396 (1979); State v. Marshall, 208 N.C. 127, 129, 179 S.E. 427, 428 (1935); State v. Kidd, 60 N.C. App. 140, 142, 298 S.E. 2d 406, 408 (1982),* disc. rev. denied, 307 N.C. 700, 301 S.E. 2d 393 (1983); [***16] *State v. Dial, 38 N.C. App. 529, 531, 248 S.E. 2d 366, 367 (1978);* 40 C.J.S. Homicide § 123(b) (1944).

* * *

...Only if defendants are required to show that they killed due to a reasonable belief that death or great bodily harm was imminent can the justification for homicide remain clearly and firmly rooted in necessity. The imminence requirement ensures that deadly force will be used only where it is necessary as a last resort in the exercise of the inherent right of self-preservation. It also ensures that before a homicide is justified and, as a result, not a legal wrong, it will be reliably determined that the defendant reasonably believed that absent the use of deadly force, not only would an unlawful attack have occurred, but also that the attack would have caused death or great bodily harm. The law does not sanction the use of deadly force to repel simple assaults. *State v. Watkins, 283 N.C. 504, 196 S.E. 2d 750 (1973).* [***18]

* * *

The evidence in this case did not tend to show that the defendant reasonably believed that she was confronted by a threat of imminent death or great bodily harm. The evidence tended to show that no harm was "imminent" or about to happen to the defendant when she shot her husband. The uncontroverted evidence was that her husband had been asleep for some time when she walked to her mother's house, returned with the pistol, fixed the pistol after it jammed and then shot her husband three times in the back of the head. The defendant was not faced [***19] with an instantaneous choice between killing her husband or being killed or seriously injured. Instead, all of the evidence tended to show that the defendant had ample time and opportunity to resort to other [*262] means of preventing further abuse by her husband. There was no action underway by the decedent from which the jury could have found that the defendant had reasonable grounds to believe either that a felonious assault was imminent or that it might result in her death or great bodily injury. Additionally, no such action by the decedent had been underway immediately prior to his falling asleep.

* * *

Additionally, the lack of any belief by the defendant -- reasonable or otherwise -- that she faced a threat of imminent death or great bodily harm from the drunk and sleeping victim in the present case was illustrated by the defendant and her own expert witnesses [***21] when testifying about her subjective assessment of her situation at the time of the killing. The psychologist and psychiatrist replied affirmatively when asked their opinions of whether killing her husband "appeared reasonably necessary" to the defendant [*263] at the time of the homicide. That testimony spoke of no imminent threat nor of any fear by the defendant of death or great bodily harm, imminent or otherwise. Testimony in the form of a conclusion that a killing "appeared reasonably necessary" to a defendant does not tend to show all that must be shown to establish self-defense. More specifically, for a killing to be in self-defense, the perceived necessity must arise from a reasonable fear of imminent death or great bodily harm.

Dr. Tyson additionally testified that the defendant "believed herself to be doomed . . . to a life of the worst kind of torture and abuse, degradation that she had experienced over the years in a progressive way; that it would only get worse, and that death was inevitable." Such evidence of the defendant's speculative beliefs concerning her remote and indefinite future, while indicating she had felt generally threatened, did not tend to [***22] show that she killed in the belief -- reasonable or otherwise -- that her husband presented a threat of imminent death or great bodily harm. Under our law of self-defense, a defendant's subjective belief of what might be "inevitable" at some indefinite point in the future does not equate to what she believes to be "imminent." Dr. Tyson's opinion that the defendant believed it was necessary to kill her husband for "the protection of herself and her family" was similarly indefinite and devoid of time frame and did not tend to show a threat or fear of imminent harm.

The defendant testified that, "I knowed when he woke up, it was going to be the same thing, and I was scared when he took me to the truck stop that night it was going to be worse than he had ever been." She also testified, when asked if she believed her husband's threats: "Yes. . . . [H]e would kill me if he got a chance. If he thought he wouldn't a had to went to jail, he would a done it." Testimony about such indefinite fears concerning what her sleeping husband might do at some time in the future did not tend to establish a fear -- reasonable or otherwise -- of imminent death or great bodily harm at the [***23] time of the killing.

We are not persuaded by the reasoning of our Court of Appeals in this case that when there is evidence of battered wife syndrome, neither an actual attack nor threat of attack by the husband at the moment the wife uses deadly force is required to justify the wife's killing of him in perfect self-defense. The Court [*264] of Appeals concluded that to impose such requirements [**15] would ignore the "learned helplessness," meekness and other realities of battered wife syndrome and would effectively preclude such women from exercising their right of self-defense.

* * *

The Court of Appeals suggests that such [***25] speculation would have been particularly reliable in the present case because the jury, based on the evidence of the decedent's intensified abuse during the thirty-six hours preceding his death, could have found that the decedent's passive state at the time of his death was "but a momentary hiatus in a continuous reign of terror by the decedent [and] the defendant merely took advantage of her first opportunity to protect herself." 89 N.C. App. at 394, 366 S.E. 2d at 592. Requiring jury instructions on perfect self-defense in such [*265] situations, however, would still tend to make opportune homicide lawful as a result of mere subjective predictions of indefinite future assaults and circumstances. Such predictions of future assaults to justify the defendant's use of deadly force in this case would be entirely speculative, because there was no evidence that her husband had ever inflicted any harm upon her that approached life-threatening injury, even during the "reign of terror." It is far from clear in the defendant's poignant evidence that any abuse by the decedent had ever involved the degree of physical threat required to justify the defendant in [***26] using deadly force, even when those threats were imminent. *HN8*The use of deadly force in self-defense to prevent harm other than death or great bodily harm is excessive as a matter of law. State v. Hunter, 315 N.C. 371, 338 S.E. 2d 99 (1986).

As we have stated, stretching the law of self-defense to fit the facts of this case would require changing the "imminent death or great bodily harm" requirement to something substantially more indefinite than previously required and would weaken our assurances that justification for the taking of human life remains firmly rooted in real or apparent necessity. That result in principle could not be limited to a few cases decided on evidence as poignant as this. The relaxed requirements for perfect self-defense proposed by our Court of Appeals would tend to categorically legalize the opportune killing of abusive husbands by their wives solely on the basis of the wives' testimony concerning their subjective speculation as to the probability of future felonious assaults by their husbands. Homicidal self-help would then become a lawful solution, and perhaps the easiest and most effective solution, to this problem.

* * *

For the foregoing reasons, we conclude that the defendant's conviction for voluntary manslaughter and the trial court's judgment sentencing her to a six-year term of imprisonment were without error. Therefore, we must reverse the decision of the Court of Appeals which awarded the defendant a new trial.

Reversed.

Bechtel v. Oklahoma, 840 P. 2d 1 (Okla.CrApp. 1992)

In contrast to the North Carolina Supreme Court, the Oklahoma Court of Criminal Appeals, in the case of *Donna Bechtel v Oklahoma*, recommended that the Battered Woman Syndrome should be a defense for justifiable homicide in the state of Oklahoma. The facts outlining the events that led to Mrs. Bechtel killing her unarmed husband are listed below.

DONNA LEE BECHTEL, Appellant, v. STATE OF OKLAHOMA, Appellee.

COURT OF CRIMINAL APPEALS OF OKLAHOMA

1992 OK CR 55; 840 P.2d 1; 1992 Okla. Crim. App. LEXIS 73; 63 O.B.A.J. 2499

September 2, 1992, Filed

OPINION: Judge Johnson

DONNA LEE BECHTEL, Appellant, was retried [**2] [1] by jury for the crime of Murder [*4] in the First Degree ....The jury returned a verdict of guilty and set punishment at life imprisonment, to which she was sentenced....

FACTS

The following facts are primarily from the testimony of [**3] the Appellant who met the victim, Ken Bechtel, in June 1981. At that time he was married, but separated, and dating another woman with whom he had been living for seven years. Appellant saw him approximately five times after their first meeting but did not start seeing him on a regular basis until he got his divorce. They were married on August 25, 1982. Although there was great conflict between her testimony and that as presented by the State, most of the balance of the facts are as presented by Appellant. We are presenting her testimony to show facts necessary to meet the first prong of our guidelines under the Battered Woman Syndrome.

She recalled that the first incidence of violence perpetrated by the victim upon her was on July 4, 1982, when around midnight, he began crying about his deceased son and, in a drunken rage, grabbed her by the head and threw her into the windshield of his boat. As she tried to get to the telephone, he started to throw canned goods out of the closet at her. She left but was caught and put in a car by Ken; while they were stopped at a stop sign, she jumped out of the car. Mr. Bechtel came around the side of the car, threw her back in, and told [**4] her not to ever do that again. Inside the car, he grabbed her head by the hair and slammed her into the window and again, told her not to get out of the car. When they arrived at her home, Appellant jumped out of the car, ran into her house and locked the doors. When Ken Bechtel threatened to kick the "m . . .f . . ." door in, Appellant responded by telling him that she had guns in her home. Mr. Bechtel eventually left. This was the first of approximately 23 battering incidents leading to the fatal shooting on September 23, 1984.

Testimony at trial revealed that the deceased committed the batterings when intoxicated and without provocation. The batterings consisted of the deceased grabbing Appellant by either her ears or hair and pounding her head on the ground, wall, door, cabinet or other available object. During many of the episodes he would sob profusely and ramble about his deceased son who was born retarded. During all of the episodes, the deceased threatened or otherwise intimidated Appellant.[2]

[**5] On three occasions, Appellant was treated in the Emergency Room. On each of the occasions, the deceased provided the information as to the cause of the injury. On one occasion, Appellant was treated for neck injury and provided with a neck collar. On the other occasions, she was treated for cuts to her hand and feet. On five occasions, Appellant sought police help. Each time the police arrived at her home, the deceased was made to leave. On one occasion, Appellant stopped at the scene of an accident and asked the policeman at the scene to remove the deceased who, in a drunken rage, was kicking the windshield and beating on the dashboard. The deceased [*5] was removed and taken to the residence and was there when Appellant arrived. Appellant was subsequently beaten by the deceased.

On several occasions, Appellant was able to escape her residence and stay overnight at various hotels. Appellant related the incidents to some of her close friends and the deceased's family. However, though some of the abuse occurred on business trips, she never told the deceased's business associates. Appellant also sought help from the deceased's family as to his alcohol problem. She made inquiries [**6] of several treatment facilities and made appointments for the deceased, who promised after later incidents to undergo treatment, but never did.

On September 23, 1984, the day of his death, the deceased returned home unexpectedly at approximately 5:30 A.M. from a hunting trip, highly intoxicated. He awakened Appellant and ordered her to get out of the bed so they could have a drink. He ordered her out on the patio where the deceased related to her and her friend, Billy Bender, who was visiting from out of state, that he had been picked up for driving under the influence by the Nichols Hills Police. Ken Bechtel continued to drink coffee with liquor. He became angry when Appellant kept turning down the jukebox whenever he would turn it up.

After about three or four hours, Appellant decided to go back to bed. Once in her bedroom, she could hear Mr. Bechtel crying. She became afraid. Aware that Ms. Bender might be in difficulty, she went to the doors of the patio to try to get Ms. Bender's attention. Finally, Ms. Bender came inside to get some cigarettes. When she tried to return to the patio, Appellant admonished her not to go back but to leave Mr. Bechtel alone to sleep it [**7] off and for her go to bed immediately. The next thing Appellant remembered was hearing the night table drawer opening and seeing the deceased with the .25 gun in his hand. He told Appellant that she would not need that G..D.. gun anymore.

As he walked towards the door leading to the backyard, she jumped up and ran to the closet where she frantically looked for her purse and keys. After retrieving her purse, she turned to go to the kitchen when a naked Ken Bechtel pulled her by the hair and threw her back on the bed. He was rambling and crying about his son Kenny and questioning her about why she was not at home when he tried to call her earlier. He held his arm against her throat. Appellant raised her leg to free herself when they both fell onto the floor. The deceased threatened to "f--k you and kill your ass." He began pounding her head into the floor. He picked her up by the head and pulled her back on the bed. He pulled her gown off and rammed his fingers into her vagina. He then climbed on top of her, held her down by placing his knees on her arms and banged her head against the headboard. He ejaculated on her face and stomach, after which he slumped on top of her. [**8] She eased from under him and went to the bathroom to wash herself.

While in the bathroom, the deceased came up behind her, grabbed the back of her head, threw her down on the floor, bit her on the left breast and finally lay his head on her lower body. During this time, Appellant tried to calm him down by repeating it's okay, it's all right. Then the telephone rang. It was a friend inquiring about his luggage. During this time, Appellant vomited. As she was trying to put on some clothes, Ken returned, accusing her of taking the friend's luggage and betting that she thought it was her "G.D." kids. He put her arm behind her back and his arm against her throat and forced her back onto the bed. At this point his eyes were glazed over and he was crying and rambling as he continued to beat her head against the headboard. He slumped on top of her.

Appellant tried to get from under him, but he would mumble whenever she made an effort. Finally, she eased herself from under him. As she sat on her knees on the floor beside the bed, she lit a cigarette, held it in one hand and her head with the other hand. As she got ready to smoke the cigarette, she heard a gurgling sound, looked [**9] up and saw the contorted look and [*6] glazed eyes of the deceased with his arms raised. Appellant reached for the gun under the bed and shot the deceased as she tried to get up and run.

SELF-DEFENSE AND THE BATTERED WOMAN

Appellant defended this case on the theory of self-defense....

* * *

This Court has held that the bare belief that one is about to suffer death or great personal injury will not, in itself, justify taking the life of his adversary. There must exist reasonable grounds for such belief at the time of the killing. (Emphasis added). Further, the right to take another's life in self-defense is not to be tested by the honesty or good faith of the defendant's belief in the necessity of the killing, but by the fact [**10] whether he had reasonable grounds for such belief. (Emphasis added). See *Hood v. State, 70 Okla. Crim. 334, 106 P.2d 271 (Okl.Cr.1940)*. Fear alone never justifies one person to take the life of another. Such fear must have been induced by some overt act, gesture or word spoken by the deceased at the time the homicide occurred which would form a reasonable ground for the belief that the accused is about to suffer death or great bodily harm. *McKee v. State, 372 P.2d 243 (Okl.Cr.1962)*; *West v. State, 617 P.2d 1362, 1366 (Okl.Cr.1980)*.

* * *

Misconceptions regarding battered women abound, making it more likely than not that the average juror will draw from his or her own experience or common myths, which may lead to a wholly incorrect conclusion. Thus, we believe that expert testimony on the syndrome is necessary to counter these misconceptions.[8]

* * *

2. REASONABLENESS AND THE BATTERED WOMAN SYNDROME

The key to the defense of self-defense is reasonableness. A defendant must show that she had a reasonable belief as to the imminence of great bodily harm or death and as to the force necessary to compel it. Several of the psychological symptoms that develop in one suffering from the syndrome are particularly relevant [**22] to the standard of reasonableness in self-defense. One such symptom is a greater sensitivity to danger which has come about because of the intimacy and history of the relationship. ...

It is during the tension-building period that the battered woman develops a heightened sensitivity to any kinds of cues of distress. *HN6*Thus, because of her intimate knowledge of her batterer, the battered woman perceives danger faster and more accurately as she is more acutely aware that a new or escalated violent episode is about to occur. See *Price v. State, 1 Okla. Crim. 358, 98 P. 447 (Okl.Cr.1908)*, where this Court held, quoting from *Allison v. United States, 160 U.S. 203, 16 Sup.Ct. 252, 40 L.Ed. 395 (1895)*:

What is or is not an overt demonstration of violence varies with the circumstances. Under some circumstances a slight [**23] movement may justify instant action because of reasonable apprehension of danger, under other circumstances this would not be so. And it is for the jury, and not for the judge passing upon the weight and effect of the evidence, to determine how this may be.

Indeed, considering her particular circumstances, the battered woman's perception of the situation and her belief as to the imminence of great bodily harm or death may be deemed reasonable.

* * *

Standards of reasonableness has been traditionally characterized as either "objective" or "subjective." Under the objective standard of reasonableness, the trier of fact is required to view the circumstances, surrounding the accused at the time of the use of force, from the standpoint of hypothetical reasonable person. Under the subjective standard of reasonableness, the fact finder is required to determine whether the circumstances, surrounding the accused at the time of the use of force, are sufficient to induce in the accused an honest and reasonable belief [*11] that he/she must use force to defend himself/herself against imminent harm.

Oklahoma's standard of reasonableness may be gleaned from past decisions of this Court and is set forth in OUJI-CR 743, which reads as follows: A person is [**25] justified in using deadly force in self-defense if that person reasonably believed that use of deadly force was necessary to protect herself from imminent danger of death or great bodily harm. Self- defense is a defense although the danger to life or personal security may not have been real, if a reasonable person, in the circumstances and from the viewpoint of the defendant, would reasonably have believed that she was in imminent danger of death or great bodily harm.

...Thus, Oklahoma's standard is a hybrid, combining both the objective and subjective standards. ...

However, in light of the jury's inquiry[9] and our decision today to allow testimony on the Battered Woman Syndrome[10] in appropriate cases, we deem it necessary to modify OUJI-CR 743 by striking the words "reasonably" and "reasonable" from such instruction. We hereby adopt a new OUJI-CR 743A instruction that will be given in all Battered Woman Syndrome cases. Such modified instruction [**27] shall read as follows:

A person is justified in using deadly force in self-defense if that person believed that use of deadly force was necessary to protect herself from imminent danger of death or great bodily harm. Self-defense is a defense although the danger to life or personal security may not have been real, if a person, in the circumstances and from the viewpoint of the defendant, would reasonably have believed that she was in imminent danger of death or great bodily harm.

* * *

3. IMMINENCE AND THE BATTERED WOMAN SYNDROME

In addition to the reasonableness standard, Oklahoma's law of self-defense also imposes the temporal requirement of imminence. The thinking is that it is unreasonable [*12] to be provoked to the point of killing well after the provocative or assertive conduct has occurred.

Furthermore, the syndrome has been analogized to the classic hostage situation in that the battered woman lives under long-term, life-threatening conditions in constant fear of another eruption of violence. ...For the battered woman, if there is no escape or sense of safety, then the next attack, which could be fatal or cause serious bodily harm, is imminent. Based on the traditionally accepted definition of imminent and its functional derivatives,[11] a battered woman, to whom the threat of serious bodily harm or death is always imminent,[12] would be precluded from asserting the defense of self-defense.

Under our "hybrid" reasonableness standard, the meaning of imminent must necessarily envelope the battered woman's perceptions based on all the facts and circumstances of his or her relationship with the victim. In Women's Self-defense Cases: Theory and Practice (1981), Elizabeth Bochnak writes:

The battered woman learns to recognize the small signs that precede periods of escalated violence. She learns to distinguish subtle changes in tone of voice, facial expression, and levels of danger. She is in a position to know, perhaps with greater certainty than someone attacked by a stranger, that the batterer's threat is real and will be acted upon.

Thus, according to the author, an abused woman may kill her mate during [**31] the period of threat that precedes a violent incident, right before the violence escalates to the more dangerous levels of an acute battering episode. Or, she may take action against him during a lull in an assaultive incident, or after it has culminated, in an effort to prevent a recurrence of the violence.[13] And so, the issue is not whether the danger was in fact imminent, but whether, given the circumstances as she perceived them, the defendant's belief was reasonable that the danger was imminent.

* * *

For the foregoing reasons, this case is REVERSED and REMANDED for a new trial, consistent with this opinion.

OPINION BY: JOHNSON, J.

Sexual Violence and Rape

Catharine A. MacKinnon

In a comprehensive analysis of 'sex equality under the law," renowned feminist scholar Catharine MacKinnon argues that rape against women is characteristic of the systemic inequality women experience in patriarchal societies. For MacKinnon, rape must be addressed through systemic reforms and societal changes.

Catharine A. MacKinnon "Reflections on Sex Equality Under Law" *Yale Law Journal* 100 (1991) 1281–1328. (Excerpts: pp. 1301–4, 1306–7)

Women are sexually assaulted because they are women: not individually or at random, but on the basis of sex, because of their membership in a group defined by gender.... Females -- adults and children -- make up the overwhelming population of victims of sexual assault. The perpetrators are, overwhelmingly, men. Men do this to women and to girls, boys, and other men, in that order. Women hardly ever do this to men.

Sexual violation symbolizes and actualizes women's subordinate social status to men. It is both an indication and a practice of inequality between the sexes, specifically of the low status of women relative to men. Availability for aggressive intimate intrusion and use at will for pleasure by another defines who one is socially taken to be and constitutes an index of social worth. To be a means to the end of the sexual pleasure of one more powerful is, empirically, a degraded status and the female position. In social reality, rape and the fear of rape operate cross-culturally as a mechanism of terror to control women. To attempt to avoid it, women are constrained in moving about in the world and walk down the street with their eyes averted. n102 Rape is an act of dominance over women that works systemically to maintain a gender-stratified society in which women occupy a disadvantaged status as the appropriate victims and targets of sexual aggression. n103

Sexual aggression by men against women is normalized. In traditional gender roles, male sexuality embodies the role of aggressor, female sexuality the role of victim, and some degree of force is romanticized as acceptable. n104 Sexual assaults frequently occur in the context of family life or everyday social events, often perpetrated by an assailant who is known to the victim. n105 In one study, one-third of American men in the sample say they would rape a woman if assured they would not get caught. The figure climbs following exposure to commonly available aggressive pornography. n106 Pornography, which sexualizes gender inequality, is a major institution of socialization into these roles. The evidence suggests that women are targeted for intimate assault because the degradation and violation and domination of women is eroticized, indeed defines the social meaning of female sexuality in societies of sex inequality. Sexual assault thus becomes a definitive act of sexualized power and masculinity under male supremacy.

Only a fraction of rapes is reported, the most frequently mentioned reason for nonreporting being fear of the criminal justice system. Women of color fear its racism particularly. Only a fraction of reported rapes is prosecuted.

Many rapes are "unfounded," an active verb describing the police decision not to believe that a rape happened as reported. n107 Only a fraction of prosecuted rapes results in convictions. Rape sentences are often short. Most rapists therefore continue to live in society either undetected or unpunished and unrehabilitated. In many instances, one must suppose that they remain unaware that they did anything even potentially culpable. n108 Perhaps these data are viewed with complacency on the unconscious belief that sexual assault is inevitable or a constant that cannot be taken seriously because it is so common. Perhaps sexual assault would not be so common if it were taken seriously.

Seen in this way, sexual assault in the United States today resembles lynching prior to its recognition as a civil rights violation. It is a violent humiliation ritual with sexual elements in which the victims are often murdered. It could be done to members of powerful groups but hardly ever is. When it is done, it is as if it is what the victim is for; the whole target population cringes, withdraws, at once identifies and disidentifies in terror. The exemplary horror keeps the group smaller, quieter, more ingratiating. The legal system is dominated by members of the same group engaged in the aggression. The practice is formally illegal but seldom found to be against the law. The atrocity is de jure illegal but de facto permitted.

Unlike the law of murder, however, before the rape law is administered, it is biased on its face. n109 Rape is typically defined as intercourse with force against one's will. Apparently this is not considered redundant, implying that women consent to sex with force all the time. Given this sadomasochistic definition of sex at the line between intercourse and rape, it is no wonder that the legal concept of consent can coexist with a lot of force. Crystallizing in doctrine a norm that animates the rape law more generally, the defense of "mistaken belief in consent" defines whether a rape occurred from the perspective of the accused rapist, not from the perspective of the victim or even based on a social standard of unacceptable force or of mutuality. n110 To a degree unlike any other crime to the person, the credibility of the victim is the issue on which turns whether any harm was done. Only in sexual assault cases is it believed, against the victim's statement to the contrary, that she may have consented to forced acts against her. The view that women seek out and enjoy forced sex is pure special pleading for the accused. This is the perspective the law has taken.

Women and men are not similarly situated with regard to sexual assault in the sense that they are not equally subject to it or equally subjected to it. But this is the inequality that indicts it, not the difference that exonerates it or exempts it from equality scrutiny.

* * *

Sexual assault, in this argument, has a special place in women's social status and the law of sexual assault has a distinctive place in the history of women's oppression by government. There is no lack of atrocities disclosing judicial bias by courts in sexual assault adjudications. n115 Condescending, demeaning, hostile, humiliating, and indifferent judicial treatment of female victims of sexual assault is not uncommon. n116 Government commits this inequality and should rectify it. Law has a choice. It can inscribe this misogyny on society yet more authoritatively, promoting sex inequality, or it can move against it by promoting sex equality. Sexual assault cannot be treated as gender neutral because sexual assault is not gender neutral. The law of sexual assault cannot be treated as private action because it is government action. n117 Women are not receiving equal protection of the laws. The equal protection clause is inconsistent with state law that promotes sex inequality. The law of sexual assault commands Fourteenth Amendment scrutiny. n118

Elizabeth J. Kramer

Elizabeth Kramer argues that male victims of rape should receive similar support and legal protections as female victims of rape. Her article explains why male rape victims are treated differently within the criminal justice system, the support community and society at-large.

Elizabeth J. Kramer. "When Men Are Victims: Applying Rape Shield Laws to Male Same-Sex Rape" New York University Law Review 73 (1998): 293–331. (Excerpts: p.293–4, 297, 304–5, 316, 317–9, 330–1)

Introduction

* * *

Alan Lane went to a friend's party one summer night. He awoke that night to find a male acquaintance raping him. [n2] Steven Dooley asked a male friend to sleep over at his parents' house after his high school prom. The friend later raped Dooley though Dooley tried to resist. [n3] Michael Blucker served five years in an Illinois prison for burglary, theft, and forgery. While there, he was raped multiple times by a gang of prison inmates. [n4] Fred Pelka was picked up by a seemingly harmless stranger while hitchhiking. The stranger later raped him by luring him into a deserted building. [n5]

The circumstances in which these men were raped varied widely. They were raped by acquaintances and strangers, by one attacker and multiple attackers, in their homes and outside their homes. They shared one common experience, however – their rapists were never prosecuted. Despite the different circumstances of their assaults, the different kinds of evidence, and the different credibility problems, all four men decided not to pursue prosecution. They did so for a [*294] number of reasons: feelings of shame, fear of retribution, concern about being perceived as gay, the negative reactions they received from the police and their families, or a combination of the above. [n6]

These four men thus became part of a largely ignored group. Despite a growing body of literature about rape law, legal commentators rarely discuss male same-sex rape, [n7] in which men are both victims and perpetrators, and the legal system's response to it. ... Because of the stigma attached to male same-sex rape, men rarely report the crime and are involved in prosecution efforts even less frequently. Thus, there are relatively few reported cases discussing male same-sex rape in any detail....

* * *

Male victims, therefore, require at least the same kind of protection that female victims receive under Rape Shield Laws, as well as additional protection that addresses their unique concerns....

* * *

Like opposite-sex rape, male same-sex rape is widely believed to be underreported. There are numerous reasons why victims of same-sex rape do not go to the police or other authorities. First, as one New York court has noted, merely by reporting the fact that they were raped, "heterosexual male victims may feel that their sexual orientation is called into question and homosexual male victims fear that their sexual preference may be revealed." [n58] Second, society's conception of masculinity has led many men to believe that they should be able to defend themselves from sexual attacks; those who are not able to do so are embarrassed and fear that authorities will not believe that the sexual contact was forced. [n59] As a result, like female victims of rape, many male victims find it humiliating to tell authorities that they have been sexually assaulted. [n60] Finally, victims of same-sex rape are reluctant to report their rape because they believe their past sexual history will be exposed at trial. [n61] This concern may be especially true of male same-sex rape victims who are homosexual, who often fear [*305] that their sexual orientation alone will cause jurors to believe that they consented to the sexual contact. [n62]

* * *

B. Cases of Male Same-Sex Rape

Implicate Bias Against Homosexuality

* * *

Anti-gay bias can be particularly virulent in cases of male same-sex rape because such cases implicate both homophobia and sexism. Men who are passive in same-sex sexual intercourse assume a role that is viewed as physically similar to that of women in opposite-sex sexual intercourse. Men who assume this passive role have been feminized, historically and today....

* * *

In addition to the bias that can confront a male same-sex rape victim because he is perceived as gay and/or feminine, there is a serious and distinct stigma associated with being a male who has been victimized. Our society, profoundly uncomfortable with men being dominated and humiliated as they are in sexual assault, believes that "victims" are women. [n135] Women can become victims of rape because their relative physical weakness and social status allow them to be dominated by men. [n136] Men, unlike women, generally do not fear being harmed in this way and thus typically do not fear rape. [n137] There seems to be little recognition of the differences in strength and social status among men, leading many people to believe that men cannot be [*318] victims of sexual assault. [n138] By undermining these assumptions, male victims of same-sex rape disturb our society's definition of "victims."

Because a man who has been sexually assaulted confounds this "men cannot be victims" stereotype, it can become difficult for other men to relate to him. As one **male rape victim** wrote, it is "precisely because [**male rape victims**] have been 'reduced' to the status of women that other men find [them] so difficult to deal with... I was held in contempt because I was a victim – feminine, hence perceived as less masculine." [n139] Due to widespread discomfort with their victimization, men who are sexually assaulted may be accused of having "wanted it" and confronted with the incorrect belief that men cannot be assaulted against their will. ...[n142] Men who report their assault also may be ridiculed by policemen who dismiss the idea that a "real man" could be raped. [n143] ...Thus, the raped man becomes subject to many of the stereotypes surrounding the rape of women – he is lying, must have asked for it, probably enjoyed it, [n146] and so on. Men need the same [*319] protection from such stereotypes and misunderstanding as women, and additional protection from the added layer of bias they confront.

* * *

Conclusion

Although the problem of male same-sex rape has been largely overlooked by state and federal legislators, the Rape Shield Laws legislators passed to protect female victims of opposite-sex rape can be- [*331] come an effective tool for protecting male victims of same-sex rape. The policy concerns that led to the adoption of Rape Shield Laws for female opposite-sex rape are largely relevant to cases of male same-sex rape. First, applying Rape Shield Laws to male same-sex rape encourages the reporting of the crime. Second, the laws limit the introduction of irrelevant prior sexual history evidence on the issue of consent. Third, Rape Shield Laws prohibit the defendant from asking the jury to infer that because the victim was sexually active in the past he is less likely to be truthful. Finally, Rape Shield Laws minimize the chance that defendants guilty of male same-sex rape will go free by disallowing inflammatory evidence. Thus, applying Rape Shield Laws to cases of male same-sex rape furthers the policy goals of such legislation.

* * *

Ultimately, Rape Shield Laws must be applied consistently and sensitively to cases of male same-sex rape if the reporting and prosecution of such crimes are to increase and improve. Male same-sex rape is a traumatic crime with serious emotional and physical consequences for its victims. Until society gives victims confidence that their privacy and dignity will be respected, victims will remain unwilling to participate in any prosecution through trial. Rape Shield Laws, written and interpreted to account for the unique bias that is implicated in cases of male same-sex rape, can become an important legal tool for providing victims with such confidence. Perhaps then society will begin to acknowledge the problem of male same-sex rape and, finally, treat its victims with fairness and compassion.

Michael M. v. Sonoma County, 450 US 464 (1981)

Like many state statutes in the past, the state of California's statutory rape law imposed criminal liability on men only. Under California law, men would be subject to criminal prosecution for engaging in sexual intercourse with a female minor between the age of 14 years old and 18 years old while women who engage in sexual intercourse with minor males of a similar age cohort face no criminal charges.[1] Two interrelated arguments were used to defend the statute. One argument was that men are more likely to be sexual aggressive than women. The other was that women, who can become pregnant, face a natural penalty that, in effect, deters them from and punishes them for sexual transgressions.

The *Michael M.* case resulted when Michael M., a 17 ½ year old male, had sexual relations with a 16 ½ year old girl. Although both parties had been drinking alcohol before the sexual encounter,[2] Michael M. was charged with statutory rape. Michael M. was convicted of statutory rape.

The United States Supreme Court had to determine the constitutionality of California's sex-based statutory rape statute. Four Justices (Rehnquist, Burger, Stewart and Powell) defended the statute. Excerpts from Rehnquist's opinion follow.

MICHAEL M. v. SUPERIOR COURT OF SONOMA COUNTY

SUPREME COURT OF THE UNITED STATES

450 U.S. 464; 101 S. Ct. 1200; 67 L. Ed. 2d 437; 1981 U.S. LEXIS 83; 49 U.S.L.W. 4273

March 23, 1981, Decided

OPINION

[*466] [***441] [**1203] JUSTICE REHNQUIST announced the judgment of the Court and delivered an opinion, in which THE CHIEF JUSTICE, JUSTICE STEWART, and JUSTICE POWELL joined.

The question presented in this case is whether California's "statutory rape" law, § 261.5 of the Cal. Penal Code Ann. (West Supp. 1981), violates the Equal Protection Clause of the Fourteenth Amendment. [HN1] Section 261.5 defines unlawful sexual intercourse as "an act of sexual intercourse accomplished with a female not the wife of the perpetrator, where the female is under the age of 18 years." The statute thus makes men alone criminally liable for the act of sexual intercourse.

* * *

The [California] Supreme Court held that "section 261.5 discriminates on the basis of sex because only females may be victims, and only males may violate the section." 25 Cal. 3d 608, 611, 601 P. 2d 572, 574. The court then subjected the classification to "strict scrutiny," stating that it must be justified by a compelling state interest. It found that the classification was "supported not by mere social convention but by the immutable physiological fact that it is the female exclusively who can become pregnant." *Ibid.* Canvassing "the tragic human costs of illegitimate teenage pregnancies," including the large number of teenage abortions, the increased medical risk associated with teenage pregnancies, and the social consequences of teenage childbearing, the court concluded that the State has a compelling interest in preventing such pregnancies. Because males alone can "physiologically cause the result which the law properly seeks to avoid," the court further held that the gender classification was readily justified as a means of identifying offender and victim. For the reasons stated below, we affirm the judgment of the California Supreme Court. [1]

...Unlike the California Supreme Court, we have not held that gender-based classifications are "inherently suspect" and thus we do not apply so-called "strict scrutiny" to those classifications. See *Stanton* v. *Stanton*, 421 U.S. 7 (1975). Our cases have held, however, that [HN2] the traditional minimum rationality test takes on a somewhat "sharper focus" when gender-based classifications are challenged.

Underlying these decisions is the principle that [HN3] a legislature may not "make overbroad generalizations based on sex which are entirely unrelated to any differences between men and women or which demean the ability or social status of the affected class." *Parham* v. *Hughes*, 441 U.S. 347, 354 (1979) (plurality opinion of STEWART, J.). But because the Equal Protection Clause does not "demand that a statute necessarily apply equally to all persons" or require "'things which are different in fact . . . to be treated in law as though they were the same,'" *Rinaldi* v. *Yeager*, 384 U.S. 305, 309 (1966), quoting *Tigner* v. *Texas*, 310 U.S. 141, 147 (1940), this Court has consistently upheld statutes where the gender classification is not invidious, but rather realistically reflects the fact that the sexes are not similarly situated in certain circumstances.

Legislature criminalized the act of illicit sexual intercourse with a minor female is a sure indication of its intent or purpose to discourage that conduct. ...

The justification for the statute offered by the State, and accepted by the Supreme Court of California, is that the legislature sought to prevent illegitimate teenage pregnancies. That finding, of course, is entitled to great deference....

We are satisfied not only that the prevention of illegitimate pregnancy is at least one of the "purposes" of the statute, but also that the State has a strong interest in preventing such pregnancy. At the risk of stating the obvious, teenage pregnancies, which have increased dramatically over the last two decades, [3] have significant social, medical, and economic consequences for both the mother and her child, and the State. [4] [*471] Of particular [***444] concern to the State is that approximately half of all teenage pregnancies end in abortion. [5] And of those children who are born, their illegitimacy makes them likely candidates to become wards of the State. [6]

We need not be medical doctors to discern that young men and young women are not similarly situated with respect to the problems and the risks of sexual intercourse. Only women may become pregnant, and they suffer disproportionately the profound physical, emotional, and psychological consequences of sexual activity. The statute at issue here [*472] protects women from sexual intercourse at an age when those consequences are particularly severe. [7]

[**1206] The question thus boils down to whether [HN4] a State may attack the problem of sexual intercourse and teenage pregnancy directly by prohibiting a male from having sexual intercourse with a minor female. [8] [***445] We hold that such a statute is [*473] sufficiently related to the State's objectives to pass constitutional muster.

Because virtually all of the significant harmful and inescapably identifiable consequences of teenage pregnancy fall on the young female, a legislature acts well within its authority when it elects to punish only the participant who, by nature, suffers few of the consequences of his conduct. It is hardly unreasonable for a legislature acting to protect minor females to exclude them from punishment. Moreover, the risk of pregnancy itself constitutes a substantial deterrence to young females. No similar natural sanctions deter males. A criminal sanction imposed solely on males thus serves to roughly "equalize" the deterrents on the sexes.

* * *

In any event, we cannot say that a gender-neutral statute would be as effective as the statute California has chosen to enact. The State persuasively contends that a gender-neutral [**1207] statute would frustrate its interest in effective enforcement. Its view is that a female is surely less likely to report [*474] violations of the statute if she herself would be subject to criminal prosecution. [9] In an area already fraught with prosecutorial difficulties, we decline to hold that [HN5] the Equal Protection Clause requires a legislature to enact a statute so broad that it may well be incapable of enforcement. [10]

* * *

There remains only petitioner's contention that the statute is unconstitutional as it is applied to him because he, like Sharon, was under 18 at the time of sexual intercourse. Petitioner argues that the statute is flawed because it presumes that as between two persons under 18, the male is the culpable aggressor We find petitioner's contentions unpersuasive. Contrary to his assertions, the statute does not rest on the assumption that males are generally the aggressors. It is instead an attempt by a legislature to prevent illegitimate teenage pregnancy by providing an additional deterrent for men. The age of the man is irrelevant since young men are as capable as older men of inflicting the harm sought to be prevented.

In upholding the California statute we also recognize that this is not a case where [**1208] a statute is being challenged on the grounds that it "invidiously discriminates" against females. [*476] To the contrary, the statute places a burden on males which is not shared by females. But we find nothing to suggest that men, because of past discrimination or peculiar [***447] disadvantages, are in need of the special solicitude of the courts. Nor is this a case where the gender classification is made "solely for . . . administrative convenience," as in *Frontiero* v. *Richardson*, 411 U.S. 677, 690 (1973) (emphasis omitted), or rests on "the baggage of sexual stereotypes" as in *Orr* v. *Orr*, 440 U.S., at 283. As we have held, the statute instead reasonably reflects the fact that the consequences of sexual intercourse and pregnancy fall more heavily on the female than on the male.

Accordingly the judgment of the California Supreme Court is

Affirmed.

Michael M. v. Sonoma County, 450 US 464 (1981)

Four Justices (Brennan, White, Marshall and Stevens) were troubled because the law placed criminal liability on men only. Excerpts from Brennan's opinion and Stevens' opinion follow.

MICHAEL M. v. SUPERIOR COURT OF SONOMA COUNTY
SUPREME COURT OF THE UNITED STATES

450 U.S. 464; 101 S. Ct. 1200; 67 L. Ed. 2d 437; 1981 U.S. LEXIS 83; 49 U.S.L.W. 4273

March 23, 1981, Decided

DISSENT BY: BRENNAN; STEVENS

DISSENT

[*488] JUSTICE BRENNAN, with whom JUSTICES [***454] WHITE and MARSHALL join, dissenting.

I

It is disturbing to find the Court so splintered on a case that presents such a straightforward issue: Whether the admittedly gender-based classification in Cal. Penal Code Ann. § 261.5 (West Supp. 1981) [**1214] bears a sufficient relationship to the State's asserted goal of preventing teenage pregnancies to survive the "mid-level" constitutional scrutiny mandated by *Craig* v. *Boren*, 429 U.S. 190 (1976). [1] Applying the analytical framework provided by our precedents, I am convinced that there is only one proper resolution of this issue: the classification must be declared unconstitutional...

II

* * *

The State of California vigorously asserts that the "important governmental objective" to be served by § 261.5 is the prevention of teenage pregnancy. It claims that its statute furthers this goal by deterring sexual activity by males -- the class of persons it considers more responsible for causing those pregnancies. [4] But even assuming that prevention of teenage [*491] pregnancy is an important governmental objective and that it is in fact an objective of § 261.5, see *infra*, at 494–6, California still has the burden of proving that there are fewer teenage pregnancies under its gender-based statutory rape law [***456] than there would be if the law were gender neutral. To meet this burden, the State must show that because its statutory rape law punishes only males, and not females, it more effectively deters minor females from having sexual intercourse. [5]

* * *

III

Until very recently, no California court or commentator had suggested that the purpose of California's statutory rape law was to protect young women from the risk of pregnancy. Indeed, the historical development of § 261.5 demonstrates that the law was initially enacted on the premise that young women, in contrast to young men, were to be deemed legally incapable of consenting to an act of sexual intercourse. [9] Because [*495] their chastity was considered particularly precious, those young women were felt to be uniquely in need of the State's protection. [10] In contrast, young men were [**1218] assumed to [*496] be capable of making such decisions for themselves; the law therefore did [***459] not offer them any special protection.

It is perhaps because the gender classification in California's statutory rape law was initially designed to further these outmoded sexual stereotypes, rather than to reduce the incidence of teenage pregnancies, that the State has been unable to demonstrate a substantial relationship between the classification and its newly asserted goal. Cf. *Califano* v. *Goldfarb*, 430 U.S., at 223 (STEVENS, J., concurring in judgment). But whatever the reason, the State has not shown that Cal. Penal Code § 261.5 is any more effective than a gender-neutral law would be in deterring minor females from engaging in sexual intercourse. It has therefore not met its burden of proving that the statutory classification is substantially related to the achievement of its asserted goal.

I would hold that § 261.5 violates the Equal Protection Clause of the Fourteenth Amendment, and I would reverse the judgment of the California Supreme Court.

JUSTICE STEVENS, dissenting.

* * *

...The question raised by this statute is whether the State, consistently with the Federal Constitution, may always punish the male and never the female when they are equally responsible or when the female is the more responsible of the two.

It would seem to me that an impartial lawmaker could give only one answer to that question. The [***462] fact that the California Legislature has decided to apply its prohibition only to [*501] the male may reflect a legislative judgment that in the typical case the male is actually the more guilty party. Any such judgment must, in turn, assume that the decision to engage in the risk-creating conduct is always -- or at least typically -- a male decision. If that assumption is valid, the statutory classification should also be valid. But what is the support for the assumption? It is not contained in the record of this case or in any legislative history or scholarly study that has been called to our attention. I think it is supported to some extent by traditional attitudes toward male-female relationships. But the possibility that such a habitual attitude may reflect nothing more than an irrational prejudice makes it an insufficient justification for discriminatory treatment that is otherwise blatantly unfair. For, as I read this statute, it requires that

one, and only one, of two equally guilty wrongdoers be stigmatized by a
criminal conviction.

* * *

Nor do I find at all persuasive the suggestion that this discrimination is
adequately justified by the desire to encourage females to inform against
their male partners. Even if the concept of a wholesale informant's
exemption were an acceptable enforcement device, what is the justification
for defining the exempt class entirely by reference to sex rather than by
reference to a more neutral criterion such as relative innocence? Indeed, if
the exempt [***463] class is to be composed entirely of members of one
sex, what is there to support the view that the statutory purpose will be
better served by granting the informing license to females rather than to
males? If a discarded male partner informs on a promiscuous female, a
timely threat of prosecution might well prevent the precise harm the statute
is intended to minimize.

Finally, even if my logic is faulty and there actually is some speculative basis
for treating equally guilty males and females differently, I still believe that
any such speculative justification would be outweighed by the paramount
interest in evenhanded enforcement of the law. A rule that authorizes
punishment of only one of two equally guilty wrongdoers violates the
essence of the constitutional requirement that the sovereign must govern
impartially.

I respectfully dissent.

People of the State of New York v. Liberta, 474 NE 2d 207 (NY 1984)

This New York case resulted from a challenge to New York's rape statute
that made rape a crime with which men only were charged. Under NY law
at the time, rape was defined as "forcible compulsion" to engage in sexual
intercourse. The state contends that men cannot be victims of rape because,
given male biology, men cannot be forced or compelled to engage in sexual
intercourse. Mr. Mario Liberta, who was convicted on first degree rape,
argued that his conviction should be overturned because the law discriminated against men. Accordingly, men should not be the only group who
was criminal liable for committing rape; women who rape men should be
subject to the same criminal prosecution as men.

The New York Court of Appeals, which is the highest state court, urged the state of New York to adopt a gender-neutral definition of rape. The Court's reasoning is excerpted below.

THE PEOPLE OF THE STATE OF NEW YORK, RESPONDENT, v. MARIO LIBERTA, COURT OF APPEALS OF NEW YORK 64 N.Y.2D 152; 474 N.E.2D 567;485 N.Y.S.2D 207;

December 20, 1984, Decided

...Section 130.35 of the Penal Law provides in relevant part that "A male is guilty of rape in the first degree when he engages in sexual intercourse with a female * * * by forcible compulsion". "Female", for purposes of the rape statute, is defined as "any female person who is not married to the actor" (Penal Law, § 130.00, subd 4).

* * *

B. THE EXEMPTION FOR FEMALES

Under the Penal Law only males can be convicted of rape in the first degree. [11] [HN10] Insofar as the rape statute applies to acts of "sexual intercourse", which, as defined in the Penal Law (see Penal Law, § 130.00) can only occur between a male and a female, it is true that a female cannot physically rape a female and that therefore there is no denial of equal protection when punishing only males for forcibly engaging in sexual intercourse with females. [12] The equal protection issue, however, stems from the fact that the statute applies to [**576] males who forcibly rape females but does [***216] not apply to females who forcibly rape males.

Rape statutes historically applied only to conduct by males against females, largely because the purpose behind the proscriptions [*168] was to protect the chastity of women and thus their property value to their fathers or husbands (see *State v Smith*, 85 NJ, at p 204, *supra*; 2 Burdick, Law of Crime, pp 218–25; Comment, Rape Laws, Equal Protection, and Privacy Rights, 54 Tulane L Rev 456, 457 [hereafter cited as "Rape Laws"]). New York's rape statute has always protected only females, and has thus applied only to males (see Penal Law, § 130.35; 1909 Penal Law, § 2010; 1881 Penal Code, tit X, ch II, § 278). Presently New York is one of only 10 jurisdictions that does not have a gender-neutral statute for forcible rape. [13]

[HN11] A statute which treats males and females differently violates equal protection unless the classification is substantially related to the achievement of an important governmental objective (*Caban v Mohammed*, 441 U.S. 380, 388; *Craig v Boren*, 429 U.S. 190, 197; *People v Whidden*,

51 NY2d 457, 460, app dsmd 454 U.S. 803). This test applies whether the statute discriminates against males or against females....

The first argument advanced by the People in support of the exemption for females is that because only females can become pregnant the State may constitutionally differentiate between forcible rapes of females and forcible rapes of males. This court and the United States Supreme Court have upheld statutes which subject males to criminal liability for engaging in sexual intercourse with underage females without the converse being true (*People v Whidden, supra; Michael M. v Sonoma County Superior Ct.*, 450 U.S. 464, *supra*). The rationale behind these decisions was that the primary purpose of such "statutory rape" laws is to protect against the harm caused by teenage pregnancies, there being no need to provide the same protection to young males (see *Michael M. v Sonoma County Superior Ct.*, 450 U.S., at pp 470–3, *supra; People v Whidden*, 51 NY2d, at p 461, *supra*).t

[*169] There is no evidence, however, that preventing pregnancies is a primary purpose of the statute prohibiting forcible rape, nor does such a purpose seem likely (see "Rape Laws", *op. cit.*, 54 Tulane L Rev, at p 467). Rather, the very fact that the statute proscribes "forcible compulsion" shows that its overriding purpose is to protect a woman from an unwanted, forcible, and often violent sexual intrusion into her body (cf. *Ballard v United States*, 430 A2d 483 [DC App]; "Rape Laws", *op. cit.*, at p 468). [14] Thus, due to the different [**577] purposes behind forcible rape laws and [***217] "statutory" (consensual) rape laws, the cases upholding the gender discrimination in the latter are not decisive with respect to the former, and the People cannot meet their burden here by simply stating that only females can become pregnant.

The People also claim that the discrimination is justified because a female rape victim "faces the probability of medical, sociological, and psychological problems unique to her gender". This same argument, when advanced in support of the discrimination in the statutory rape laws, was rejected by this court, and it is no more convincing in the present case. "[An] '"archaic and overbroad" generalization' * * * which is evidently grounded in long-standing stereotypical notions of the differences between the sexes, simply cannot serve as a legitimate rationale for a penal provision that is addressed only to adult males" (*id.*, quoting *Craig v Boren*, 429 U.S., at p 198, *supra*; cf. *Orr v Orr*, 440 U.S., at p 283, *supra*; Tribe, Constitutional Law, p 1066).

Finally, the People suggest that a gender-neutral law for forcible rape is unnecessary, and that therefore the present law is constitutional, because a woman either cannot actually rape a man or such attacks, if possible, are extremely rare. Although the "physiologically impossible" argument has been accepted by several courts (see *People v Reilly*, 85 Misc 2d 702, 706–7; *Brooks v State*, 24 Md App 334; *Finley v State*, 527 SW2d 553 [Tex Crim App]), it is simply wrong. The argument is premised on the notion that a man cannot engage in sexual intercourse unless he is sexually aroused, and if he is aroused then he is consenting to intercourse. "Sexual [HN12] intercourse" however, "occurs upon any penetration, however slight" (Penal Law, § 130.00); this degree of contact can be achieved without a male being aroused and thus without his consent.

As to the "infrequency" argument, while forcible sexual assaults by females upon males are undoubtedly less common than [*170] those by males upon females this numerical disparity cannot by itself make the gender discrimination constitutional. Women may well be responsible for a far lower number of all serious crimes than are men, but such a disparity would not make it permissible for the State to punish only men who commit, for example, robbery (cf. *Craig v Boren*, 429 U.S., at pp 200–4, *supra*).

[HN13] To meet their burden of showing that a gender-based law is substantially related to an important governmental objective the People must set forth an "'exceedingly persuasive justification'" for the classification (*Mississippi Univ. for Women v Hogan*, 458 U.S. 718, 724; *Kirchberg v Feenstra*, 450 U.S. 455, 461), which requires, among other things, a showing that the gender-based law serves the governmental objective better than would a gender-neutral law (*Orr v Orr*, 440 U.S., at pp 281–2, *supra*; "Rape Laws", *op. cit.*, 54 Tulane L Rev, at p 468; cf. *Michael M. v Sonoma County Superior Ct.*, 450 U.S., at p 464, *supra*). [HN14] The fact that the act of a female forcibly raping a male may be a difficult or rare occurrence does not mean that the gender exemption satisfies the constitutional test. A gender-neutral law would indisputably better serve, even if only marginally, the objective of deterring and punishing forcible sexual assaults. The only persons "benefitted" by the gender exemption are females who forcibly rape males. As the Supreme Court has stated, "[a] gender-based classification which, as compared to a gender-neutral one, generates additional benefits only for those it has no reason to prefer cannot survive equal protection scrutiny" (*Orr v Orr*, 440 U.S., at pp 282–3, *supra*).

Accordingly, we find that section 130.35 of the Penal Law violates equal protection [**578] [***218] because it exempts females from criminal liability for forcible rape.

* * *

Liberta v. Kelly, 839 F. 2d 77 (2d Cir. 1988)

The United States Court of Appeals for the 2nd Circuit reviewed the New York Court of Appeals' decision in *People v. Liberta* which declared that New York's first degree rape statute unconstitutionally discriminated against men. As the excerpt below shows, the 2nd Circuit Court cited the United States Supreme Court's decision in *Michael M. v. Sonoma County* in upholding the law.

Mario R. Liberta, Petitioner-Appellant, v. Walter R. Kelly, Superintendent, Attica Correctional Facility, Respondent-AppelleeUNITED STATES COURT OF APPEALS FOR THE SECOND CIRCUIT

839 F.2d 77; 1988 U.S. App. LEXIS 1640

February 9, 1988, Decided

* * *

We turn ... to Liberta's claim that the limitation in Section 130.35's prohibition of rape to males violates the equal protection clause. The Supreme Court has consistently held that [HN6] a "party seeking to uphold a statute that classifies individuals on the basis of their gender must carry the burden of showing an 'exceedingly persuasive justification' for the classification." *Mississippi Univ. for Women v. Hogan*, 458 U.S. at 724 (quoting *Kirchberg v. Feenstra*, 450 U.S. 455, 461, 67 L. Ed. 2d 428, 101 S. Ct. 1195 (1981)). [**16] "The burden is met only by showing at least that the classification serves 'important governmental objectives and that the discriminatory means employed' are 'substantially related to the achievement of those objectives.'" *Id.* (quoting *Wengler v. Druggists Mut. Ins. Co.*, 446 U.S. 142, 150, 64 L. Ed. 2d 107, 100 S. Ct. 1540 (1980)). ...Moreover, the equal protection clause does not "demand that a statute necessarily apply equally to all persons" or " 'require things which are different in fact ... to be treated in law as though they were the same.'" *Rinaldi v. Yeager*, 384 U.S. 305, 309, 16 L. Ed. 2d 577, 86 S. Ct. 1497 (1966) (quoting *Tigner v. Texas*, 310 U.S. 141, 147, 84 L. Ed. 1124, 60 S. Ct. 879 (1940)). [**17] Accordingly, [HN7] a statute containing a gender-based classification must be upheld "where the gender classification is not invidious, but rather realistically reflects the fact that the sexes are not similarly situated in certain circumstances." *Michael M. v. Superior Court*, 450 U.S. 464, 469, 67 L. Ed. 2d 437, 101 S. Ct. 1200 (1981) (plurality opinion).

We disagree with the New York Court of Appeals' failure to give any weight to the very realistic concerns that underlie Section 130.35's application only to males. [3] In particular, we cannot agree with the dismissal of the argument that rape of males by females is so extraordinary or even nonexistent as not to warrant specific legislative concern. ...

[**18] We note that the Court of Appeals made no claim that evidence of female rapes of males actually exists. We also note that the definition of "sexual intercourse" as involving "any penetration, however, slight" is necessary to prevent males from raising defenses concerning completion of an act of sexual intercourse. The fact that [HN8] that definition creates a possibility of female rape does not render Section 130.35 unconstitutional where such events are virtually or wholly nonexistent. ....Certainly the Constitution does not require legislatures to anticipate virtually nonexistent or purely hypothetical events in drafting penal statutes. Indeed, we find it inconceivable that males who rape should go free solely because the legislature focused on a real problem, rape of women by men, with verified attendant physical and psychological trauma, and failed to act on a hypothetical problem, rape of men [**19] by women.

We also disagree with the New York Court of Appeals's dismissal of the state's argument that women who are raped also face the danger of unwanted pregnancy. As the Eighth Circuit has observed:

Although . . . prevention of unwanted pregnancy is not, standing alone, a plausible purpose of a forcible rape statute, the fact that only women can become pregnant and only if attacked by a man implies that a male assailant can impose a unique harm on a female victim. A male can impose the fear of and, in some cases, the actuality of an unwanted pregnancy. No woman can impose this harm on a man and no assailant can impose this harm on a person [**20] of the same sex. Only women can become pregnant and thus only they can fear an unwanted pregnancy or be forced to undergo the physical, emotional, ethical, and financial consequences of such a pregnancy.

[HN9] Women and men thus are not similarly situated with regard to rape. Rape is unquestionably a crime that requires male participation as a practical matter, and only male rape of a female can impose on the victim an unwanted pregnancy. These facts, in our view, provide an "exceedingly persuasive justification," *Mississippi Univ. for Women v. Hogan*, 458 U.S. at 724, for a statute that provides heightened sanctions for rapes committed by men. Moreover, it cannot be contended that a rape statute punishing [**21] only men "demean[s] the ability or social status" of either men or women, Parham v. Hughes, 441 U.S. 347, 354, 60 L. Ed. 2d 269, 99 S. Ct. 1742 (1979), particularly in the context of a penal code that prohibits coercive sexual conduct by women. The exclusion of women from the scope of Section 130.35, therefore, does not deny men equal protection of the laws.

Affirmed.

Notes

1   It should be noted that, under California law, "anyone, regardless of gender, can be guilty of engaging in lewd, lascivious act including consensual sexual intercourse with a child under the age of 14 years old. Also, any person can be criminally prosecuted for molesting, annoying or contributing to the delinquency of anyone under 18 years old."

2   There was a dispute over whether the girl actually consented to the sexual intercourse. The United States Supreme Court focused on the constitutionality of the California statute that placed all criminal liability on the men.

Questions

1   Do battered women need special protection under the law? Should society protect battered women from their abusive partners even if the victims refuse assistance?

2   Why are male victims of sexual assaults treated differently than female victims of sexual assaults? Do you think that sexual assault affects male victims and female victims in the same way?

3   Should battered women be forced to assist police and prosecutors in convicting their batterers? What do mandatory prosecution policies suggest about the rational capacity of women to assess their best interests?

4   Should a man be able to use a battered "man's" syndrome defense after he kills his abusive, but sleeping, wife?

5   Do you agree with Catharine MacKinnon's argument that rape is a manifestation of the systematic inequality that women constantly experience in American society? Why is rape so common in the US?

Suggested Reading

Ayyildiz, Elisabeth. "When Battered Women's Syndrome Does Not Go Far Enough: The Battered Woman as Vigilante." *American University Journal of Gender and the Law* 4, 1995, 141–66.

Coughlin, Anne M. "Excusing Women." *California Law Review* 82, 1994, 1–92.

Dershowitz, Alan. *The Abuse Excuse.* New York: Little, Brown and Company, 1994.

Estrich, Susan. "Rape." *Yale Law Journal* 95, 1996, 1087–148.

Goodmark, Leigh. "Autonomy Feminism: An Anti-Essentialist Critique of Mandatory Interventions in Domestic Violence Cases." *Florida State University Law Review* 37, 2009, 1–48.

Hanna, Cheryl. "No Right to Choose: Mandated Victim Participation in Domestic Violence Prosecutions." *Harvard Law Review* 109, 1996, 1849–910.

Holmes, Anna. "The Disposable Woman." *New York Times,* 2011, www.nytimes.com

Kinports, Kit. "Deconstructing the 'Image' of the Battered Woman: So Much Activity, So Little Change: A Reply to the Critics of Battered Women's Self-Defense." *St. Louis University Public Law Review* 23, 2004, p. 155–91.

Klein, Richard. "An Analysis of Thirty-five Years of Rape Reforms: A Frustrating Search for Fundamental Fairness." *Akron Law Review* 41, 2008, 981–1057.

Kramer, Elizabeth J. "When Men Are Victims: Applying Rape Shield Laws to Male Same-Sex Rape." *New York University Law Review* 73, 1998, 293–331.

MacKinnon, Catharine A. "Reflections on Sex Equality Under Law." *Yale Law Journal* 100, 1991, 1281–328.

Novotny, Patricia. "Rape Victims in the (Gender) Neutral Zone: The Assimilation of Resistance?" *Seattle Journal for Social Justice* 1, 2003, 743–51.

Rumney, Phillip N. S. "In Defence of Gender Neutrality." *Seattle Journal of Social Justice* 6, 2007, 481–512.

Walker, Lenore W. *Battered Woman.* New York: Harper and Collins, 1979.

Wolf, Naomi. "Why Rape is Different?" *Project Syndicate,* 2011, Chinadaily.com.cn

6

Marriage and Parenthood

Introduction

The American family today is in flux and, some would argue, in crisis. Prior to the 1960s, few American marriages ended in divorce and most American children were reared in two-parent households. Yet today close to half of these marriages end in divorce while about half of American mothers under 30 are unmarried.[1] Many factors have contributed to these changes including a decline in traditional religious belief, a significant rise in poverty, the prevalence of no-fault divorce, and the impact of the sexual revolution. Some traditionalist thinkers also attribute the unsettled nature of American family life to the achievements of feminism and, more recently, of the gay rights movement which they view as underminning the moral and legal foundations of traditional marriage and parenthood. Reformers applaud these achievements, however, for giving women and gays greater dignity and autonomy and view the current unsettled state of American family life more positively. The debates featured in this chapter, which concern sex roles within marriage, same-sex marriage, and the rights and duties of fatherhood, reflect these different perspectives.

Sex Roles within Marriage

All three of these debates have their roots in the doctrine of separate spheres which shaped the concepts of marriage and parenthood for much of our history. This doctrine, as we saw in Chapter 1, rests on a strong version of the natural difference argument which a majority of both sexes endorsed until well after the first stirrings of American feminism. While early Americans considered men and women equal in certain respects, they believed that nature destined them to play wholly different roles in life. Men, they held, were naturally fit to provide for, protect, and govern their families, albeit with their wives' consent. Women, on the other hand, were considered more naturally suited for managing the home, for shaping family mores and, most important, for having and nurturing children. American lawmakers and moralists supported this strict division of labor by denying women social and political rights and by consigning them to the private sphere.

During the course of American history, the feminist movement pursued a robust civil rights agenda which challenged most of the legal supports and the moral justifications for the doctrine of seperate spheres. Feminists also weakened the social supports for this doctrine by persuading a broad majority of Americans to accept the educational and work-related aspirations of women. Over time, American women attained at least rough legal parity with men and enjoyed unprecedented economic, political, social, and educational opportunities. This expansion of sexual equality greatly reduced the scope of the doctrine of separate spheres. Virtually no proponents of this doctrine, for example, would deny today's women the right vote, to sit on juries, to attend college, to serve in the military, or to enter professional life.

Yet despite these momentous shifts in American law and public opinion, the separate spheres doctrine still continues to influence American family life. Most husbands are still the chief providers and protectors of their families while most wives are still the chief homemakers and caregivers even if they work full-time. Many feminists blame these family dynamics for making women economically and psychologically vulnerable in marriage (and even more so in cases of divorce) and for preventing them from attaining their rightful place in the external world.[2] They think, therefore, that the final battle for sexual equality in America must be fought within the family itself.

Susan Moller Okin argues that winning this most difficult battle requires a frontal assault on natural difference arguments as they exist today. "Moving away from gender is essential," she writes, "if we are to be at all true to our democratic ideals." In her ideal version of America, "one's sex would have no more relevance than one's eye color or the length of one's toes."[3] Under these circumstances, husbands and wives would share paid and unpaid work equally and play virtually interchangeable roles within the family. This altered division of labor, she argues, would strengthen American families by making their domestic arrangements more just than they currently are. Women would be healthier, more independent, more economically productive, and better citizens; men would be more empathic and more directly involved in the lives of their children; and children would be more likely to grow up as independent and fair-minded adults.[4]

Such arguments for a less gendered version of family life have not, of course, gone unchallenged. Traditionalists, such as Steven E. Rhoads, maintain that strengthening sex-based roles in marriage is the best means for revitalizing the American family. Drawing on scientific evidence from the fields of biology and evolutionary psychology, Rhoads claims that sex differences are "large, deeply rooted, and consequential," and that they must be respected in order for families to flourish.[5] Most women, in his view, naturally put family first, while men tend to care most about their careers. Thus, women commonly prefer to marry men who are superior to them in earnings, status, and power, while men largely prefer to marry women who are likely to be more devoted to them and to their children than to their own careers.[6]

Same-Sex Marriage

The most significant, hotly contested family issue in America today concerns the legal status of same-sex marriage. At first glance, this controversy seems unrelated to the principle of sexual equality which we have so far considered solely in relation to men and women. Yet we believe that same-sex marriage does raise important issues regarding this principle, partly because it involves questions of equality and fairness, and partly because it challenges a core premise of the natural difference doctrine, namely that men and women each play unique and essential roles within healthy family life.

According to this doctrine, marriage is by definition a legal, monogamous relationship between a man and a woman. Gay marriage advocates argue that this view of marriage unjustly discriminates against same-sex couples whom they consider equal to opposite-sex couples in virtually all respects. Several states have accepted this view and granted same-sex couples the right to marry by court decree, by legislation, and by popular referendum. Many more states, however, have prohibited same-sex marriage by constitutional amendment. Congress also passed the Defense of Marriage Act (DOMA) in 1996 which still prevents the national government from legally recognizing same-sex unions, although the relevant section in DOMA is currently subject to consitutional challenge.

Perhaps the most interesting chapter in the brief history of America's same-sex marriage controversy occurred in California, where the status of same-sex marriage was very hotly contested. The California Supreme Court's decision legalizing same-sex marriage in 2008 was overturned later that year by the passage of Proposition 8, a proposed state constitutional amendment which restricted marriage in California to heterosexuals. In the case of Perry v. Schwarzenegger (2010), US District Court Judge Vaughn R. Walker invalidated this amendment on equal protection grounds, both because banning gay marriage unjustly discriminates against gay individuals and beacuse it is not rationally related to any legitimate state interest.[7]

In his opinion, Judge Walker addressed the question of how the law should define marriage, which has become a key issue in the same-sex marriage debate. While marriage in his view is an evolving institution, it is and has always been "the right to choose a spouse and, with mutual consent, join together and form a household."[8] Its purpose is to provide individuals with the long-term psychological, material, and social benefits that governments and societies extend to legally recognized marriages. Gender, according to Judge Walker, is not essential to marriage thus understood. Thus, the amendment's restriction of marriage to heterosexuals is merely an anachronism, an "artifact of a time" when inter-racial marriage was forbidden and the now discredited doctrine of separate spheres held sway.[9]

While some traditionalists concede that homosexual couples deserve to enjoy most of the civil benefits marriage provides, they argue that the chief purpose of this institution is not to serve adults, but to provide a legal and social framework for the having and rearing of children. In their view, every child has a right to be reared by its biological parents—a right that the state has an interest in protecting even if it cannot always be realized. They consider this right more fundamental and important than the right of gay adults to marry. Legalizing same-sex marriage, they claim, would imperil children's rights by breaking the necessary definitional link between marriage and parenthood and by rejecting the principle that every child needs a mother and a father. Weakening this principle, they fear, will also damage current efforts to promote responsible fatherhood at a time when fatherless households in America are becoming less the exception than the rule.[10]

Judge Walker responded to these arguments by citing evidence which, in his view, shows that legalizing same-sex marriage will not adversely affect children. According to this evidence, same-sex and opposite-sex parents are equal in all respects, and having gay rather than straight parents has no discernible bearing on a child's welfare. California law already recognizes this fact, he noted, by permitting gay parents to adopt children and by treating them exactly the same as their straight counterparts. The supporters of Proposition 8, he suggested, are probably more interested in mistreating a vulnerable minority than in seeking to promote a legitimate state interest in protecting children.[11]

Fathers and Children

This chapter's third set of debates, which has received less public attention than the first two, concerns the relationship between fathers and children. These debates highlight efforts by reformers to challenge laws and policies regarding custody and procreation which have traditionally favored women on natural difference grounds. In recent years, fathers have prevailed in some cases. In 1972, for example, the US Supreme Court overturned an

Illinois state law which denied unwed fathers the same right to rear their children that unwed mothers enjoyed.[12] Also, when family courts now consider the "best interests of the child" in custody disputes, they tend to favor fathers more frequently that they did in years past.

Men have been much less successful, however, in their efforts to achieve equality with women in procreative matters, where the biological differences between the sexes are most pronounced. In *Roe v. Wade* (1973) the Supreme Court held on due process grounds that a state cannot stop a woman from ending her pregnancy until the fetus becomes viable. She also has an absolute right to carry the child to term. The father has no legal rights regarding the mother's decision to abort the fetus or have the child, nor can he put the newborn up for adoption against her wishes. If the mother decides to rear the child, he must assume legal and financial responsibility for it despite his previously stated unwillingness to do so.[13]

The reading selections in this section of Chapter 6 concern efforts to address this situation. The case of *Planned Parenthood v. Danforth* (1976), involved a Missouri law which required a married woman to obtain the consent of her spouse before having an abortion during the first trimester of her pregnancy. The plaintiffs, a Planned Parenthood facility and two physicians, challenged this law on behalf of all Missouri doctors who perform abortions and their patients.

The Supreme Court, which heard this case on appeal, struck down the Missouri law on the grounds that it violated a woman's due process rights set forth in Roe v. Wade. Speaking for the majority, Justice Harry Blackmun argued that after Roe, a state cannot delegate a "veto power" to a spouse with respect to an abortion when the state itself has no constitutional authority in the matter. He admits that ideally "the decision to terminate a pregnancy should be one concurred in by both the wife and her husband." Yet he pointed out that the right to privacy is an individual right, and that when spouses disagree, only one can prevail. Under Roe, biology settles disputes between men and women. Since the mother "physically bears the child" and is "more directly and immediately affected by the pregnancy" than the father, the balance must weigh "in her favor."[14]

In his dissent, Justice White argued that Missouri legislators intended to protect the father's interest, not the state's interest, in the unborn child. Thus, the court erred by assigning "a greater value" to a mother's desire to end "a potential human life" than to a father's desire to allow the fetus to "mature into a live child." In White's view, the father's interest in the child's fate, which may be profound, is constitutionally equal to the mother's interest and "should not be extinguished" by her "unilateral decision."[15]

The case of *Dubay v. Wells* (2007)[16] also involved efforts to achieve equal reproductive rights for men in the aftermath of Roe v. Wade. Here, however, a father sought the right **not** to assume the responsibilities of parenthood. After Dubay and Wells became romantically involved, Dubay informed

Wells that he did not want to become a father. Wells responded that she was infertile and additionally that she would use birth control during their sexual relations. Nonetheless, Wells became pregnant and carried the child to term over Dubay's objections.[17]

After the child was born, Wells sought child support and other expenses under the Michigan Paternity Act which holds "parents of a child born out of wedlock . . . responsible for the necessary support and education of the child." Dubay challenged the constitutionality of this part of the law on the grounds that it denied him the same right to disclaim parenthood that Wells enjoyed via her abortion rights. The 6th Circuit Court, which heard this case on appeal, rejected Dubay's claim holding that no parent, male or female, can legally "sever his or her financial responsibilities to the child after the child is born." [18]

In recent years, scholars troubled by these decisions have proposed alternative approaches. Some have argued that local family courts provide the best venue for balancing parental rights and interests when determining the fate of a pregnancy. *Danforth* permits this option, they contend, because its ruling prohibits state legislatures from requiring spousal consent for an abortion, but says nothing about the prerogatives of local courts.[19]

Other scholars have proposed statutes which would allow unmarried fathers, like Dubay, to "opt out" of the legal rights and duties of parenthood under certain conditions. These might include the father's having forewarned the mother prior to sexual intercourse that he will not assume these rights and obligations, the father's offering to pay for an abortion or consenting to adoption, and the mother's using fraud or misrepresentation when entering into sexual relations with him. Neither of these two strategies is likely to succeed unless the American public becomes more willing to expand the rights of men with respect to procreation than is currently the case. [20]

Notes

1 David Blankenhorn, *The Future of Marriage*. New York: Encounter Books, 2007, 5. Jason de Parle and Sabrina Tavenise, "For Women Under 30, Most Births Occur Outside of Marriage." *New York Times*, February 17, 2012.

2 Susan Mollar Okin, *Justice, Gender, and the Family*. New York: Basic Books, 1989, 139, 170.

3 Okin, *Justice*, 172, 171.

4 Ibid., 179, 184.

5 Steven E. Rhoads, *Taking Sex Differences Seriously*. New York: Encounter Books, 2004, 4.

6 Ibid., 248, 258–60.

7 Perry v. Schwarzenegger, 2010 US Dist. LEXIS 78817 (ND Cal. 210).

8 Ibid. at 187.

9 Ibid.

10 Perry v. Brown 671 F. 3rd 1052, Amicus Brief, National Organization for Marriage et al., 3–4, 7–8, 16, 21.

11 Perry v. Schwarzenegger, 2010 US Dist. LEXIS 78817 (ND Cal. 210) 206, 207.

12 Stanley v. Illinois, 405 US 645 (1972).

13 Roe v. Wade, 410 US 113 (1973).

14 Planned Parenthood v. Danforth, 428 US 52 (1976) at 69–71.

15 Ibid., at 93–4.

16 Dubay v. Wells 506 F.3d 422 (6th Cir. 2007) http://caselaw.findlaw.com/us-6th-circuit/1467603.html 1–11.

17 Ibid., 2.

18 Ibid., 4–5.

19 For a summary of these arguments see Andrea M. Sharrin, "Note: Potential Fathers and Abortion: A Woman's Womb is Not a Man's Castle," *Brooklyn Law Review* 55, Winter 1990, 1359–404 at 1385, 1386.

20 Erika M. Hiester, "Note: Child Support Statutes and the Father's Right Not to Procreate," *Ave Maria Law Review* 2, Spring 2004, 213–41. See also Melanie G. McCulley, "The Male Abortion: The Putative Father's Right to Terminate His Interests in and Obligations to the Unborn Child." *Journal of Law and Policy* 1, 1998, 1–55.

READINGS

Sex Roles within Marriage

Susan Moller Okin (1946–2004)

Susan Moller Okin was a prominent feminist author who argued that gender belongs at the core rather than at the margins of political philosophy. The selection below comes from her most famous work, *Justice, Gender, and the Family*.

Okin, Susan Moller. *Justice, Gender, and the Family*. New York: Basic Books, 1989. (Excerpts: pp. 170–1, 175, 176, 179, 183–5, 186)

Conclusion: Toward a Humanist Justice

The family is the linchpin of gender, reproducing it from one generation to the next. As we have seen, family life as typically practiced in our society is not just, either to women or to children. Moreover, it is not conducive to the rearing of citizens with a strong sense of justice. In spite of all the rhetoric about equality between the sexes, the traditional or quasi-traditional division of family labor still prevails. Women are made vulnerable by constructing their lives around the expectation that they will be primary parents; they become more vulnerable within marriages in which they fulfill this expectation, whether or not they also work for wages; and they are most vulnerable in the event of separation or divorce, when they usually take over responsibility for children without adequate support from their ex-husbands. Since approximately half of all marriages end in divorce, about half of our children are likely to experience its dislocations, often made far more traumatic by the socioeconomic consequences of both gender-structured marriage and divorce settlements that fail to take account of it. I have suggested that, for very important reasons, the family *needs* to be a just institution, and have shown that contemporary theories of justice neglect women and ignore gender. How can we address this injustice?

This is a complex question. It is particularly so because we place great value on our freedom to live different kinds of lives, there is no current consensus on many aspects of gender, and we have good reason to suspect that many of our beliefs about sexual difference and appropriate sex roles are heavily influenced by the very fact that we grew up in a gender-structured society....

I shall argue here that any just and fair solution to the urgent problem of women's and children's vulnerability must encourage and facilitate the equal sharing by men and women of paid and unpaid work, of productive and reproductive labor. We must work toward a future in which all will be likely to choose this mode of life. A just future would be one without gender. In its social structures and practices, one's sex would have no more relevance than one's eye color or the length of one's toes. No assumptions would be made about "male" and "female" roles; childbearing would be so conceptually separated from child rearing and other family responsibilities that it would be a cause for surprise, and no little concern, if men and women were not equally responsible for domestic life or if children were to spend much more time with one parent than the other. It would be a future in which men and women participated in more or less equal numbers in every sphere of life, from infant care to different kinds of paid work to high-level politics. Thus it would no longer be the case that having no experience of raising children would be the practical prerequisite for attaining positions of the greatest social influence.... If we are to be at all true to our democratic ideals, moving away from gender is essential. Obviously, the attainment of such a social world requires major changes in a multitude of institutions and social settings outside the home, as well as within it.

* * *

Moving Away from Gender

First, public policies and laws should generally assume no social differentiation of the sexes. Shared parental responsibility for child care would be both assumed and facilitated... If we start out with the reasonable assumption that women and men are equally parents of their children, and have equal responsibility for both the unpaid effort that goes into caring for them and their economic support, then we must rethink the demands of work life throughout the period in which a worker of either sex is a parent of a small child. We can no longer cling to the by now largely mythical assumption that every worker has "someone else" at home to raise "his" children.

* * *

It is impossible to predict all the effects of moving toward a society without gender. Major current injustices to women and children would end. Men would experience both the joys and the responsibilities of far closer and more sustained contact with their children than many have today. Many immensely influential spheres of life—notably politics and the professional occupations—would for the first time be populated more or less equally by men and women, most of whom were also actively participating parents.

This would be in great contrast to today, when most of those who rise to influential positions are either men who, if fathers, have minimal contact with their children, or women who have either forgone motherhood altogether or hired others as full-time caretakers for their children because of the demands of their careers....

* * *

Protecting the Vulnerable

* * *

Thus, while protecting those whom gender now makes vulnerable, we must also put our best efforts into promoting the elimination of gender.

The increased justice to women that would result from moving away from gender is readily apparent. Standards for just social institutions could no longer take for granted and exclude from considerations of justice much of what women now do, since men would share in it equally. Such central components of justice as what counts as productive labor, and what count as needs and deserts, would be greatly affected by this change. Standards of justice would become *humanist,* as they have never been before. One of the most important effects of this would be to change radically the situation of women as citizens. With egalitarian families, and with institutions such as workplaces and schools designed to accommodate the needs of parents and children, rather than being based as they now are on the traditional assumption that "someone else" is at home, mothers would not be virtually excluded from positions of influence in politics and the workplace. They would be represented at every level in approximately equal numbers with men.

In a genderless society, children too would benefit. They would not suffer in the ways that they do now because of the injustices done to women.... Equality of opportunity to become what we want to be would be enhanced in two important ways by the development of families without gender and by the public policies necessary to support their development. First, the growing gap between the economic well-being of children in single-parent and those in two-parent families would be reduced. Children in single-parent families would benefit significantly if fathers were held equally responsible for supporting their children, whether married to their mothers or not; if more mothers had sustained labor force attachment; if high-quality day care were subsidized; and if the workplace were designed to accommodate parenting. These children would be far less likely to spend their formative years in conditions of poverty with one parent struggling to fulfill the functions of two. Their life chances would be significantly enhanced.

Second, children of both sexes in gender-free families would have (as some already have) much more opportunity for self-development free from sex role expectations and sex-typed personalities than most do now. Girls and boys who grow up in highly traditional families, in which sex difference is regarded as a determinant of everything from roles, responsibilities and privileges to acceptable dress, speech, and modes of behavior clearly have far less freedom to develop into whatever kind of person they want to be than do those who are raised without such constraints.... Even now, in most cases without men's equal fathering, both the daughters and the sons of wage-working mothers have been found to have a more positive view of women and less rigid views of sex roles; the daughters (like their mothers) tend to have greater self esteem and a more positive view of themselves as workers, and the sons, to expect equality and shared roles in their own future marriages. We might well expect that with mothers in the labor force *and* with fathers as equal parents, children's attitudes and psychologies will become even less correlated with their sex In a very crucial sense, their opportunities to become the persons they want to be will be enlarged.

Finally, it seems undeniable that the enhancement of justice that accompanies the disappearance of gender will make the family a much better place for children to develop a sense of justice. We can no longer deny the importance of the fact that families are where we first learn, by example and by how we are treated, not only how people do relate to each other but also how they *should*. How would families not built on gender be better schools of moral development? First, the example of co-equal parents with shared roles combining love with justice, would provide a far better example of human relations for children than the domination and dependence that often occur in traditional marriage. The fairness of the distribution of labor, the equal respect, and the *inter*dependence of his or her parents would surely be a powerful first example to a child in a family with equally shared roles. Second, as I have argued, having a sense of justice requires that we be able to empathize, to abstract from our own situation and to think about moral and political issues from the points of view of others.... including others who are different from ourselves.

* * *

For those whose response to what I have argued here is the practical objection that it is unrealistic and will cost too much, I have some answers and some questions. Some of what I have suggested would not cost anything, in terms of public spending, though it would redistribute the costs and other responsibilities of rearing children more evenly between men and women. Some policies I have endorsed, such as adequate public support for children whose fathers cannot contribute, may cost more than present policies, but may not, depending on how well they work. Some, such as subsidized high-quality day care, would he expensive in themselves, but also might soon be offset by other savings, since they would enable those who would otherwise be full-time child carers to be at least part-time workers.

...But even if my suggestions would cost, and cost a lot, we have to ask: How much do we care about the injustices of gender? How much do we care that women who have spent the better part of their lives nurturing others can be discarded like used goods?...How much do we care that those who raise children, *because* of this choice, have restricted opportunities to develop the rest of their potential, and very little influence on society's values and direction? How much do we care that the family, our most intimate social grouping, is often a school of day-to-day injustice? How much do we *want* the just families that will produce the kind of citizens we need if we are ever to achieve a just society?

Steven E. Rhoads

Steven E. Rhoads teaches in the Woodrow Wilson Department of Government and Foreign Affairs at the University of Virginia where he specializes in ethics and politics, economics and public policy, and sex and gender differences in public policy. The selection below is taken from his most recent book, *Taking Sex Differences Seriously*.

Rhoads, Steven E. *Taking Sex Differences Seriously*. New York: Encounter Books, 2004. (Excerpts: pp. 4–5, 6, 248, 249, 252, 253, 254, 255, 256, 259, 261, 262, 263).

...When discussing the lives of men and women, we now use the term *gender* far more often than sex....The term *gender difference* reflects the assumption that any distinctions between the sexes' traits, values, interests, skills and behaviors arise from society's rigid gender roles, which channel people's thoughts and actions in stereotypical directions.

This book goes against that grain. It argues that sex differences are large, deeply rooted and consequential. Men and women still have different natures and, generally speaking, different preferences, talents and interests. The book presents evidence that these differences can be explained in part by hormones and other physiological and chemical distinctions between men and women. Thus they won't disappear unless we tinker with our fundamental biological natures.

* * *

I see my task as explaining why the sex differences discussed are profound and why they should affect the way we think about specific policies and cultural issues. Despite the unconventional nature of the argument, I do not think my burden of proof is high. I will not consider my argument disproved if some of my evidence is questioned. There is so much of it that what remains will be enough to challenge the dominant ideology of the last thirty years that sees men and women as having fundamentally equivalent natures and goals. Such an ideology, I believe, cannot withstand scrutiny. We need a new view of gender for a new century.

CONCLUSION

* * *

What Most Women Want

...Most women want most of all a loving husband and children. They have always been more attracted to people than to things. They love strong long-term relationships; casual uncommitted sex soon loses its attractions if ever indeed it had any. The marital ideal—one man and one woman bound in body and soul, sharing, comforting, communicating through good times and bad—is very appealing even, or perhaps particularly, in a cynical age. This vision includes romantic and committed sex along with children, to whom most women have been drawn since childhood and who seem even more precious once pregnancy and breastfeeding bathe women in hormonal pleasure.

* * *

...Given the priorities that most women give to family on the one hand and job on the other, it seems unlikely that the job gains of the last forty years have compensated for the deterioration that has occurred on the home front. A 1995 poll found that more than twice as many women thought the feminist movement had made it harder to combine jobs and families as thought the movement had made it easier. Similarly, a 1998 poll found that about five times as many men *and* women thought changing gender roles had made it harder for marriages to be successful as thought it had made it easier. And whatever the cause, women are far less likely to get the marriages and children they say they want than in the past....

* * *

Although the national media might make us think that Mr. Moms are popping up all over, they are not. For one thing, women are rarely attracted to such men. Sociologist Catherin Hakim surveys the evidence and concludes, "Even the most qualified and high-earning women reject role reversal in favor of a partner who is at least equal, preferably superior, in earnings, status or power." Hakim...agrees with me that women, even more than men, prefer gendered roles in which the husband spends more time earning money. She finds that the women's movement has not narrowed the gender gap in this regard....

What Most Men Need

* * *

...[M]en are less attracted to and less well equipped for marriage than women. Men, nonetheless, need marriage. Communities of unmarried young men are prone to engage in violence and predatory sex. Compared with the married, young unmarried men tend to be lazy and unfocused. Or worse, they may drop out of society altogether, or undermine it. Unmarried men are five times more likely than unmarried women to be homeless and they disproportionately fill our prisons.

* * *

Married men usually take well to the provider role. Even among those with top educational credentials, men are more likely than women to choose a job because it offers better financial prospects. Polls show that men are more likely than women to depend upon work for a sense of purpose and identity....

Despite its constraints, work caters to a part of men's nature. It allows them to roam beyond the family fire. It provides a competitive outlet. A salary gives a tangible indicator of progress. Men who marry and who plan a family have more motivation to work hard, and with rising personal responsibilities, their work effort and salaries rise concurrently....

Men are more aggressive than women, and they more regularly seek to dominate. Dominance, assertiveness and the drive that sustains ambition are thought to belong to the same behavioral family. In the workplace, men are more likely than women to grab the floor in meetings and to claim credit, whether deserved or not, for the ideas that carry the day. Women seem to care more about protecting the feelings of subordinates; men worry more about hurting the feelings of their bosses....

This male drive, however, does not extend to the domestic sphere. Even in those few modern American families where the parents try to share child care equally, the husbands often push for more paid care so there are fewer total hours they must divide with their spouses....The fathers in families where time with children is shared equally acknowledge that their wives are more emotionally involved with the children, often to the extent that they find it harder to concentrate on other tasks when away from them. In contrast, husbands in two-career families are more stressed than wives if child care breaks down and they must stay home from work to tend to children.

Marital Dynamics and Vulnerabilities

The theme of female vulnerability recurs throughout this book. Because women tend to bond with those they sleep with, men's more cavalier attitude about sex can leave women bitter and emotionally devastated. Pregnancy, delivery and nursing can drain women's energy, often leaving them in need of being nurtured themselves. Women's outsized love of their children produces a bond that makes them more dependent on their husbands to provide the resources enabling them to spend as much time with their children as they wish.

* * *

That so much of women's happiness is dependent on a good marriage and happy children makes women especially vulnerable. One study of full-time dual-career couples found that problems at work increased psychological distress equally for men and women, but that problems in the marriage led to much more distress for women than for men. Women's vulnerability affects their physical as well as their mental health....

Men's distress in marriage has other sources entirely. Husbands' mental and physical health deteriorate when they think their wives are failing in the domestic arena or when they feel that they themselves are not fully meeting their providing and protecting duties. Husbands are happy in their marriage if their wife is attractive—and more attractive than they are—and if she performs well domestic tasks such as cooking and shopping....

Women's Work

The biggest issues in contemporary marriages surround women's work, in and out of the home. Women like to care for children much more than men do, and they also like housework more than men do. ...There is reason to think that such differences have a biological basis....

* * *

Most women would prefer...days made up of part-time work outside the home or full-time homemaking. Today, cultural pressures to work and even the preferences of many men prevent women from bringing such days into being.

* * *

The result is angry, exhausted mothers desperate for a house that looks and feels like a home and for more time with their children. One way out would be for women to start telling their boyfriends, husbands and the rest of the world that they are not the same as men are. Being constantly on the go in a competitive world may work for men but not for many women who want to get pregnant or who want to nurse. They need to relax. And carrying and delivering a baby can be exhausting. Nursing takes time. In order to be fulfilled emotionally and psychologically, mothers need to spend enough time with the kids. And, as corroborated by study after study, the kids need more time with their mothers....

This philosophy will usually require men to provide the business plan. Men like challenges. Women might ask them to step up and be real providers, leaving the women more time and capacity to better fulfill the domestic role.

Such a scenario sounds regressive in an era like our own that pays plenty of lip service to a revolutionary approach to sex roles, but it's pretty much what most men and women believe works best even today. Especially after marriage, most men and women in the United States and western Europe continue to support a division of labor in which men are ultimately responsible for breadwinning and women for the domestic realm. This division continues to produce happy and stable couples, and it enables men to be manly, protective, and competent....

* * *

In one way, men and women in a traditional marriage both get exactly what they want... [W]hen asked how they would like to be described, men use words like *dominant, assertive, independent.* Women asked the same question say *loving, generous, sensitive.*

If marriage means bringing together one person with a taste for assertion and another with a taste for generosity, we should not be surprised to find that the former is, in some sense, the head of the family. This doesn't mean he rules like an absolute dictator. Indeed, it's still quite common to hear of small, feminine women who have their strong, masculine husbands "wrapped around their little fingers." Happy women usually rule indirectly. They can rule because their husbands love and want to please them. They can also rule because, as psychological studies have demonstrated, women can read men better than men can read women. What matters, then, is only that men be the ostensible heads of households. In such cases, both parties emerge happy.

* * *

...If we took sex differences seriously, we would not be looking for new ways to weaken the historic role of men in the family. By challenging the titular familial leadership of the male and undermining the centrality of his role as provider for his family, modernity has reduced the number of men to whom marriage seems desirable....

Wives doubtful about whether to grant titular household leadership to husbands should realize they may not have to give up much more than the title. Some studies have shown that husbands overestimate their decision-making power, while wives underestimate theirs...

A woman who seeks power outside the family through a dominant and aggressive personality will have to be as agile as Spiderman if she is to be happily married as well. My female students often warm to ... another type of female power, which is "something subtler, the force that creates relationships, binds families and builds societies." This is a kind of power we desperately need. It is past time for both sexes to appreciate its importance.

Same-Sex Marriage

Perry v. Schwarznegger, 210 U.S. Dist. LEXIS 78817 (2010)

In May 2008, the California Supreme Court held in the case *In re Marriage Cases* that state statutes limiting marriage to heterosexual applicants violated the California Constitution. The following month, same-sex couples were able to marry in California. In November, 2008, California's electorate adopted Proposition 8, a constitutional amendment that restored the opposite-sex limitation on marriage. In May, 2009, the American Foundation for Equal Rights filed suit in the U.S. District Court for the Northern District of California challenging the validity of Proposition 8 on behalf of the two same-sex couples. In the case of Perry v Schwarznegger

(2010), U.S. District Chief Judge Vaughn R. Walker invalidated Proposition 8 on the grounds that it violated the Due Process and Equal Protection Clauses of the Fourteenth Amendment to the U.S. Constitution. In February, 2012 a divided three judge panel of the U.S. Ninth Circuit Court of Appeals upheld the decision of the District Court. The proponents of Proposition 8 appealed the case to the U.S. Supreme Court in July, 2012, which is going to hear the case in the 2012–13 term.

KRISTIN M PERRY, SANDRA B STIER, PAUL T KATAMI and JEFFREY J ZARRILLO, Plaintiffs, CITY AND COUNTY OF SAN FRANCISCO, Plaintiff-Intervenor, v **ARNOLD SCHWARZENEGGER,** in his official capacity as Governor of California; ...

No C 09-2292 VRW

UNITED STATES DISTRICT COURT FOR THE NORTHERN DISTRICT OF CALIFORNIA

2010 U.S. Dist. LEXIS 78817

August 4, 2010, Filed

JUDGES: VAUGHN R WALKER, United States District Chief Judge.

III
CONCLUSIONS OF LAW[3]

DUE PROCESS

[HN9]The *Due Process Clause* provides that no "State [shall] deprive any person of life, liberty, or property, without due process of law." *US Const Amend XIV, § 1.* Due process protects individuals against arbitrary governmental intrusion into life, liberty or property. When legislation burdens the exercise of a right deemed to be fundamental, the government must show that the intrusion withstands strict scrutiny.

THE RIGHT TO MARRY PROTECTS AN INDIVIDUAL'S CHOICE OF MARITAL PARTNER REGARDLESS OF GENDER

[HN10]The freedom to marry is recognized as a fundamental right protected by the *Due Process Clause.*

The parties do not dispute that the right to marry is fundamental. The question presented here is whether plaintiffs seek to exercise the fundamental right to marry; or, because they are couples of the same sex, whether they seek recognition of a new right.

HN11To determine whether a right is fundamental under the [*184] *Due Process Clause*, the court inquires into whether the right is rooted "in our Nation's history, legal traditions, and practices." *Glucksberg, 521 US at 710*. Here, because the right to marry is fundamental, the court looks to the evidence presented at trial to determine: (1) the history, tradition and practice of marriage in the United States; and (2) whether plaintiffs seek to exercise their right to marry or seek to exercise some other right. Id.

Marriage has retained certain characteristics throughout the history of the United States. See FF 19, 34–5. Marriage requires two parties to give their free consent to form a relationship, which then forms the foundation of a household. FF 20, 34. The spouses must consent to support each other and any dependents. FF 34–5, 37. The state regulates marriage because marriage creates stable households, which in turn form the basis of a stable, governable populace. FF 35–7. The state respects an individual's choice to build a family with another and protects the relationship because it is so central a part of an individual's life. See *Bowers v Hardwick, 478 US 186, 204–5, 106 S. Ct. 2841, 92 L. Ed. 2d 140 (1986)* (Blackmun, J, dissenting).

HN12Never has the state inquired into procreative [*185] capacity or intent before issuing a marriage license; indeed, a marriage license is more than a license to have procreative sexual intercourse. FF 21. "[I]t would demean a married couple were it to be said marriage is simply about the right to have sexual intercourse." *Lawrence, 539 US at 567*. The Supreme Court recognizes that, wholly apart from procreation, choice and privacy play a pivotal role in the marital relationship. See *Griswold, 381 US at 485–6*.

Race restrictions on marital partners were once common in most states but are now seen as archaic, shameful or even bizarre. FF 23–5. When the Supreme Court invalidated race restrictions in Loving, the definition of the right to marry did not change. *388 US at 12*. Instead, the Court recognized that race restrictions, despite their historical prevalence, stood in stark contrast to the concepts of liberty and choice inherent in the right to marry. Id.

The marital bargain in California (along with other states) traditionally required that a woman's legal and economic identity be subsumed by her husband's upon marriage under the doctrine of coverture; this once-unquestioned aspect of marriage now is regarded as antithetical to the notion [*186] of marriage as a union of equals. FF 26–7, 32. As states moved to recognize the equality of the sexes, they eliminated laws and practices like coverture that had made gender a proxy for a spouse's role within a marriage. FF 26–7, 32. Marriage was thus transformed from a male-dominated institution into an institution recognizing men and women as equals. Id. Yet, individuals retained the right to marry; that right did not become different simply because the institution of marriage became compatible with gender equality.

The evidence at trial shows that marriage in the United States traditionally has not been open to same-sex couples. The evidence suggests many reasons for this tradition of exclusion, including gender roles mandated through coverture, FF 26–7, social disapproval of same-sex relationships, FF 74, and the reality that the vast majority of people are heterosexual and have had no reason to challenge the restriction, FF 43. The evidence shows that the movement of marriage away from a gendered institution and toward an institution free from state-mandated gender roles reflects an evolution in the understanding of gender rather than a change in marriage. The evidence did not [*187] show any historical purpose for excluding same-sex couples from marriage, as states have never required spouses to have an ability or willingness to procreate in order to marry. FF 21. Rather, the exclusion exists as an artifact of a time when the genders were seen as having distinct roles in society and in marriage. That time has passed.

The right to marry has been historically and remains the right to choose a spouse and, with mutual consent, join together and form a household. FF 19–20, 34–5. Race and gender restrictions shaped marriage during eras of race and gender inequality, but such restrictions were never part of the historical core of the institution of marriage. FF 33. Today, gender is not relevant to the state in determining spouses' obligations to each other and to their dependents. Relative gender composition aside, same-sex couples are situated identically to opposite-sex couples in terms of their ability to perform the rights and obligations of marriage under California law. FF 48. Gender no longer forms an essential part of marriage; marriage under law is a union of equals.

Plaintiffs seek to have the state recognize their committed relationships, and plaintiffs' relationships [*188] are consistent with the core of the history, tradition and practice of marriage in the United States. Perry and Stier seek to be spouses; they seek the mutual obligation and honor that attend marriage, FF 52. Zarrillo and Katami seek recognition from the state that their union is "a coming together for better or for worse, hopefully enduring, and intimate to the degree of being sacred." *Griswold, 381 US at 486.* Plaintiffs' unions encompass the historical purpose and form of marriage. Only the plaintiffs' genders relative to one another prevent California from giving their relationships due recognition.

Plaintiffs do not seek recognition of a new right. To characterize plaintiffs' objective as "the right to same-sex marriage" would suggest that plaintiffs seek something different from what opposite-sex couples across the state enjoy — namely, marriage. Rather, plaintiffs ask California to recognize their relationships for what they are: marriages.

* * *

PROPOSITION 8 DOES NOT SURVIVE RATIONAL BASIS

Proposition 8 cannot withstand any level of scrutiny under the *Equal Protection Clause*, as excluding same-sex couples from marriage is simply not rationally related to a legitimate state interest....

Proponents put forth several rationales for Proposition 8, which the court now examines [*201] in turn: (1) reserving marriage as a union between a man and a woman and excluding any other relationship from marriage; (2) proceeding with caution when implementing social changes; (3) promoting opposite sex parenting over same-sex parenting; (4) protecting the freedom of those who oppose marriage for same-sex couples; (5) treating same-sex couples differently from opposite-sex couples; and (6) any other conceivable interest.

PURPORTED INTEREST #1: RESERVING MARRIAGE AS A UNION BETWEEN A MAN AND A WOMAN AND EXCLUDING ANY OTHER RELATIONSHIP

Proponents first argue that Proposition 8 is rational because it preserves: (1) "the traditional institution of marriage as the union of a man and a woman"; (2) "the traditional social and legal purposes, functions, and structure of marriage"; and (3) "the traditional meaning of marriage as it has always been defined in the English language." Doc #605 at 12–13. These interests relate to maintaining the definition of marriage as the union of a man and a woman for its own sake.

HN18Tradition alone, however, cannot form a rational basis for a law. *Williams v Illinois, 399 US 235, 239, 90 S. Ct. 2018, 26 L. Ed. 2d 586 (1970).* The "ancient lineage" of a classification does not make it rational. [*202] *Heller, 509 US at 327.* Rather, the state must have an interest apart from the fact of the tradition itself.

The evidence shows that the tradition of restricting an individual's choice of spouse based on gender does not rationally further a state interest despite its "ancient lineage." Instead, the evidence shows that the tradition of gender restrictions arose when spouses were legally required to adhere to specific gender roles. See FF 26–7. California has eliminated all legally mandated gender roles except the requirement that a marriage consist of one man and one woman. FF 32. Proposition 8 thus enshrines in the California Constitution a gender restriction that the evidence shows to be nothing more than an artifact of a foregone notion that men and women fulfill different roles in civic life.

The tradition of restricting marriage to opposite-sex couples does not further any state interest. Rather, the evidence shows that Proposition 8 harms the state's interest in equality, because it mandates that men and women be treated differently based only on antiquated and discredited notions of gender. See FF 32, 57.

Proponents' argument that tradition prefers opposite-sex couples to same-sex [*203] couples equates to the notion that opposite-sex relationships are simply better than same-sex relationships. Tradition alone cannot legitimate this purported interest. Plaintiffs presented evidence showing conclusively that the state has no interest in preferring opposite-sex couples to same-sex couples or in preferring heterosexuality to homosexuality. See FF 48–50. Moreover, [HN19]the state cannot have an interest in disadvantaging an unpopular minority group simply because the group is unpopular. *Moreno, 413 US at 534.*

The evidence shows that the state advances nothing when it adheres to the tradition of excluding same-sex couples from marriage. Proponents' asserted state interests in tradition are nothing more than tautologies and do not amount to rational bases for Proposition 8.

PURPORTED INTEREST #2: PROCEEDING WITH CAUTION WHEN IMPLEMENTING SOCIAL CHANGES

Proponents next argue that Proposition 8 is related to state interests in: (1) "[a]cting incrementally and with caution when considering a radical transformation to the fundamental nature of a bedrock social institution"; (2) "[d]ecreasing the probability of weakening the institution of marriage"; (3) "[d]ecreasing the probability [*204] of adverse consequences that could result from weakening the institution of marriage"; and (4) "[d]ecreasing the probability of the potential adverse consequences of same-sex marriage." Doc #605 at 13–14.

Plaintiffs presented evidence at trial sufficient to rebut any claim that marriage for same-sex couples amounts to a sweeping social change. See FF 55. Instead, the evidence shows beyond debate that allowing same-sex couples to marry has at least a neutral, if not a positive, effect on the institution of marriage and that same-sex couples' marriages would benefit the state. Id. Moreover, the evidence shows that the rights of those opposed to homosexuality or same-sex couples will remain unaffected if the state ceases to enforce Proposition 8. FF 55, 62.

The contrary evidence proponents presented is not credible. Indeed, proponents presented no reliable evidence that allowing same-sex couples to marry will have any negative effects on society or on the institution of marriage. The process of allowing same-sex couples to marry is straightforward, and no evidence suggests that the state needs any significant lead time to integrate same-sex couples into marriage. See Background to Proposition [*205] 8 above. Consider, by contrast, *Cooper v Aaron, 358 U.S. 1, 7, 78 S. Ct. 1401, 3 L. Ed. 2d 5, 79 Ohio Law Abs. 452 (1958)* (recognizing that a school district needed time to implement racial integration but nevertheless finding a delay unconstitutional because the school board's plan did not provide for "the earliest practicable completion of desegregation"). The evidence shows that allowing same-sex couples to marry will be simple for California to implement because it has already done so; no change need be phased in. California need not restructure any institution to allow same-sex couples to marry. See FF 55.

Because the evidence shows same-sex marriage has and will have no adverse effects on society or the institution of marriage, California has no interest in waiting and no practical need to wait to grant marriage licenses to same-sex couples. Proposition 8 is thus not rationally related to proponents' purported interests in proceeding with caution when implementing social change.

PURPORTED   INTEREST   #3:   PROMOTING   OPPOSITE-SEX
PARENTING OVER SAME-SEX PARENTING

Proponents' largest group of purported state interests relates to opposite-sex parents. Proponents argue Proposition 8: (1) promotes "stability and responsibility in naturally procreative [*206] relationships"; (2) promotes "enduring and stable family structures for the responsible raising and care of children by their biological parents"; (3) increases "the probability that natural procreation will occur within stable, enduring, and supporting family structures"; (4) promotes "the natural and mutually beneficial bond between parents and their biological children"; (5) increases "the probability that each child will be raised by both of his or her biological parents"; (6) increases "the probability that each child will be raised by both a father and a mother"; and (7) increases "the probability that each child will have a legally recognized father and mother." Doc #605 at 13–14.

The evidence supports two points which together show Proposition 8 does not advance any of the identified interests: (1) same-sex parents and opposite-sex parents are of equal quality, FF 69–73, and (2) Proposition 8 does not make it more likely that opposite-sex couples will marry and raise offspring biologically related to both parents, FF 43, 46, 51.

The evidence does not support a finding that California has an interest in preferring opposite-sex parents over same-sex parents. Indeed, the evidence [*207] shows beyond any doubt that parents' genders are irrelevant to children's developmental outcomes. FF 70. Moreover, Proposition 8 has nothing to do with children, as Proposition 8 simply prevents same-sex couples from marrying. FF 57. Same-sex couples can have (or adopt) and raise children. When they do, they are treated identically to opposite-sex parents under California law. FF 49. Even if California had an interest in preferring opposite-sex parents to same-sex parents — and the evidence plainly shows that California does not — Proposition 8 is not rationally related to that interest, because Proposition 8 does not affect who can or should become a parent under California law. FF 49, 57.

To the extent California has an interest in encouraging sexual activity to occur within marriage (a debatable proposition in light of *Lawrence, 539 US at 571*) the evidence shows Proposition 8 to be detrimental to that interest. Because of Proposition 8, same-sex couples are not permitted to engage in sexual activity within marriage. FF 53. Domestic partnerships, in which sexual activity is apparently expected, are separate from marriage and thus codify California's encouragement of non-marital sexual [*208] activity. *Cal Fam Code §§ 297-299.6*. To the extent proponents seek to encourage a norm that sexual activity occur within marriage to ensure that reproduction occur within stable households, Proposition 8 discourages that norm because it requires some sexual activity and child-bearing and child-rearing to occur outside marriage.

Proponents argue Proposition 8 advances a state interest in encouraging the formation of stable households. Instead, the evidence shows that Proposition 8 undermines that state interest, because same-sex households have become less stable by the passage of Proposition 8. The inability to marry denies same-sex couples the benefits, including stability, attendant to marriage. FF 50. Proponents failed to put forth any credible evidence that married opposite-sex households are made more stable through Proposition 8. FF 55. The only rational conclusion in light of the evidence is that Proposition 8 makes it less likely that California children will be raised in stable households. See FF 50, 56.

None of the interests put forth by proponents relating to parents and children is advanced by Proposition 8; instead, the evidence shows Proposition 8 disadvantages families [*209] and their children.

PURPORTED INTEREST #4: PROTECTING THE FREEDOM OF THOSE WHO OPPOSE MARRIAGE FOR SAME-SEX COUPLES

Proponents next argue that Proposition 8 protects the *First Amendment* freedom of those who disagree with allowing marriage for couples of the same sex. Proponents argue that Proposition 8: (1) preserves "the prerogative and responsibility of parents to provide for the ethical and moral development and education of their own children"; and (2) accommodates "the *First Amendment* rights of individuals and institutions that oppose same-sex marriage on religious or moral grounds." Doc #605 at 14.

These purported interests fail as a matter of law. *HN20*Proposition 8 does not affect any *First Amendment* right or responsibility of parents to educate their children. See *In re Marriage Cases, 183 P3d at 451–2.* Californians are prevented from distinguishing between same-sex partners and opposite-sex spouses in public accommodations, as California antidiscrimination law requires identical treatment for same-sex unions and opposite-sex marriages. *Koebke v Bernardo Heights Country Club, 36 Cal. 4th 824, 31 Cal. Rptr. 3d 565, 115 P3d 1212, 1217–18 (Cal 2005).* The evidence shows that Proposition 8 does nothing other than eliminate [*210] the right of same-sex couples to marry in California. See FF 57, 62. Proposition 8 is not rationally related to an interest in protecting the rights of those opposed to same-sex couples because, as a matter of law, Proposition 8 does not affect the rights of those opposed to homosexuality or to marriage for couples of the same sex. FF 62.

To the extent proponents argue that one of the rights of those morally opposed to same-sex unions is the right to prevent same-sex couples from marrying, as explained presently those individuals' moral views are an insufficient basis upon which to enact a legislative classification.

PURPORTED INTEREST #5: TREATING SAME-SEX COUPLES DIFFERENTLY FROM OPPOSITE-SEX COUPLES

Proponents argue that Proposition 8 advances a state interest in treating same-sex couples differently from opposite-sex couples by: (1) "[u]sing different names for different things"; (2) "[m]aintaining the flexibility to separately address the needs of different types of relationships"; (3) "[e]nsuring that California marriages are recognized in other jurisdictions";

and (4) "[c]onforming California's definition of marriage to federal law."
Doc #605 at 14.

Here, proponents assume a premise [*211] that the evidence thoroughly
rebutted: rather than being different, same-sex and opposite-sex unions
are, for all purposes relevant to California law, exactly the same. FF 47–50.
The evidence shows conclusively that moral and religious views form the
only basis for a belief that same-sex couples are different from opposite-sex
couples. See FF 48, 76–80. The evidence fatally undermines any purported
state interest in treating couples differently; thus, these interests do not
provide a rational basis supporting Proposition 8.

* * *

A PRIVATE MORAL VIEW THAT SAME-SEX COUPLES ARE INFERIOR TO OPPOSITE-SEX COUPLES IS NOT A PROPER BASIS FOR LEGISLATION

In the absence of a rational basis, what remains of proponents' case is an
inference, amply supported by evidence in the record, that Proposition 8
was premised on the belief that same-sex couples simply are not as good
as opposite-sex couples. FF 78–80. Whether that belief is based on moral
disapproval of homosexuality, animus towards gays and lesbians or simply
a belief that a relationship between a man and a woman is inherently better
than a relationship between two men or two women, this belief is not a
proper basis on which to legislate. See *Romer, 517 US at 633*; *Moreno,
413 US at 534*; *Palmore v Sidoti, 466 US 429, 433, 104 S. Ct. 1879, 80 L.
Ed. 2d 421 (1984)* (HN22"[T]he [*214] Constitution cannot control [private
biases] but neither can it tolerate them.").

The evidence shows that Proposition 8 was a hard-fought campaign
and that the majority of California voters supported the initiative. See
Background to Proposition 8 above, FF 17–18, 79–80. The arguments
surrounding Proposition 8 raise a question similar to that addressed in
Lawrence, when the Court asked whether a majority of citizens could use
the power of the state to enforce "profound and deep convictions accepted
as ethical and moral principles" through the criminal code. *539 US at
571*. The question here is whether California voters can enforce those
same principles through regulation of marriage licenses. They cannot.
HN23 California's obligation is to treat its citizens equally, not to "mandate
[its] own moral code." Id (citing *Planned Parenthood of Southeastern Pa
v Casey, 505 US 833, 850, 112 S. Ct. 2791, 120 L. Ed. 2d 674, (1992)*).
"[M]oral disapproval, without any other asserted state interest," has never
been a rational basis for legislation. *Lawrence, 539 US at 582* (O'Connor, J,

concurring). Tradition alone cannot support legislation. See *Williams, 399 US at 239*; *Romer, 517 US at 635*; *Lawrence, 539 US at 579*.

Proponents' purported [*215] rationales are nothing more than post-hoc justifications. [HN24]While the *Equal Protection Clause* does not prohibit post-hoc rationales, they must connect to the classification drawn. Here, the purported state interests fit so poorly with Proposition 8 that they are irrational, as explained above. What is left is evidence that Proposition 8 enacts a moral view that there is something "wrong" with same-sex couples. See FF 78–80.

The evidence at trial regarding the campaign to pass Proposition 8 uncloaks the most likely explanation for its passage: a desire to advance the belief that opposite-sex couples are morally superior to same-sex couples. FF 79–80. The campaign relied heavily on negative stereotypes about gays and lesbians and focused on protecting children from inchoate threats vaguely associated with gays and lesbians. FF 79–80; See PX0016 Video, Have You Thought About It? (video of a young girl asking whether the viewer has considered the consequences to her of Proposition 8 but not explaining what those consequences might be).

At trial, proponents' counsel attempted through cross-examination to show that the campaign wanted to protect children from learning about same-sex marriage [*216] in school. See PX0390A Video, Ron Prentice Addressing Supporters of Proposition 8, Excerpt; Tr 132:25-133:3 (proponents' counsel to Katami: "But the fact is that what the Yes on 8 campaign was pointing at, is that kids would be taught about same-sex relationships in first and second grade; isn't that a fact, that that's what they were referring to?"). The evidence shows, however, that Proposition 8 played on a fear that exposure to homosexuality would turn children into homosexuals and that parents should dread having children who are not heterosexual. FF 79; PX0099 Video, It's Already Happened (mother's expression of horror upon realizing her daughter now knows she can marry a princess).

The testimony of George Chauncey places the Protect Marriage campaign advertisements in historical context as echoing messages from previous campaigns to enact legal measures to disadvantage gays and lesbians. FF 74, 77–80. The Protect Marriage campaign advertisements ensured California voters had these previous fear-inducing messages in mind. FF 80. The evidence at trial shows those fears to be completely unfounded. FF 47–9, 68–73, 76–80.

[HN25]Moral disapproval alone is an improper basis on which to deny [*217] rights to gay men and lesbians. The evidence shows conclusively that

Proposition 8 enacts, without reason, a private moral view that same-sex couples are inferior to opposite-sex couples. FF 76, 79–80; *Romer, 517 US at 634* ("[L]aws of the kind now before us raise the inevitable inference that the disadvantage imposed is born of animosity toward the class of persons affected."). [HN26]Because Proposition 8 disadvantages gays and lesbians without any rational justification, Proposition 8 violates the *Equal Protection Clause of the Fourteenth Amendment.*

CONCLUSION

Proposition 8 fails to advance any rational basis in singling out gay men and lesbians for denial of a marriage license. Indeed, the evidence shows Proposition 8 does nothing more than enshrine in the California Constitution the notion that opposite-sex couples are superior to same-sex couples. Because California has no interest in discriminating against gay men and lesbians, and because Proposition 8 prevents California from fulfilling its constitutional obligation to provide marriages on an equal basis, the court concludes that Proposition 8 is unconstitutional.

IT IS SO ORDERED.

/s/ Vaughn R Walker

VAUGHN R WALKER

United States District Chief Judge

NATIONAL ORGANIZATION FOR MARRIAGE

The National Organization for Marriage is a non-profit political organization established in 2007 to work against the legalization of same-sex marriage in the United States. It serves as a national resource for opponents of same-sex marriage initiatives at the state and local level. The following selection is taken from its amicus brief in Perry v. Brown.

Perry v Brown 67 F. 3rd 1052, Amicus Brief, National Organization for Marriage, et. al. (2012) (Excerpts: pp. 3, 4, 5, 6, 7–8, 9–12, 14–15, 16–17, 21)

INTRODUCTION

This brief argues that same-sex marriage works a profound change in the public meaning of marriage; this change in public definition from "sexual union of male and female" to "union of any two persons" clearly severs the connections between marriage and its core historic civil mission: increasing the likelihood that children will be born to and raised by their mother and father. If it is rational for the plaintiffs to be concerned about the meaning of the word, it is rational for 7 million California voters to be concerned as well.

I. REDEFINING MARRIAGE TO INCLUDE SAME-SEX COUPLES WILL CHANGE THE PUBLIC MEANING AND PURPOSE OF MARRIAGE IN A WAY THAT WILL WEAKEN OR SEVER ITS RELATIONSHIP TO PROCREATION IN THE PUBLIC MIND

A. Marriage is intrinsically linked to procreation in law and society

Sexual unions of male and female are unique: they alone can make new life, and when they do so will either connect (or disconnect) children from mothers and fathers....It is this biological reality that has given rise to the marriage relationship, not just in America, but across all cultural, ethnic, religious and tribal lines throughout recorded history.

* * *

How does marriage as an enduring and exclusive sexual union of male and female serve the state's interest in procreation and child well-being? The connection is two-fold: First, every child conceived by a married couple begins life with a mother and father precommitted to caring for him or her together. Almost no child conceived in any other sexual union receives this great benefit. Additionally, every person who remains faithfully married, whether they have children together or not, is much less likely [to] create fatherless children in alternate relationships. Every married couple minimally serves the public purpose of marriage and none contradict the link between marriage and procreation.

* * *

Reasonable people may believe that marriage promotes the state's interest in encouraging children to be born to a mother and father who are committed both to one another and to the children their union may create. This alone is sufficient to uphold Proposition 8 under rational basis review.

B. The public meaning of marriage matters.

The State's definition of marriage helps shape the cultural understanding of what marriage is and what purposes it serves. Legally redefining marriage as "the union of any two persons," particularly through the blunt instrument of constitutional mandate, will weaken or sever the connection in the public square between marriage and procreation, elevating adult desires for love and commitment over the needs of children as the defining public purpose of marriage in law.

The ability of the law to shape public understanding of social institutions has long been recognized. Scholars have explained that marriage law regulates opposite-sex relationships by providing a bright line marker that would be difficult or impossible for any individual to sustain alone.

* * *

The norms that constitute the social institution are aspirational in nature. That means these normative models "are not and never were the descriptions of any universal empirical reality."...They are nevertheless important for promoting the social ideal and lifting the empirical reality.

The definition of marriage is one way the law of marriage helps further this civic purpose: our laws give a baseline definition of who is or is not married, providing a shared framework from which concepts such as out-of-wedlock pregnancies, or even adultery, can be understood....

C. Same-sex marriage will disconnect marriage in law from its public purpose of promoting responsible procreation.

After same-sex marriage, marriage in law will have no obvious or intrinsic relationship to childbearing, connecting natural parents to their children, or to providing children with mothers and fathers. If two men are a marriage, then marriage is clearly, and in a new public way, no longer about procreation, no longer about natural parenthood, and no longer about connecting mothers and fathers to children. Our historic conception of marriage will be replaced (in a definitive new way) by a new legal conception of marriage.

Two ideas are in conflict here: one is that children deserve mothers and fathers and marriage is intrinsically oriented towards serving this vital purpose. The other idea is that adult interests in forging romantic relationships of choice (i.e. to marry the person they love) are more important than recognizing and protecting the natural family. This latter idea is at the heart of the idea that same-sex marriage is a civil right. And it is the core idea that must be rejected if the state's interest in marriage is to be sustained.

* * *

The trial court rejected this first view, asserting that procreation has never been a purpose of marriage because elderly people and infertile people have always been allowed to marry. But throughout the period during which judges were explicitly and repeatedly affirming that marriage is about procreation, the elderly were allowed to marry and infertility was no bar....

* * *

Elderly couples and childless couples are all part of the natural lifecycle of marriage. They do not contradict the idea that a key purpose of "an enduring, exclusive sexual union of male and female" is responsible procreation. By contrast, the forced inclusion of same-sex couples into the category "marriage" will be a dramatic transformation in the meaning of marriage in law, and as the law influences cultural norms, in the public mind.

If same-sex unions are deemed just the same as unions of husband and wife, it becomes difficult to see how marriage could have any public relationship to its great historic task of producing families in which the mother and father who make the baby raise the baby in love together. This court will have declared that marriage is not about children; rather it is primarily about adult interests, with no particular relationship to children at all. The idea that marriage is important for children's well-being will be privatized not publicly shared, undermined rather than reinforced, in the law. The idea that marriage matters because children need a mother and father will be stigmatized as irrational bigotry.

It is very reasonable for California voters to believe that government promotion of this new idea of marriage would have its most lasting effect over time, as the next generation's attitudes toward marriage, childbearing, and the importance of mothers and fathers are shaped by a new legal regime.

Same-sex marriage informs our culture that two fathers or two mothers are not only just as good as a child's own mother and a father, *they are just the same*. If two mothers are just the same as a child's own mother and father, for example, why can't a single mother living with her mom (the child's grandmother) do just as well as a married mother and father? Why are dads relevant at all?

Consistently regulating acts of sexual passion so they do not produce fatherless children—whether through abstinence, contraception, confining one's relationships to marriage partners, or potential partners—is hard, very hard, especially for young people. Same-sex couples do not have these issues, and society need not worry about the effects of their sexual activity in the same way. If these goals of marriage are key, they do not fit. If they fit, these goals are probably not key to marriage.

If the ruling below is upheld, can an advocate for reducing divorce or unmarried childbearing still say, "Marriage really matters because children need a mom and a dad? With the advent of gay marriage, this public argument will no longer make sense in a new way. The law of marriage will clearly and obviously be repudiating this as a core public purpose of marriage.

D. Supporters and opponents of gay marriage agree that redefining marriage will transform marriage and its public meaning.

Many voices argued for Proposition 8 on the grounds that same-sex marriage would sever the link between marriage and children. Even more significantly, many gay marriage advocates agree, concluding that the redefinition of marriage would radically transform marriage as we know it.

* * *

Perhaps a new genderless vision of marriage disconnected from procreation or the ideal that children need a mother and father would be a good thing for our society. Or perhaps not. The point here again is not that this court must necessarily endorse the view that redefining marriage will radically disconnect marriage from procreation—but when both those who support and those who oppose gay marriage are predicting a dramatic change, the concerns of California voters must be seen as rational as well.

This is especially true when the district court essentially validated the worst fears of voters. In its decision below, the district court first eliminated procreation from the history of marriage altogether, then privatized this purpose of marriage, and finally attempted to stigmatize those who hold that view as irrational bigots. In this progression, the court first denied that procreation has ever been a public purpose of marriage..., suggesting instead that Proposition 8 is supported only by private moral views..., and finally concluding that, in the absence of a public justification, those private moral views produce an inference of bigotry, supportable only by moral disapproval of homosexuality, animus toward gays and lesbians, or heterosexist superiority....

In such a context, not only will the law find it more difficult to connect mothers and fathers with children, but civil society will as well under the weight of such judicial disapproval as was expressed in the trial court opinion....

II. GAY MARRIAGE MAY UNDERMINE MALE WILLINGNESS TO SACRIFICE FOR CHILDREN BY UNDERMINING THE IDEA THAT CHILDREN NEED THEIR FATHERS.

When law and society discard as irrational bigotry the traditional understanding of marriage, it is fatherhood that is likely to be most profoundly affected. The retreat from marriage in recent years does not produce equal numbers of single fathers and single mothers. Sex between men and women makes babies, even in a society with constitutional rights to abortion and contraception. When society simply weakens its support for the ideal that children should be cared for by both the man and the woman who made them, children end up disproportionately in the care of solo mothers. What will happen when the law and society rejects that view altogether as irrational bigotry? If the district court has its way, we will find out.

The children themselves are at a substantially increased risk for a wide array of outcomes: poverty, infant mortality, mental and physical illness, school failure, juvenile delinquency, sexually transmitted disease. The mothers themselves face higher rates of negative outcomes and a structural gendered inequality that a child support check does not erase....

Defining marriage as the union of a husband and wife recognizes a core biological reality—that each child has a parent of each sex. Marriage encourages those who are responsible for creating children, both fathers and mothers, to jointly assume responsibility for raising the child—mitigating the gendered inequality which frequently occurs when single mothers bear the burdens of parenting alone.

As the district court's opinion makes crystal clear, same-sex marriage announces that we have discarded as irrational bigotry the idea that gender or biology matters. It can hardly be questioned that encouraging parental responsibility in general is an important social good. Given the high number of men who do not care for the children created by acts of sexual passion, encouraging natural parents to feel responsible for their children is also an important good.

* * *

Marriage cannot mean two contradictory things simultaneously. While marriage may have different meanings for individuals, when the law defines marriage for public purposes, that definition has consequences. The law can either endorse the idea that marriage is the union of a husband and wife united for the benefit of their children, or the idea that marriage's primary purpose is to publicly acknowledge and validate the loving relationships of consenting adults regardless of sex. When the law endorses the latter idea it is changing the public meaning of marriage in ways that will make the social task of giving more children effective and loving fathers harder.

* * *

Fathers and Children

Planned Parenthood v. Danforth 428 U.S. 52 (1976)

This case involved a challenge to a Missouri state law which required minors to obtain parental consent and married women to obtain spousal consent before proceeding with an abortion. The U.S. Supreme Court struck down both provisions of this law. Below are excerpts from the plurality opinion written by Justice Blackmun and from the dissent written by Justice White.

Planned Parenthood of Central Missouri et al., v.

Danforth, Attorney General of Missouri, et. al.

No. 74-1151

SUPREME COURT OF THE UNITED STATES

428 U.S. 52; 96 S. Ct. 2831; 49 L. Ed. 2d 788; 1976 U.S. LEXIS 13

July 1, 1976, Opinion delivered *

JUDGES: Burger, Brennan, Stewart, White, Marshall, Blackmun, Powell, Rehnquist, Stevens.

OPINION BY: BLACKMUN

(3) With the written consent of the woman's spouse, unless the abortion is

certified by a licensed physician to be necessary in order to preserve the life of the mother.

C

[***LEdHR8] [8]The spouse's consent. Section 3(3) requires the prior written consent of the spouse of the woman seeking an abortion during the first 12 weeks of pregnancy, unless [*68] "the abortion is certified by a licensed physician to be necessary in order to preserve the life of the mother." [9]

> 9 It is of some interest to note that the condition does not relate, as most statutory conditions in this area do, to the preservation of the life or *health* of the mother.

The appellees defend § 3(3) on the ground that it was enacted in the light of the General Assembly's "perception of marriage as an institution," Brief for Appellee Danforth 34, and that any major change in family status is a decision to be made jointly by the marriage partners. Reference is made to an abortion's possible effect on the woman's childbearing potential. It is said that marriage always has entailed some legislatively imposed limitations: Reference is made to adultery and bigamy as criminal offenses; to Missouri's general requirement, Mo. Rev. Stat. § 453.030.3 (1969), that for an adoption of a child born in wedlock the consent of both parents is necessary; to similar joint-consent requirements imposed by a number of States with respect to artificial insemination and the legitimacy of children so conceived; to the laws of two States requiring spousal consent for voluntary sterilization; and to the long-established requirement of spousal consent for the effective disposition of an interest in real property. It is argued that "[r]ecognizing [**2841] that the consent of both parties is generally necessary... to begin a family, the legislature has determined that a change in the family structure set in motion by mutual consent should be terminated only by mutual consent," Brief for Appellee Danforth 38, and that what the legislature did was to exercise its inherent policy-making power "for what was believed to be in the best interests of all the people of Missouri." *Id.,* at 40.

The appellants, on the other hand, contend that § 3(3) obviously is designed to afford the husband the right unilaterally to prevent or veto an abortion, whether or [*69] not he is the father of the fetus, and that this not only violates *Roe* and *Doe* but is also in conflict with other decided cases. See, *e.g., Poe* v. *Gerstein,* 517 F. 2d 787, 794–6 (CA5 1975), appeal docketed, No. 75-713; *Wolfe* v. *Schroering,* 388 F. Supp., at 636–7; *Doe* v. *Rampton,* 366 F. Supp. 189, 193 (Utah 1973). They also refer to the situation where the husband's consent cannot be obtained because he cannot be located. And they assert that § 3(3) is vague and overbroad.

In *Roe* and *Doe* we specifically [***805] reserved decision on the question whether a requirement for consent by the father of the fetus, by the spouse, or by the parents, or a parent, of an unmarried minor, may be constitutionally imposed. 410 U.S., at 165 n. 67. We now hold that [HN5] the State may not constitutionally require the consent of the spouse, as is specified under § 3(3) of the Missouri Act, as a condition for abortion during the first 12 weeks of pregnancy. We thus agree with the dissenting judge in the present case, and with the courts whose decisions are cited above, that the State cannot "delegate to a spouse a veto power which the state itself is absolutely and totally prohibited from exercising during the first trimester of pregnancy." 392 F. Supp., at 1375. Clearly, since the State cannot regulate or proscribe abortion during the first stage, when the physician and his patient make that decision, the State cannot delegate authority to any particular person, even the spouse, to prevent abortion during that same period.

[***LEdHR9A] [9A]We are not unaware of the deep and proper concern and interest that a devoted and protective husband has in his wife's pregnancy and in the growth and development of the fetus she is carrying. Neither has this Court failed to appreciate the importance of the marital relationship in our society. See, *e.g., Griswold* v. *Connecticut,* 381 U.S. 479, 486 (1965); *Maynard* v. *Hill,* 125 U.S. [*70] 190, 211 (1888). [10] Moreover, we recognize that the decision whether to undergo or to forgo an abortion may have profound effects on the future of any marriage, effects that are both physical and mental, and possibly deleterious. Notwithstanding these factors, we cannot hold that the State has the constitutional authority to give the spouse unilaterally the ability to prohibit the wife from terminating her pregnancy, when the State itself lacks that right. See *Eisenstadt* v. *Baird,* 405 U.S. 438, 453 (1972). [11]

10 "We deal with a right of privacy older than the Bill of Rights – older than our political parties, older than our school system. Marriage is a coming together for better or for worse, hopefully enduring, and intimate to the degree of being sacred. It is an association that promotes a way of life, not causes; a harmony in living, not political faiths; a bilateral loyalty, not commercial or social projects. Yet it is an association for as noble a purpose as any involved in our prior decisions." *Griswold* v. *Connecticut,* 381 U.S., at 486.

[***LEdHR9B] [9B]

11 As the Court recognized in *Eisenstadt* v. *Baird,* "the marital couple is not an independent entity with a mind and heart of its own, but an

association of two individuals each with a separate intellectual and emotional makeup. If the right of privacy means anything, it is the right of the *individual,* married or single, to be free from unwarranted governmental intrusion into matters so fundamentally affecting a person as the decision whether to bear or beget a child." 405 U.S., at 453 (emphasis in original).

The dissenting opinion of our Brother WHITE appears to overlook the implications of this statement upon the issue whether § 3(3) is constitutional. This section does much more than insure that the husband participate in the decision whether his wife should have an abortion. The State, instead, has determined that the husband's interest in continuing the pregnancy of his wife always outweighs any interest on her part in terminating it irrespective of the condition of their marriage. The State, accordingly, has granted him the right to prevent unilaterally, and for whatever reason, the effectuation of his wife's and her physician's decision to terminate her pregnancy. This state determination not only may discourage the consultation that might normally be expected to precede a major decision affecting the marital couple but also, and more importantly, the State has interposed an absolute obstacle to a woman's decision that *Roe* held to be constitutionally protected from such interference.

[*71] It [***806] [**2842] seems manifest that, ideally, the decision to terminate a pregnancy should be one concurred in by both the wife and her husband. No marriage may be viewed as harmonious or successful if the marriage partners are fundamentally divided on so important and vital an issue. But it is difficult to believe that the goal of fostering mutuality and trust in a marriage, and of strengthening the marital relationship and the marriage institution, will be achieved by giving the husband a veto power exercisable for any reason whatsoever or for no reason at all. Even if the State had the ability to delegate to the husband a power it itself could not exercise, it is not at all likely that such action would further, as the District Court majority phrased it, the "interest of the state in protecting the mutuality of decisions vital to the marriage relationship." 392 F. Supp., at 1370.

We recognize, of course, that when a woman, with the approval of her physician but without the approval of her husband, decides to terminate her pregnancy, it could be said that she is acting unilaterally. The obvious fact is that when the wife and the husband disagree on this decision, the view of only one of the two marriage partners can prevail. Inasmuch as it is the woman who physically bears the child and who is the more directly and immediately affected by the pregnancy, as between the two, the balance weighs in her favor. Cf. *Roe v. Wade,* 410 U.S., at 153.

We conclude that § 3(3) of the Missouri Act is inconsistent with the standards enunciated in *Roe* v. *Wade*, 410 U.S., at 164–5, and is unconstitutional. It is therefore unnecessary for us to consider the appellants' [*72] additional challenges to § 3(3) based on vagueness and overbreadth.

DISSENT

MR. JUSTICE WHITE, with whom THE CHIEF JUSTICE and MR. JUSTICE REHNQUIST join, concurring in part and dissenting in part.

In *Roe* v. *Wade*, 410 U.S. 113 (1973), this Court recognized a right to an abortion free from state prohibition. The task of policing this limitation on state police power is and will be a difficult and continuing venture in substantive due process. However, even accepting *Roe* v. *Wade*, there is nothing in the opinion in that case and nothing articulated in the Court's opinion in this case which justifies the invalidation of four provisions of House Committee Substitute for House Bill No. 1211 (hereafter Act) enacted by the Missouri 77th General Assembly in 1974 in response to *Roe* v. *Wade*. Accordingly, I dissent, in part.

I

Roe v. *Wade, supra,* at 163, holds that until a fetus becomes viable, [**2852] the interest of the State in the life or potential life it represents is outweighed by the interest of the mother in choosing "whether or not to terminate her pregnancy." 410 U.S., at 153. Section 3 (3) of the Act provides that a married woman may not obtain an abortion without her husband's consent. The Court strikes down this statute in one sentence. It says that "since the State cannot... proscribe abortion... the State cannot delegate authority to any particular person, [*93] even the spouse, to prevent abortion...." *Ante*, at 69. But the State is not -- under § 3 (3) -- delegating to the husband the power to vindicate the *State's* interest in the future life of the fetus. It is instead recognizing that the husband has an interest of his own in the life of the fetus which should not be extinguished by the unilateral decision of the wife. [1] It by no means follows, from the fact that the mother's interest in deciding "whether or not to terminate her pregnancy" outweighs the *State's* interest in the potential life of the fetus, that the husband's interest is also outweighed and may not be protected by the State. A father's interest in having a child -- perhaps his only child – may be unmatched by any other interest in his life. See *Stanley* v. *Illinois,* 405 U.S. 645, 651 (1972), and cases there cited. It is truly surprising that the majority finds in the [***819] United States Constitution, as it must in order to justify the result it reaches, a rule that the State must assign a greater value to a mother's decision to cut off a potential human life by abortion than to a father's decision to let it mature into a live child. Such a rule cannot be found there, nor can it be found in *Roe v. Wade, supra.* These are matters which a State should be able to decide free from the suffocating power of the federal judge, purporting to act in the name of the Constitution.

> 1 There are countless situations in which the State prohibits conduct only when it is objected to by a private person most closely affected by it. Thus a State cannot forbid anyone to enter on private property with the owner's consent, but it may enact and enforce trespass laws against unauthorized entrances. It cannot forbid transfer of property held in tenancy by the entireties but it may require consent by both husband and wife to such a transfer. These situations plainly do not involve delegations of legislative power to private parties; and neither does the requirement in § 3 (3) that a woman not deprive her husband of his future child without his consent.

[*94] In describing the nature of a mother's interest in termininating a pregnancy, the Court in *Roe v. Wade* mentioned only the post-birth burdens of rearing a child, 410 U.S., at 153, and rejected a rule based on her interest in controlling her own body during pregnancy. *Id.,* at 154. Missouri has a law which prevents a woman from putting a child up for adoption over her husband's objection, Mo. Rev. Stat. § 453.030 (1969). This law represents a judgment by the State that the mother's interest in avoiding the burdens of child rearing do not outweigh or snuff out the father's interest in participating in bringing up his own child. That law is plainly valid, but no more so than § 3 (3) of the Act now before us, resting as it does on precisely the same judgment.

Dubay v. Wells 506 F.3d 422 (6th Cir., 2007)

This case involved a challenge to the Michigan Paternity Act which requires parents of a child born out of wedlock to provide financial support for that child. Dubay, the father of a child born against his strongly expressed wishes, challenged the law on the grounds that it denied him the same right to disclaim parenthood that Wells, the mother of the child, had via her abortion rights. The U.S. Court of Appeals for the Sixth Circuit affirmed the Michigan law on the grounds that the needs of a child for support from both parents outweigh any of the circumstances surrounding its birth. Excerpts from the appellate court's decision appear below.

DUBAY V. WELLS

UNITED STATES COURT OF APPEALS, SIXTH CIRCUIT

506 F. 3d 422 (6th Cir., 2007) http://caselaw.findlaw.com/us-6th-circuit/1467603.html, 1-11. (Excerpts from: pp. 2, 3, 4–6)

OPINION

I. BACKGROUND

* * *

In the fall of 2004, Dubay and Wells became involved in a romantic relationship. At that time, Dubay informed Wells that he had no interest in becoming a father. In response, Wells told Dubay that she was infertile and that, as an extra layer of protection, she was using contraception. Dubay, in reliance on these assurances, participated in a consensual sexual relationship with Wells.

The parties' relationship later deteriorated. Shortly thereafter, and much to Dubay's surprise, Wells informed Dubay that she was pregnant, allegedly with Dubay's child. Wells chose to carry the child to term and the child, EGW, was born on an unspecified date in 2005. During the pregnancy and birth of the child, Dubay was consistently clear about his desire not to be a father.

A few weeks after EGW's birth, the County brought a paternity complaint against Dubay in the Saginaw County Circuit Court under the Michigan Paternity Act. Wells and the County sought a judgment of filiation, child support, reimbursement for delivery of the child, and other statutory and equitable relief. Dubay requested a stay so that the constitutional issues presented by the litigation could be resolved, but the trial court denied that request. Dubay thereafter brought this action against Wells and the County in federal district court, seeking relief under 2 U.S.C. 1983.

In his amended complaint,...Dubay alleged that the application of the Michigan Paternity Act to his case violated the Equal Protection Clause of the Fourteenth Amendment as well as Article 1, Section 2 of the Michigan Constitution, which loosely parallels the Equal Protection Clause....

...On July 17, 2006, the court issued an opinion and order dismissing Dubay's complaint with prejudice....

* * *

On appeal, Dubay challenges...the district court's dismissal of his. ...claim.

* * *

II. DISCUSSION

A. THE MICHIGAN PATERNITY ACT DOES NOT VIOLATE DUBAY'S RIGHT TO EQUAL PROTECTION

* * *

2. Analysis

.....Dubay alleges that the Michigan Paternity Act violates the Equal Protection Clause of the Fourteenth Amendment, which guarantees that "[n]o state shall...deny to any person within its jurisdiction the equal protection of the laws."...

* * *

Dubay argues that the enforcement of the Michigan Paternity Act against him denies him the equal protection of the law in two ways. First and foremost, Dubay argues that the Michigan statutes deny him the equal protection of the law by affording mothers a right to disclaim parenthood after engaging in consensual sex (i.e., through abortion) while denying that right to fathers. Second, Dubay contends that Michigan law denies men equal protection by making it easier for a woman to place a child in adoption or drop the newborn off at a hospital or other social service agency. An examination of these claims under our equal protection jurisprudence, however, reveals that they lack merit.

The Equal Protection Clause of the Fourteenth Amendment "is essentially a direction that all persons similarly situated should be treated alike."... However, "the Fourteenth Amendment does not deny to [the] State the power to treat different classes of persons in different ways."...In reviewing state legislation for an equal protection violation, "we apply different levels of scrutiny to different types of classifications."...In general, we start with the presumption that the statute is valid. ...To overcome this presumption, the party challenging the statute must demonstrate that the statute is not rationally related to a legitimate government purpose. ...If the legislation's official classification is based on gender, however, the justification must be "exceedingly persuasive."...For such classifications, the burden is on the state to demonstrate that the legislation serves "important governmental objectives and that the discriminatory means employed are substantially related to the achievement of those objectives."...Finally, classifications affecting fundamental rights "are given the most exacting scrutiny."... Under strict scrutiny, a regulation infringing upon a fundamental right will only be upheld if it is narrowly tailored to serve a compelling state interest....

Dubay cannot prevail under any of these equal protection theories. First, strict scrutiny does not apply because the Michigan Paternity Act does not affect any of Dubay's fundamental rights. In *N.E. v. Hedges,* we found that the right to privacy, articulated in the Supreme Court's substantive due process jurisprudence, does not encompass a right to decide not to become a parent after conception and birth....In doing so, we explicitly rejected the argument, which Dubay raises in his brief, that "fairness" dictates that men should receive a right to disclaim fatherhood in exchange for a woman's right to abortion....Our discussion clarified that it is not a fundamental right of any parent, male or female, to sever his or her financial responsibilities to the child after the child is born....Thus, to the extent that Dubay claims that Michigan is not affording him equal protection of the law by denying men, but not women, "the right to initiate consensual sexual activity while choosing to not be a parent,"...his argument must fail.

Second, we do not need to apply intermediate scrutiny because the Michigan Paternity Act does not discriminate on the basis of gender. The statutory provisions that impose the obligation of support upon Dubay, and similarly situated fathers, are gender neutral. ("The *parents* of a child born out of wedlock are liable for the necessary support and education of the child." (emphasis added). ...By requiring the identification of a mother and a father for the child and by demanding that both these parents provide support to the child, the Michigan statutes do not discriminate against either sex in imposing parenting obligations and, thus, do not need to be reviewed under intermediate scrutiny.

Finally, the Michigan Paternity Act withstands rational basis review because it is rationally related to a legitimate government purpose...."The underlying purpose of the Paternity Act is to ensure that the minor children born outside a marriage are provided with support and education."...This is undoubtedly a legitimate, and an important, governmental interest... Moreover, the means that the statute uses to achieve this end-requiring support from the legal parents, and determining legal fatherhood based on the biological fatherhood-is substantially, let alone rationally, related to this legitimate, and probably important, government purpose. Accordingly, we find that Dubay has raised no viable equal protection challenge to the Michigan Paternity Act.

* * *

Because Dubay has no legal basis for his claim that the Michigan Paternity Act and other unspecified statutes violate the Equal Protection Clause, he cannot show that the County's application of these laws to his case has deprived him of his constitutional rights as required for this...action. Therefore, we hold that the district court properly dismissed Dubay's case for "failure to state a claim upon which relief can be granted."

* * *

Erika M. Hiester

Erika M. Hiester was the Notes Editor of the *Ave Maria Law Review* in 2002–3. She received her J.D degree from the Ave Maria School of Law in 2003.

Hiester, Erika M. "Note: Child Support Statutes and the Father's Right Not to Procreate." Ave Maria Law Review 2 (Spring 2004) 213–41. (Excerpts: pp. 213–17, 218, 227–8, 233–4, 238, 240–1)

Introduction

Since its legalization in 1973, abortion has been the cause of death for more than forty-two million unborn children. [n1] The controversy surrounding Roe v. Wade [n2] has not abated in the thirty years following the decision. Americans are still no closer to a consensus regarding this volatile and deeply divisive issue, which is central to most current political struggles and frequently informed by moral and religious beliefs. [n3] This note, however, will not address the merits, or lack thereof, of the legal underpinnings of Roe v. Wade and its progeny. [n4] Rather, this note will consider whether or not those who maintain the right to abortion must accept that it takes two to procreate; and that if choice is essential, a man must also have the right to choose. The modern legal culture has failed to acknowledge a man's right to procreate, or more importantly his right not to procreate. [n5]

This note posits that child-support laws and welfare regulations creating an automatic obligation to pay child support upon the [*214] establishment of biological paternity deprive men of their fundamental right to procreation,....

I. Understanding the Problem

In holding that the right of privacy founded in the Fourteenth Amendment was "broad enough to encompass a woman's decision whether or not to terminate her pregnancy," [n8] the Supreme Court in Roe opened the door to a myriad of questions. [n9] Among these were questions relating to the rights of the unborn child and the rights of the father of the child. The Court answered the first question by determining that the unborn child was not a person within the meaning of the Fourteenth Amendment, and thus had no rights. [n10] The question of the rights of the father was similarly disposed of in [*215] later Supreme Court cases. While recognizing a man's interest in his offspring, [n11] the Court has nonetheless consistently held that a father has no right to interfere with the woman's right to choose. [n12] Thus, while recognizing a woman's right to terminate her pregnancy, to be the master (or mistress) of her own procreative capabilities, the courts and the legislatures have simultaneously trampled upon a man's right to be the master of his own procreative capabilities.

Since 1942, the Court has recognized the fundamental right to procreation. [n13] Yet, under current law, a man's right concerning procreation begins and ends with the woman's decision. The mere fact that the woman is the carrier of the unborn child gives her, in the Court's opinion, the sole ability to make the important decision for both herself and the child's father of whether the two shall be parents. [n14]

A pregnant woman has three options under the current regime. Under the shield of privacy, she may carry the child to full term and raise the infant; she may place the child she has carried to term for adoption; or she may terminate her pregnancy through an abortion. [n15] Her right to an abortion cannot be restricted until the child reaches viability. [n16] Following viability, her right is practically unfettered; the only restriction is a state's ability to proscribe abortions at this point that are not performed for the life or the health of the mother. [n17] The [*216] right to an abortion attaches to a woman regardless of whether she is married. [n18] In addition, an unmarried mother may place a child she has carried to term for adoption. [n19] In this regard, the law places the question of whether a woman will face the financial responsibilities and other entanglements of child rearing squarely in the woman's own hands.

On the other hand, a man who has impregnated a woman has no rights with regard to the developing child. The laws of this country afford him no recourse. A man may not interfere with the woman's right to terminate her pregnancy; [n20] he may not force her to undergo an abortion or to place the child for adoption. [n21] Furthermore, the law places no obligation upon the mother to tell the father that he is the father of her child. [n22] Neither does the law permit a man to avoid responsibility for a child whom the mother chooses to raise herself. [n23] [*217] Thus the question of whether a man is to face all the entanglements of fatherhood is also placed squarely in the hands of the mother. At the moment of conception, under the current law, the only decision left to the father's determination is what kind of a father he is going to be.

......Together, the right to bear or beget a child and the right to abortion are the foundation of the right to procreate. Obligatory child support based upon a biological relationship effectively strips a man of his right to procreate, as this right has been constructed by the modern legal culture, while leaving the woman's right intact.

The fundamental injustice in allowing a woman to evade responsibility while requiring a man to pay has not been completely ignored. In the past decade, commentators have acknowledged the discriminatory treatment of men and women in regard to their reproductive rights. Some have attempted to justify the disparate treatment by asserting a woman's superior right because she must bear the burden of pregnancy. [n25] Others have argued for equal protection for men, proposing statutes that allow for a man to [*218] terminate his relationship with the child. Neither the legislatures nor the courts, however, have responded to rectify this inequality.

* * *

III. Constitutional Guarantees: Due Process and Liberty

* * *

....In the abortion context, the question of control regarding procreation has consistently been decided in the woman's favor. Women alone have the capacity to carry a child; therefore, the Supreme Court has favored them with the sole authority to terminate pregnancies. [n84] Conversely, and necessarily, women also have the sole authority to decide to continue pregnancies. [n85]

Under current law, the right to an abortion is a woman's right alone. This may seem obvious insofar as it is only a woman who has the ability to become pregnant. Depriving a man of an equal right to terminate a pregnancy, however, ignores the biological fact that a woman and a man have contributed equally to the pregnancy. Viewed as an element of procreational autonomy, which includes the right not to procreate as well as the right to procreate, the right to abortion is more than just the right to terminate a pregnancy. It is the right to terminate procreation. The right to an abortion critically alters the relationship between pregnancy and procreation.

Pregnancy is no longer synonymous with procreation. Instead, abortion destroys the union between conception and procreation. For the sake of procreational autonomy, the crucial question after the legalization of abortion becomes "when does procreation happen?" While the recognition of a woman's right to terminate a pregnancy is itself appalling because of the termination of an unborn child, the failure of the law to recognize the right of a man to terminate a pregnancy leads to a disturbing dichotomy in how procreation is defined. For a woman, procreation is not actually recognized until [*228] she has given birth to a baby or, during pregnancy, at the point of viability when the state's interest in the unborn child may be recognized. For the man, procreation occurs at the moment of conception because his active role ends and his duties and obligations are fixed at that moment. This inequality seriously burdens a man's right to procreational autonomy. Due to the fundamental nature of the right of procreational autonomy, the state may not burden it without a compelling state interest.[n86]

* * *

IV. Fourteenth Amendment Protections

* * *

The law may not treat similarly situated individuals differently. [n119] Failure to allow a man the option of terminating his "procreative act" treats similarly situated men and women differently. Both stand in the same position concerning potential to be parents to the unborn child. Yet, the law allows a woman to terminate that potential while not affording a similar right to the man. Instead, the law recognizes the parental relationship of the man at the point of conception. [n120]

While child-support statutes do not per se infringe upon the right to procreate, that right is implicated because the statutes usually assign a parental obligation based upon a genetic relationship. [n121] In other words, child-support laws enable or legitimize different treatment of men with regard to the exercise of procreational autonomy. All that is required to enforce a child-support obligation against a man is the mere fact of his genetic relationship to the child. [n122] On the other hand, because a woman has the right to terminate her pregnancy, child-support obligations can never be enforced against her without her consent to the existence of a parental obligation. Although the very existence of the child might be deemed procreation, it is not until the law recognizes or enforces parental rights or obligations that procreation is realized. [n123] Therefore, when the law recognizes a parental obligation against the will of the "parent," it forces procreation on that individual and infringes on the fundamental right of procreational autonomy. In the same way that forcing a woman to bear a child, and therefore parental responsibility, against her will burdens her procreational autonomy, forcing a man [*234] to bear parental responsibility against his will burdens his right of procreational autonomy.

* * *

This does not mean that a man should be able to avoid responsibility for his procreative actions. The father and the mother both share responsibility for the conception. It does not necessarily follow, however, that both parties are responsible for the birth of the [*238] child. For the law to be logically consistent in its treatment of the men and women, if the father does not want the child, if he is not ready to accept the responsibilities of parenthood, his choice not to procreate should not be unilaterally overridden by the choice of the mother.

* * *

Allowing the father of a child the right to exercise his right of procreation and to decide not to become a parent will undoubtedly have repercussions for the mother. The mother may become solely financially responsible for the child. The knowledge that she cannot rely on the father for support may affect her decision whether to undergo an abortion or whether to place the child for adoption. Since, however, it is her decision alone that will bring the child into the world, placing additional cost on her shoulders would not create an unjust result. In addition, although the father's decision may affect the mother's decision, any impact cannot be any more of an infringement on her right to procreate than the mother's choice to terminate the child is on the father's right to procreate when he wants to keep the child. When the mother chooses to terminate her pregnancy, she has irrevocably exterminated the child of the father. She has frustrated any procreative intent he may have had and any desire he had for the child to live. On the other hand, a father's refusal to become a father does not have the same irrevocable effect. Neither does his action have the effect of frustrating the procreative desire of the other party. His refusal to become a father may increase the difficulty of the mother's decision, but the decision of whether to keep the child will still belong to her.

[*241]

Conclusion

Despite claims of equality and responsibility, current legal trends are hypocritical. The current law claims for a woman that which it refuses for a man: the ability to choose parenthood. Instead, the law imposes parenthood on a man solely as a result of the choice of the woman. Allowing a man equal protection by the ability to voluntarily terminate his paternal rights may be distasteful, contrary to custom and history, and bad public policy, but these are not legitimate reasons for refusing to give legal protection to fathers. ....The ability to refuse parenthood is the result of the right to abortion. A child cannot be a child at conception for the man and not until birth for the woman. If the woman can avoid responsibility for the child by having an abortion, the man must have a similar right. It is inequitable and unjust to force responsibility on him for the choices made by the mother of his child.

Questions

1   How important are sex roles in American family life today and in American life generally? Will these roles increase or diminish over time?

2   How desirable are the dramatic changes taking place in American family life today? Is the American family changing for the better or for the worse?

3   Why is same-sex marriage so controversial today? What are the best arguments for and against same-sex marriage?

4   How important is it that children are reared by their biological parents? What are the advantages and disadvantages for children who live with their biological parents and for children who experience alternative forms of parenthood?

5   Why is it so difficult for men and women to achieve equality in matters concerning procreation? What light does this shed on the question of whether the biological differences between the sexes are morally, socially, and politically significant?

Suggested Reading

Okin, Susan Moller. *Justice, Gender, and the Family*. New York: Basic Books, 1989.

Rhoads, Steven E. *Taking Sex Differences Seriously*. New York: Encounter Books, 2004.

Rauch, Jonathan. *Gay Marriage: Why it is Good for Straights, Good for Gays, and Good for Americans*. New York: Holt Paperbacks, 2004.

Blankenhorn, David. *The Future of Marriage*. New York: Encounter Books, 2007.

Corvino, John and Gallagher, Maggie. *Debating Same-Sex Marriage*. New York and London: Oxford University Press, 2012.

7

Sexual Equality in America— Now and in the Future

Introduction

We shall conclude our book by briefly reviewing how sexual equality has evolved in American society, examining what sexual equality means to Americans today, and considering the prospects for this principle in our country's future. Our goal here is not merely to summarize and predict, but rather to take this last opportunity to underscore our central arguments. These are first, that the best American debates about sexual equality stem from genuine differences of opinion about complex issues and therefore deserve careful study; second, that the core question which animates most of these debates is whether the biological differences between the sexes have moral, social and political significance; and third, that we must approach these debates with an open mind and a willingness to learn from all points of view.

Past and Present

As we have seen, the dominant paradigm governing the relations between the sexes in early America was the doctrine of separate spheres. This doctrine was based on the premise that men and women are equal in natural rights, but sufficiently different by nature to justify their assuming different roles in life. Men were expected to provide for the material wellbeing of their families and their communities and to exercise civil rights commensurate with these responsibilities. Women were expected to manage their households, nurture their children, and shape their moral character. Since women's lives were considered private by nature, they had few civil rights.

These rights were considered superfluous for women because the relevant men in their lives protected their interests which supposedly conformed to their own.

This traditional paradigm began to dissolve with the rise of American feminism in the mid-nineteenth century. The early reformers, as we have seen, argued that sexual equality in the United States must mean at least this: no artificial barriers should prevent women from fully participating in American society, exercising a full array of civil rights, and pursuing happiness according to their own lights. Over time, these reformers successfully used the American passion for equality to enlist both the law and public opinion on behalf of this principle. Traditionalists who tried to block these efforts were increasingly put on the defensive. At some point in time, perhaps during the late 1960s, the reformers forged a new American consensus regarding sexual equality which guaranteed women the same opportunities as men in virtually all spheres of life.

Once the United States reached this historical turning point, many of the debates regarding sexual equality that so bitterly divided previous generations of Americans simply came to an end. Virtually no one, for example, now objects to the fact that there are and will always be women voters, jurors, soldiers, university students, athletes, professionals, clergy, and politicians. Moreover, even women who choose the vocations of marriage and motherhood will never again be confined to the domestic sphere or subject to laws which give their husbands arbitrary power over them, their property, and their children. Men now also benefit from this increase in equality by having access to occupations, avocations, and parental roles that were traditionally reserved for women.

Yet the defeat of the Equal Rights Amendment by traditionalists in 1982 also marked an important watershed in American history. This event, which dealt a serious blow to the hopes of reformers, suggests that the American passion for sexual equality has limits, and that many Americans still want the law to differentiate between the sexes under some circumstances. Indeed, some feminists themselves have come to acknowledge the moral significance of sex differences. Carol Gilligan claims, for example, that women naturally speak "in a different voice" than men do, a voice that is rooted more in caring and relationships than in a weighing of rights.[1]

Looking Ahead

How will the principle of sexual equality fare under these circumstances? In the post-ERA era, the Supreme Court has determined the constitutionality of American laws which distinguish between the sexes on natural difference grounds. As we have seen, the Court's standard for adjudicating such laws is whether the men and women affected by them are similarly or differently situated. The Court will uphold a sex-based law that in its judgment operates fairly and is substantially related to an important, clearly stated governmental objective. Yet if the Court determines that the law distinguishes between the sexes arbitrarily or without good cause, it will declare this law unconstitutional.

Perhaps the most important currently operative sex-based law is the Selective Service Act of 1980. This law requires men, but not women, to register for the draft partly on the grounds of the long-held belief that women are naturally unfit for combat duty. Yet many service women now serve in combat roles with explicit Defense Department approval and with little public outcry despite the recent rise in female combat-related casualties. This change in public opinion occurred partly because technology now often shields women warriors from direct hand-to-hand fighting while still enabling them to engage effectively with the enemy. Yet despite this change, few people now seek to make the Selective Service System more egalitarian with respect to sex. Nor can we predict how the Defense Department, the Supreme Court, or the American public would respond to an effort to require young women to register for the draft. This may depend, of course, on whether Congress ever seeks to reinstate the draft, or if the country faces an imminent and prolonged threat to its national security.

As we have seen, Americans are now engaged in a series of fierce debates regarding the nature of the family. Indeed, both reformers and traditionalists are dissatisfied with the status quo and seek to reform the American family in different ways—the first by blurring and the second by maintaining or strengthening its traditional sex-roles. We believe that this debate over sex-roles will continue well into the future. It is unlikely, for example, that most Americans will soon, if ever, unambiguously endorse either the genderless version of the family that some reformers favor or the soft version of the doctrine of separate spheres that traditionalists prefer.

In this fluid situation, most couples with children will probably decide for themselves which work and childcare arrangements are best for them. Yet few think that the percentage of male homemakers, or stay at home dads, will increase significantly in the years to come unless adverse economic circumstances dictate otherwise. Thus, most future American mothers will probably continue to sacrifice at least some of their career aspirations or their earning power to the traditional tasks of having and caring for their young.

It is also hard to assess the prospects for same-sex marriage in the United States. The modern gay rights movement which began in 1969 has made Americans more favorably disposed toward gay men and women than at any time in the past. This change is reflected in governmental and business policies which forbid discrimination on the basis of sexual orientation.

Although hate crimes and prejudice against gay individuals still frequently occur, more gays now live "out of the closet" than ever before and often enter the mainstream of American life, including the armed services, with relatively little rancor. These developments seem to bode well for the future of gay marriage which is now legal in several states and is supported by many political leaders, the media elite, the icons of popular culture, and, according to some accounts, the great majority of younger citizens.

Yet well over half the states now have constitutional amendments banning same-sex marriage and, barring a decision supporting gay marriage rights by the Supreme Court, these amendments will be difficult to overturn. This evidence suggests that many Americans are quite reluctant to change the traditional understanding of marriage which supports biological parenthood and has deep roots in both our secular and our religious past.

At this point, it is also hard to predict how the concept of parenthood will evolve. It is fairly clear, for example, that future American children will be less likely than ever to live together with both their biological parents regardless of how Americans come to understand the nature of marriage. The determinative factors here include a persistently high divorce rate, an increase in the number of children born out of wedlock, a rise in the number of gay couples and single individuals who choose to become parents, and advances in reproductive technology. Some reformers see these developments as hopeful signs that the American family is evolving in new, more diverse, and ultimately healthier ways. Traditionalists fear, however, that the further decline of biological parenthood will adversely affect both our nation's children and our entire moral and social fabric.

The most interesting debates regarding sexual equality in the future will probably focus on the ways that advances in science and technology have changed family life. Many gay couples, single individuals, and even married heterosexual couples could not have become parents, for example, without the use of sperm banks, egg donors, in vitro fertilization, and surrogate mothers. Yet these advances pose daunting challenges for those moralists seeking to reform the American family as well as for American lawmakers and judges. Who, for example, is the legal mother of a child whose genetic inheritance comes from one woman, who is brought into the world by another, and who is reared by a third? What does the concept of paternal responsibility mean when the law permits one sperm bank donor to produce as many as 150 children?[2]

Modern science and technology also provide new options for transgendered Americans, the latest group seeking to expand the scope of sexual equality. These individuals are biologically born into one sex, but emotionally identify with the other. Transgendered Americans can now change their gender identity through hormone therapy and surgery, and their willingness to alter their bodies through painful and costly procedures suggests that biology does strongly affect an individual's psychological make-up. Despite the fact that most individuals who physically change their sex report experiencing great satisfaction, they are likely to continue to face significant prejudice in the foreseeable future. Transgendered Americans also raise difficult questions with respect to the law. Should the law define an individual's sexual identity in terms of inherent biology or in terms of personal preference and physical appearance? State courts now differ on this issue and a national effort to achieve consensus seems highly unlikely at any time soon.[3]

If the past and present are any guides, future American debates on sexual equality will be very thought provoking, very contentious, and very difficult to resolve. In this book, we have offered you, our readers, a wide range of materials which treat the principle of sexual equality from various viewpoints and perspectives. We have also presented these materials in a debate format, partly to show you that no one side in future controversies regarding this principle will likely have a monopoly on the truth. We hope that this approach has helped prepare you to think about these controversies with empathy and insight. As with all great moral and political principles in American life, the fate of sexual equality rests at least partly in your hands.

Notes

1 Carol Gilligan, *In a Different Voice: Psychological Theory and Women's Development*. Cambridge: Harvard University Press, 1993.

2 Jacqueline Mroz, "One Sperm Donor, 150 Offspring," *New York Times*, September 5, 2011.

3 See In re Estate of Marshall Gardiner, 42 P3d. 120 (Kansas, 2002) and MT v. JT, 140 NJ Super 77 (NJ 1976).

Questions

1 Do men and women enjoy genuine equality of opportunity in today's America? What factors, if any, could now make this ideal more real?

2 What should Americans do to improve the relations between the sexes in the future? Should new efforts be made to pass the Equal Rights Amendment?

3 How has reproductive technology affected the relations between the sexes in the United States? Should American law limit the use of reproductive technology? If so, how?

4   What light do the problems faced by transgendered Americans shed on our quest for a just version of sexual equality? Will these Americans ever be fully accepted in the mainstream of American life?

5   What new insights regarding sexual equality in America have you acquired from reading this book?

Suggested Reading

Gilligan, Carol. *In a Different Voice: Psychological Theory and Women's Development*. Cambridge: Harvard University Press, 1993.

Berg, Barbara J. *Sexism in America: Alive, Well, and Ruining our Future*. Chicago: Chicago Review Press, 2009.

Venker, Suzanne and Schlafly, Phyllis. *The Flipside of Feminism: What Conservative Women Know—and Men Can't Say*. Washington: World Net Daily Books, 2011.

Lublin, Nancy. *Pandora's Box: Feminism Confronts Reproductive Technology*. Lanham, MD: Rowman & Littlefield, 1998.

Teich, Nicholas. *Transgender 101: A Simple Guide to a Complex Issue*. New York: Columbia University Press, 2012.

INDEX

Proposition 8 275–6, 289–300 *see also*
National Organization for
Marriage
Protect Marriage campaign 299

rape 214, 251–70
male victims of 254–7, 264–70
statutory 257–64
Rape Shield Laws 254–7
rational basis test 31, 32–3, 57–8
Reed v. Reed (1971) 32, 38–40, 46–7
Reeves v. Swift Transportation Co.
(6th. Cir. 2006) 177–9
reformers 3–4
Rehnquist, Chief Justice William
47–50, 89, 91–5, 168–70,
197–201, 258–61
Rhoads, Steven E. 274–5, 284–9
Roe v. Wade (1973) 38, 277, 310–11,
315–16 *see also* abortion
Rosen, Leora 105
Rostker v. Goldberg (1981) 66, 91–7

same-sex marriage 275–6, 289–306,
325–6
Scalia, Antonin Justice 87, 89–91,
110, 125–9
schools *see also* education
single sex 109–110, 118–29
sport in 109–11, 129–38
Selective Service Law 66 *see also*
Military Selective Service
Act (1980) *and Rostker v.
Goldberg* (1981)
Semiramis of Ninevah 12
Seneca Falls convention 9, 19, 24, 64
separate spheres doctrine 4, 8, 10, 63,
273–4, 323–4
sex 4, 284–9
sexual assault 214, 252–70 *see also*
domestic violence *and* rape
sexual equality 323–7
Simpson, Nicole Brown 229–30
Simpson, O. J. 229–30
Simpson III, Judge Charles R. 183–5
Sixth Amendment 65, 79–82
slavery 29
Stanton, Elizabeth Cady 9, 19–24, 64

State v. Chase (Ore. 1922) 74–6
statutory rape 257–64 *see also* rape
Stevens, Justic John 47, 157–61,
263–4
Stewart, Justice Potter 142–4
Stone, Judge Harlan Fiske 30
suffrage 63–4, 69–72
Suk, Julie C. 202–7
Supreme Court, United States 29–34
Sykes, Circuit Court Judge 175–7

Taylor v. Louisiana (1975) 65, 79–82
Title VII 111–14, 189–90, 194–6, 205
*see also City of Los Angeles
Department of Water and
Power v. Manhart* (1978)
and Dothard v. Rawlinson
(1977) *and General Electric
Co. v. Gilbert et al.* (1976)
and *Hall v. Nalco Co.*
(ND Ill. 2006) *and Hall v.
Nalco Co.* (7th Cir. 2008)
*and Torres v. Wisconsin
Department of Health and
Social Services* (7th Cir. 1988)
*and Wallace v. Pyro Mining
Co.* (WD Ky. 1990)
Title IX 109, 129–38
Tocqueville, Alexis de 8–10, 14–16
*Torres v. Wisconsin Department of
Health and Social Services*
(7th Cir. 1988) 147–56
traditionalists 3–4
transgender 326–7
Truth, Sojourner 7, 25–6
two-tiered approach 30–1, 36

United States v. Carolene Products
(1938) 30–1
United States v. Virginia (1996) 110,
118–29

VAWA (Violence Against Women Act,
the) 228
violence *see* domestic violence *and*
rape
Violence Against Women Act, the
(VAWA) 228